What I say unto you, I say unto all, Watch.
(Mark 13:37)

DISCERNERS

ANALYZING **CONVERGING PROPHETIC SIGNS** FOR THE END OF DAYS

TERRY JAMES

GENERAL EDITOR

PRESS

DISCERNERS

ANALYZING CONVERGING PROPHETIC SIGNS FOR THE END OF DAYS

First Printing

Published by RR PRESS

RR Press
P.O. Box 969
Benton, AR 72018

ISBN: 9781087058368

All Scripture quotations are from the King James Version unless otherwise noted.
Cover and design by Brent Spurlock, Green Forest, AR.
Printed in the United States of America

www.raptureready.com

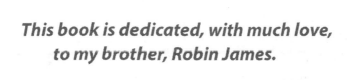

*This book is dedicated, with much love,
to my brother, Robin James.*

ACKNOWLEDGMENTS

THIS IS A BOOK truly a *labor of love*. The *love* is for the Lord of Heaven shared by all of the authors who have poured their considerable talents and time into the writing of these chapters.

My deep appreciation to each of my colleagues and friends who have been so generous in agreeing to contribute to *Discerners: Analyzing Converging Prophetic Signs for the End of Days*. May your collective effort bring forth great fruit for God's harvest.

My love and thanks to Angie Peters, my daughter in my heart, for another of many, many editing masterpieces accomplished for our books together. She holds my work-life together.

To Dana Neel, another of my *daughters*, my deep love and appreciation for making this book come to life through our self-publishing effort. Her superb business acumen and dedication means everything in bringing this book to publication.

To Brent Spurlock, my deep thanks for providing expert counsel and for contributing his very special design talents to this book's production.

To my long-time friend, Jim Fletcher, my profound thanks for helping guide us through the process as we produced and distributed *Discerners*. I'm thankful for such brothers in my Christian family.

As always, my thanks and deepest love for Margaret; Terry, Jr.; Nathan; Kerry; and Jeanie. They help form the nucleus of a life that might not otherwise be productive.

To Todd Strandberg, another indispensable family member, who is also my partner in raptureready.com, the great website he founded: my love and my appreciation for the preface to this book.

My heartfelt gratitude for the Christian friendship and love of Howard and Terri Lieber in contributing so much to this effort on behalf of our Lord.

Thanks to you, the reader of our volume on the importance of being a discerner in these closing days of the Age of Grace. May the Lord bless you with that supernatural ability to understand these troubling although exciting days just ahead.

To our Lord Jesus Christ, my greatest love and adoration. Without Him neither this book nor anything else would matter.

—Terry James

CONTENTS

PREFACE

TODD STRANDBERG

LATELY WE HAVE HEARD the term "fake news" being used to describe misreporting by news outlets. All too often, that term of condemnation is well deserved. We are lied to by this world's media and by many others. After all, Satan is called "the prince of the power of the air," the primary medium that is used to carry the falsehood he spreads.

He does all within his power to misdirect the creation he wants to destroy—that is, God's creation called man. If he can get humanity headed down the path to destruction, he can disrupt the Creator's plan to have with Him men, women, and children He wants in His heavenly family for eternity.

The devil certainly has made progress in doing just that—convincing human beings to go down the broad road that leads to the abyss. He continues to do all he can to cause as many as possible to be detoured from entering the "narrow gate" that leads to salvation.

Satan's efforts to divert people from coming to the Savior are ramping up. This can be observed in every area of life in this nation and around the planet. His coming against all that is godly can't be missed or denied by the *believer,* the *Christian* who has his or her *spiritual ears* and *spiritual* eyes set in the *discernment* mode.

None of what is happening in the devil's attempts to bring about the end of anything and everything that is godly and righteous should take the discerner by surprise. The Christian is commanded by the Lord to "look up and lift up your head" when we see all these things begin to come to pass.

Jesus said this is the time when "your redemption draws near" (Luke 21: 28).

We're in a time when all signs given by Jesus and the Old and New Testament prophets are *converging*. They're all coming together right before our spiritual ears and eyes.

Christians are expected to be discerners while these things are beginning to come to pass. And that, of course, is what this book is about. Each writer has laid out the signals that point to the Second Coming of Jesus Christ. These signs are everywhere one looks, and this means that Christ's call to His Church—His *Bride*—must be near. He must even now be standing at the doorway of Heaven getting ready to shout, "Come up here!" (Revelation 4:1).

INTRODUCTION

TERRY JAMES

JESUS LOOKED DIRECTLY AND deeply into the eyes of the pious religion-ists and elitist legalists (the Pharisees and Sadducees). His omniscient, penetrating, piercing gaze saw into their very souls. These religious zealots and lawyers sought to disprove the claims by His followers that He was sent from God. They wanted Him to immediately perform a private miracle for them, thinking, no doubt, that He would fail, giving them fodder for their attacks against Him.

Jesus, in answer to their probing demands for a sign, said:

> "When it is evening, ye say, It will be fair weather: for the sky is red. And in the morning, It will be foul weather to day: for the sky is red and lowring. O ye hypocrites, ye can discern the face of the sky; but can ye not discern the signs of the times?" (Matthew 16:2–3)

He then said:

> "A wicked and adulterous generation seeketh after a sign; and there shall no sign be given unto it, but the sign of the prophet Jonas." And he left them, and departed. (Matthew 16:4)

He warned His disciples then to beware of the religionists and legal-ists who add to or take away from true doctrine, thereby corrupting truth. Jesus commanded His followers to be discerning in regard to those whose "leaven" (destructive influences) corrupts truth.

Jesus' forewarning reminds of those today who seek to alter or even eliminate the truth of Bible prophecy. Peter, Christ's close disciple and an apostle, echoed Jesus' words to some extent when he said the following:

> Knowing this first, that there shall come in the last days scoffers, walking after their own lusts, And saying, Where is the promise of his coming? for since the fathers fell asleep, all things continue as they were from the beginning of the creation. For this they willingly are ignorant of, that by the word of God the heavens were of old, and the earth standing out of the water and in the water: Whereby the world that then was, being overflowed with water, perished: But the heavens and the earth, which are now, by the same word are kept in store, reserved unto fire against the day of judgment and perdition of ungodly men. (2 Peter 3:3–7)

Today, it's understandable that the humanistic scientists, sociologists, and political elitists of the world hate the thought of there being a God who is one day going to upset their applecart. But, the tragic fact is that many within so-called Christendom, including even high-profile evangelical pastors and leaders, also scoff at Bible prophecy as irrelevant to the present hour. They question, in mocking tone, this "promise" we believe the Bible teaches about the coming catastrophic intervention into the affairs of this corrupted, rebellious human condition.

The Rapture—particularly the pre-Trib Rapture—is more often than not berated with scathing invective by a number of the scoffers—though intricate, in-depth studies prove beyond doubt the truth of the pre-Trib Rapture.

In regard to truth about the pre-Trib Rapture of all believers of the Church Age, we can almost hear repeated in the scoffing the familiar, smirking, words once whispered to the first man and woman in the Garden of Eden: "Yea, hath God said?"

Many among the so-called clergy have no discernment about or even interest in Bible prophecy whatsoever. They mockingly invite us to show them a sign, but they really don't believe there are any. They point out that everything is as it was from the beginning, the way things have always been.

There have always been those, like us, they proclaim, who say Armageddon is at hand, that Bible prophecy is on its way to fulfillment.

It seems to me that if He were physically present during our time, Jesus would confront today's mocking sign-seekers with the same condemnation He used in the above passage. This is because, like the Pharisees and Sadducees of Christ's time, the modern versions of those "hypocrites" want only to scoff at Bible prophecy and to prove the Rapture isn't true.

I believe the Lord would repeat to these scoffers today:

> A wicked and adulterous generation seeketh after a sign; and there shall no sign be given unto it, but the sign of the prophet Jonas.

The heart of His words is the sign given through the prophet Jonah, who was in the great fish's belly three days and three nights, foreshadowing the death, burial, and resurrection of Christ centuries afterward.

Christ would indicate, in effect, that even if they weren't actually a part of that "wicked generation," certainly they were acting as if they were. He would tell these that there is no other sign for those who are in this category but the sign of Jonah.

By this condemnation He would be—as He did to those in that earlier time—telling them that the only way they could understand the signs of the time is to *believe*—to believe He was in their presence by believing in Him for salvation of their souls.

Jesus, alone, can provide discernment through spiritually regenerated hearts and minds. Until they know Christ for salvation, they remain blind to all going on around them.

Paul the apostle said it this way:

> But the natural man receiveth not the things of the Spirit of God: for they are foolishness unto him: neither can he know them, because they are spiritually discerned. (2 Corinthians 2:14)

With this condemnation and exhortation straight from the mouth of the Creator of all that is, those who do know Christ as Savior should take serious stock of their own mocking, scoffing attacks on Bible prophecy.

God expects His people, of whatever era or generation, to be *discerners* during the time when they inhabit the planet. Each and every person has the ability to discern the times in which they live their given increments of history. The Holy Spirit indwelling them gives this supernatural ability to *discern* what God wants them to know. They can choose not to be discerners, but the ability is there if they will but appropriate it.

It's Time to Discern the Times

We must look at factors most relevant to today's believers in examining Jesus' words of condemnation to those He called "hypocrites." The Pharisees and Sadducees of His day couldn't recognize the signs all around showing clearly that the Messiah was among them. They were spiritually blind because they could not or would not understand the sign of Jonah. They refused the truth of God's redemptive plan. Jesus was and is at the heart of that redeeming process. (Christ would soon be in the grave for three days and nights, then be resurrected, just as Jonah was three days and nights in the belly of the great fish.) They wouldn't acknowledge Jesus Christ as their Messiah; therefore, they qualified to have the Lord call them "hypocrites."

How so? Because they claimed to know the plan of God for Israel through their reading from the holy writings, but they denied the very power thereof. They had a form of godliness, while missing totally the very One among them who came to seek and save the lost of Israel—and the world. They were hypocrites by not discerning all the miracles and wonders surrounding Jesus' ministry, rather choosing to hate Him and wanting to do away with Him because He threatened their power over the people they were supposed to teach about Heaven's truth.

Christians of this day and hour, for the most part, are falling into the same trap that held those earlier hypocrites in its hellish jaws. Too many believers today, sitting under the tutelage of prophecy-denying or prophecy-ignoring pastors and teachers, are not discerning the blatantly prophetic times within which this generation is positioned.

Scripture exhorts us to understand our times and their prophetic import. We'll look briefly at two such exhortations from God's Word, then explore elements within the human condition today that make these heavenly instructions so specific to this late hour of mankind's history.

Prophecy Threatens Establishment Clergy

Judaizers of Jesus' time of ministry on earth were afraid He represented a threat to their power over the people. So, too, Christ coming back to this planet to set it aright must be looked at as a threat by some who rail against Bible prophecy that appears about to unfold. Their sometimes quite lucrative power bases might be lost if and when such a stupendous event occurs. Even exploring Scriptures from the pulpit about such matters might be detrimental to the status quo of ministry financial business and beyond.

Jesus' powerful verbal chastisement of the religionists of that day, like all of His teachings, speak to the need for discernment in these days so near the end of the age. Jesus *is* the very *Word* (John 1:1). He, through Holy Spirit-inspired writers of that Word, have much to say about things to come. We are commanded to look for things that are coming, according to Bible prophecy.

Paul the apostle wrote:

> Looking for that blessed hope, and the glorious appearing of the great God and our Saviour Jesus Christ. (Titus 2:13)

Luke recorded Jesus' own words about discernment as the Lord sat upon the Mount of Olives. He described world conditions and disturbing events that will unfold at the very end of the age, and wrapped up by saying:

> And when these things begin to come to pass, then look up, and lift up your heads; for your redemption draweth nigh. (Luke 21:28)

Believers alive at the time of Christ's next intervention into the affairs of mankind, then, are commanded to be watchful. They are to be *discerning* of the times. They are to strive to understand the signs all around them that indicate Christ is about to deliver them from the horrors He had just prophesied. When those believers see these signs begin to come to pass, their Redeemer will be on the cusp of keeping His promise of Revelation 3:10:

> Because thou hast kept the word of my patience, I also will keep thee from the hour of temptation, which shall come upon all the world, to try them that dwell upon the earth.

Signs for the Discerning Christian

Can there be any doubt that the conditions and activities God's Word predicts will be prevalent while the end of the age approaches are now being played out before our eyes? The similarities between the biblical descriptions and the reports we witness on our never-ending newscasts are stunning.

Man's atrocities against his fellow man are pandemic. Stories of debased human behavior are so numerous that what once would have been hardcopy, front-page headlines are now relegated to electronic, cyberspace pages farther back because even more heinous stories overshadow them.

Jesus Himself prophesied about the generation that would inhabit the earth at the time of His Second Advent:

> But as the days of Noah were, so shall also the coming of the Son of man be. (Matthew: 24:37)

He said, while discoursing with His disciples on the Mount of Olives, that that generation, like the pre-Flood society of Noah's day, will be "eating and drinking, marrying and giving in marriage" (Matthew 24:38). Like in the time of Noah, society will be conducting business as usual, having become desensitized to the perversities going on around them. They would be even more desensitized to any consideration of the things of God and the fact that divine judgment was already on the way.

Daniel the prophet said: "And the end of it shall be with a flood" (Daniel 9:26), meaning a flood of incorrigibly wicked behavior and a flood of God's wrath and judgment poured upon that unrepentant, blasphemous people of the apocalypse. Jesus said the generation alive at the end of the age will be immersed in doing what is right in their own eyes, just as the antediluvians. The people of that earlier, doomed generation were marrying, partying, and busily engaging in commerce while their perversions, debaucheries, violence, and blasphemies were simply well accepted, even welcomed ingredients within the cultural and societal mixture of the time. Jesus said that they were carrying on as usual "until the day that Noah entered into the ark, And knew not until the flood came, and took them all away, so shall also the coming of the son of man be" (Matthew 24:28–39).

Jesus was saying that people living at the time of His return will have become so rebellious that they will have rejected the notion of a Creator God. Their thinking will have become so reprobate, their consciences so seared, that many will no doubt even forget that such a God was ever said to have existed! Christ's coming will be so swift and startling that it will be analogous to the horror of that long-ago, worldwide deluge that destroyed all but those who were found righteous in God's eyes. Just prior to that Flood, Enoch disappeared, translated into the presence of the God with whom he walked righteously (Genesis 5:24). Noah and his family were supernaturally preserved upon the raging sea that engulfed the entire earth (Genesis 8).

Jesus also drew the parallel between the time of the destruction of the cities of Sodom and Gomorrah and the days that will immediately precede the consummation of the age:

> Also as it was in the days of Lot; they did eat, they drank, they bought, they sold, they planted, they built; But the same day that Lot went out of Sodom, it rained fire and brimstone from heaven, and destroyed them all. Even thus shall it be in the day when the Son of man is revealed. (Luke 17:28–29)

Peter the apostle wrote about Lot's days of interaction with the people of Sodom:

> For that righteous man [Lot] dwelling among them, in seeing and hearing, vexed his righteous soul from day to day with their unlawful deeds. (2 Peter 2:8)

Peter then went on to imply the type of behavior that greatly disturbed Lot—the sort of behavior that inevitably brings on Almighty God's indignation and judgment:

> But chiefly them that walk after the flesh in the lust of uncleanness, and despise government. Presumptuous are they; self-willed, they are not afraid to speak evil of dignities…. But these, as natural brute beasts, made to be taken and destroyed, speak evil of the things that they understand not, and shall utterly perish in their own corruption, And shall receive the reward of unrighteousness, as they that count it pleasure to revel in the daytime.
>
> Spots they are and blemishes, reveling with their own deceiving while they feast with you. Having eyes full of adultery and that cannot cease from sin; beguiling unstable souls; an heart they have exercised with covetous practices; cursed children, Who have forsaken the right way, and are gone astray….
>
> These are wells without water, clouds that are carried with the tempest, to whom the mist of darkness is reserved forever. For when they speak great swelling words of vanity, they allure through the lusts of the flesh, through much wantonness, those that are just escaping from them who live in error. While they promise them liberty, they themselves are the servants of corruption; for of whom a man is overcome, of the same is he brought in bondage. (2 Peter 2:8–19)

God's Word speaks powerfully of His opinion about the vile activities that were commonplace during Lot's day warning all generations that His righteous judgment must and will fall on those who engage in ungodly enterprises:

> Even as Sodom and Gomorrah, and the cities about them in like manner, giving themselves over to fornication, and going after strange flesh, are set forth for an example, suffering the vengeance of eternal fire. In like manner also

these filthy dreamers defile the flesh, despise dominion, and speak evil of dignities…these speak evil of those things which they know not; but what they know naturally, as brute beasts, in those things they corrupt themselves. Woe unto them! For they have gone in the way of Cain…. Raging waves of the sea, foaming out their own shame; wandering stars, to whom is reserved the blackness of darkness forever. (Jude 7–13).

The Holy Scripture then rolls before the mind's eye of our imagination the awesome truth contained within the words, "It is a fearful thing to fall in the hands of the living God" (Hebrews 10:31). As the book of Jude continues:

And Enoch also, the seventh from Adam, prophesied of these, saying, Behold, the Lord cometh with ten thousands of his saints, To execute judgment upon all, and to convict all that are ungodly among them of all their ungodly deeds which they have ungodly committed, and of all their hard speeches which ungodly sinners have spoken against him. These are murmurers, complainers, walking after their own lusts; and their mouth speaketh great swelling words, having men's persons in admiration because of advantage. But, beloved, remember ye the words which were spoken before by the apostles of our Lord Jesus Christ; How they told you there should be mockers in the last time, who should walk after their own ungodly lusts. These are they who separate themselves, sensual, having not the Spirit. (Jude 14–19)

Apologies to Sodom and Gomorrah

Ruth Bell Graham is attributed to have made the statement, in the context of surveying the growing wickedness she observed in her nation, that if God did not judge the United States, He would surely have to apologize to the cities of Sodom and Gomorrah. Many years have passed since Mrs. Graham allegedly made that (in my opinion, very correct) assessment. Does the fact that the United States hasn't been obliterated by fire and brimstone, all of its population consumed in a thermonuclear holocaust or by supernatural fire from the heavens, mean that we, as a nation, are improving to the extent the Almighty will not judge like He did those ancient cities? Or does it mean that Mrs. Graham was wrong?

One thing is sure: God is never wrong and thus never needs to apologize for His actions. He is the same yesterday, today, and forever (Hebrews 13:8). His immutability is perfectly consistent as recorded throughout His Word. Thankfully, and praise His Holy Name, so is His quality of mercy, His slowness to anger and wrath—or else the little, though tremendously prideful, creature called man would have ceased to exist long ago.

Mrs. Graham dramatically made the frightening (but true) point that sin ultimately brings death to individuals and to nations who transgress God's laws and refuse to repent. God's judgment might, in some cases, seem slow in falling as man counts finite time, but God's judgment is certain! This brings us to the question: Where does America—and for that matter, the world—stand in relationship to sin, repentance, and God's judgment like that which consumed the wicked cities of Sodom and Gomorrah? Has the TV soap opera like hedonism in which our society has gleefully bathed made the days of our lives, as the world turns, cleaner for all my children— and yours? Or have the filth and scum simply been loosened from the bottom of the world's bathtub and brought to the surface through glamour and aggrandizement to the point they stick to and permeate our lives while they, at the same time, provide a putrefying cesspool environment for sin germs to incubate and for soul-destroying infection to spread?

Examination, Diagnosis of and Prognosis for a Sick World

The authors of *Discerners: Analyzing Converging Prophetic Signs for the End of Days,* go into great depth to explore the issues and events of our day that, we believe, indicate the lateness of the prophetic hour. Read carefully each chapter to determine if you agree that Jesus must even at this moment be getting ready to fulfill Revelation 3:10.

Most adults in America today would, if honesty prevailed, acknowledge that our culture has changed markedly during the course of the last decade. Many of those adults—especially those of us fifty years of age and older—would have to admit, if that same degree of honesty held firm, that societal conditions in America and the world have suffered phenomenal degeneration despite spectacular technological breakthroughs and sometimes heroic efforts to better mankind's lot. That the human race is in rapid decline doesn't surprise Christians who are discerning—that is, those who are spiritually attuned to the prophetic warnings of their Heavenly Father's written Word.

> Evil men and seducers shall become worse and worse, deceiving and being deceived. (2 Timothy 3:13)

> This know also, that in the last days perilous times shall come, for men shall be lovers of their own selves, covetous, boasters, proud, blasphemers, disobedient to parents, unthankful, unholy, Without natural affection, trucebreakers, false accusers, incontinent, fierce, despisers of those that are good, Traitors, heady, high-minded, lovers of pleasures more than lovers of God, Having a form of godliness, but denying the power of it.... For of this sort are they who creep into houses, and lead captive silly women laden with sins, led away with various lusts, Ever learning, and never able to come to the knowledge of truth. (2 Timothy 3:1–7)

Does any of that seem familiar? Indeed, hasn't the entertainment industry, even down to and including pornography of the vilest sort daily crept into our houses and "led captive silly women"—and, incidentally, "silly men"? Are not our fallen human lusts whipped into ever-heightening frenzies while we see mankind's most wicked imaginings glamorously advertised on our television screens? Is it any wonder that our national and world societies have, in biblical terms, "gone the way of Cain"?

Paul the apostle, in that 2 Timothy account, warned that the last-days generation will pay the price for its self-sufficient, self-centered godlessness:

> For their folly shall be manifest to all men. (2 Timothy 3:9)

Manifestations of a Sin-Diseased Society

The fact that we live in a world that grows sicker by the minute is undeniable except to the most ostrich-like among us. A head-in-the-sand approach to life might, for a time, provide a degree of insulation against the worsening conditions closing in on even the most isolated havens of safety. Nonetheless, the time seems to be rapidly approaching when this generation will reach the fever pitch of that ancient one described by Paul in his letter to the Romans. Those people, like many—perhaps the majority—of those who are alive today, apparently thought the conditions that engulfed them were merely normal for the times in which they lived. They failed to detect the rising, killing temperature of their societal fever like in the perhaps trite but appropriate proverbial story of the frog simmering, then finally boiling to death, in a pot of water because the rise in temperature was so gradual he could not sense the change. Could it be that this generation, like those in Noah's day and like those about whom Paul wrote, are failing to or woefully refusing to read the thermometer of our time? Is *discernment* something that is as extinct as the dodo bird?

Paul wrote God's thoughts to all generations—perhaps particularly to those who will be alive at the time of Christ's return—about the course of degenerate human conduct that inevitably brings the Almighty's righteous judgment. We find that condemning message in Romans 1:18–32.

Although I deal later in the book with Paul's description of the Lord's condemnation of any rebellious, anti-God generation, I'll touch on it to some extent here. And our authors deal in-depth with these things throughout the following chapters. Our present time fits perfectly Paul's analysis of what brings on God's ultimate wrath and judgment.

Again, I address these condemning matters of Romans chapter 1 in the conclusion to this book. But we'll first look at them here.

Case Histories Then and Now

This generation, if reports coming in minute by minute are accurate, is indeed raging toward a precipice beyond which lurks the black abyss of apocalypse. Certainly, world society has for some time now been exhibiting all the symptoms prevalent during the time of the ancients, symptoms of the sin virus-engendered incorrigibility that caused a loving God to give the patient up to self-willed self-destruction.

Notice that Paul writes in Romans 1:28 that "God gave them over to a reprobate **mind**" (emphasis added).

That generation, like the ancients of Sodom and Gomorrah who would come later, were of one unchangeable mindset: They would rather perish than change! They were all in agreement. They were inalterably determined that each had the right to do what was right in his own eyes.

Undoubtedly, these judgment-bound societies termed doing what was right in their own eyes "freedom of choice." They pursued their own form and concept of life, liberty, and happiness totally apart from the loving God who created them. In their willful right to choose, obstinacy lay the chains of their enslavement to sin and, ultimately, God's wrath and destruction. It took the gushing waters of a broken earth and an angry, deluging sky to cleanse the sin-sick world of pre-Flood days. It took the fire and brimstone conflagration sent by a God of righteous judgment to purify that area of the earth's surface occupied by the cities of Sodom and Gomorrah during Lot's day.

Symptoms of Degenerative Sin Disease—Then and Now

God's Holy Word speaks bluntly about the cause and effect of sin disease that ravaged the earliest reported civilizations. Considering the Holy Spirit's words spoken through Paul's pen, it's clear that the people of those ancient civilizations flatly rejected the truth of God, although He plainly manifested Himself to them.

> Because, when they knew God, they glorified Him not as God, neither were thankful, but became vain in their imaginations, and their foolish heart was darkened. Professing themselves to be wise, they became fools. (Romans 1:21–22)

Let's briefly attempt to dissect what God's Word tells us was a systemic infection within that antediluvian society, with the hope of discerning similarities between the state of moral decay during their time on earth as compared to our own.

Symptom #1: Idolatry—The Antediluvian

Paul reported that the corrupted ancients:

> ...changed the glory of the incorruptible God into an image made like corruptible man, and birds, and four-footed beasts, and creeping things. Wherefore, God also gave them up to uncleanness through the lusts of their own hearts, to dishonor their own bodies between themselves, Who exchanged the truth of God for a lie, and worshipped and served the creature more than the Creator. (Romans 1:23–25)

God's first statement in Paul's letter is frighteningly unequivocal:

> For the wrath of God is revealed from heaven against all ungodliness and unrighteousness of men, who hold the truth in unrighteousness. (Romans 1:18)

After stating that He has clearly made Himself known to humankind through the creation that surrounds them, God exposes that early generation's unthankfulness and points an omniscient finger of guilt toward their idolatrous betrayal, the particular act that seems most egregious to Him.

Those people had "changed the glory of the incorruptible God into an image made like corruptible man." In other words, this generation, although they knew that God is God, nonetheless rejected Him and His own declaration to Himself, the Godhead (the Trinity—God the Father, God the Son, and the Holy Spirit).

"Let us make man in our image" (Genesis 1:26.). These willful people, in effect, said to the Almighty, "We are not made like unto your image; rather, we will make you into whatever image we choose!" They were obviously saying further, "We, like Lucifer, choose to become gods ourselves! Even though we are creatures, we choose to worship and serve ourselves—that is, do what is right in our own eyes rather than worship and serve You."

That generation, like Lucifer—who is that old serpent, Satan, and the devil—thereby exhibited the sinful attribute God says He hates above all others: PRIDE.

The writer of Proverbs records for us God's opinion of this most heinous sin:

> These six things doth the Lord hate; yea, seven are an abomination unto him: A proud look. (Proverbs 6:16–17)

Idolatry, then, springs from then orbits the iniquitous thing called pride. When idolatry becomes full-blown—i.e., a state of arrogance manifests itself through determination to usurp the very throne of the eternal God—He apparently quits dealing with that individual or generation, and allows their minds to become reprobate. The mindset becomes darkened by sin to the point that insanity rather than rationality rules not only the physical mind, but spiritual discernment as well. When that point of incorrigibility is reached and God lets people do what is right in their own eyes, human society is very soon turned upside down.

Almighty God, using His people, Israel, to speak not only to the generation of that time but to all generations and all nations, warns of the consequences of becoming so vile that God allows reprobate mentality to have its way:

> Woe unto them who call evil, good, and good, evil; who put darkness for light, and light for darkness; who put bitter for sweet, and sweet for bitter! Woe unto them who are wise in their own eyes, and prudent in their own sight!... Therefore, as the fire devoureth the stubble, and the flame consumeth the chaff, so their root shall be as rottenness, and their blossom shall go up as dust, because they have cast away the law of the Lord of hosts, and despised the word of the Holy One of Israel. Therefore is the anger of the Lord kindled. (Isaiah 5:20–25)

God expounds further through the prophet Isaiah about such prideful nations and individuals:

Ah, sinful nation, a people laden with iniquity, a seed of evildoers, children that are corrupters; they have forsaken the Lord, they have provoked the Holy One of Israel unto anger, they are gone away backward.

Why should ye be [dealt with through correction] anymore? Ye will revolt more and more; the whole head is sick, and the whole heart faint. From the sole of the foot even unto the head there is no soundness in it, but wounds, and bruises, and putrefying sores. They have not been closed, neither bound up, neither mollified with ointment. (Isaiah 1:4–6).

Isaiah then puts forth the terrifying fact that in God's foreknowing mind, these and all such reprobate peoples will suffer terribly. In God's thoughts, their fall is already an accomplished thing:

Your country is desolate, your cities are burned with fire, your land, foreigners devour It In your presence, and it is desolate, as overthrown by foreigners. (Isaiah 1:7)

When Pride Equals Death

God told Adam and Eve that if they ate of the fruit that was forbidden, they would surely die. They nonetheless succumbed to the serpent's tempting appeal to their pride—the implied promise that if they ate of the fruit, they would be "as God." So pride, the sort that causes human beings to desire to usurp Almighty God's authority, is poison to those who fall to its alluring tug, just as God warned. God's warning about the fatally toxic effects of disobedience was true. Every person inevitably gives up his or her physical existence to death. Pride, then, is not a characteristic that leads to a more desirable quality of life, as those who preach self-esteem would have it, but it is a fallen human trait that has always brought death to all mankind.

A tragic manifestation of humanistic pride equaling death is most clearly seen in the human historical record. Every civilization, culture, and society that has gone so deep into idolatry as to have exchanged "the truth of God for a lie" has had as a common practice in their idol worship the insane horror of child sacrifice.

History is replete with accounts of human sacrifice to pagan gods. Almost always, those sacrifices involve the most vulnerable. Children, young women, and sometimes the aged were most often selected by those who practice these abominable acts to placate their insatiable gods. We have all read of the Incas and the Aztecs, the ancient Hawaiians, and many other so-called civilizations whose hearts became so sin-blackened that their foolish minds grew dark—and human sacrifice was the ultimate result. However, it is a sad truth that those heathens were not the only societies to reach that depth of depravity.

God wrote through Jeremiah the prophet:

> Because of all the evil of the children of Israel and of the children of Judah, which they have done to provoke me to anger, they, their kings, their princes, their priests, and their prophets, and the men of Judah, and the inhabitants of Jerusalem. And they have turned unto me the back, and not the face; though I taught them, rising up early and teaching them, yet they have not hearkened to receive instruction.
>
> But they set their abominations in the house, which is called by my name, to defile it. And they built the high places of Baal, which are in the valley of the Son of Hinnom, to cause their sons and their daughters to pass through the fire unto Molech; which I commanded them not, neither came it into my mind, that they should do this abomination, to cause Judah to sin. (Jeremiah 32:32–35)

The Contemporary Heathen

There is no way the people of today would do the foolish and even insane acts historically attributed to those ancient heathen! Such might be the wishful acclamation of the most optimistic in the current world—especially in America. Surely an overwhelming majority of Americans would never fall prey to idolatry that, for example, "changed the glory of the incorruptible

God into an image made like corruptible man, and birds, and four-footed beasts, and creeping things." Oh no?

With the primary god of this age, mammon (money), haven't the affluent among our ranks, individually and collectively, fashioned the idols we've chosen to worship into forms that pleasure our own imaginations? Instead of worshipping the Creator, don't we rather bend the knee to our cars, boats, and sports teams—many of which we've named after birds, four-footed beasts, creeping things, and signs of the zodiac? Do we not sit for hours at a time before our computer or TV screens, amused at the debased activities we see, some of which might have made even the ancient pagans blush? The debasing goings-on draw our transfixed attention, in many cases resulting in turning over to their mesmerizing devices our children who desperately need nurturing. Are these not altars from which emanate the images made like corruptible man?

But surely we aren't among the generation of earth dwellers that has reached the point at which God has given us over to a collective reprobate mind. We would never allow child sacrifice, which is one of the sure manifestations of a totally reprobate civilization. Really?

Since *Roe v. Wade* was upheld by the Supreme Court of the land, more than sixty million babies have been aborted. Under the auspices of the secular religion called humanism, these little ones continue to be judged as nothing more than self-created possessions subject to disposal, should the women carrying them so choose. And now there is a growing number of those who demand that even born children be subject to being murdered following their births. Abortion on demand has generated a multibillion-dollar industry based on infanticide. By far, the greater number of abortions are performed for ridding the person and/or people involved of the child who would, they fear, interfere with their own, self-centered lifestyle. The majority are abortions of convenience, contraception after the fact of, in most cases, illicit sexual activity.

If God judged Israel for turning her back on Him, rebellion that brought a mindset so darkened by sin that they offered children in sacrifice to pagan Gods, will He not judge America? No other nation has been more blessed with the light of God's truth. Yet daily, under the full sanction of the United States government, thousands of our children are passed through the fires of abortion, sacrificed to the gods of convenience and pleasure and hedonism under the specious claim that a woman has a right to do what she wishes with her own body. In this convoluted way, freedom of choice becomes the willful demand to do what is right in their own eyes. In effect, she proclaims herself to be godlike. Child sacrifice, then, is idolatry come to fruition.

Symptom #2: Sexual Perversion

Paul the apostle, under inspiration, gave the second most pronounced manifestation of any society that has totally turned its back on the loving God who has, time and time again, called for it to turn from its course of wickedness. In spite of the liberal theological acrobatics some theologians and even secular humanists go through to try to explain away this and other accounts of sexual perversions that inevitably come to a hopelessly godless people, history attests that societal decay ends in the death throes of the basest kind of sexual depravity.

The Antediluvians

Paul writes of the decadent societal characteristic that is second only to immersion in idolatry:

> God gave them up unto vile affections; for even their women did exchange the natural use for that which is against nature. And likewise also the men, leaving the natural use of the woman, burned in their lust one toward another, men with men working that which is unseemly, and receiving in themselves the recompense of their error which was fitting. (Romans 1:26–27).

Historical accounts of Greece and Rome, and to a lesser extent, of other civilizations, validate and expand upon Paul's brief but graphic description of the sexual cesspool in which these ancients ultimately became mired. No rational denial can be made of the fact that Paul reported homosexuality to be the most glaring manifestation of that society's incorrigibility.

We should note that these people were so submerged in sexual pruri-ence—particularly male homosexuals—that they were "receiving in them-selves the recompense of their error, which was fitting." It is an appropriate speculation that this must have been AIDS and/or hepatitis, or something similar. It is interesting, too, that God said in this account that these homo-sexuals were receiving judgment in their bodies because of the error (the sin) of their homosexual activities.

The Contemporary Heathen

To review the past several decades with regard to how homosexuality has evolved from being kept in our culture's closet to being accepted now as an "alternate lifestyle" would be boringly redundant because of our familiar-ity with the facts. We've been fed daily doses of desensitizing hyperbole intended to convince us to accept that terrible, dehumanizing activity as not only normal, but as "gay." What God calls "vile" modern society calls "gay."

Perhaps nothing more needs to be said about how thinking in our gen-eration has become so reprobate that evil is now called good, and good is now called evil. Not only is what God called "abomination" now called "gay," but those who give a clarion call back to morality and point out the mind-darkened sin-error of such perversion are vilified as "intolerant bigots" at best or as "homophobic Nazi- types" at worst.

Those who view wanting to marry someone of the same sex as being against the order God established are called "haters." Those who believe that allowing grown men to use a public restroom while women and girls are using the same one is perverted are called insensitive to gender identity. Those who believe that changing genders is wrong are called intolerant and out of touch with the changing times.

Discerning the Signs

Many symptoms of systemic sin sickness boil to the surface and erupt for all to see between the time a society determines to turn its back on God and the time a people become so wicked that God gives up pleading for them to repent because their hearts and minds can't be turned again to Him. It is incumbent upon Christians, who have the capability to discern the signs pointing to how near is the time when God's judgment must fall, to be *watchmen on the wall*.

Discerners: Analyzing Converging Prophetic Signs for the End of Days is a book we prayerfully trust will help the reader who is a believer in Jesus Christ become *watchmen on the wall*.

Each chapter's author has presented, I believe, Holy Spirit direction for discerning these strange but exciting times so near when Jesus will step out on the clouds of glory and call all who are born again to Himself (Revelation 4:1).

How sick is the patient?

What is the prognosis for the sin sickness that courses through the life's blood of this generation? We must seek answers to these questions by first examining our own lives. Society, culture, and civilization are no better or worse collectively than its individual members. The sickness that afflicts one afflicts all. The good news is there is a cure. And the cure is the GOOD NEWS—the good news of the gospel of Jesus Christ, who came to seek and save every person from the darkness of sin. God is "not willing that any should perish, but that all should come to repentance" (2 Peter 3:9).

Jesus Christ alone can regenerate the hearts and minds of fallen man and restore him to health and newness of life. If you haven't done so, take the cure.

Accept Jesus Christ this moment as your Savior and your Lord.

> That if thou shalt confess with thy mouth the Lord Jesus, and shalt believe in thine heart that God hath raised him from the dead, thou shalt be saved. For with the heart man believeth unto righteousness; and with the mouth confession is made unto salvation. (Romans 10:9–10)

CHAPTER 1

"PERILOUS TIMES" PROPHECY BEYOND AMAZING

LARRY SPARGIMINO

'M GOING TO MAKE an admission that might shock some of my readers: I am a humanist. In fact, I'm going to make another possibly shocking admission: I am also a feminist.

Before you consign me to eternal perdition, allow me to clarify. I am a *biblical* humanist and a *biblical* feminist. When we hear the words "humanism" and "feminism," we think left-wing humanism and left-wing feminism. But the fact is, progressives, left-wingers, atheists, and God-haters are neither humanists nor feminists. It is impossible for those who reject the authority of the Bible and the lordship of Jesus Christ to be on the side of men and women, boys and girls.

As we look at the "perilous times" of Scripture, we see a growing number of evils that are destructive to human life and sanity. Things like sex-change reassignment surgery and hormone treatment, gender fluidity, the legalization of prostitution, marriage to robots, third-trimester abortion, and the war on freedom of speech and religious liberty are dehumanizing and represent Satan's final goal of completely erasing the image of God in man. The Lord Jesus Christ wants us to enjoy the abundant life (John 10:10); Satan is preparing mankind for abundant misery (John 8:44; 1 John 2:18).

> This know also, that in the last days perilous times shall come. (2 Timothy 3:1)

God inspired the Apostle Paul by the Holy Spirit to write about "perilous times" in the last days. While the Holy Spirit fully knew the depths of the perversity and ugliness of the end times, it is doubtful If Paul, as the human vehicle of divine revelation, knew the full extent of how perilous the "perilous times" would be.

I have been commenting on the culture war, writing on Bible prophecy, and seeking to "connect the dots" for almost thirty years. Thirty years ago, the times were dark. Yet I did not realize how much darker they would get and how quickly all of that would unfold. As I watch the latest developments in human rebellion and rage against God and His blessed ways, I realize that these are perilous times "beyond amazing." If the Lord tarries and the Rapture trumpet does not yet sound, I am convinced that the darkness will get yet darker.

In the early 1980s, Drs. Emil Gaverluk and Rob Lindsted did a series of radio programs on the *Watchman on the Wall* broadcast of Southwest Radio Church dealing with the exponential curve and how it explains the increasing perversity of the expression of human depravity. In mathematics, the exponential curve reflects the fact that there is more of everything and that there is an acceleration in the rapidity with which this increase is taking place.

For thousands of years, man fought with primitive weapons that remained, for centuries, at the same primitive level of lethality. But within the last half century, we now have weapons that seem to have emerged from a sci-fi novel. For thousands of years, man had traveled no more than twenty to thirty miles an hour. The speed of horses in one century remained the same for many centuries; yet within the last half century, we have broken the sound barrier many times over. Because of the exponential curve, the way human depravity is now able to express itself has intensified and been magnified many times over. There is another aspect to the exponential curve that we will delve into later in this chapter, but at this point, we simply want to point out the increasing peril we are facing in these last days.

The Gaverluk-Lindsted programs were originally published in booklet form under the title *Suddenly No More Time!* In 2003, Dr. Noah Hutchings asked me to write a full-length book for Southwest Radio Church under the same title. In the years that have passed since writing that book, I am increasingly amazed at how the exponential curve is taking us to depths of evil I never imagined.

Because of the rapid advance of technology and the growing depravity of humanity, I believe that it is even doubtful whether Paul and Timothy understood what we would see today. There is something desperately wrong with man. Science and technology have a way of magnifying it. We were good at killing each other when we only had sticks and stones, but mass murder becomes much easier with nuclear weapons.

When Philip went to Samaria, we see the Spirit of God mightily at work: "For unclean spirits, crying with loud voice, came out of many that were possessed with them…. And there was great joy in that city" (Acts 8:7–8), yet Simon was active "and bewitched the people of Samaria" (vs. 9).

In later times, even in times of revival and church growth, we still see apostasy. Chuck Smith, Greg Laurie, and others associated with the early years of Calvary Chapel saw how the Lord transformed an unlikely generation in the 1970s, yet there were those who fell away.

> When he was a teenager, Greg [Laurie] saw some who'd come to faith in Jesus, their faces wet with tears. Yet a few weeks later, they'd dropped away. One girl said that she just couldn't get that feeling back anymore. A guy said that his dog had gotten hit by a car, and if God had allowed that to happen, then he couldn't follow Him. Another guy confessed that he missed weed and sex too much to try to walk the straight and narrow with Jesus.[1]

Current events, however, right here in our beloved America show an intensifying of evil—an evil beyond evil. So, when is this all going to come to a head? When will the Omega Point be reached? Second Timothy 3:1 tells us that it will be in "the last days."

Ray Stedman (d. 1992) relates that when he was in grade school, he was filled with fear, concerned about the terrible times that had come upon America. "I was confident," he writes, "that the 'terrible times' were being fulfilled in that day, years ago. The Great Depression was beginning; there was much trouble and strife in the United States.... Already the looming threat of World War II was gathering on the horizon."

In a blog, Stedman noted, however, that on the Day of Pentecost, Peter quoted the prophecy of Joel, in which the prophet said that "in the last days" God would pour His Spirit upon all flesh (Acts 2:17). "That, Peter said, was beginning to be fulfilled on the Day of Pentecost, almost two thousand years ago."

> Again and again in our Western world, we have had periods of relative peace and prosperity, only to have them interrupted by terrible times of stress and agony that repeatedly invades human affairs. So these words are not necessarily a prediction of the last days for the church; rather, they are a recognition of the cycle of days like this that will keep coming. And, of course, *one of them is going to be the last one* [italics supplied by LS].[2]

Yet, if we add one other item to the mix, we get a clearer picture of the last of the last days. That item is prophetic convergence. There have always been famines, floods, and freakish phenomena in the skies. However, when we see that God, in His providential arrangement of time and history, is synchronizing things so that they are all coming together at once—and keeping in mind that Israel is now a nation—there is high likelihood that we are now in that last cycle of days Stedman was referencing, i.e., "one of them is going to be the last one."

Enter the Romantic Robots

With the increasing popularity of sexbots—even brothels are featuring them—and the rising number of divorces, experts are predicting that human-robot marriage will be legal by 2050.

As I write this, there was a recent "Love and Sex with Robots" weekend at Goldsmith University in London. David Levy, author and expert on sex and intimacy with robots, believes there is going to be a sharp rise in such activity when the public at large realizes all the advantages, with hardly any disadvantages, to a robot-human marriage. Adrian Cheok, computing professor at City University London and director of the Mixed Reality lab in Singapore, says that sexbots could fulfill perverse male sexual fantasies and that robot-human marriages will have an overwhelmingly positive effect on society. Cheok believes that some people just weren't made for marriage, yet they need companionship with the opposite sex.[3]

Marriage—between two humans, one male and one female—is an ordinance of God. It can be a sanctifying experience. Putting two people together under the same roof with little kids coming in to the world has a way of chipping the rough edges off of us. It's one of the ways God brings maturity to His children. However, what will society be like when maladjusted people never grow up because their mates are machines?!

Though this seems like a scary thought, we are definitely being prepared for human-robot relationships. We already have chat apps and bots that can be our "friends," provide a wide range of entertainment, and help us with our political views. Human life, relationships, and pleasure can be augmented by mixed-reality experiences that allow us to carry our "significant other" in our pockets, thus merging fantasy with reality. Our "significant other" is traditionally thought of as our spouse. Is it possible to have our affection drawn away from our spouse by a gadget?

Creating Your Own Boyfriend

Have you ever heard someone say, "My boyfriend doesn't understand me"? Quartz online offered a helpful piece—at least the author, Fei Liu, thinks it's helpful. She wrote an article titled, "I'm Building a Robot Boyfriend—And You Can, Too." This love machine has a name, Gabriel2052. The author writes:

> Gabriel2052[']s library of motor movements will know what I'm turned on by, his fingertips ghosting across the back of my neck with the right force-per-unit area. His motorized parts will know how to spread goosebumps across my skin, and his sensors will detect when my breath quickens in response.[4]

More recent innovations in robotics are being announced on an almost daily basis. The recent rise of "self-aware robots" has brought us a major step closer to man's creation of a "machine capable of thinking for itself from scratch"—i.e., without prior programming by a human. Engineers at Columbia University claim to have smashed one of the biggest barriers in the field of robots after a mechanical arm, which had not been programmed with any instructions, began performing practical tasks after just a few hours of "learning." The team claimed this as the first time a robot has shown the ability to "imagine itself," thereby working out what its purpose is and how to perform it. The robotic arm spent some thirty-five hours moving about at random while intensive machine-learning and computing was going on. After a time, the robot began successfully performing exercises, picking up objects, and placing them elsewhere. Professor Hod Lipson, who leads the Creative Machines lab where the research was carried out, said, "This is perhaps what a newborn child does in its crib, as it learns what it is."[5]

"Without natural affection" (2 Timothy 3:3)

Now that society has been dumbed down and consciences have been seared, the law of God, chiseled on the heart, has been chipped away. How has this happened? How is it that we are now descending to the point that we are "without natural affection"—meaning that we're at the point where we're more animalistic than even the animals?

The Tightening Noose

There is a process that is becoming more and more evident. Alarmism and a natural revulsion always seem to precede the next slip into every advance into perversion, but then, the human psyche adjusts, and the weird, bizarre, outlandish, and that which is totally against God—same-sex marriage, sex reassignment surgery—becomes normalized and generally accepted. At first, porn raised a general revulsion, then, with Internet dating and Snapchat sexting, it was accepted into modern life. One by one, these technologies and moral downgrades slipped in under our moral radar, for a time creating a wave of panic and alarm. However, as people adjusted, these perversions were normalized and became a part of life. So, too, with the general acceptance of marijuana, even for recreational use, even in traditionally conservative states like Oklahoma. (However, as a resident of Oklahoma, I can say that the general public was apathetic about opposing it even though many ministries and conservative groups sought to warn about its health dangers.) First there is an almost universal ban, then a national ban, and while that ban is still in place, states begin their acceptance. While *Roe v. Wade* opened the floodgates, now the whole dam has crumbled. Liberals cleverly assured everyone that abortion should be "safe, legal, and rare." Now, this vile practice has become "healthcare and a woman's right." Some women even parade and boast, "I love my abortions."

Virginia Governor Ralph Northam now wants to be "civil" about killing newborns. He ended his response to questions about approving third-trimester abortions by saying, "So again, as I said in my comments about this earlier, we can agree to disagree, but let's be civil about it." Dr. Michael L. Brown responds the way we all should:

> What? Let's "agree to disagree" about the ethics of infanticide? Let's be civil about terminating the life of a newborn? With respect, sir, that is not going to happen. Not as long as there are Americans with a conscience. Not as long as there are Americans with a heart. We do recognize that abortion can sometimes be an agonizingly difficult choice for a pregnant woman, like a 16-year old raped by her drunken uncle. While we still say that abortion was the wrong choice, we do not condemn the teen as a moral monster.... Gov. Northam, we will never "agree to disagree" with you about infanticide. As Vice President Pence wrote, what you're advocating "is morally reprehensible and evil."[6]

If things go the way the Left hopes, it will soon be illegal to teach abstinence-only sex ed in Colorado's public schools. No kidding! A Colorado bill backed by Planned Parenthood and the American Civil Liberties Union characterizes abstinence-only sex ed as insufficient and lacking and does not meet the requirements of the curriculum. Teachers would be required to include "the relational or sexual experiences of lesbian, gay, bisexual or transgender individuals" in their lessons without using "shame-based or stigmatizing language or instructional tools." In case you missed the point, the Bible, or Bible-based curricula, is forbidden.

Most public schools in Colorado have taught "comprehensive" sex-ed courses since 2013, but some charter and rural schools opted out of doing so. This current bill will remove that option, requiring schools to teach either the proposed sex-ed curriculum or nothing at all.[7]

Surgery That Doesn't Heal

If you were a surgeon and someone asked you to perform surgery that would not help the patient in any way, was not needed, would produce a wound that would not heal, would not make the individual feel better, and would produce suicidal tendencies in the patient, do you think you would perform the surgery? In the case of gender dysphoria, doctors perform a surgery that amputates perfectly healthy body parts simply because the patient feels he or she was born in the wrong body.

The *New York Times* printed a shockingly honest, first-person article about Andrew Long Chu, a man who identifies as a woman and is raising money for sex-reassignment surgery that he admits will be harmful. In the piece, Chu says that he knows the transition will not make him happy. "Until the day I die," he writes, "my body will regard [the result of this surgery] as a wound…(that) will require regular, painful attention to maintain." Unbelievably, Chu even admits that the transition process and treatments have made him more miserable and the hormones he is being given have made him suicidal. John Stonestreet, president of the Chuck Colson Center for Christian Worldview and BreakPoint cohost, writes: "As hard—brutal even—as this piece is to read, please do. It's a look behind the curtain of a harmful ideology to which our entire culture is currently bowing down."[8]

Better Yet, Choose Your Race, Age, or Even Species!

While the transgender community is adamant that people should be allowed to choose their gender, and some jurisdictions have incorporated that idea into law, a new poll indicates that a substantial portion of British adults believes people should also be allowed to choose their age…and race…and even their species.

The survey, a project of ComRes, interviewed 2,002 British adults ages eighteen and up online in September of 2018. One in three respondents support those over eighteen being allowed to self-define their race. Twenty percent supported those over eighteen being able to self-define their age. Stunningly, it also found 10 percent "support those who wish to define as a non-human species." The UK's Coalition for Marriage, a conservative British organization that supports traditional marriage, said:

> Worryingly the poll found significant support for those who want to self-define their race (32 percent), their age (19 percent) and even their species (10 percent). Among young people, these figures were higher in every category. Thirty-four percent of 18–24 year olds backed the right to choose your race, 23 percent their age and 18 percent their species.[9]

These individuals are to be pitied and prayed for. They and multitudes of others entrapped by humanistic ideologies are the best proof for biblical Christianity. They have rejected it. Their lives are in shambles. They are so far from the real world that they don't even realize it. Fact, fantasy and fiction are blurred together. Their motto could very well be, "Just because it's fiction doesn't mean it's not real."

"Despisers of those that are good" (2 Timothy 3:3)

In the world of media, with its far-left tilt, one's Christian faith—especially that of a person in high office—is a target for mockers.

The women of ABC News' *The View* took a shot at Vice President Mike Pence's Christian faith, mocking the former governor of Indiana for talking to Jesus. They even called it a "mental illness." Joy Behar joked, "Can he talk to Mary Magdalene without his wife in the room?"[10]

She was referring to the vice president's rule that he would not be seen in public with a woman unless his wife was present. It's a good rule, one that is underscored by the many sexual harassment cases popping up. Yet, the vice president was mocked by Jia Tolentino, who said he "refuses to dine extramaritally." She said Pence's practice is hindering women from gaining positions of authority in the corporate world.[11]

The vice president's wife, Karen, was also slammed for teaching at a Christian school that prohibits "homosexual activity." This has thrown the LGBT crowd into a rage—reminding us of Psalm 2, which asks: "Why do the heathen rage?" Yet, Robert W. Tuttle, a professor at George Washington Law School, told the *Washington Post* that Immanuel Christian School's language on sexuality is typical of conservative Christian institutions and that the Second Lady is well within her rights to teach there. The standards of Immanuel Christian school, as found on page 11 of the school's employment application, includes words and phrase such as:

> I understand that the term "marriage" has only one meaning: the uniting of one man and one women in a single, exclusive covenant union as delineated in Scripture and that God intends sexual intimacy to occur only between a man and a woman who are married to each other.... Moral misconduct which violates the bona fide occupational qualifications for employees includes, but is not limited to, such behaviors as the following: heterosexual activity outside of marriage (e.g., premarital sex, cohabitation, extramarital sex), homosexual or lesbian sexual activity, polygamy, transgender identity, and other violations of the unique roles of male and female.[12]

Actor Neal McDonough was fired from the ABC series *Scoundrels* in 2010 for refusing to engage in sex scenes with his co-star Virginia Madsen. McDonough has been married to model Ruve Robertson since 2003 and the couple shares five children. McDonough told a reporter that he's so dedicated to his wife that he still refuses to do love scenes with other actresses. "I won't kiss any other woman because these lips are meant for one woman," he said.[13] In this cultural climate, it is becoming evident that more and more professions are not for those who wish to follow the standards of the Bible.

While I don't want to set up President Trump as a "paragon of virtue," Donald Trump has backed several issues that resonate well with Christians—support for Israel, support for life, fiscal responsibility, and religious liberty, for example. Yet the MAGA hat ("Make America Great Again" red hat) has drawn anger and abuse for those who wear it. During the third straight day of student protests against the outcome of the presidential election, several students beat up a fifteen-year-old who was wearing a MAGA hat. In San Antonio, Texas, a teen who made national news after having his MAGA hat angrily stolen in a Whataburger restaurant has received a replacement cap personally signed by Mr. Trump.[14] Several more incidents prove that wearing a MAGA hat in America could be dangerous to life and limb.

One could write pages and pages showing how the Left despises basic Christian morality and those who identify with it. Family, home, marriage, church attendance, and identifying with Christianity all seem to throw so-called tolerant liberals into a fit of rage. Like a pack of hungry dogs after a hapless fawn, they snarl, growl and bite. It would be easy to conclude that this is part of the judicial hardening that the Apostle Paul speaks of with the words, "For this cause God gave them up" (Romans 1:26). Paul continues a few verses later, "Who knowing the judgment of God, that they which commit such things are worthy of death, not only do the same, but have pleasure in them that do them" (vs. 32).

"Having a form of godliness, but denying the power thereof" (2 Timothy 3:5)

The apostle is not referring to lost people on the outside of professing Christendom, but to lost people who are a part of the visible church, whose hearts have never been changed by the grace of God. The word "apostasy" never refers to pagans who have not believed, but to those who have fallen away from their profession of faith, thus showing that they are "professors but not possessors."

It's not hard to recognize a person who is a "news freak." That person stays on top of current events and can talk up a storm about what is happening in today's world. Nor is it hard to recognize a sports enthusiast. He or she spends time listening to the words of the members of their favorite team. The same is true with those who have spent time with God. You can recoqnize them by the focus of their life, what grabs their hearts, and their willingness to talk about their faith. These are the people who want more of God, not more of the blessings He imparts. In his excellent book, *More of God,* R. T. Kendall writes:

> If you are like many people in the church, today, you want more *from* God more than you want more *of* God. Wanting more *of* God is desiring Him for what He is in Himself. Paul prayed that the Ephesians would "be filled with all the fullness of God" (Eph. 3:19). Wanting more *from* God is *using* Him to accomplish your goals. Wanting more *of* God is partaking of the "divine nature, having escaped from the corruption that is in the world because of sinful desire" (2 Pet. 1:4). Wanting more *from* God is seeking Him to get what you want.[15]

Unfortunately, coldness in the American church and apostasy in the pulpits of America is going big time. Dr. Ron Rhodes reports that pastors are now defecting from the faith. Jerry DeWitt had been a pastor in the Bible Belt, but the problem of evil and all the extreme suffering some people experience was more than he could handle. He finally wrote a book titled *Hope After Faith: An Ex-Pastor's Journey from Belief to Atheism.* There are actually websites devoted to apostasy. One website aimed at apostate pastors and others, *Recovering from Religion*, affirms, "If you are one of the many people who have determined that religion no longer has a place in your life, but are still dealing with the after-effects in some way or another, *Recovering from Religion* may be just the right spot for you."[16]

These are the casualties from health-and-wealth preaching. Big TV stars and Christian personalities have led many to believe that if they follow Christ, they will be able to "name it and claim it." When this doesn't happen, people turn from "religion." It is a good thing when people turn from "religion"—that's not biblical Christianity. Sometimes, however, they have been so burned by unscriptural promises that they embrace atheism and secularism. If you expect more from God and don't get it, you will depart from Him.

"Ever learning and never able to come to the knowledge of the truth" (2 Timothy 3:7)

A multitude of people have a lot of "head knowledge" about Christianity and the Bible. With the Internet and "distance learning," there are many more opportunities than ever before to know about Bible history, language and linguistics, church history, and many other disciplines that were, until only a few years ago, available only to the "theologically privileged." Now, however, just about anyone who wants to learn more about the Bible can do so.

Linguistic tools enabling the user to plumb the depths of Greek and Hebrew words and gain a knowledge of Bible archeology are all at our fingertips. I don't want to deny my great gratitude to the Lord for the "tools" that have been prepared for Bible study. However, we must not only seek to know the Book. We must seek to know the Author of the Book.

Our goal must always be to know God, not just to know about God. There are many false substitutes. God has much more planned for us than for us to just become nice people. He wants to flood our lives with the same power that raised Christ from the dead (Ephesians 1:19–20). The Blessed Trinity is not simply seeking to civilize us and help us be productive citizens; He wants us to be Christlike. While I agree that getting a good grip of basic Bible doctrines and theology is important, we need to remember that theology can be like porn: There is the imagination of a relationship without the risk. The Bible is indeed a book of propositional truths that are eternally valid because they come from the Eternal God. However, the Bible is also a roadmap to God. As we get into the details of studying the map and maybe even arguing over our understanding of the map, we get so engrossed in the map that we fail to make the journey.

When Paul writes that there are some who are never able to come to the "knowledge of the truth," we need to know that there are two words for "knowledge." One word is *gnosis,* which can describe cognitive knowledge, knowing about something. But that is not the word the apostle uses in 2 Timothy 3:7. There, he uses the word *epignosis*, which means "full knowledge." There are some who are always learning but who are never able to come to the "full knowledge" of the truth.

> Now as Jannes and Jambres withstood Moses.... But
> they shall proceed no further: for their folly shall be manifest
> unto all men, as theirs also was. (2 Timothy 3:8–9)

Jannes and Jambres are the names given in early Jewish extrabiblical writings to the Egyptian magicians who opposed Moses (Exodus 7:8–13). While 2 Timothy 3 is about terrible times and terrible people, they're not all terrible people. Notice what Paul says about the terrible people: "They shall proceed no further: for their folly shall be manifest unto all men, as theirs also was."

A few verses later, in verse 13, the apostle writes: "But evil men and seducers shall wax worse and worse, deceiving, and being deceived." The text does not say that "all men shall wax worse and worse." Who will "wax worse and worse"? Those who are "deceiving, and being deceived." Some will be like those who knew the folly of Jannes and Jambres. They recognized these false workers of evil.

As a pastor, prophecy researcher, and author, I watch the news carefully. I see the same phenomenon happening over and over: "Pushback." I first noticed it in Islamic countries. There was pushback against radical Islam. ISIS had been brutal and had taken many lives; yet, as a result, Muslims are examining their faith as never before, and they're asking some hard questions. Many are even converting to Christ. More Muslims have converted to Christ in the last ten years than in all the previous centuries combined.[17]

Similarly, homosexuals are trying hard to dominate the world with a massive push to make homosexuality "normal." Yet, there is pushback. Homosexuals are finding liberty in Christ and speaking against liberal legislators who want to make it a criminal offense to give biblical counsel to homosexuals who want to leave that lifestyle.[18] As Paul wrote about Jannes and Jambres, "But they shall proceed no further: for their folly shall be manifest unto all men, as theirs also was."

Earlier I spoke about my book, *Suddenly No More Time*. Take a chessboard and place one penny on the first square, two on the second, four on the third—doubling the number on each subsequent square. On the thirteenth square you would have 4,096 pennies! By doubling, you have 1 penny, then

2, then 4. After that, you have 8, 16, 32, 64, 128, 256, 512, 1,024, 2,048, and, finally, 4,096 pennies—simply by doubling. We cannot escape the sudden leap in the number of pennies.

When I first wrote *Suddenly No More Time,* I applied the exponential increase to bad things. Yes, there is an exponential increase in evil and in the ways of disseminating it. However, we need to notice that there is also a parallel expansion and increase in things that are *good.* Technology can be used for evil, but it can also be used for good. Every year, more and more people are celebrating Christmas and Easter than ever before. The Word of God is going out and impacting lives for good.

It was somewhat gratifying to see the pro-life response to Governor Andrew Cuomo of New York and Governor Ralph Northam of Virginia, both of whom are arguing for infanticide. Keep it up, men. At this rate we will have an overwhelmingly pro-life population that realizes the implication of pro-choice theology. We can be encouraged that doctors, scientists, social scientists, Christian writers, and pastors have made their position loud and clear. It has been gratifying to see God's people rise up against things that are clearly not in His will. Christians in America have been soft and drowsy. It took the disaster of 9/11 to remind us of the danger from radical Islam.

Radical Leftists Drive Away Jobs and Mega Bucks

It's always good when eyes are opened to evil and people see danger. The Democratic Party is laced with socialists; more people are realizing that. Some Democrats know that this will spell the death of the party. Trump will win in the next presidential election unless the radical left-wingers in the Democratic party are reined in. They are bad for the party because they attack success, prosperity, and the jobs that make success and prosperity possible.

When Amazon announced it had changed its mind on its plans to build its second headquarters (HQ2) in New York City because of the hostility of New York socialist lawmakers, notably Democratic Congresswoman Alexandria Ocasio-Cortez (AOC), many New Yorkers—even Democratic progressives—were upset. Amazon released a statement that gave the reason the company was pulling out:

> While polls show that 70% of New Yorkers support our plans and investment, a number of state and local politicians have made it clear that they oppose our presence and will not work with us to build the type of relationships that are required to go forward with the project we and many others envisioned in Long Island City.

Even leftist leaders in New York like Governor Andrew Cuomo and New York City Mayor Bill de Blasio lamented losing the benefits of Amazon's HQ2, which included a pledge from the tech giant to create twenty-five thousand jobs, paying an average of $150,000 per year in exchange for a slew of city and state tax breaks and subsidies worth up to $3 billion.[19] Not only do leftists kill babies, they're also adept at killing the economy.

"For Their Folly Shall Be Manifest"

As we see from 2 Timothy 3:9, not everyone is defecting from the faith or softening the message so that it is more palatable to the politically correct crowd. A good example is Pastor Robert Jeffress, currently pastor of the First Baptist Church of Dallas, Texas. Though he pastors a megachurch, he is politically incorrect—fiercely so. In his book, *Outrageous Truth…7 Absolutes You Can Still Believe,* Jeffress points out that if you don't believe that truth is currently hated by a large number of people, just try making any one of the following comments around the breakroom at work or even at a church dinner: "Only Christians will go to heaven; everyone else is going to hell." "The husband is the head of the family." "Homosexuality is a perversion." "Then just sit back and watch the fireworks explode!" Jeffress says in his book. "You'll most likely hear the terms *intolerant, bigot, uneducated,* and *arrogant* hurled at you." Jeffress deals with several other "outrageous truths" as well, such as "Every Other Religion Is Wrong," "God Sends Good People to Hell," and "Evolution is a Myth."

When Jeffress was pastor of First Baptist Church in Wichita Falls, Texas, a member of the church brought him copies of two children's books from the local library: *Daddy's Roommate* and *Heather Has Two Mommies*. The former won the Lambda Literary Award for Gay Men's Small Press Book Award (1990). Both books tell the story of a child being raised by a homosexual couple. It just so happened that the week the books were brought to Pastor Jeffress' attention, his sermon was on God's destruction of Sodom and Gomorrah. He read from *Daddy's Roommate,* then said, "Here's a library book—purchased with your tax dollars—promoting sodomy, which is illegal in the state of Texas." He then said, "It is time for God's people to say 'Enough!'"[20]

In 1990, when Rick Scarborough became pastor of First Baptist Church of Pearland, Texas, he found that not one member of the church was involved in civil government as an elected official at any level. That all changed when Scarborough went to a school assembly "in which a cute, petite, bubbly, twenty-four-year-old coed" spoke to students and described "in great detail every form of sexual expression you can imagine." She displayed a condom, "today's amoral solution for the host of afflictions that accompany illicit sex." She stretched it, made jokes about the male anatomy, and announced, 'Condoms are 94 percent effective in combating AIDS when used correctly.'" Scarborough stood up in the assembly and challenged her, "Ma'am, where did you get your statistics of 94 percent? I have read a lot on the subject, but I have never heard anyone suggest condoms are 94 percent safe." To make a long story short, Pastor Scarborough went public. The parents were outraged and the school board was replaced.[21]

A Reminder: God Is Still God

We don't want to minimize the intensity of evil and the reality of Satan. Nevertheless, we need to remember that divine power is still being manifested today. I would encourage my readers to read Lee Strobel's new book, *The Case for Miracles: A Journalist Investigates Evidence for the Supernatural.* It's a thorough investigation that opens with an interview with a well-known skeptic who was once a professing Christian but is now an atheist. It also deals with situations in which God did not perform a miracle.

An atheist turned Christian, Strobel was the award-winning legal editor of the *Chicago Tribune* and is the best-selling author of several books whose titles all have the words, *The Case for...*

The Case for Miracles presents a number of medically verified healings. At the beginning of the book, Strobel tells of Pastor Duane Miller, who served in a Baptist congregation in Brenham, Texas. One Sunday morning, the pastor could hardly speak. Over a three-year period, Miller saw sixty-three physicians. His case was scrutinized by a Swiss symposium. The conclusion: Miller would never speak normally again.

Despite his protestations, his former Sunday school class at First Baptist Church of Houston asked him to come and share with them. They provided a special microphone to amplify Miller's soft, and raspy voice. His class said they loved and respected him so much that they wanted him to come. They would record whatever words he could utter.

Miller said a few words from Psalm 103. He read the third verse, where it says God "heals all your diseases." Miller later reported, "With my tongue I was saying, 'I still believe that God heals,' but in my heart, I was screaming, '*But why not me, Lord?*'"

When Miller came to the next verse, which says the Lord "redeems your life from the pit," he said to the class, "I have had and you have had in times past *pit* experiences." As soon as he said the word "pit," the choking sensation that he had experienced for the last three years disappeared. His voice slowly returned. The audience gasped, then began to shout and cheer, shout and laugh.

This amazing change was captured on audiotape and went viral. Miller pastors Pinnacle Church in the Cedar Lake area and has a daily program on a Dallas radio station—he uses his voice to tell others about what God did in his life. The audiotape can be accessed at www.nuvoice.org.[22]

I don't want this chapter to be a gloomy catalog of the unbelievable wickedness occurring in our country and world today. We need to always keep God's grace and power in our minds. "The god of this world" (2 Corinthians 4:4) is certainly not the God of the universe.

"Yea, and all that will live godly in Christ Jesus shall suffer persecution" (2 Timothy 3:12)

The House Church Movement in China, perhaps better called "the Unregistered Church Movement" (UCM), since some unregistered churches don't meet in houses but in church buildings and refuse to register with the Chinese Communist Party (CCP), is one of the sterling examples of what the above verse means. Paul Hattaway, an insider and chronicler of the UCM, gives a picture of what the church could face in our hostile Western world: "Apparently the [Chinese] government is using a new method to deal with people when they arrest them. Instead of beating them, they are drugging them with a mind-altering chemical that diminishes the person's mental capacity."[23]

The Shandong Revival in China was perhaps one of the greatest revivals of the twentieth century. The invasion of Shandong by the Japanese in 1937 and the brutality of the Chinese government under Mao Tse-tung in the 1940s put an end to the open manifestations of revival in China, but the fires of revival still burn.

Mao was a monster—one of the many antichrists who are harbingers of THE Antichrist (1 John 2:18)—and was adept at making horrific threats: "Whoever wishes to oppose Communism must be prepared to be mauled and torn to pieces by the people. If you have not yet made up your mind about being mauled and torn to pieces, it would be wise for you not to oppose Communism." Mao ridiculed people of faith and promised that he would harass and murder dissenters: "There certainly will be those who refuse to change until they die. They are willing to go see God carrying their granite heads on their shoulders. That will be of little consequence."[24]

China's Social Credit System

Imagine going to book a flight and the agent politely pauses, looks up at you, and says that you are blacklisted. Your "social credit" score shows that you have been doing some things that don't sit well with the government. You are being punished, and part of the punishment is that you can't travel out of the country to visit relatives in America. You're shocked. You haven't even gotten a traffic ticket before. "There must be some mistake," you tell the agent. She insists that she can't get you a flight. You're getting a little perturbed and raise your voice. She looks to the right, nods, and—before you know it—there are two gentlemen in black coats, one on your right and the other on your left. They each grab your arms.

Beijing is seeking to implement its controversial "social credit" system, which allows the government to closely monitor and judge each of its 1.3 billion citizens based on their associations, activities, friends, and church attendance. The system will be fully functional by 2020. This system makes it difficult for those who are deemed "untrustworthy" to have any mobility. Not only is travel restricted, but people with low credibility scores have their low scores publicly disclosed on a regular basis. That may lead to some being dismissed from employment. Companies don't want a "subversive" person on staff—otherwise, they will not get government contracts. People who attend an unregistered church or who put their kids in private Christian schools rather than in government schools won't be able to travel.

The social credit system is already functional in some areas, and in recent months, the Chinese state has blocked millions of people from booking flights and getting tickets on high-speed trains. By May of 2018, the government had already blocked 11.14 million people from flights and 4.25 million from taking high-speed train trips.[25]

Unbelievable advances in technology are underscoring—in red—the prophecies of Scripture. The coming Tribulation period, and the Scriptures that graphically describe it, must not be allegorized. We may think it is hard now, but for those who are left behind, it will be so bad they will wish they had not been left behind.

Prophecy reveals that the Antichrist won't just be against Christianity, but against all deities "who opposeth and exalteth himself above all that is called God, or that is worshipped; so that he as God sitteth in the temple of God, showing himself that he is God" (2 Thessalonians 2:4). Earth will become "the prison planet."

After reading this, you might think, "Stop the world. I want to get off!"

It won't happen until the Rapture:

For the Lord himself shall descend from heaven with a shout, with the voice of the archangel, and with the trump of God and the dead in Christ shall rise first: Then we which are alive and remain shall be caught up together with them in the clouds, to meet the Lord in the air and so shall we ever be with the Lord. Wherefore comfort one another with these words. (1 Thessalonians 4:16–18)

CHAPTER 2

ESCALATING EVIL SEDUCERS

DON MCGEE

THE PRESENCE AND INFLUENCE of evil is a growing phenomenon, and this growth is in direct proportion to the nearness of the coming of Jesus for His Church. The reasons for the modern exponential increase in iniquity are many, but in these pages two will be presented for consideration. First is the attraction humans have toward the religion of humanism and second is their obsession with the expansion of knowledge and its unhindered, rapid access.

The texts referenced are 2 Timothy 3:1–13 and Romans 1:18 and following, both of which were written by the Apostle Paul. These are easily understood in context of the last days by seekers of truth, but unfortunately, they're not so readily accepted by those unwilling to know the truth.

The influence of humanism has convinced most people that biblical Scriptures are essentially the writings of ignorant religious fanatics and must, therefore, be rejected. This argument says that the human race has progressed only by exploiting its innate godhood by focusing attention upon sophisticated, contemporary reasoning. Therefore, there must be no turning back to religious fantasy. The archaic and repressive must forever be dismissed and replaced by a well-informed human religion that is progressive and liberating.

Christians associate the prophetic significance of the above Scriptures with their implied warning that humanity needs to go back to the old paths in order to correct societal disfunction. Contemporary thinkers, on the other hand, associate them with going back to the days of horse-carried mail and using blood-sucking leaches for treating illness. They believe that twenty-first century life and biblical truths are mutually exclusive. Satan has effectively deceived humanity into believing that what God said two thousand years ago about anything, especially about the future, is a liability that impedes human progress. That is not true.

In the eighteenth and nineteenth centuries, houses, barns, and furniture were handmade with simple tools. Logs were hand hewn and joints were mitered, mortised, and dovetailed with care and precision. These were slow processes that required patience and focused attention, but they have stood both the test of time and the test of long-term value.

But things began to change drastically with the introduction of tools and techniques that saved time and heavy labor. Steam power and large circular saws with massive carriages that enhanced production became the benchmarks of the building trades in those days. These were good things in and of themselves, and they promoted economic growth, adding a much-needed measure of relief to those used to hard living.

But a measure of compromise came with this cutting-edge innovation because it led to an unnecessary emphasis on production at the expense of quality. Unfortunately, this unwarranted trade-off continues.

Today, craftsmen use electric woodworking machines to produce large pallets of rapidly cut and milled lumber that can quickly be assembled and shipped to consumers. Everyone from the tree farmer and the millwright to the retailer and the consumer is pleased—that is, until the long-term quality that is expected begins to become far too rare, or until something happens that the computer-controlled machine is incapable of interpreting and correcting.

The need for skilled handcraftsmanship has been replaced with the only the skills necessary to turn on a machine. This is acceptable and even beneficial in many circumstances, but what has been lost is the craftsman's nature, his character, and the personal touch of his hand that used to be seen in something as simple as a hammer handle. The special relationship between an independent, conscientious craftsman's personal touch and his project has been replaced with the cold indifference between a sweat-free, metal machine and a piece of cheap fiberboard. This difference is what makes old, hand-forged tools and antique, hand-made, solid wood furniture so valuable today.

But human souls are not mass-produced dead pieces of wood being machined into cheap, third-rate boards by a metal saw. A human soul is a living entity that will spend eternity in one of two places and is thus in need of God's loving and personal touch. In these last days, the warm, personal touch of our loving Creator is vehemently rejected in favor of cold, human, finite reasoning based upon mass-produced secular knowledge, little of which has anything to do with God.

The result is what we now see before us: Immortal human souls are being brainwashed by religious humanism, which relies upon the exponential increase of secular knowledge in its hopeless effort to prolong the life of the earth and humanity's ability to live upon it.

People are being led to believe that every person is a god unto himself or herself, that our vast learning has allowed us to escape the orbit that a deceptive and cruel God has imposed upon us, and that we're quite capable of doing whatever needs to be done for our survival and continued evolution. This sounds a lot like what we read in the first five verses of Genesis 3.

The deception of the twenty-first century is greater than that of earlier days because the expansion rate of secular knowledge is greater than ever. The nucleus of this newly discovered knowledge is most often godless and superficial, with the result being the escalation of humanity's estrangement from God. This is exactly what Paul had in mind in our texts.

Amazingly, many who profess Christianity have also been deceived by this misplaced emphasis on human achievement. We see this clearly in the doctrine of some Christian denominations, those who say the world will be won to Jesus through the efforts of the Church—which is blatantly contrary to Paul's words in both texts. This belief system whereby the Church will present the redeemed world to her Lord as some sort of gift, is commonly known as postmillennialism. This, of course, is ludicrous and will never happen.

God the Father will present the kingdoms of this world to the Son, according to Psalm 2. Thus, the Church as His bride will be on the receiving end of this gift, not on the giving end.

In the meantime, humanity will not only continue its obsession with wickedness, but will do so with an increasing addiction to it. The slide into evil is by choice, and it's escalating because of the growing influence of the religion of humanism and the exponential increase in access to knowledge. Most won't admit that this path will end in cataclysmic destruction, and even those who suspect things may conclude this way refuse to face this inevitability.

Evil is increasing in both presence and influence today. We must not miss the fact that this prophetic fulfillment is an unmistakable sign that God's intervention into the affairs of the world is imminent. This intervention will not be what most people think of as the Battle of Armageddon, but it will be the removal of His Church from the earth. The reader, therefore, should be left with the conviction that things aren't going to get better, and the critical moment of God's intervention could very well be the next moment.

It's necessary at this point to address an often-misunderstood truth. Though we're to be thankful for positive advances in technology, nothing done by human mind or hand will ultimately solve the problems of this world because our advances are mechanical and superficial. They don't reach the spiritual condition of the human soul because they can't.

No political party's policies of any kind—economic, foreign, environmental, educational, social, etc.—will ever contribute anything of substance toward genuine human betterment. In fact, the policies of most political parties are toxic to spiritual healing and advancement.

Yes, we should make informed voting choices because most political groups are more noxious than others, but in the end, we're never to forget that humans, because of sin, are irreparably broken spiritually when left to our own devices. Only God can fix that, but humanism rejects His offer.

This fact isn't overwhelmingly accepted, but it is true because God said it, and even common sense clearly indicates it.

Twenty-first century civilization has morally digressed to the point that most every kind of evil is justified by using the pseudo legitimacy of human religion and secular knowledge. The validation and acceptance of what has been historically defined as evil is no longer simply being offered for society's reconsideration, but its purveyors are now demanding that those evils be accepted as a normal part of life—and even this isn't enough for them. They're demanding that innocent children in government schools be indoctrinated with such teaching. Those who refuse to accept this revisionism are increasingly being dismissed and marginalized, often with harshness and even violence.

There are many ways to document the escalating depravity of society, but just the effort to revise the definition of evil is enough to stand upon its own. The fact that this has so permeated unregenerate human hearts that they insist upon plenary endorsement of their evil agenda is clear evidence of full-blown, unreserved rebellion against God. In earlier times, Western civilization at least tried to offer a pretense of godliness and morality, but even that's no longer the case. Now, reprobates glory in their shame with an increasing in-your-face brashness.

In this chapter, we'll first consider the influence that humanism, with its insatiable appetite for knowledge, is having upon people who don't want God's presence in their lives to any degree. Next, we'll look at some recent examples of the resulting societal degradation, and we will conclude with a few thoughts on what we might see if Jesus delays His return much longer.

Humanism and the Explosion of Knowledge

Consider what is driving this rapidly worsening situation by looking at 2 Timothy 3.

Many consider this to be Paul's description of the Church in the last days, and that is indeed applicable. Christians have been warned in Scripture about those within the Church who would corrupt the message of the gospel, and this is indeed happening. Jesus and Peter referred to this specifically in Matthew 7:15 and 2 Peter 2:1. However, 2 Timothy 3 is contextually broad enough to also apply to the condition of the secular world in those same last days, and this is equally obvious.

For Satan to be successful in his efforts to destroy those God loves, he must construct a false scenario through which he can deceive humanity. This scenario was the one he used in the Garden of Eden, and he is effectively using it today with even more determination. His strategy consists of a false religion whereby man is the object of worship, along with a form of justification for self-worship. The religion is humanism, and the justification for it is the vast accumulation of secular knowledge. The premise is we don't need God because we are smart enough to take care of ourselves.

There is a natural spinoff to this spiritually lethal mixture. Prior to Paul's words in verse 13, where he said both societal and spiritual degradation will increase, he listed several things that would be involved in the increase of evil. The presence and influence of these evils have always been abetted by three powerful characteristics of fallen humanity, and this is especially the case in these last days. These can be labeled as narcissism (lovers of self), materialism (lovers of money), and hedonism (lovers of pleasure).

Clearly, these traits have nothing to do with needs associated with normal life. God expects His people to take care of their families and themselves, to earn enough money to meet obligations if possible, and to enjoy righteous pleasure. In fact, God says that if a man refuses to work when he is able, then he is not to be fed (2 Thessalonians 3:10).

However, humanism demands that we love ourselves first, because self-love is the preeminent love. This lays the foundation for materialism and hedonism, and it offers soothing justification to anyone who just might have a pricked conscience about their obviously corrupt, man-inspired religion.

Humanism also leads people to believe that accumulating material things is the natural way to live, because life on earth is all there is. This religion says that we only live once, so we should get all we can get, and we should get it now. Thus, humanism declares that possessing many things is the way the world validates a person's sophistication, wisdom, and success. It becomes the standard by which personal social value is measured.

Finally, humanism stresses pleasure at the expense of everything else. Even for aged reprobates on the cusp of eternity, pursuing one's desires effectively suppresses any momentary pause a person might have had to consider his or her future.

Many Christians believe that most humanists are atheists, because atheism allows them to satisfy their lusts in any way desired without fear of ultimate accountability. It may be that for this reason, a pedophile or serial rapist will follow and even escalate his lust without conscience. The plain-sense definition of a psychopath is "one who is without remorse for his crimes," and atheistic humanism goes a long way in removing remorse.

The religion of humanism enthusiastically embraces all three of these practices, though they're based upon the hellish lie that people are inherently gods and therefore will never be held accountable to a higher authority. In the same way Adam and Eve fell for the lie at the beginning while innocent, people today whose hearts are not innocent are falling for it with reckless abandon.

The situation described in 2 Timothy 3 can be further divided into two broad types of sin. One is more physical in nature and has to do with people who press beyond the normal satisfaction of needs and desires to a point of overindulgence. The pursuit of excess then becomes the most important reason for existence. Secularists focus all their time, talent, and effort on things that may be important enough in their own right, but when given undue emphasis become liabilities.

At this point, such things become obsessions that are temporal and contribute little to the most important aspect of being human, which has more to do with spiritual matters than physical. Of course, to the natural person, this kind of life sounds embarrassingly cheesy, boring, and without real joy and reward.

It has often been said that Satan can exploit the failures of a Christian to a much greater degree than he can use the outright rebellion of a sinner. This is often true, and is the reason he sets traps for Christians to influence them to make choices from a purely carnal perspective. This taints the spiritual life of believers and destroys their witness for Jesus in the eyes of the secular world.

The second type of sin is more spiritual in nature and has to do with secular society's growing resentment toward everyone—and everything—that is good and holy. This hostility is often hellish, brutal, and merciless. Said another way, of all the words a person might use to describe the last-days rebellion of humanity, "hatred toward God" is the most inclusive way to put it.

The hostility connected with these last-days characteristics is a deep and seething, visceral hatred for God, His Word, and His people. Further, it's directed toward any sense of morality, whether cultural or scriptural. The heat of this hatred cauterizes rebellious human hearts to the point that any conviction of social conscience, much less any direct conviction by the Holy Spirit, is summarily rejected. This is likely the same kind of hatred Satan has for God, and it may be a precursor of the hatred Antichrist will direct toward the Jewish people during the final part of the Tribulation.

The world has always included people of an evil and base nature. They were seen worldwide in the days of Noah and Lot and the great world empires Daniel described, and have been evident in the history of the twentieth century. Joseph Stalin, Adolf Hitler, Idi Amin, Pol Pot, and Che Guevara are just several among the many examples that could be cited.

But this text's description of the escalating depravity of humanity in the last days is unique because it is rooted in humanism, which is being justified in the eyes of secular people by the vast knowledge being discovered by researchers along with easy access to this knowledge. This wasn't understood in detail by Paul two thousand years ago or even by those deeply spiritual commentators of just a few decades ago.

The explosion of knowledge in the last days feeds humanism like an unlimited supply of fuel feeds a raging inferno. Though denied by secularists who resent the idea that they need God in their lives, in reality, they're practicing religious fanatics who become easily energized by what they call the progression of human knowledge. They're convinced that increasing their knowledge about the world is a manifestation of their human deity and forms the ultimate goal of evolution.

More than anything else, this clearly shows how depraved and deceived a human heart can be.

In Daniel 12:4, God told the prophet this would happen, though Daniel couldn't have understood how. He, along with those who lived just a hundred years ago, had no point of reference for measuring, much less comprehending, what we're witnessing today with the accumulation of and easy access to vast amounts of information.

Further, God referred to false knowledge in His words to Job in chapters 38ff. Specifically, in verse 2, God asks Job a rhetorical question wherein He expresses bemusement at Job's spiritual shallowness. He asks who it is that darkens, or obscures, God's counsel. Then He speaks of words that are without knowledge, referring to Job and his three friends who were all blind to the facts of Job's situation.

This is the case today. With growing vileness, humanism is obscuring what God has said about the world, human life, and eternity. And the vast knowledge (and the immediate access people have to it) is not real knowledge, because it does nothing to emphasize God's love for people and their desperate need for God. In that context, what is called "knowledge" is simply empty words, like the nonsensical babblings of a drunken fool.

This outbreak of knowledge is not only unprecedented, but wasn't even imaginable just a few years ago. In fact, it's so new and unique that the same world that thrives on it doesn't know how to handle it.

An article entitled "Modern Science and the Explosion of New Knowledge" published in *Biophysical Chemistry* noted that the evolution of technical knowledge has led to serious problems.[26] Those problems include the worldwide, uneven distribution of young people and science, the development of super specializations, and the problems associated with trying to teach this vast amount of information to others. And that article was published more than twenty years ago!

An Internet search on the explosion of knowledge and the speed at which it is produced leaves most people with the idea that the information is not only too vast to comprehend, but also that much of it is obsolete almost as soon as it is published. This is a phenomenon too confusing for most to fully understand.

This modern age of information has indeed benefitted humanity to a degree, but it isn't always easy to objectively quantify and qualify this new information along with its easy access. As an example, we can easily educate ourselves about physical health with accurate information on the Internet, but at the same time, we can get precise information on how to bypass a neighbor's home-security system for nefarious purposes.

What this vast and readily available knowledge hasn't done is help humanity's much-needed reconciliation with God. Paul said in verse 7 that in these last days people will be "always learning and never able to come to the knowledge of the truth." In fact, it seems to be estranging people of all cultures and classes from their Creator, with no exceptions. Multitudes are being led to believe that God doesn't exist or is irrelevant at best. These people are being deceived into thinking that civilization's only hope for long-term survival is whatever panacea human effort can provide in the way of information and knowing how to put that information into action.

The immediate access to vast and sundry secular information both in text and in image has accelerated the influence of all religions whose god is not God, which is another way to frame humanism. This results in mortal minds filled with information but human hearts that have no inkling about Jesus. People whose minds and hearts have thus been corrupted form the masses Paul described in 2 Timothy 3.

The human heart is inherently evil simply in its normal state (Jeremiah 17:9). Even people with some degree of moral responsibility don't generally want to hear about God, Jesus, the Bible, sin, forgiveness, Heaven, Hell, or anything else having to do with spiritual matters because they are humanists—though they may not clearly understand that they are. When easy access to deceptive secular knowledge is added to their regular state of evil, the result is most often the exponential rise of disregard for God.

Why is this so? At least one reason is that evil human hearts are naturally drawn away from God by the lure of deceptive secular knowledge because it promises independent godhood for humanity. This is what happened in the Garden of Eden and again at Babel (Genesis 11), and it is being repeated today at a much greater rate.

Much of what enthralls the masses today is like rancid vapor—repulsive, short-lived, and of no value. In 1 Timothy 6:20, Paul described this "worldly and empty chatter" as false knowledge. Yet it is being invited into the minds of our children under the guise of education, though it is false or at best not entirely accurate. A good example of this might be a secular television channel's presentation on some aspect of the Bible, like the Battle of Armageddon, by a highly credentialed, liberal theologian who skillfully warps the truth. Scroll to yet another channel and a viewer might hear a famous scientist declare that the earth is billions of years old.

Most people who don't give a second thought to what God says on any subject suddenly become spellbound by these shamans, and they accept their words as fact. This is like students who check their critical thinking skills at the door of a biology class where evolution is taught as scientific truth.

Never in history has Satan had such an arsenal at his disposal. Though Paul and Timothy didn't know about the Internet, they knew Satan would have access to an instrument of some kind that he would use as a catalyst for the exponential increase of evil in the last days. The growing influence of humanistic religion, along with the unlimited access to vast storehouses of secular knowledge, is tailor-made for his efforts.

Culture began to be degraded after the Fall. This is demonstrated by the fact that most ancient cultures were characterized by every perversion imaginable. However, modern Western culture as Americans know it is relatively new to the rapidly increasing corruption being seen today, and most Baby Boomers believe this slide into the amoral abyss can be traced to the mid twentieth century. That means most people alive today can't critically analyze humanism's deification of man and its close connection to the accumulation of knowledge and data because they have known nothing else.

For those who wish to objectively examine modern society, it becomes readily obvious that godliness and morality began to be omitted in the raising of post-World War II generations. Satan was subtle at first with his plan, but by the 1960s, it was in full-blown assault mode. The humanistic rejection of godliness and morality quickly became the norm in education, music, literature, and movies. Soon this attitude went from the mere rejection of morality-infused education to outright revulsion toward it.

After the war, American society began to radically change. Various groups of men, many of whom were veterans feeling a sense of disenfranchisement and disillusionment, began to coalesce. Some of those groups eventually morphed into antisocial movements such as outlaw motorcycle gangs. Wives and moms got a taste of independence while working in factories during the war, and many liked it so much they never returned to being homemakers. That was a big leap toward the societal shift favoring two-income families with daycare facilities raising their children. Still, American social structure was yet to hit bottom.

But things changed forever in 1967 with the hippie culture's Summer of Love celebration in San Francisco's Haight-Ashbury district. This event alone signaled that a volatile point in American social stability had been reached, and it only needed a detonator to push American culture onto a very steep and slippery slope. It came full force that summer after America's spiritually neglected young people came under the influence of people like Harvard's Timothy Leary and acid-rock music's Janis Joplin, among many others.

Vanity Fair, in its June 2012 issue, described the Summer of Love by saying:

> In a 25-square-block area of San Francisco, in the summer of 1967, an ecstatic, Dionysia mini-world sprang up like a mushroom, dividing American culture into a Before and After unparalleled since World War II.[27]

Following this West Coast phenomenon, similar events such as Woodstock in New York in 1969 and Celebration of Life in McCrea, Louisiana, in 1971 began springing up around the nation. Culturally, the rules had been changed and the consequences could not be stopped.

An amoral subculture in Western civilization began to grow and exert influence like an aggressive cancer—and it wasn't just happening in America. Western Europe had already died spiritually, with humanism rampant and prevailing in every quarter. Socialism and Christian higher criticism were already having their degrading influence on a continent whose religious, political, and economic leadership believed consolidation at any cost was the goal they should pursue.

Modern culture has been changed without regard to national borders. And, like the proverbial scrambled egg, it can never be unscrambled. The world has begun its last-days slide into degradation and the rate is increasing. It seems that Satan has engineered a phenomenon that has no terminal velocity. This climate and attitude set the cast for the molding of modern rebellion against God, and the consequences are being felt in every aspect of life each day.

Examples of Escalating Godlessness

In what ways is last-days godlessness being seen?

Consider the legitimization of the homosexual agenda along with transgenderism; abortion on demand; the rampantly anti-God attitudes proudly proclaimed publicly; the gutter-level vulgarity in music, film, and even in common conversation; the propagation of open marriages; the rejection of the institution of marriage; government-imposed ownership of the minds of children; and the growing popularity of socialism among the entitlement crowds, etc. And this is just part of what is intensifying. Another issue, one closely connected to this cauldron of corruption, is the nonchalant attitude of those elected to bring this situation into check.

Still, something else is escalating: the frustration Christians and others who are against this societal revolution are feeling. Though Christians know these things will be, they're continually exasperated that so-called Christian Bible teachers, pastors, and preachers, along with pseudo-conservative politicians, are generally not wholly involved in fighting these things. Christians familiar with Bible prophecy take great comfort in knowing that soon Jesus will take control of the secular world and there will suddenly be a new way of doing business at city hall. But until then, their vexation continues.

However, more important than our exasperation is God's. We don't know at what point He will withdraw His hand from the affairs of humanity, but we know He will. Second Timothy 3 describes the escalating degeneration of planet earth in the last days, but it is from Romans 1:18ff that we see that those things will provoke God to wrath, and that He will eventually give up on His proactive, redemptive efforts.

This should surprise no one, for God did essentially the same thing in Genesis 6. Yet, multitudes of self-described Christian leaders, along with their followers, continue to speak of God's patience and love in such a way as to imply He will never react drastically to continued human rebellion. This is an abominable religious dogma for which those proponents will soon have to answer.

The Romans 1 text explicitly says God, as His patience runs out, will give rebellious people over to impurity, degrading passions, and a depraved mind—things for which they will pay the ultimate penalty. These verses are not welcome in modern pulpits where deceived people are of the opinion that God is all about blind, milquetoast love, and that He should actually be pleased to have them on His side. That these plain words of warning are not from man but from God Himself makes no impression upon them. This is a form of practical atheism.

Modern, progressive religious thinking is born from the idea that in the last three hundred years, God's people have grown up and therefore no longer need Him. They see themselves as having matured spiritually and, like children who have grown beyond the common Christmas and Easter myths, they no longer see Scripture as infallible truth but as mere precepts they can now subjectively interpret and apply using a more highly refined spirituality.

From Charles Darwin, Frederick Nietzsche, Thomas Huxley, John Dewey, and others comes the modern foundation of the humanist religion. From Tim Berners-Lee, Fujio Masuoka, Steve Jobs, Elon Musk, and others comes the modern superhighway of information-gathering, information-storage, and communication. The lives of these men and many others like them have been brought together in a narrowing apex of human thinking and technological development in the twenty-first century in such a way as to influence the path of human history as no others.

These developments in combination with each other have resulted in what we're seeing today in man's estrangement from God. Why is this so, when so much of what we can do today is beneficial? Because, when left to their own intellect and devices, humans can't balance what is eternally important with what is temporarily expedient.

One more example will suffice for this chapter, but before it is mentioned, it's necessary to make some things very clear. We now live in what modernists call a progressive society. By that, they want people to believe that our newfound interdependency and vast collection of data are the panacea all humanity has been waiting for.

Modernists tell us to forget God, the Bible, and Christianity because these things are not only obsolete but have a repressive effect upon human progress. Most of them believe God doesn't exist anyway. They say that absolutes don't exist, that every word and every action must be considered in its situational context, and that words and actions must never be interpreted within the context of Judeo-Christian values.

Only in that way can vile profanities and abominable perversions be placed on the public table for discussion, consideration, and implementation without the bright light of biblical morality being shown upon them. Only within the parameters of this modern subculture have such evil ideas been able to gain social traction. Not many decades ago, these would have been rejected hands down.

We may be sure that the following is simply one more modern illustration of the evil that has been part of godless society for millennia, but we may also be sure that never has evil held more rapid influence upon humanity than the present. In context of this chapter, it seems clear that the godless religion of humanism combined with the instantaneous access people have to vast sources of information play a major role in this influence.

A modern practice that has become politically and socially recognized and accepted is transgenderism, something even the ancient pagans understood was not possible. This is much more than a person wishing to be a crossdresser or transvestite. These people physically alter their bodies via surgery and hormone treatment in their attempts to change their gender, though the word "alter" better describes their efforts than "change."

Those who practice this perversion claim to identify with the opposite sex and make every effort to alter themselves physically, chemically, and emotionally In order to reach their self-imposed identity. That such a thing is impossible is of no matter to their corrupt minds as they fall headlong into the horrific tragedy their attempts bring.

Modern culture has socially, legally, and medically granted moral standing to this perversion. Social and political correctness now demand that all people everywhere accept transgenderism as a normal alternative lifestyle. This is the same path that the homosexual agenda used, and because our culture has become so greatly estranged from God, transgenderism has now been accepted as well.

Homosexuals not only can marry, but are now welcomed into various denominations' clergy. Those who identify with the opposite sex can now use public restroom facilities without fear of being arrested. Celebrities are now being paraded before the public as models of the transgender movement. And today innocent children are seeing major corporations advertising on television using as props married homosexuals who are raising children as a normal family. God pronounces a great woe upon those who would cause an innocent child to stumble!

There can be no wonder that God has given them up to their impurity, their degrading passions, and their depraved minds. Such last-days escalation could not be possible without His abandonment.

From a practical viewpoint, this is causing problems in many aspects of social interaction, including sports competition. Olivia Caldwell, in her December 3, 2017, report, said that men who compete as women have an unfair advantage over women. The report said that even with hormone therapy, a man may still have up to three times the testosterone as a woman.[28]

This is having a ripple effect on junior varsity competition all the way up to the professional leagues. Just a few years ago, this couldn't have been imagined by anyone.

But this isn't about sports competition. It's about the rejection of what God determines for a person at conception. Put another way, these are creatures saying to the Creator that their impossible and diabolical choices are valid and that God's sovereignty is not. Such a person implies that God made a mistake, that they are angry with Him for that mistake, and that they will stop at nothing to correct it according to their own thinking.

Further, some parents are now deciding to let their children make up their own minds as to their gender at some later date in their lives. This is the wholesale warping of a child's mind that will skew and corrupt most every decision that child will make the rest of his or her life.

But the core of transgenderism is not gender dissatisfaction. It is the exponential influence of humanistic religion that has seized upon a species of knowledge that is toxic to the human soul. Researchers tout their so-called accomplishments and predict a glorious future for humanity, all the while putrefying in their spiritual deadness.

Not only does sound research clearly show the exponential rise in the 2 Timothy 3 characteristics of the last days, but anybody with a rational mind can see it just as clearly. Statistics are not needed.

That the world is escalating into a narrowing spiral of wretched evil in these last days cannot be doubted.

The Future Should the Lord Tarry

The great enlightened empires of Greece and Rome rested upon the shoulders of renowned scholars and philosophers whose pursuit of knowledge and debate characterized their civilizations, as did their cultures' acceptance of perversion. Their written work is still a part of university study, and they're often quoted in almost every field of academic endeavor. But their knowledge did not bring them closer to their Creator; in fact, it alienated them from God. This is clearly seen in the accounts of the Apostle Paul as Luke recorded them in Acts.

This is being repeated today, only with growing intensity. So, what new perversions might be coming, at least in our own country?

No one can specifically predict the kinds of vileness that humans will propagate as we wait for Jesus to take His Church off this planet. We can be no more specific than the facts that God has given us through His Word allow us to be. Still, we've seen glimpses into the kinds of degradation that will be fostered upon the world in the future. Of course, these will no longer be experienced by the Church once she is removed, but they will continue to be a very real part of life on this earth after the Rapture.

Most Americans are patriotic and are proud of our armed forces. This is a good thing to a degree, but when we begin to believe our liberty is contingent upon our powerful military and not upon God, we're in trouble. Because of this misplaced confidence, we're seeing God gradually lower His protective hedge of our nation. This is very clearly seen by the degrading changes in our armed forces. These are malignant and will one day metasta-size to a point where our defense will suddenly fail when it will be tested in the face of a direct military threat.

The American military is being touched by humanism and its much-touted social progression. Christian chaplains may not invoke Jesus' name in a prayer for fear of offending a non-Christian who may hear the prayer. The Military Association of Atheists and Freethinkers (MAAF) is demanding that the military implement humanist chaplains in order to serve atheists, agnostics and humanists on active duty.

The fallout from these and other such efforts will be to silence Christian chaplains who take biblical stands on doctrinal and moral issues because the biblical worldview does not fit in a spiritually and morally inclusive military.

The idea of an inclusive military also carries with it the inclusion of women in any future conscription. This is anathema to many families, but is being strongly encouraged at this moment. Without regard to the arguments of liberal progressives, the fact is that warfighting, especially combat, is not something for which women are physically designed. It appears that the progressive armies of the world, including the vaunted Israel Defense Forces, are now having to admit this.

A woman's inherent vulnerability and that vulnerability's ripping emotional impact on husbands, children, parents, and siblings is impossible to measure. The lie that women are as capable as men when it comes to warfighting is so inadequate and shameful that it defies common sense. Despite the tremendous liability of placing women in such situations, the supporters of this senseless agenda are incessant in their efforts.

Such a liability is seen when a man naturally shifts his focus from the highly intense combat situation before him to the gut-wrenching thought that a woman next to him is about to be wounded, killed, or captured. This inherent protection mindset is a God-given part of a man's psyche and cannot be compensated for by indoctrination or training. Forget what is found in movies and books, because that is all hogwash constructed by digital technology fueled by politically correct fantasy.

In the most basic of combat training, a private soldier learns that the two most important responsibilities of a military leader are his mission and his men, in that order. Those currently making military policy in the United States have never known an all-male fighting force and therefore do not know how this makes a difference in the success of a mission and thus the security of a nation.

On a culturally broader scale, there is another near-future probability associated with the Romans and 1 Timothy texts.

Because in the practice of humanism there is no right or wrong, no Heaven or Hell, and no accountability for choices, the sanctity of an individual life—young or old—takes a backseat to what this religion calls "the common good." Look for this to become even more barbaric in practice.

The sanctity and value of a person's life will become situational with someone other than that person making the evaluation. That is already being done with the practice of infanticide, commonly called abortion. In the not-so-distant future, we will see the cold-blooded murder of unwanted children after they are placed into the "defective" classification by parents and/or a government bureaucracy. It was done in Nazi Germany, and it's being done in some countries today—specifically, Belgium and the Netherlands.[29] In Belgium, some of the killings have involved non-terminal patients, and in some cases, psychiatrists have given lethal injections—or offered to do so—to young adults under what has been referred to as "dubious circumstances."

Physician-assisted suicide is legal in some states in America presently. Will America accept active or passive euthanasia as a matter of legal policy? Probably. When a nation's conscience becomes callused by atheistic humanism, it is a short step to licensed murder, especially when it is for so-called public benefit. That alone is a sign of government totalitarianism and cruelty.

What are we to do about what we presently see and what we believe is coming? Some Christians believe they shouldn't bring children into this world, and most people can understand that conviction. However, we aren't to think that God has lost control of this planet and that we should withdraw into a spiritual cocoon to be outside the reach of evil influences. That's the wrong way to think. This is akin to the old idea that we should sell all possessions, put on white robes, and migrate to a mountaintop to await Jesus' return.

What we are to do is what God has called us to do, collectively as the Church and individually, all the while placing our trust in His sovereignty. Only in this way can we "snatch some from the fire," which brings salvation to those so snatched and great glory to our Lord for His love, grace, and mercy.

In closing, note that Romans 2:5, while referring to the obstinate reprobates of chapter 1, gives sober and clear warning that their increasing rebellion serves only to store up God's wrath upon them. His impending judgment will be perfectly righteous, and it will come upon them without mercy.

Technological advancement and its benefits to humanity cannot be denied—and no one wants to deny them. However, we're to never lose sight of the fact that undirected ambition that springs from human motives alone does not draw people closer to God, but rather alienates them. It instinctively operates outside God-given parameters and always results in a worldview that is irreparably defective due to sin. Complete destruction immediately followed by eternal judgment is the inevitable consequence.

This not only describes the horrific last days of mankind, as our texts very clearly indicate, but also points to an escalation that cannot be stopped or even slowed.

CHAPTER 3

DESCENDING DARK DELUSION

JEFF KINLEY

FROM MY CHILDHOOD, MAGICIANS have always fascinated me. From Houdini and Blackstone to Copperfield and Blaine, I've long been impressed by the illusionary skills of such great performers. Not too long ago, a dear friend invited my wife and me to see an illusionist who was performing at a theater in Branson, Missouri, not too far from where I live. This performer possessed all the skills and flair of a seasoned Vegas headliner. Accompanied by his lovely assistants, he performed one trick after another, wowing hundreds of wide-eyed spectators. He then brought several audience members onstage, only to fool them up close with carefully choreographed deceptions and sleight-of-hand. His handsome appearance and immaculate, stunning wardrobe—along with his quick wit and well-planned one-liners—quickly secured him a place in the hearts of every person there that evening.

Then, as the stage went dark, he stepped forward into the spotlight to tell us about his final and most spectacular illusion. The lights came on, and suddenly an actual helicopter materialized behind him. The performer then went on to claim that he was about to make the same helicopter disappear before our very eyes. What followed was a frenzy of movement onstage, as our eyes darted back and forth from the magician to his assistants and the huge helicopter. All the while, heart-pounding cinematic music blared over the loudspeakers.

Then came the climactic moment. A circular curtain slowly lowered around the helicopter, and after the illusionist made a few hand gestures and dance steps, the music abruptly stopped and the lights went out. Then, before we could take another breath, there came a flash of blinding light and an explosion of smoke. The curtain quickly lifted, revealing a blank space onstage where they helicopter once sat. The aircraft had seemingly disappeared—vanished into thin air!

The crowd let out a collective gasp and spontaneously erupted into a standing ovation. The illusionist promptly stepped forward, breaking into a million-dollar smile and bowing proudly to receive his well-deserved adulation. The curtain closed to celebratory music, and the show was over. Hundreds of stupefied eyewitnesses left the theater scratching their heads and wondering how the amazing showman could've done such a thing. How could he have so effectively fooled us all?

Professional illusionists are masters of their trade. They're skilled performers and experts in the art of misdirection and deception. But stages like the one in Branson, along with those in Las Vegas, aren't the only places where you'll find such trickery and deceit. Far from the dazzling lights of carefully staged magic performances, the Bible tells us that another kind of deception is coming to mankind. And this one has nothing to do with mere entertainment.

Scripture says that in the end times, a *world* delusion is coming, one that will deceive the bulk of humanity. But what's different about this trickery is that, unlike those who attend a magic show, the future participants won't be aware they are being deceived.

The Apostle Paul wrote to the Thessalonians:

> Then that lawless one will be revealed whom the Lord will slay with the breath of His mouth and bring to an end by the appearance of His coming; *that is*, the one whose coming is in accord with the activity of Satan, with all power and signs and false wonders, and with all the deception of wickedness for those who perish, because they did not receive the love of the truth so as to be saved. *For this reason*

God will send upon them a deluding influence so that they will believe what is false, in order that they all may be judged who did not believe the truth, but took pleasure in wickedness. (2 Thessalonians 2:8–12, italics added)

So, it's clear from Scripture that a time is coming when the whole earth will fall under a grand delusion. The means through which this global deception will take place is the Antichrist, the Man of Sin. He himself is directly energized by Satan. Paul says this devilish activity will take place during the last three and half years of the Tribulation. With his signs (whether they prove to be illusionary in nature or actual miracles), he will nevertheless convince the world that he is indeed "God." Billions will worship him as such (see Revelation 13:8, 11–15; 14:9, 11; 16:2; 19:20; 20:4). This is the culmination of Satan's long-sought objective—to be worshipped as God (Isaiah 14:13–14). Through the Antichrist, he will finally realize that depraved desire.

But what makes this bizarre phenomenon so perplexing is that God Himself initially sends this delusion. One may be inclined to think this sounds uncharacteristic, cruel, or antithetical to God's essence and character. After all, doesn't He *want* people to come to faith in Him? Doesn't Scripture say as much in 2 Peter 3:9? If this is true, why would He then cause the world to be deceived by lies that will effectively prevent people from salvation? These are fair and legitimate questions, and ones that, fortunately, are answered for us in God's Word.

The first clue God gives us comes from the very passage we just read. Second Thessalonians 2:10 tells us the specific reason for their godless gullibility: "because they did not receive the love of the truth so as to be saved." In other words, according to Paul, these billions are merely reaping the consequences of a lifetime's rejection of the gospel and Jesus Christ. During their lives, they repeatedly refused to repent and believe God's truth. As a result, those living in the last half of the seven-year Tribulation will not be given a second chance. Though others will be saved during this period, those who fall under this end-times delusion seal their destiny forever (Revelation 7:14, 13:8).

This highlights a sobering spiritual principle, one repeated elsewhere in the Bible. Though there is freedom of choice for every person, there is no freedom concerning the consequences our choices bring. Let that sink in for a few seconds.

We see this principle explained in Romans 1. Here, Paul unfolds a cause-effect relationship between the suppression of truth and the judgment of God. It begins with rejecting the evidence God has provided to mankind concerning His divine nature and creative activity in the heavens and the earth (Romans 1:18–20). This evidence, Paul claims, is undeniable proof that there is a God. When someone chooses to suppress this truth and refuses to acknowledge God, their hearts become (even more) darkened and their minds are thrown into confusion (1:21). Now, without the truth of God to form and guide their thinking, they erroneously believe themselves to now be the highest seat of authority and wisdom. They place themselves above the Bible and the Creator. As a result, verse 22 tells us, God says they are "fools" (Greek: *moros*). And because they have cast God out of their life's equation, they begin worshipping other things, including the creation it-self (1:23). For this reason, the Creator initiates a judgment protocol, which involves giving them over to their own immoral passions and perverse de-sires, including all forms of lesbianism and homosexuality (1:24–27).

This divine judgment is currently unfolding in America, where almost every strain of sexual deviance and perversion is not only being tolerated and accepted, but also legislated, promoted, and publicly celebrated. The culmination of this incremental judgment (referred to by many as "aban-donment wrath") is that God literally turns those engaging in these activi-ties over completely (releases them) to a depraved mind (1:28). This means that their minds are thoroughly saturated in sin. There is no longer any room for conscience, decency, common sense morality, or Judeo-Christian values. What happens when a community, culture, or planet falls under this type of judgment? The most godless culture imaginable, very much like the days of Noah (1:29–32; Genesis 6; Matthew 24:37–39).

Paul's description of this abandonment wrath in Romans 1 is but a pre-view of the coming delusion we read about in 2 Thessalonians 2.

So, what will this Tribulation delusion look like? What do we know?

First, keep in mind that the very nature of deception is that you don't know you're being deceived. In fact, you're convinced of its veracity. You think it's the truth. You sincerely believe, even to the point of vehemently defending your beliefs. This will be the ultimate brainwashing of humanity.

Second, this delusion involves the world believing a lie concerning the Antichrist, specifically the lie that states he is a messiah, and even God Himself.

Third, this delusion includes the worship not only of Antichrist, but also of demonic entities (Revelation 9:20–21). The Tribulation will be an era of renewed supernatural phenomena. Miraculous occurrences will be both overt and commonplace, far more so than they are during the Church Age. There will be supernatural judgments of God via the seal, bowl, and trumpet judgments (Revelation 6–16), the two witnesses (Revelation 11), demonic manifestations, both known and unknown (Revelation 9), and through the Antichrist and False Prophet (Revelation 13).

Perhaps, as many Satan worshippers believe today, these Tribulation demons may even promise power, enlightenment, or some sort of deliverance from God's terrible judgments. Certainly, Revelation indicates there will be an explosion of dark occult practices, along with rampant drug abuse and every imaginable sexual excess and perversion (Revelation 9:20–21).

Fourth, the destiny of those who are deluded is eternal damnation— torment day and night forever in the Lake of Fire, without any reprieve or rest (Revelation 14:9–11; 20:11–15).

These are sobering truths. However, the precursors to this prophecy are being felt even now.

During the Second World War, Joseph Goebbels, minister of propaganda for Hitler's Nazi Party, famously said:

> If you tell a lie big enough and keep repeating it, people
> will eventually come to believe it. The lie can be maintained
> only for such time as the State can shield the people from

the political, economic and/or military consequences of the
lie.[30]

In other words, the bigger the lie, the more people who will eventually believe it, as long as you just keep repeating it. That statement itself may initially be hard to believe. But it only further highlights the depths of depravity to which humanity can plummet. A lie can be so shocking that it would, at first, appear truly *un*believable. But over time, it can have the opposite effect. Fifty years ago, if you (or the president, or the majority of the media) boldly claimed that an unborn child wasn't really a human being, you would have been laughed at as ludicrous and condemned by society as morally reprehensible. Yet, that very lie has been repeated throughout the past decades to the point that it is now embraced by a large percentage of politicians, radical feminists, lawyers, actors, and members of the media. Today, we live in a culture where more than half (58 percent) of Americans believe abortion should be legal.[31]

This is part of Satan's current "Big Lie." His delusion.

However, the Antichrist won't have the luxury of having lots of time on his side. He has a limited open window through which to seize his moment. So, he will have to expedite the delusion by promoting Satan's boldest and most convincing miracle of all:

Being raised from the dead.

Of course, since this ultimate deception hasn't happened yet, we must ask, "Are we seeing any foreshadowings of this last-days phenomenon?"

I believe we are.

Besides his letter to the Thessalonians, elsewhere the Apostle Paul prophesied, along with Peter and Jude, that in the Tribulation days, there would be a massive falling away from the faith and a deterioration of doctrine.

However, leading up to that time, he also says we will see this falling away and deterioration in culture and in the Church.

But the Spirit explicitly says that in later times some will
fall away from the faith, paying attention to deceitful spirits

and doctrines of demons, by means of the hypocrisy of liars seared in their own conscience as with a branding iron, men who forbid marriage and advocate abstaining from foods which God has created to be gratefully shared in by those who believe and know the truth. (1 Timothy 4:1–3)

But realize this, that in the last days difficult times will come. For men will be lovers of self, lovers of money, boastful, arrogant, revilers, disobedient to parents, ungrateful, unholy, unloving, irreconcilable, malicious gossips, without self-control, brutal, haters of good, treacherous, reckless, conceited, lovers of pleasure rather than lovers of God, holding to a form of godliness, although they have denied its power; Avoid such men as these. (2 Timothy 3:1–5)

But false prophets also arose among the people, just as there will also be false teachers among you, who will secretly introduce destructive heresies, even denying the Master who bought them, bringing swift destruction upon themselves. Many will follow their sensuality, and because of them the way of the truth will be maligned; and in their greed they will exploit you with false words; their judgment from long ago is not idle, and their destruction is not asleep. (2 Peter 2:1–3)

Know this first of all, that in the last days mockers will come with their mocking, following after their own lusts, and saying, "Where is the promise of His coming? For ever since the fathers fell asleep, all continues just as it was from the beginning of creation." For when they maintain this, it escapes their notice that by the word of God the heavens existed long ago and the earth was formed out of water and by water, through which the world at that time was destroyed, being flooded with water. But by His word the present heavens and earth are being reserved for fire, kept for the day of judgment and destruction of ungodly men. (2 Peter 3:3–6)

We've seen this type of apostasy at various times and in varying degrees throughout Church history. However, these passages make it clear that it will come to a climax in the days before the Tribulation and leading up to Christ's return.

Where are we currently seeing evidence of this type of delusion? Following are some examples of modern satanic deceptions:

1. "All roads lead to God." It doesn't matter what religion you are or what name you use to refer to God. Heaven is a state of mind. There is good in all religions, and thus all have a legitimate path to Heaven. You may remember the ancient Indian fable about the blind men and the elephant. Apologist Greg Koukl summarizes the parable this way.

> The first blind man put out his hand and touched the side of the elephant. "How smooth! An elephant is like a wall."
>
> The second blind man put out his hand and touched the trunk of the elephant. "How round! An elephant is like a snake."
>
> The third blind man put out his hand and touched the tusk of the elephant. "How sharp! An elephant is like a spear."
>
> The fourth blind man put out his hand and touched the leg of the elephant. "How tall! An elephant is like a tree."
>
> The fifth blind man reached out his hand and touched the ear of the elephant. "How wide! An elephant is like a fan."

The sixth blind man put out his hand and touched the tail of the elephant. "How thin! An elephant is like a rope."

An argument ensued, each blind man thinking his own perception of the elephant was the correct one. The Rajah, awakened by the commotion, called out from the balcony. "The elephant is a big animal," he said. "Each man touched only one part. You must put all the parts together to find out what an elephant is like."[32]

Now enlightened by the Rajah's wisdom, the blind men reached agreement. "Each one of us knows only a part. To find out the whole truth we must put all the parts together."

This is precisely what some wish to do with God today, arguing that every religion contributes a "part" of Him, but no religion possesses the complete, correct truth about Him. In fact, according to the Bible, God has a name (Yahweh), and Jesus has a claim (to be God and the *only* way to Heaven)!

2. "Truth is subjective, not objective." There is no unchanging standard by which we can view and interpret reality or judge morality. *We*—not Christianity—decide and declare our own truth. We are, in essence, gods (if you remember, the opportunity to become like God was the original temptation to Eve in the Garden in Genesis 3). We see this today with sexual and gender identity issues, as well as in the defiant claim of a woman's "right over her own body." This goddess-like sovereignty is pandemic in our culture.

3. "Morality is malleable." What was considered taboo by the previous generation is now tolerable. We're increasingly often being told that we must accept all peoples and their views, and include them in the life of Jesus' Church because "that's the loving and Christlike thing to do." But is it? And who decides what moral values and standards are to be honored? This is apparent through both legal and social

demands that Christians capitulate to in answer to the demands of those of the homosexual, transgender, and pedophile persuasions. This (im)moral pressure is also being applied as it relates to abortion, in that we must not prevent a woman's right from being freely exercised according to her will.

4. "The Bible is an outdated, ancient book, and impractical for the modern world." The Creation account is no longer seen as credible, and certainly is not "scientific." The Bible's clearly stated morality and design for marriage, as well as about the role of women, has been all but torpedoed by postmodern thought. Even within many mainstream denominations and evangelical churches, neo-orthodox theology concerning these issues is on the rise.

In fact, all of the above heresies are creeping into the Church today. This, I believe, is a direct result of pastors who are not themselves thoroughly convinced of Scripture's infallibility, inerrancy, and unchanging authority. And, combined with their own cowardice, they end up leading the sheep astray. Further, this is precisely what Paul commanded Timothy NOT to do. Consider the following strong exhortations for pastors:

> In pointing out these things to the brethren, you will be a good servant of Christ Jesus, constantly nourished on the words of the faith and of the sound doctrine which you have been following. But have nothing to do with worldly fables fit only for old women. On the other hand, discipline yourself for the purpose of godliness; for bodily discipline is only of little profit, but godliness is profitable for all things, since it holds promise for the present life and also for the life to come. It is a trustworthy statement deserving full acceptance. For it is for this we labor and strive, because we have fixed our hope on the living God, who is the Savior of all men, especially of believers. Prescribe and teach these things. (1 Timothy 4:6–11)

> Until I come, give attention to the public reading of Scripture, to exhortation and teaching. Do not neglect

the spiritual gift within you, which was bestowed on you through prophetic utterance with the laying on of hands by the presbytery. Take pains with these things; be absorbed in them, so that your progress will be evident to all. Pay close attention to yourself and to your teaching; persevere in these things, for as you do this you will ensure salvation both for yourself and for those who hear you. (1 Timothy 4:13–16)

Retain the standard of sound words which you have heard from me, in the faith and love which are in Christ Jesus. Guard, through the Holy Spirit who dwells in us, the treasure which has been entrusted to you. (2 Timothy 1:13–14)

But evil men and impostors will proceed from bad to worse, deceiving and being deceived. You, however, continue in the things you have learned and become convinced of, knowing from whom you have learned them, and that from childhood you have known the sacred writings which are able to give you the wisdom that leads to salvation through faith which is in Christ Jesus. All Scripture is inspired by God and profitable for teaching, for reproof, for correction, for training in righteousness; so that the man of God may be adequate, equipped for every good work. (2 Timothy 3:13–17; 4:1–5)

I solemnly charge you in the presence of God and of Christ Jesus, who is to judge the living and the dead, and by His appearing and His kingdom: preach the word; be ready in season and out of season; reprove, rebuke, exhort, with great patience and instruction. For the time will come when they will not endure sound doctrine; but wanting to have their ears tickled, they will accumulate for themselves teachers in accordance to their own desires, and will turn away their ears from the truth and will turn aside to myths.

But you, be sober in all things, endure hardship, do the work
of an evangelist, fulfill your ministry. (2 Timothy 4.1–5)

Though it is an increasingly unpopular statement to make these days, doctrine and what we believe are not secondary or minor issues. They are primary and critical to our faith, at least according to Jesus, Paul, James, and Jude. But why? What real difference does it make what we believe, just as long as we love one another and do good to our neighbor—right? Isn't that what God really cares about? Isn't doctrine divisive?

First, doctrine can be divisive, but it doesn't have to be. Second, truth itself is divisive when infiltrated by lies. But also consider that:

- Sound doctrine reveals the mind and character of God. Apart from what the Bible teaches, we have no guarantee that our view of God is correct.

- Believing sound doctrine is the difference between eternal life and death, obedience and disobedience, worship and idolatry. God's revealed truth is what leads us to Jesus and Heaven. We cannot worship a god about which we know nothing for sure. And to worship a god of our own thinking is the essence of idolatry.

- False teachers exist, and they are not passive. Rather, they're quite aggressive in their dissemination of their delusions. Like the illusionist I spoke of at the beginning of this chapter, they are skilled at their craft.

- Satan hates God and His people. He is a liar, deceiver, and the father of lies (John 8:44).

- Sound doctrine insulates and protects us from error and the deceptions so prevalent in our culture.

- We can't fully (or always) trust our own thoughts. We desperately need God's unchanging truth to purify, calibrate, and transform our thinking into His (Romans 12:2).

Many today are downplaying and minimizing doctrine, shoving it to the side for the sake of love, unity, community, and even evangelism/outreach. But "love" is not enough because it doesn't exist apart from the One who created it. Love and unity are based in Christ and what He has done for us; it is not based from within ourselves. Love is more than a feeling or emotion (which can mislead and deceive), but rather is rooted in the truth, God's truth. Evangelism isn't enough, because we have no saving message to communicate apart from what God has revealed in His Word. God's truth is the wellspring of our love, unity, community, fellowship, and evangelism. Apart from it, none of those things have any ultimate or lasting meaning.

So, what are we, as believers, to do in light of the present falling away from the faith? Here are some practical and helpful principles to help you in your spiritual relationship with Christ and in your everyday dealings with worldly values.

- Know the truth. Get into the Word regularly (John 17:17).

- Nourish yourself with the truth. Don't just get it into your head. Feed on it with your soul. Let it be your milk and meat (Philippians 1.9–11; Colossians 1:9–10; 1 Peter 2:2).

- Develop biblical discernment (Hebrews 5:1–11:14). This discernment (sound judgment/wisdom) only comes from habitually immersing yourself into God's Word, seeking more than just the surface truths. It means you want to know the deep things of Scripture. Biblical discernment will protect you from being deluded by the lies of the world and the devil. It's not something you get just from reading a book or attending a conference. Instead, it's life skill you learn over time, through much practice.

- Reject unbiblical thinking in your own heart (2 Corinthians 10:3–5). Once you recognize subtle lies of the enemy, turn those thoughts over to Christ and remind yourself of a biblical truth that addresses it.

- Contend for the truth (Jude 1:3). Every believer—not just pastors, teachers, or apologists—is called to defend God's truth and character. Train yourself in exactly how to wrestle for the truth in today's world. This doesn't mean you have to correct every wrong you see (especially on social media). But it does mean that we must all learn to "make a defense to everyone who asks…to give an account for the hope that is within [us], yet with gentleness and reverence" (1 Peter 3:15).

This is part of what it means to be a discerner in the world today. Becoming this kind of believer protects us from falling under even the most subtle of Satan's deceptions! And in the process, we can help lead others out of the darkness as well!

CHAPTER 4

DANIEL'S LAST DAYS TO-AND-FRO FRENZY

BY NATHAN E. JONES

HOW DO WE KNOW the end times are upon us and that Jesus Christ is returning soon? One of the surest ways we can know is through the incredible end-times sign of technology. God has revealed in the Bible that when certain centuries-old prophecies concerning future technology, especially those that greatly increase knowledge and travel, become a part of everyday life, then the final days of this age leading up to Christ's Millennial Kingdom will have at last come upon us. The long-ago prophesied technologies that we now take for granted prove that Jesus is returning soon.

The Technology Scale

Before we take a look into this jaw-dropping end-times sign, let me first ask you a question: How do you feel personally about technology? Do you love it, and consider yourself a technophile? Or do you hate it, and are proud of the label "technophobe"? Or, are you just floating in blissful ambivalence somewhere in the middle of the love-to-hate technology scale?

For those who dislike technology, or who at least keep a wary eye upon it, you probably have some good reasons for feeling that way. When struggling to operate the latest and greatest gizmo, maybe merely turning it on frustrates you. We've all felt irritated when using some new piece of tech—and we've also felt so much better after hurling the device against the wall! Maybe the nerd factor keeps you at a distance. You avoid shopping at Best

Buy at all cost, worried that upon entering you'll be transformed into the next Steve Urkel. Who would ever want to end up as a social stigma in suspenders? Or, maybe you fear that technology will eventually become so advanced that it will evolve and, once it reaches self-awareness, it will seek to destroy all of humanity with an army of glowing-eyed, Schwarzenegger-like Terminators. Why take the chance on having our own creations rebel against us just as we've been doing with God? Or, maybe in the process of assimilating all of this tech into our lives and even into our bodies, we worry that we'll lose our humanity and become more Borg than organism.

For those who love technology, I believe the real reason we create so many new devices is that we like to find creative ways to torment our pets. It's true! Who hasn't turned on the vacuum cleaner and received a good laugh out of watching the dog bolt for cover? Or, gotten some kind of demented glee out of watching the cat frantically chase the penlight's beam zigzagging around the carpet? Or, chuckled as the fish took a ride up the bubble stream glugging out of the tank's treasure chest? Or, taken a wiener dog scuba diving? (Well, maybe not that.)

With all of our human ingenuity, you'd think we'd at least use our creativity for more constructive purposes. But alas, for all our creative genius, we humans tend to misuse our ingenuity more than we use it. We create many of our new technologies in the name of convenience, but in the end, they often end up making us look quite silly. Who in a public bathroom hasn't waved dripping hands in front of an automatic dispenser and had the device mock us by refusing to eject a paper towel? Or, cursed a leaf blower for blowing leaves from one side of the yard back to the same spot again? Or, spent every Christmas Eve untangling a Gordian knot forged out of those little blinking tree lights? Or, had a smart phone's autocorrect wish a spouse, "Happy birthday, dead husband"? Or, when mounting lasers to the heads of sharks? Well, maybe not the last one either, but you get the point. Rooms full of corporate gadget-makers have long been belly laughing at our expense.

Where do I personally fall on the love-to-hate technology scale? I made it through college on a typewriter, even though a fully-equipped computer lab lay at my disposal. But, then, I got over my reticence and devoted my early career to being a Web developer and designer. And, now as an Internet and television evangelist, I've embraced the tremendous benefits of our modern-day communications technology because it provides unlimited possibilities for sharing the gospel with the world. I may not be the first in line to shell out obscene amounts of money for the latest iPhone, but then, neither am I the last. A simple Appalachian cabin would suit me fine, just as long as a wireless connection to my Netflix account was readily available. I'd imagine most of us fall along that point on the scale.

Technology Defined

Before moving any farther into our look at how today's technology heralds the end times, we first need to define terms, because you are going to read the word "technology" a whole lot in this chapter. The Greek word *tekhnologia* provides the root of our English word "technology," meaning "the systematic treatment of art and skill." The *Science Dictionary* clarifies Aristotle's nebulous definition with "the use of scientific knowledge to solve practical problems." But, is science absolutely necessary to solve our problems? Maybe technology is more about "the practical application of knowledge." That's a pretty good definition. Or, how about this one? "The sum of the ways in which social groups provide themselves with material objects of their civilization." I believe these curious definitions tend to beat around the bush, so I'm going to give you my own definition technology: "Applying what you know to fix problems and make stuff." Technology, therefore, is not just the gizmos and gadgets we make, but the technical skills and creativity it takes to invent and forge these tools.

The Origins of Knowledge

So, technology does what again? It fixes problems and it makes stuff. For those who dislike technology, fixing problems and making stuff isn't so bad, right? Right, because I'm now going to prove that technology can certainly be a good thing. After all, do you know where knowledge and the wisdom to properly wield technology comes from? It originates directly from God Almighty

The Source of Knowledge

Job once asked, "Can anyone teach God knowledge?" (Job 21:22). The obvious answer is no; no one can teach an all-knowing God. Job later referred to God as, "Him who is perfect in knowledge" (Job 37:16). That means that God is absolute, flawless, and perfect. He is the ultimate in knowing all things. He even knows all things down to the tiniest minutia, such as the number of hairs on each of our heads (Luke 12:7).

The prophet Isaiah asked similar rhetorical questions: "With whom did He take counsel, and who instructed Him, and taught Him in the path of justice? Who taught Him knowledge, and showed Him the way of understanding?" (Isaiah 40:14). Nobody! God is the Author and the Creator. All that ever was to be known, is known, or will be known has been authored by God. To have real knowledge means to know what God already knows.

You can understand, then, why the Apostle Paul cried out: "Oh, the depth of the riches both of the wisdom and knowledge of God! How unsearchable are His judgments and His ways past finding out!" (Romans 11:33). That means everything mankind has ever known has originated from God. It also means that when we finally get to Heaven and live with our omniscient Savior forever and ever, we will also continually learn forever and ever. We'll never catch up to what God already knows, because what He knows is infinite, just as He is infinite. Isn't that exciting? Christians will have an eternity of learning and growing ahead of us.

The Keeper of Knowledge

Not only is God the *source* of knowledge, but He is also the *keeper* of knowledge. The Proverbs reveal that "the eyes of the Lord preserve knowledge" (Proverbs 22:12). In other words, God protects knowledge as if it were a commodity. Paul explained the reason as "in whom are hidden all the treasures of wisdom and knowledge" (Colossians 2:3). God sees both wisdom and knowledge as treasure. He doles out those treasures as He sees fit, keeping the keys to certain scientific breakthroughs hidden until

He wants mankind to at last discover them. Bear in mind that wisdom, like technology, is simply the practical application of knowledge. Therefore, God, as the keeper of wisdom is, therefore, also the keeper of technology.

The Provider of Knowledge

God may be the source and the keeper of knowledge, but He's also generous in sharing what He knows. He then becomes the provider of knowledge, therefore technology. That means all the technologies mankind has invented and taken credit for, well, it can be argued that they in truth came from the very mind of God—the Provider—when He saw fit to release that knowledge.

The Proverbs teach that, "For the Lord gives wisdom; from His mouth comes knowledge and understanding" (Proverbs 2:6). When E. F. Hutton talks, people listen, but every time God talks, we learn something eternal. That's why it's so important that we read God's Word.

The author of Ecclesiastes wrote, "For God gives wisdom and knowledge and joy to a man who is good in His sight" (Ecclesiastes 2:26). How are we good in His sight? How do we please God? By doing His will, for "whatever we ask we receive from Him, because we keep His commandments and do those things that are pleasing in His sight" (1 John 3:22).

That the all-knowing God of the universe is the source, keeper, and provider of all knowledge is, to quote Donald Trump, "Yuge!" It's so huge, in fact, that I must stop for a second and point this out again, for I'm going to keep making the argument that the technology we have today was given to us by God only when He saw fit to give it to us. Former President Obama once accused our nation's companies, saying, "You didn't make that." He meant that without government's help, our companies could never have ever made the widgets and services that they make. Obama was wrong about the government part (and about pretty much everything else), but he would have been correct if he had attributed the production of our technology to God. God provided the knowledge and inspiration to produce certain technologies at key times He designated, all because He is the provider of knowledge.

The prophet Daniel added to this vital point: "He gives wisdom to the wise and knowledge to those who have understanding" (Daniel 2:21). Here we learn that God gives even more knowledge, and the wisdom to apply that knowledge, to those who know how to utilize it. If you happen to be knowledgeable and wise, it's because the Holy Spirit has made you that way. Paul added, "For to one is given the word of wisdom through the Spirit, to another the word of knowledge through the same Spirit" (1 Corinthians 12:8). God made each of us with a certain level of knowledge, skills, and wisdom; we each apply those to fixing our problems and making stuff.

Promises Concerning Knowledge

Did you know that God has made certain promises concerning knowledge? Young Timothy learned from his mentor, Paul, that when it comes to the knowledge about salvation, God "desires all men to be saved and to come to the knowledge of the truth" (1 Timothy 2:4). Who does God want to have the knowledge of the truth of salvation and so be saved? All of mankind! Every one of us. Whether people accept that saving knowledge or not, well, that's up to them. But, when it comes to knowledge concerning salvation, God provides that freely.

Titus learned from Paul that the hope of eternal life in God, who cannot lie, was promised before time began (Titus 1:1–2). God promised the knowledge about salvation before the beginning of time, and long before mankind had ever sinned.

Living Without Knowledge

We'd agree that there are many smart people out there who clearly have a good amount of knowledge. And, we'd agree that there are just as many people out there who clearly are lacking in knowledge. (Many work in Congress.) What happens when people lack knowledge?

Proverbs tells us, "The fear of the Lord is the beginning of wisdom, and the knowledge of the Holy One is understanding" (Proverbs 9:10). If you have no knowledge of the Holy One, what do you really have? Nothing! Without respect for God and a desire to seek Him and learn about Him, our manmade knowledge becomes absolutely worthless. This verse is an emphatic declaration that the first step to attaining true knowledge must begin with accepting the fact that there is a God, if we are to really know anything at all.

If we don't first begin our quest for attaining knowledge by acknowledging there is a God and follow that by identifying Him as the God of the Bible, then we end up with the opposite of knowledge, which is ignorance. Take, for instance, Paul's warning to Timothy to "guard what was committed to your trust, avoiding the profane and idle babblings and contradictions of what is falsely called knowledge" (1 Timothy 6:20). So, there's godly knowledge, and then there's mankind's knowledge. Mankind's knowledge is rarely built upon God's knowledge, so it ends up being, in reality, not even knowledge at all. Mankind's knowledge, apart from God's knowledge, is false and worthless. (Can we say "evolution"?) So-called knowledge apart from God turns geniuses into ignoramuses.

Ignorance has consequences. God, through the prophet Hosea, bemoaned, "My people are destroyed for lack of knowledge" (Hosea 4:6). Without knowing Jesus Christ as Savior, we die unforgiven of our sins and face an eternal punishment for our rebellion against God in Hell. Not knowing the source and provider of knowledge, especially when it comes to the knowledge concerning salvation, is literally killing us in this life and ultimately in Hell in the next life.

The Destiny of Knowledge

Does knowledge have a destiny? The Bible tells us so, and it's twofold.

First, "Whether there is knowledge, it will vanish away" (1 Corinthians 13:8). That manmade earthly knowledge that we're so keen on stoking, which puffs up so many egos and leads so many people astray from the saving knowledge of Jesus Christ, will all end—and someday soon.

Second, that manmade earthly knowledge we put so much stock into will ultimately be replaced: "For the earth will be filled with the knowledge of the glory of the Lord, as the waters cover the sea" (Habakkuk 2:14). God's knowledge is all that matters, for manmade knowledge will be replaced totally, universally, and forever by the wonderful truth of God—the source, keeper, and provider of knowledge.

The Benefits of Technology

That brings us back to my initial question: How do you feel personally about technology? After all, now that you know God is the source and provider of all true knowledge, and that knowing Him is the ultimate application of that knowledge, ergo wisdom, then is using His knowledge to create technology inherently bad? I would argue that since God Himself is a Creator who made His children in His image to also be creators, and that He doles out knowledge as He sees fit for the purpose of leading mankind to invent new technologies, then technology is inherently good. After all, don't we all have the need from time to time to fix problems and make stuff?

When mankind shivered out there in the wild in the cold of night, they figured out how to make a fire, then control the fire, then safely bring the fire indoors. When their legs grew weary from walking and saddle-sore from riding, they invented the wheel and buggy, and later the monster truck. When heavy earthen pots became too burdensome to carry back and forth from the well, they designed irrigation systems and mastered glass-blowing to create lightweight pitchers, and eventually the Thermos. When people got tired of burning their hands over an open fire while cooking their latest kill, they invented the charcoal grill and invited all their friends over for a BBQ. And, when their backsides grew red and raw from using pinecones in the outhouses, the Chinese (God bless them) invented toilet paper. Who can argue with the benefits of these technologies? These, and so many more like them, fix mankind's problems.

So, technology: Good or bad? I'd conclude that technology is inherently good, but with this caveat, in the wrong hands, it can certainly can be misused.

The Progress of Technology

When I was a kid back in the 1980s, I faced some serious dilemmas. The tough decisions I was forced to make affected my life so monumentally that, should I have ended up making the wrong choices, they would have forever sent me down the dark path of social obscurity. VHS or Betamax? Kodak 35mm film or Polaroid camera? Sony Walkman or Sound Burger 33 1/3 RPM record player? Slide deck or overhead projector? Commodore 64 or Apple Macintosh? Nintendo NES or Sega Master System? Transformers or Gobots? As you can see, the '80s were a minefield of new technologies to navigate. Choose wrongly, and you may end up like Donovan from the movie *Indiana Jones and the Last Crusade.*

Unless you're a toddler playing with your mother's Android, you have enough history to look back and see that technology has changed a lot—a whole lot—over the last few decades. Let's not even talk in decades, but in just years. The child attaining adulthood today can with a shudder look back to 2002 when there was no Wikipedia, no Gmail, no social media like Facebook and Twitter, no cloud computing, no tablets, no smartphones, and certainly no high-speed Internet connectivity. Remember the sound a modem made when connecting a surfer to the World Wide Web? Ask ten-year-olds that question today and they couldn't even tell you. Even Bob Dylan couldn't have imagined how much things would be changing when way back in the stone ages of 1963 he sang *The Times They Are a-changin'.*

Times a-changin' wasn't always the way things were, though. For thousands of years of human history, life remained pretty much the same. Sure, every three hundred years or so, the world eked out a technological innovation that revolutionized the world, moving humanity from, say the Bronze Age to the Iron Age. But, for the most part, limitations in travel left most inventions cordoned off to a tiny corner of the world. But, then, AD 1454 finally arrived, and the German goldsmith Johannes Gutenberg released the very first mobile, reusable type press (like an antique photocopier). At last, knowledge could be mass copied onto paper and be distributed far and wide. The age of the printed book revolutionized the world, and Gutenberg started with the fount of all knowledge—the Bible.

It'd be hundreds of years later before other monumental inventions transformed society: Eli Whitney and the cotton gin, Thomas Newcomen and the steam engine, Samuel Morse and the telegraph, Thomas Edison and the light bulb, Alexander Graham Bell and the telephone, Alexander Fleming and antibiotic penicillin, Guglielmo Marconi and the radio, Philo Taylor Farnsworth and the television, William Shockley and team the transistor, and Jack Kilby and Robert Noyce the microchip.

Were you surprised to learn from history classes that the most world-changing technologies were invented in the last 150 years or so? And, as we got closer to our own day and age, each technological discovery came about faster and faster and faster, and each grew more and more and more powerful, as one invention was built on top of another on top of another. This increasingly rapid acceleration of technological discovery has been called the exponential curve. Our technology has been experiencing an exponential growth as one discovery builds upon another at an increasingly faster and faster pace.

Let's just look at the exponential curve of computers, for instance. The old joke is, "How do you know when your computer is obsolete?" The answer: "When you take it out of the box." That's not too far from the truth, though. Computer companies tend to double computer processing speeds every eighteen months. Known as Moore's Law, this is just one manifestation of the greater trend in how all technological change happens to be occurring at an exponential rate. By 2023, computers are expected to possess the processing speed equivalent to that of the human brain. By 2045, in a mere quarter of a century, Moore's Law predicts that we will possess computers that have the computational ability equivalent to that of the entire human race!

The exponential curve is not limited to computers. Other technologies in biomedicine, space science, chemical engineering, human engineering, and all the other sciences have been climbing faster and steeper up their own exponential curves with each passing day. It's expected that in the next five years the world's technology will be thirty-two times more advanced than it is today. It's also been estimated that 65 percent of today's kindergarteners, once they finally graduate from college, will end up working in completely new jobs that, at this time, don't yet even exist.

This exponential curve in all areas of technology reminds me of another exponential curve, one Jesus described in the Bible. The apostles once asked Jesus, "What will be the sign of your coming, and of the end of the age?" (Matthew 24; Luke 21; Mark 13). Jesus answered by providing ten signs that would reveal when His Second Advent would be upon us. A marked increase in false prophets and false messiah, wars and rumors of wars, earthquakes, famines, plagues, fearful events, signs in the sky, the persecution of Christians, and the world's focus on Jerusalem would encompass the first nine signs, with the tenth sign involving the unnatural disasters that will directly precede the Messiah's return. Jesus added that these signs would increase in frequency and intensity, much like a woman's birth pains, the closer we come to His return. Exponential curves become, in and of themselves, their own sign that marks the advent of the Messiah's return to this earth.

Technology in the Old Testament

How does the intersection of the two exponential curves—the end-times-signs curve and the technology curve—indicate that Jesus Christ is returning soon? Before we dive deep into answering that question, I want to back up a bit and confront a general misconception. Let's take a moment to look at technologies historically found in the Bible, particularly way back in the very beginnings of the Old Testament. Since we're looking at God's Word for the answer to where technology is going, we first need to bust a myth. Men like famed astronomer Neil deGrasse Tyson have scoffed that "God is an ever receding pocket of scientific ignorance." Atheists like him claim that the Bible is merely a "religious book" filled with primitive people tromping around in the mud and hating science. As we take a look into the Bible, we'll see that's certainly not the case. The Bible is just full of science.

Pre-Flood Technologies (4000-2348 BC, Covering 1,652 Years)

Let's, like H. G. Wells, hop into our time machine and travel back to the age before the Flood. Let's look at the era between the Creation, say 4000 BC, to 2348 BC, when creation scientists calculate the Flood occurred. This era covers some 1,652 years. Let's explore some of the various technologies that early people used to fix their problems and make stuff.

Agriculture. "Then the Lord God took the man and put him in the Garden of Eden to tend and keep it" (Genesis 2:15). Even before the Fall of mankind, Adam and Eve were working the land. Horticulture, botany, farming, and all the agrarian sciences were being discovered, and new technologies and tools were invented to handle agricultural work. And, we're talking about just two people figuring all of this out. Our ancient parents must have been incredibly intelligent people!

Textiles. "And they sewed fig leaves together and made themselves coverings" (Genesis 3:7). As soon as Adam and Eve sinned and realized they were walking around in the buff, they ran off behind a tree and sewed some clothes together. They didn't just lick and stick a bunch of leaves all over themselves. They had at least already invented the needle and thread. They knew how to make textiles.

Weaponry. "So He drove out the man; and He placed cherubim at the east of the garden of Eden, and a flaming sword which turned every way, to guard the way to the tree of life" (Genesis 3:24). Even before Adam and Eve were expelled from the Garden of Eden, weaponry like swords already existed in the heavenly realm. Genesis records that two angels flashed a flaming sword back and forth to prevent mankind from accessing the Tree of Life. The first couple had observed Heaven's arsenal before needing to learn how to construct their own weaponry to ward off the velociraptors.

Tools. "Now Abel was a keeper of sheep, but Cain was a tiller of the ground" (Genesis 4:2). How did Abel shear his sheep? He had to invent the clipper and the comb. And, did Cain dig with his hands? No, he invented tools such as hoes, rakes, sickles, and other farm implementations. Cain wouldn't have been able to farm very well without these tools. Even as early as the second generation, humanity had developed tools.

Construction. "And he [Cain] built a city" (Genesis 4:17). After Cain had killed his brother and was ordered by God to wander the earth, Cain went right ahead and disobeyed God by building an entire city. Sure, there may once have been people living in caves, but cavemen? No! The earliest of peoples possessed the ability to build buildings.

Mining. "Tubal-Cain, an instructor of every craftsman in bronze and iron" (Genesis 4:22). All the way back to the earliest chapters in Genesis, mankind possessed the technology to mine metals, refine the ores in furnaces, utilize measuring devices, and work with blacksmith's tools. They constructed pickaxes, drills, and chisels in order to mine the earth.

Shipbuilding. "Make yourself an ark of gopherwood" (Genesis 6:14–16). Noah was asked to build a boat—and not just any boat, but probably the most massive boat the world up to that point had ever seen. Sure, the task took him a hundred years or so to accomplish, but it still takes a lot of technology to build a boat. Noah knew how to cut, fell, and shape wood. He had the ability to measure lengths with various measuring devices. He needed a crane. And, did Noah even know how to sail? He would have needed some knowledge about yachting. The ability to build and master ships was already in existence by Noah's day.

Fermentation. "And Noah began to be a farmer, and he planted a vineyard. Then he drank of the wine" (Genesis 9:20–21). Almost as soon as Noah got out of the ark, what did he do? He cultivated vines, constructed vats, fermented grapes, and then got passed-out drunk. Noah had earlier mastered how to distill alcohol. People have long been searching for a stiff drink.

Post-Flood Technologies (2347–1 BC, Covering 2,347 Years)

Even in those early days, back when people were starting all over again after the Flood, Noah's descendants had problems that needed fixing and so they continued to make stuff.

Medicine. "And Joseph commanded his servants the physicians to embalm his father. So the physicians embalmed Israel" (Genesis 50:2). Ancient Egypt had medical personnel who were proficient in various plant remedies, chemistry, and healing treatments. They even knew how to pre-serve dead bodies against the dry desert elements. Egyptians were master doctors at the time. Even some of today's medical methodology originat-ed back in those ancient lands.

Transportation. "And He took off their chariot wheels, so that they drove them with difficulty" (Exodus 14:25). This very first mention of the wheel in the Bible shows that ancient people relied on this vital bit of tech-nology to travel and transport cargo. Ancient people weren't just exhaust-ing themselves from pushing pallets around, but they used wheel technol-ogy to increase their productivity and get themselves home from work faster in time for dinner.

Language and Writing. "Then the Lord said to Moses, 'Write this for a memorial in the book'" (Exodus 17:14). By Moses' day, people had already long mastered verbal and written languages, recording words on clay tablets and antique forms of paper. Adam actually had already invented language back when God had commanded him to name everything. So, no: Ancient people didn't go around grunting and saying "Oog!" Language has been around since the beginning, and the written language has ex-isted for thousands of years. Even today, writing continues to be an ad-vanced skill.

Tentmaking. "So you shall speak to all who are gifted artisans…and He has filled him with the Spirit of God, in wisdom and understanding, in knowledge and all manner of workmanship" (Exodus 28:3, 35:31). These passages tell the story of the construction of the Tabernacle, which be-came the most ornate tent ever seen in early Israel. Tentmaking involves all sorts of skills in weaving and design work, metallurgy, and textiles. Here again, God who is the source of all knowledge, provided His people with the skills and abilities to craft such a magnificent pavilion.

Musical Instruments. "Praise Him with the sound of the trumpet; praise Him with the lute and harp! Praise Him with the timbrel and dance; praise Him with stringed instruments and flutes" (Psalm 150). Have you ever learned how to play a musical instrument? Just think about how complicated most musical instruments are. They involve a combination of all sorts of craftsman's skills, artistically implemented. Plus, music is a language all of its own, and a mathematically complicated one at that.

So, this whole belief that ancient man started off as a bunch of uneducated, grunting primitives who pulled their women along by their hair and lived in dank caves is pure nonsense. Mankind's ability to combine intellect and knowledge in order to discover and invent new technologies that would fix their problems and make stuff has been around ever since God first created Adam and Eve. After all, God is the source of all of mankind's knowledge, which He shared with our ancient ancestors.

Signs of Technology

Let's at last take a look at where the technological exponential curve is leading us. Let's look at the signs of technology revealed in the Bible that point to the fact that we are now living in the end times and that indicate Jesus will soon return. The following are, I believe, nine of the most prominent signs of technology.

#1) Increase in Knowledge

The first sign is the sign of knowledge. Not only does this sign stand out particularly as the most revealing of all the technological signs, but it also provides the foundation that the others in this list build upon.

We find the source text for this prophecy in the book of Daniel. "But you, Daniel, shut up the words, and seal the book until the time of the end; many shall run to and fro, and knowledge shall increase" (Daniel 12:4). Daniel had been listening across many chapters to an angel pronouncing a mind-blowing message from God. Through the angel, God revealed the rise and fall of great empires, leading eventually to a global empire led by a world ruler whom the Apostle John would later call the Antichrist. Of course, all these great empires were still future from Daniel's perspective, so he was quite perplexed over all he was hearing. Rubbing his forehead in confusion, he asked the angel for an explanation. To his dismay, no luck! The angel basically told Daniel that he could never understand these prophecies because too much needed to happen first. This would include a great increase in mankind's knowledge, which would mark the "time of the end," or end times (Daniel 12:9). Only those living in the end times and who were "wise" would at last understand these prophecies and recognize that the exponential increase in knowledge heralded the soon return of the Messiah (Daniel 12:3,9).

Have you ever considered that, just a hundred years ago, all that most people learned throughout their entire lifetime equaled the information contained in one Sunday edition of the *New York Times*? Our ability today to practically consume that same amount of data on a daily basis shows just how far mankind's knowledge has increased in such a short time.

What technologies have helped us facilitate the advent of this massive explosion in the growth of knowledge? You probably answered "computers," and you'd be absolutely correct (high-five yourself). Not only has the exponential curve in all areas of computer technology increased our knowledge to stupendous levels, but computers have aided in all the major scientific discoveries of our day. We don't need to cram all these facts into our brains anymore, either, for the ability to easily store and access data means we can continue to learn like we've never learned before in human history.

Today's exponential increase in knowledge points to the fact that Jesus Christ is returning soon.

#2) Increase in Transportation

Notice in that same prophecy, the angel told Daniel that, besides a great increase in knowledge, "many shall run to and fro" (Daniel 12:4). This second sign, a tremendous increase in the distance and speed of travel, would also occur in the same context, that being the end times. God was revealing that, once people begin to run to and fro, both farther and faster, the final years before Christ returns to set up His Millennial Kingdom will finally be upon us.

Stop and think how people traveled just a single century ago. Most roads weren't even paved yet, and were traveled with horse-drawn wagons. Watch on YouTube the video of San Francisco from back in 1909 and you will see far more horses than horseless carriages. People rarely, if ever, left their hometowns. Animal domestication and the early beginnings of decent roads, then bicycles, balloons, boats, and simple automobiles were developing technologies, but they weren't widely received. Since the early part of the twentieth century, mankind went on to invent airplanes and jets, and we've even left the Earth's atmosphere in rockets and space shuttles. It used to take months for people to travel by boat overseas, but now we travel that same distance abroad in mere hours. In today's world, people are always on the move, just as the angel prophesied to Daniel.

Today's exponential increase In travel points to the fact that Jesus Christ is returning soon.

#3) The Mark of the Beast

The third sign involves technologies that will make the Mark of the Beast the terror of the world. The Book of Revelation forewarns, "He causes all, both small and great, rich and poor, free and slave, to receive a mark on their right hand or on their foreheads, and that no one may buy or sell except one who has the mark or the name of the beast, or the number of his name" (Revelation 13:16–17).

Let me provide you with a little context concerning the Mark of the Beast. A seven-year Tribulation period is coming when God will pour out His wrath upon the world, just as He did during the days of the Flood. Revelation reveals that at the midpoint of the Tribulation, the Antichrist and his False Prophet will set up a system of commerce whereby people cannot buy or sell unless they have sworn allegiance to the Antichrist. They do so by writing his name or the number 666 on their right hand or forehead.

What kinds of technologies would be required to control the world's commerce? The Apostle John could visibly read the name and number etched on the people who had sworn their allegiance to the Antichrist, so some kind of tattooing is certainly involved. Magnetic inks can store a person's personal, financial, and health information; then, digital readers would scan the ink in order to authorize whether that person is allowed to buy and sell. Maybe a RFID microchip is also involved, embedded in a rice-sized glass case underneath the readable mark.

Global commerce also needs a way to collect the countless terabytes of information, so would require the constructing of giant data centers to store a planetary population full of data. That data would need to move lightning fast, using high-speed-Internet connectivity, complex ecommerce systems, wireless networks, billion-dollar satellites, and so on.

The closest system we have today to the Mark of the Beast is China's social credit score, which has already been instituted in their more populated cities. The Chinese government has positioned millions of cameras everywhere in order to spy on their citizens. Computer algorithms then rate each citizen's allegiance to the government, granting benefits to those who are more loyal and restrictions on those the computer deems as not being patriotic enough. Just imagine that horribly restrictive system instituted on a global scale! All these ecommerce technologies, which make today's buying and selling so much easier, are all coming together so that the Antichrist can control the world's commerce, and thereby all of the people under his rule.

A lot of fear surrounds taking the Mark of the Beast, and rightly so, for those who take it, God says, will have lost their hope of becoming saved. But, we today should have no fear of accidently taking the Mark, for it will not be instituted until halfway through the Tribulation, well after the Church has been raptured into Heaven. Therefore, don't sweat chips and barcodes and credit cards. They have nothing to do with the Mark of the Beast…yet.

Today's global ecommerce network points to the fact that Jesus Christ is returning soon.

#4) Evangelism

The fourth is actually a wonderful sign, for it's a positive one, prophesying that the entire world will be evangelized in the end times: "And this gospel of the kingdom will be preached in all the world as a witness to all the nations, and then the end will come" (Matthew 24:14).

God wants the Church to preach the Good News of His salvation to the entire world, so He's provided us with powerful communication tools for sharing the gospel. Today's exponential curve in communications technology has played a vital role in reaching more of the world for Christ than has ever been reached in the previous nineteen centuries. Technologies such as cameras and microphones, televisions and tablets, smartphones and cell towers, communications networks and satellites, the Internet and the airwaves, big media and social media all work together to form the largest pulpit the world has ever known.

And while all these breathtaking technologies are leading people to Christ by the thousands each day, the entire world, as Jesus referred to it, will not all hear the gospel before the Rapture happens. That blessing awaits the Second Coming at the end of the Tribulation. Communications technologies will continue to spread the gospel to the post-Rapture world. In addition, God will send forth 144,000 Jewish evangelists, the two witnesses, and even the ospel angel to preach throughout the whole world. Every person on the planet will be evangelized by the end of the Tribulation. God will leave no person without a chance to choose His Son and so be saved.

Today's communications technologies point to the fact that Jesus Christ is returning soon.

#5) Image of the Antichrist

The fifth sign involves the "living" image of the Antichrist. "He performs great signs, so that he even makes fire come down from heaven on the earth in the sight of men.... He was granted power to give breath to the image of the beast, that the image of the beast should both speak and cause as many as would not worship the image of the beast to be killed" (Revelation 13:13–15).

Revelation reveals that during the Tribulation, the Antichrist will order his False Prophet to set up an image of himself in the newly built Jewish Temple and will order the world to worship him as if he were God. This is the same scenario all over again, when the Babylonian King Nebuchadnezzar set up a statue of himself and ordered everybody to worship it. Daniel tells of how Shadrach, Meshach, and Abednego refused and so were thrown into a fiery furnace. This is all going to happen again during the Tribulation, but instead of chucking people into ovens, the False Prophet will rain down fire and incinerate those who refuse to worship the Antichrist.

How will the False Prophet make fire fall down from the sky and consume people? Assuming there's nothing supernatural going on, let's look at the technologies involved in producing pyrotechnics. Maybe John was referring to jets or drones dropping bombs and other incendiary weapons. And, satellite-based weapon systems, such as missile or laser systems, could simply zap people from high up in orbit. Remember that the Antichrist must use technology because he is a counterfeit. His False Prophet will not be a real miracle maker, so will use today's military technology to destroy people with the touch of a button.

What's so peculiar about the story of this image is that John reveals that it was given life. Nebuchadnezzar's statue didn't get up and walk around and sing and dance and all that; it didn't even move. But, the image of the Antichrist will appear to be alive! Assuming there's nothing supernatural involved in making the illusion of a living statue, such as the demonic possession of an object, statues still cannot move. They lack the proper joints and musculature.

What kinds of technology could the False Prophet use, then, to make an image move? John may have been the very first person to watch television. The Antichrist's image may appear at regular intervals on a person's TV set or mobile device, and once broadcast, everyone is expected to fall down and worship his image. Or, the image may involve robotic and artificial intelligence (AI) technologies. How about a fully functional hologram? Japan especially has been hard at work developing both robotics and holographic technologies. Why, for years now, one of Japan's biggest pop stars has been Hatsune Miku who is a fully interactive hologram that sings in live concerts. With the proper Alexa-like technology, the Antichrist's living image, be it robot or hologram, could fully interact with his adoring acolytes.

Today's weapons and robotic technologies point to the fact that Jesus Christ is returning soon.

#6) Population Explosion

The sixth sign of technology that points to the fact that we are living in the end times involves a great population explosion. Revelation reveals, "Then the sixth angel poured out his bowl on the great river Euphrates, and its water was dried up, so that the way of the kings from the east might be prepared" (Revelation 16:12). Prepare the way for what? "Now the number of the army of the horsemen was two hundred million; I heard the number of them" (Revelation 9:16). What happens to this army? "And the winepress was trampled outside the city, and blood came out of the winepress, up to the horses' bridles, for one thousand six hundred furlongs" (Revelation 14:20).

In context, as the Tribulation winds mercifully to a close, the Antichrist's empire begins to crumble due to a number of rebellions led by various sub-rulers. Just as the Antichrist squashes a rebellion in Africa, he must turn his loyal forces north to deal with a rebellion coming from the East. Both armies meet in the Valley of Armageddon located in northern Israel. While these armies are busy slaughtering each other, they will see Jesus and His armies returning out of the heavens and unite against Him. The King of Kings will easily defeat the world's armies just by speaking. The blood from the vanquished armies will flow as high as a horse's head for a staggering 180 miles!

By the end of the Tribulation, most of the world's population will have been wiped out, and still these prophesied kings of the East can amass a two-hundred-million-man army. This prophecy must have blown John's mind, for in his first-century day, there were only two hundred million people living on the whole earth. How, then, does the human population get so large that, despite the massive death toll of the Tribulation, the East can assemble such a staggeringly large army? How do we have the billions we now have today? The answer: medicine. As each successive generation produces more and more people, aided by medicines that greatly reduce infant mortality and keep people healthier and allow us to live longer, we've reached a massive global population numbering nearly eight billion. China and India have been able to mount a two-hundred-million-soldier army ever since the 1960s and could easily do so during the Tribulation. The exponential curve strikes again!

Today's medical technologies point to the fact that Jesus Christ is returning soon.

#7) Nuclear Weapons

The seventh sign of technology involves the inevitable release of the world's nuclear arsenal. Both the Old and New Testaments describe the destruction of much of the world by a series of nuclear cataclysms.

"Then behold, at eventide, trouble! And before the morning, he is no more" (Isaiah 17:1–14; Jeremiah 49:23–27). In context, Isaiah and Jeremiah prophesied the destruction of the oldest city on the planet—Damascus—by Israel suddenly and in just one night. How do you destroy an entire city in just one night? Israel will have to use a nuclear bomb.

"Men's hearts failing them from fear and the expectation of those things which are coming on the earth, for the powers of the heavens will be shaken" (Luke 21:26). In this verse, Jesus prophesied that the horrors unleashed during the Tribulation will actually cause heart attacks.

> Then the sky receded as a scroll when it is rolled up, and every mountain and island was moved out of its place. And the kings of the earth, the great men, the rich men, the commanders, the mighty men, every slave and every free man, hid themselves in the caves and in the rocks of the mountains, and said to the mountains and rocks, "Fall on us and hide us from the face of Him who sits on the throne and from the wrath of the Lamb! For the great day of His wrath has come, and who is able to stand?" (Revelation 6:14–17).

The sixth seal judgment uncannily describes what a nuclear blast looks like and how the people will hide in caves to escape all the destruction and radiation these bombs will rain down upon them.

"The first angel sounded: And hail and fire followed, mingled with blood, and they were thrown to the earth. And a third of the trees were burned up, and all green grass was burned up" (Revelation 8:7). The first trumpet judgment describes yet another cataclysm that sounds very much nuclear in nature.

"By these three plagues a third of mankind was killed—by the fire and the smoke and the brimstone which came out of their mouths" (Revelation 9:18). During the sixth trumpet judgment, demonic creatures will be let loose to incinerate millions with their nuclear fire-like breath.

"And this shall be the plague with which the Lord will strike all the people who fought against Jerusalem: their flesh shall dissolve while they stand on their feet, their eyes shall dissolve in their sockets, and their tongues shall dissolve in their mouths" (Zechariah 14:12). Zechariah describes what will happen to the Antichrist's armies upon the Messiah's return. No nukes may be involved, but the weapon of the Messiah's own words will produce the same effect as the setting off of a nuclear bomb.

Many of God's judgments during the Tribulation sound like a first-century man's attempt to explain a nuclear holocaust. Many believe that the two atomic bombs dropped on Hiroshima and Nagasaki during World War II have been the only atomic weapons released, but no, in the last seventy-plus years, over twenty-five hundred nuclear warheads have been set off in testing. Nine countries have stockpiled an estimated fifteen thousand nuclear weapons, with eighteen hundred always standing at alert and prepped for immediate launch. The fact that the world hasn't already annihilated itself in a nuclear holocaust proves that God's restraining hand is holding mankind's worst destructive proclivities at bay. But, that time will end when God's restraining influence will be taken away, along with the Church, at the Rapture. During the first year or so after the Tribulation begins, half of the world's population will perish. A nuclear holocaust is indeed about to be unleashed upon this world, and one day soon.

The technologies involved in the making of nuclear weapons are among the most complex technologies ever developed. Heavy metal mining and refinement, nuclear containment, nuclear plants, submarines and silos for delivery, missiles for deployment—all these super-duper advanced technologies have been in development for decades. The world sleeps, blissfully unaware of the constant threat of nuclear self-annihilation.

Today's nuclear technologies point to the fact that Jesus Christ is returning soon.

#8) Space Science

The eighth sign of technology involves our cutting-edge space-science technologies, particularly the International Space Station (ISS), that we utilize in our attempt to explore outer space. The source verse reads, "How you are fallen from heaven, O Lucifer, son of the morning! How you are cut down to the ground, you who weakened the nations!" (Isaiah 14:12). Other translations of this Isaiah passage render Lucifer's name as the "Morning Star."

During the Tribulation, Satan—the Morning Star—will possess and be worshiped through the Antichrist. Because the earth will face utter annihilation due to God's twenty-one judgments as described in Revelation, I've often wondered where Satan and the Antichrist would feel safe and able to rule unimpeded, insulated from all the disasters ravaging the planet. As the International Space Station orbits over the earth, it can best be viewed from the ground during the mornings, and looks like a bright star sailing slowly across the heavens. That's led the ISS to be nicknamed the "Morning Star." How would one escape a world that is being annihilated, to sit safely from on high, in order to rule over the world? Most likely from high up in orbit.

The eighth sign of technology I consider a tentative sign, though. I have no biblical proof that the Antichrist will rule from up in orbit. But, with the space station costing somewhere between $150 billion and half a trillion dollars, the ISS must have more of a long-term purpose than just seeing how earthworms float.

Today's space science technologies point to the fact that Jesus Christ is returning soon.

#9) Limitations

The ninth and final sign of technology in this list actually has to do with technology's limitations. Have you ever considered that our technology has limits? It does!

For one, supplies of rare earth metals are running dangerously low. Did you know that the computer, tablet, and smartphone (that are surely an arm's length away from you) are made of rare earth metals? The metals used to make these advanced technologies, those we've become so dependent on, can only be found in certain places, and the supplies are quickly dwindling. Nearly 95 percent of these metals can only be found in hostile countries such as China and Afghanistan. Unless alternatives can be synthesized, our ability to build laptops, cell phones, TVs, you name it, is quickly going to disappear. Once the limited amounts of these rare earth metals run out, so will much of today's technology.

Also, are there limits to how far our technology will take us into outer space? It appears, according to the Bible, not very far. The prophet Zechariah prophesied that *all* the nations of the earth will be gathered against Jerusalem in the last days (Zechariah 12:1–3). Once Jesus returns, He will defeat the armies of the Antichrist gathered against the city of Jerusalem. Once these armies are destroyed, Jesus will then send His angels to collect every single person and gather them together for what's called the "sheep-goat judgment" (Matthew 25:31–46). Since all the remnants of the nations will stand before Jesus Christ and be judged, there can be no people living on space stations, lunar colonies, Martian colonies, extra-earth settlements, or safely tucked away on spaceships traveling beyond our solar system. This gathering of every human being against Jesus at Armageddon, and then again at the sheep-goat judgment, means that humanity will still be confined to the earth. Our optimistic hope of settling outer space will not be happening, at least in this age, according to these limits set in the Bible.

Technology during the Tribulation will have also reached its limit. If four prophesied catastrophic earthquakes shake the world apart, what will happen to all the mountains? They will be leveled. What happens to cell towers during earthquakes? They fall over. What happens when solar flares burn the sky? The radiation destroys the satellites and interferes with communications. What happens when the oceans are filled with blood and dead sea creatures clog the waters? Ships can't bring oil and goods to port, so distribution channels are disrupted. I could go on and on with disaster scenarios, but you know that even in the tamest of rainstorms our power companies struggle to keep the lights on. Now, imagine the whole world ravaged by endless natural, manmade, and divine disasters. That's why I believe that by the end of the Tribulation, most of our technology, mankind's last crutch and our own Tower of Babel, will be rendered useless. The prophets indicated that by the end of the Tribulation, the survivors will be out fighting with bows and arrows and horses again. Certainly there must still be tanks and other technological weapons of war that I'm sure the Antichrist will protect. But still, God appears to eliminate much of the world's technology so that by the end of the Tribulation, desperate people are left with nothing to kill each other with but primitive weaponry.

Knowledge, travel, the Mark of the Beast, evangelism, the image of the Antichrist, a great population explosion, nuclear weapons, space science, and now the limitations of our technology—all point to the fact that Jesus Christ is returning soon.

App-lication

I hope I've made my case that the sign of technology, which is merely one of many categories of end-times signs, points to the fact that Jesus Christ is returning soon. Knowing this wonderful day will inevitably arrive, how then should we apply this truth to our own lives? Is there an app for that?

Recognize the Times

First, when you've at last accepted the fact that the Lord could return at any moment, and by looking through the filter of the Bible at all these wondrous yet fearful events playing out before us, you will begin to recognize the times in which we are living. You'll be comforted knowing that God's got it all under control, He has a great big plan in place, and His children play a vital role in that plan. Life, therefore, isn't meaningless, but purposeful. Christians are called to serve God in these dark times, so serve Him with all our unique talents, gifts, time, money, and experience.

For those of you who haven't yet accepted Jesus Christ as your Savior, but now recognize that we are living in the end times, the realization should act like an alarm clock buzzing you awake to the fact that the world doesn't have much time left. We are all living on borrowed time.

Therefore, embrace the fact that God loved the world so much that He gave His one and only Son, and that whosoever believes in Him should not perish, but have eternal life (John 3:16). Respond to the Holy Spirit's leading, praying from your heart in faith and repentance something like: "Dear, Jesus, please forgive me of my sins and be my Lord and Savior." And, He will do just that. Jesus Christ will free you of the guilt of your sins and transform you into a brand-new person. He will also grant you the blessed hope of knowing that, one day soon, Jesus is coming to take you up to Heaven to live with our Heavenly Father forever. Our Lord, our Savior, the one who loves us so much and who calls us His children, He has an eternal plan for your life. Embrace it! Don't flip another page without having accepted Jesus Christ as your personal Savior.

Utilize to E-vangelize

And, second, knowing that our Savior will be returning soon, consider how you can utilize all of this great to-and-fro technological frenzy that God has given us to e-vangelize the world for Jesus Christ. After all, did you know that as of 2018, 88 percent of the people in the United States access the Internet? China's Internet access has quickly grown from 10 percent to 54 percent of the population in just a decade. Overall, you can now reach out to 55 percent of the entire world through the Internet, and that number is climbing up an exponential curve as well. Even language barriers may be a thing of the past, as translation software continues to improve.

That means over half of the world is now available at your fingertips. So, go, get online! Share the gospel by post, pin, tweet, subtweet, text, blog, chat, message, meme, mention, notify, sponsor, comment, call, hashtag, trend, favorite, handle, feed, curate, emote, engage, like, friend, influence, reach, outreach…

CHAPTER 5

FINAL EMPIRE FORMING

DAYMOND DUCK

THE PURPOSE OF THIS chapter is to comment on four passages of Scripture pertaining to the coming world government: Daniel chapter 2, Daniel chapter 7, Luke 17:22–37 and Revelation 13:1–10. We'll discuss why some believe this coming world government is shaping up.

Introduction

The book of Daniel is often called "apocalyptic" literature. The word "apocalypse" means the unveiling or revealing, so apocalyptic literature unveils or reveals things. The book of Daniel unveils or reveals evil, the source of evil, God's judgment upon evil, and the ultimate victory of God's people over evil.

The book of Revelation is also called "apocalyptic" literature. The word "revelation" comes from the Greek word *apokalupsis*. Like the book of Daniel, Revelation unveils or reveals things. It unveils or reveals the coming world government and how Jesus will deal with it.

The events in the book of Daniel were future to the prophet Daniel, but most (not all) of his prophecies have already been literally fulfilled. They've been so accurately fulfilled that critics have long claimed that Daniel couldn't be the real author of the book.

For example, hundreds of years before it happened, Daniel predicted that the Roman Empire would come into being and that it would break up

(Daniel 2:33, 40). That literally happened, so the critics say someone had to write the book of Daniel after those events were fulfilled. The critics simply refuse to admit that God revealed the events before they happened (Isaiah 46:10). They want people to believe Daniel is a book of history.

It's important to remember that Jesus called Daniel a prophet (Matthew 24:15); that a complete and accurate copy of the book of Daniel was found with the Dead Sea Scrolls; that many scholars believe the Dead Sea Scrolls were hidden about two hundred years before the birth of Jesus; and that the book of Daniel was written in a style and words that were very common in ancient Babylon. All this is evidence that Daniel was written before the Roman Empire broke up.

It's also important to remember that Revelation calls itself a book of prophecy at least five times (Revelation 1:3, 22:7, 10, 18, 19). It reveals future events. Some of those events, such as the ability to track all buying and selling, were unbelievable to people who lived almost two thousand years ago, but they're close to becoming reality today.

Daniel and Revelation are sometimes called the bookends of Bible prophecy. They support each other. They also support all the prophecies in the books between them. There are no contradictions among any of these books.

Other than being prophetic, the fundamental message of the two books is the sovereignty of God and the encouragement and hope that Jesus' return has for Christians and Jews. God loves His people. He intends for Christians and Jews to have a wonderful future. He wants everyone to make the right moral choices, because evil exists and everything is moving toward the end of the age.

There is a God. He is all-powerful and still on the throne. At the proper time, Jesus will intervene in the awful events that will be taking place on earth. He will deal with the evil. He will establish His Kingdom of peace, justice, and righteousness on earth. Wonderful things are on the way.

Daniel was way ahead of his time because he revealed many things about the coming Antichrist that no other Old Testament writer conveyed, and Daniel did it more than 2,500 years before that lawless one will appear on earth. In fact, Daniel revealed so many characteristics of the Antichrist that he is sometimes called "the prophet of the Antichrist."

Here are just a few of the things Daniel revealed:

- The Antichrist will start out small and grow in power (Daniel 8:9).

- He will be a deceiver and cast the truth to the ground (Daniel 8:12).

- He will get his power from Satan (Daniel 8:23).

- He will erect an image of himself at the rebuilt Temple (Daniel 9:27).

- He will show no regard for the desire of women (Daniel 11:37).

- He will divide the land of Israel for gain (Daniel 11:41).

- He will capture many countries (Daniel 11:42–43) (More will be said about this when we get to Daniel chapter 7.)

Daniel revealed the Tribulation period when he said:

> And at that time [the time of the end] shall Michael stand up, the great prince which standeth for the children of thy people: and there shall be a time of trouble, such as never was since there was a nation even to that same time: and at that time thy people [Israel] shall be delivered, every one that shall be found written in the book. (Daniel 12:1)

Jesus said it this way:

> For then shall be great tribulation, such as was not since the beginning of the world to this time, no, nor ever shall be. (Matthew 24:21)

Daniel and Jesus both talked about the time of the end.

Daniel said:

> But thou, O Daniel, shut up the words, and seal the book, even to the time of the end: many shall run to and fro, and knowledge shall be increased. (Daniel 12:1)

Jesus said it this way:

> And this gospel of the Kingdom shall be preached in all
> the world for a witness unto all nations; and then shall the
> end come. (Matthew 24:14)

This is the point: Those who discount the book of Daniel come dangerously close to saying that Jesus was wrong when He called Daniel a prophet
and talked about things that are in the book of Daniel. They are clearly ignoring what the Holy Spirit revealed.

One more thing and we will get into the topic of this chapter. Recall that
there were no chapter-and-verse divisions in the original manuscripts of the
books of Daniel and Revelation. At the end of Daniel 11, God revealed several facts about the Antichrist and the time of the end. At the beginning of
Daniel 12, God told Daniel that the archangel Michael will stand up for the
Jews at the time of the end, and there will be a time of trouble unlike anything that the world has ever experienced. The Jews will survive that time of
trouble and there will be a resurrection of the dead.

At that point, God told Daniel to shut up and seal the book, "even to the
time of the end." He said, "many shall run to and fro, and knowledge shall be
increased." The end of the age will be marked by a vast explosion of travel
and knowledge (planes, computers, etc.). Daniel wanted to know more. But
God told Daniel a second time that "the words are closed up and sealed...
till the time of the end" (Daniel 12:9).

Notice that the prophecies in the book of Daniel were sealed only until
the time of the end. This means those prophecies would be unsealed (understandable) when the time of the end arrives. Many prophecy teachers
believe that time has arrived.

Revelation contains an interesting event about a sealed book in Heav-
en that Jesus unsealed (perhaps the book or the scroll of Daniel). John was
caught up into Heaven, where he stood before the throne of God (Revelation 4:1). Jesus was seated on the throne with a seven-sealed scroll (or book)
in His hand. John wept much because the scroll (or book) was sealed, and
he wanted to know what was in it, but no one was worthy to unseal it (Revelation 5:1–4).

An angel told John not to cry because the Lion of the tribe of Judah who looked like a lamb that was slain was worthy to unseal the scroll (or book). Jesus unsealed it. He revealed details about many of the prophecies Daniel wanted to know more about when God told him to seal up his book.

Jesus not only called Daniel a prophet, but He also expanded on the prophecies of Daniel in the Revelation. It's important to understand this, because this chapter is going to move from fulfilled prophecy in Daniel to unfulfilled prophecy in Daniel and Revelation that appears to be coming on the scene in our generation.

Daniel 2

Prophecy teachers love to use timelines, and the book of Daniel contains two. The first is God's timeline of Gentile events, or more specifically, Gentile world governments, also called the "times of the Gentiles" (Daniel 2:1–49). The second is God's timeline of Jewish events, also called "Daniel's seventy weeks of years" (Daniel 9:24–27).

God's timeline of Gentile events (the times of the Gentiles) is Nebuchadnezzar's dream about a great statue. The timeline starts at the top of the statue's head with Babylon and ends at the tip of the statue's toes with the Second Coming of Jesus. It identifies all of the Gentile world governments that would come into being between Babylon and the Second Coming of Jesus. It reveals that the times of the Gentiles must run their course before the Second Coming of Jesus. It also reveals that the Second Coming of Jesus is premillennial (the Second Coming will take place before the Millennial Kingdom on earth).

God's timeline of Jewish events starts with a command to restore and rebuild Jerusalem and ends with the Second Coming of Jesus. It reveals the exact day Jesus would make His triumphal entry into Jerusalem at His First Coming and that all seventy weeks of Daniel must run their course before the Second Coming of Jesus.

These two timelines disclose dozens of prophecies that history has proven to be 100 percent accurate up to this time. This chapter will focus on the Gentile timeline.

The Times of the Gentiles (Gentile World Governments)

It was the second year of King Nebuchadnezzar's reign when he had a dream that troubled him. He called in some of his advisors and wise men and asked them to tell him what he had dreamed and what his dream meant. They couldn't do it.

After some back and forth, King Nebuchadnezzar issued an order to have all of his wise men killed. The commander of his palace guard went to arrest Daniel, but the young prophet asked for time to come up with the dream and its meaning. His request was granted.

Daniel believed that God could tell him what he needed to know. He went to Shadrach, Meshach, and Abednego and asked them to join him in prayer for God's mercy concerning the matter. They prayed and went to bed.

During the night, God revealed the dream and its prophetic meaning to Daniel. The young prophet responded:

> Blessed be the name of God for ever and ever: for wisdom and might are his: And he changeth the times and the seasons: he removeth kings, and setteth up kings: he giveth wisdom unto the wise, and knowledge to them that know understanding. (Daniel 2:20–21)

Daniel worshipped our awesome God. He is wise. He ends one age and begins another. He removes one leader and raises up another. He reveals hidden things that no one knows. He is the very source of revelation and knowledge.

Daniel told the commander of the king's guard that God had given him the king's dream and its meaning. Daniel was rushed into the presence of the hot-headed king. It was obvious to Daniel that Nebuchadnezzar doubted the ability of God.

Never doubt the ability of God. He told of the virgin birth before it happened. He revealed that Jesus would be born in Bethlehem Ephratah before it happened. He said that Jesus would be crucified before it happened.

Moses asked, "Is any thing too hard for the Lord?" (Genesis 18:14). And Jeremiah declared, "Nothing is too hard for the Lord" (Jeremiah 32:17). Paul said, I am "persuaded that what He has promised, He is also able to perform" (Romans 4:21). God knows the future better than we know the past.

Daniel told the king there is a God in Heaven who "revealeth secrets, and maketh known to the king Nebuchadnezzar what shall be in the latter days" (Daniel 2:27–28). There is a God in Heaven who can reveal the future. He has let us know what shall be in the latter days. He put it into the Bible because He wants every generation, including all of us, to know these things.

Daniel told the king that he dreamed about a great statue that had a head of gold, a chest and arms of silver, a belly and thighs of brass, and legs of iron. The legs broke into pieces and came back together with feet of iron mixed with clay. A Rock struck the statue on its feet; the statue crumbled into dust, and the wind blew it away. Nothing was left. The Rock that struck the statue started to grow.

It grew into a great mountain and filled the whole earth.

After describing his dream to the king, the prophet told Nebuchadnezzar what it meant.

The Head of Gold

First, Daniel explained the statue's head of gold:

> Thou, O king, art a king of kings: for the God of Heaven hath given thee a kingdom, power, and strength, and glory. And wheresoever the children of men dwell, the beasts of the field and the fowls of the heaven hath he given into thine hand, and hath made thee ruler over them all. Thou art this head of gold. (Daniel 2:37–38)

God allowed King Nebuchadnezzar to rule over every human being and living creature on earth. Starting in the days of Daniel, Babylon was the first Gentile world kingdom.

Daniel added that everything the king had was a gift from God. The good things we enjoy (such as our life, our freedoms, our possessions) are gifts from God. James said, "Every good gift and every perfect gift is from above" (James 1:17).

The Chest and Arms of Silver

Second, Daniel moved down to the statue's chest and arms of silver:

> And after thee shall arise another kingdom inferior to
> thee. (Daniel 2:39)

"After thee" means after Babylon's Gentile world kingdom will have run its course. "Shall arise another kingdom" means a second Gentile world kingdom would arise.

Daniel told us how that was fulfilled in chapter 5. Babylon was surrounded by a great army. King Belshazzar wanted to show that he wasn't afraid of that great army; he wasn't even afraid of God.

He threw a party, invited a thousand of his lords, wives, and concubines, and foolishly decided to defy the God of Heaven in front of his guests. He sent for the sacred vessels that his grandfather Nebuchadnezzar had stolen from the Jewish Temple in Jerusalem. He drank wine out of them.

Suddenly, the ghostly fingers of a great hand appeared and wrote on the wall:

> Mene, Mene, Tekel, Upharsin.... Thou art weighed in the
> balances, and art found wanting.... Thy kingdom is divided
> and given to the Medes and Persians. (Daniel 5:25–28)

The God of Heaven had decided that Babylon's days were over. He had judged the head of gold and found it unworthy to lead a Gentile world government. He decided that the Medes and Persians would replace Babylon's Gentile world government.

This is amazing. The prophet Jeremiah predicted that Babylon would fall seventy years after Babylon conquered Judah (Jeremiah 25:12–13). Seventy years passed, Babylon was an armed fortress, and it seemed impossible that Babylon could fall. But Babylon fell in one night—exactly seventy years after Babylon conquered Judah.

The destiny of every nation is in the hands of the God of Heaven. He can bring down any nation He wants to bring down in one night—anytime He wants.

Many people are rightly concerned about America's future. Their concern needs to be translated into confession, repentance, and prayer in the Church—or the God of Heaven may bring America down. He brought Babylon and her leaders down in one night. He can bring America and her leaders down in one night.

The Belly and Thighs of Brass

Third, Daniel moved down to the statue's belly and thighs of brass. He said, "another third kingdom of brass shall bear rule over all the earth" (Daniel 2:39). "Another third kingdom" means this is the third of three Gentile world kingdoms. "Shall bear rule over all the earth" means these are world kingdoms.

Daniel didn't identify this third Gentile world kingdom. But Scripture and history reveal that it was the kingdom of Greece led by Alexander the Great. God gave Alexander the Great a brilliant military mind, but he was an immoral person. God cut him down in the prime of his life, and his kingdom broke up.

The Upper Part of the Statue's Legs

Fourth, Daniel moved down to the upper part of the statue's legs. He said, "The fourth kingdom shall be strong as iron" (Daniel 2:40). Most scholars agree that this fourth kingdom was the Roman Empire. History has adequately recorded that the Romans replaced the Greeks. Rome was the major power on earth when Jesus came the first time.

The Church began during this kingdom. Records show that the early Church was very interested in Bible prophecy. Many of its early leaders were fascinated with the accuracy of Daniel's prophecies. They were amazed that Daniel had accurately predicted the fall of the kingdom of Babylon, the rise and fall of the kingdom of the Medes and Persians, the rise and fall of the kingdom of Greece, and the rise of the Roman Empire. They knew these prophecies had been literally fulfilled and they were living in the time of the fourth Gentile world kingdom. They longed for their Roman oppressor to fall and their persecution to stop.

The Lower Part of the Statue's Legs

Fifth, Daniel moved down to the lower part of the legs of iron. He said they would "break into pieces and bruise" (Daniel 2:40) and predicted that the Roman Empire would break into pieces or nations. Then, those nations would bruise and fight wars.

Many early Church members were persecuted by the Romans: beaten with whips, stabbed with swords, burned at a stake, and fed to lions, etc. They prayed for God to bring down the Roman Empire.

The Roman Empire eventually split into two legs: eastern and western. Following that, the two legs split into pieces or nations. Some nations ultimately fought each other. No human being knows what a day will bring forth. But the God of Heaven foretold exactly what would happen to the Roman Empire, and He did so hundreds of years before the Roman Empire came into existence.

The Feet of the Statue

Sixth, Daniel moved down to the statue's feet of iron mixed with clay. He didn't identify this Gentile world government, but he had already said that there is a God in Heaven who reveals secrets, and he made known to the king what would happen in the latter days (Daniel 2:28).

Daniel looked way off into the future and revealed that a last Gentile world government would exist at the end of the age. Other Scriptures teach that it will exist for seven years and be destroyed at Jesus' Second Coming (Daniel 9:27).

Daniel said, "There shall be in it the strength of the iron" (Daniel 2:41). The strength of this last Gentile world government will come from the nations of iron that were once part of the Old Roman Empire. Today, they're called the European Union.

The clay represents other groups of nations that will partner with the European Union to form one last Gentile world government. This is what globalism and global governance are all about. It's the coming New World Order, or the coming one-world government.

The feet have ten toes, which represent ten kings. Daniel said, "In the days of these kings shall the God of Heaven set up a kingdom, which shall never be destroyed" (Daniel 2:44). The last Gentile world government will have ten subdivisions (ten groups of nations with a leader over each group). It's important to understand that these are groups of nations that form a world government, not nations that make up the European Union. The EU is just one toe (no doubt one of the big ones).

The Rock

Seventh, Daniel explained the Rock that struck the statue on its feet. This Rock is Jesus. King David said, "The Lord is my rock" (Psalm 18:2) and the Rock is "our God" (Psalm 18:31).

Jesus will come back (in His Second Coming, not the Rapture) after the arrival of the ten kings to destroy this last Gentile world kingdom and establish His own kingdom. Concerning the Rock, Daniel said, in the days of this future world kingdom:

> ...shall the God of Heaven set up a kingdom, which
> shall never be destroyed: and the kingdom shall not be left
> to other people, but it shall break in pieces and consume
> all these kingdoms, and it shall stand for ever. (Daniel 2:44)

Globalism and the New World Order

Globalism and the New World Order are not ordinary events, they're signs of an approaching world government that will be destroyed at the end of the age by the Second Coming of Jesus. The Bible describes this approaching world government in chilling terms. It will be a satanic world government dominated by an evil man during the Tribulation period.

This man will be a tyrant from the bottomless pit whom many writers and preachers call the Antichrist. He will lie, blaspheme, and do the bidding of Satan. He'll confirm a Middle East peace treaty that begins the Tribulation period, and will take control of databases and track all buying and selling.

He will persecute and kill many who believe during the Tribulation period.

During his seven-year reign, natural disasters, persecution, plagues and war will kill two-thirds to three-fourths of those on earth.

Evidence That the Final Empire is Forming

The Bible clearly teaches that the Antichrist will come and rule over a world government (Daniel 7:23, 9:24–27; Matthew 24:15; 2 Thessalonians 2:3-4; Revelation 13:7–8). Two things are required for this to happen: There must be a decline in nationalism or patriotism, and there must be a rise in globalism or world government. Both of these are happening right now in our generation, the generation that has witnessed the return of the Jews to the Promised Land (Matthew 24:32–35).

Consider the following as evidence of a decline in nationalism or patriotism: efforts to ignore and abandon the US Constitution; people being evicted from their apartments or communities for flying the US flag; demonstrators burning the American flag; a strong push for open borders; the elimination of voter ID and letting illegal aliens vote; people chanting "death to America;" the growing disdain for America's military; NFL football players refusing to stand during the national anthem; and the destruction of national monuments in the US.

And consider the following as evidence of a rise in globalism or world government: efforts to create a New World Order; agreements to merge nations and surrender national sovereignty; calls to strengthen the United Nations; the formation of groups of nations such as the European Union; calls for a world government by 2030; the rise of multiculturism; the creation of world courts, a World Health Organization, a World Trade Organization, etc.; the effort to create a global ethic; and group meetings such as the World Government Summit.

On September 25, 2018, President Trump addressed the UN General Assembly. Reporters said he "espoused a nationalist doctrine that underscored his administration's tensions with the UN." He told the UN, "We will never surrender American sovereignty to an unelected, unaccountable global bureaucracy," and added, "America is governed by Americans." Then, he continued, "We reject the ideology of globalism, and we embrace the doctrine of patriotism." Shortly after that he added, "America will always choose independence and cooperation over global governance, control, and domination."

The fact that the president of the United States told the UN General Assembly, "We will never surrender American sovereignty to an unelected, unaccountable global bureaucracy" should be adequate proof that there is an effort to establish a world government.

On January 7, 2019, Pope Francis presented his annual "State of the World" message before a group that included diplomats from many nations. According to news reports, the main focus of the pope's message was global warming, global government, global citizenship, and things like that. He believes the solution to most of the world's problems is less national sovereignty and more multilateralism.

On January 21, 2019, media darling and socialist, Alexandria Ocasio-Cortez, said, "The world is gonna end in twelve years if we don't address climate change." To understand this, it's necessary to remember that the UN has a goal to establish a world government by 2030. In essence, three weeks after 2018 ended, Alexandria Ocasio-Cortez was saying, if the world doesn't accept climate change and meet the UN's goal of a world government by 2030, the world will end three weeks later.

That is her opinion, and it has been followed by similar statements from Bernie Sanders and Beto O'Rourke. God says otherwise. But the effort to establish a world government is real and appears to be ready to bear fruit.

Signs That Patriotism Is Declining and Globalism Is Rising

First, on November 6, 2018, President Trump traveled to Chattanooga, Tennessee, to speak at a rally on behalf of Marsha Blackburn's campaign for the United States Senate. A musician named Lee Greenwood attended and sang his famous patriotic song, "God Bless the USA."

About ten thousand people joined in with Mr. Greenwood, and while they were singing, President Trump walked onto the stage. People in the audience who were opposed to him started chanting "Racist country! Racist song!" This evidenced a decline in nationalism or patriotism in the US.

Second, about the same time, it was reported that globalists at the UN don't like Trump's "America First" policies. They're offended that a leader of a great nation would put the welfare of his nation above their globalist agenda.

They are not alone. In many nations, citizens are unhappy with their leaders and demanding change. There have been riots in France, Belgium, and the Netherlands. The reasons are varied, but there is one common complaint: Citizens are fed up with leaders who put the desires of the globalists above the good of the people.

Third, on November 3, 2018, it was reported that the UN Refugee Agency commanded President Trump to let the caravan of immigrants approaching the US-Mexico border into America. A UN agency can't force the president of the United States to comply with its orders, but notice that it tried.

American citizens need to understand that globalists are using immigration to destabilize nations and create a crisis that will allow them to bring in world government. Globalism and open borders (not the cost of a wall) are the real issue that led to the partial US government shutdown in December 2018.

Fourth, on November 11, 2018, President Trump attended the Paris Peace Forum to observe the hundredth anniversary of the end of World War I. French President Macron called nationalism (putting America first) treason. He defended the United Nations and the European Union, saying patriotism means putting world government first.

For whatever it's worth, the patriots in the US fight and die to protect the Americans, not the UN or world government. Mr. Macron was trying to redefine patriotism, demonize President Trump's America First policy, and support the UN and the merger of nations. The decline of nationalism (patriotism) and the rise of globalism (world government) are signs that the last world government is rising.

Fifth, German Chancellor Angela Merkel was also at the Paris Peace Forum. She said, "Close international cooperation on the basis of shared values that are enshrined in the UN charters: This is the only way to overcome the horrors of the past and pave a new future."

She was also attacking Trump's nationalism, or America-First policy, and saying that nations must accept the values of the UN (one of the most corrupt organizations on earth). It is her opinion that the world's problems are so great that a world government is the only thing that can solve them.

Sixth, on November 13, 2018, the UN Human Rights Committee adopted a document called General Comment No. 36 that says nations must legalize abortion in cases of rape, incest, health of the mother, and unviable pregnancy. Several nations condemned this committee for exceeding its authority. Nevertheless, it was trying to force nations to follow UN wannabe world government dictates.

Seventh, on February 5, 2019, in his State of the Union address, President Trump said, "The United States will never become a socialist country." He added, "America was founded on liberty and independence—not government coercion, domination, and control. We are born free, and we will stay free." He was responding to the fact that some in the US, EU, and UN support the establishment of a socialist world government.

Daniel Chapter 7

About fifty years after Nebuchadnezzar's dream about the statue with the head of gold, chest and arms of silver, etc., Daniel dreamed about four great beasts coming up out of the sea (Daniel 7:1–3). His dream bothered him, and when he got the interpretation, he said his thoughts greatly troubled him (Daniel 7:15, 28).

He was told that these four great beasts are "four kings (or kingdoms) which shall arise [appear in Daniel's future] out of the earth" (Daniel 7:16–17). But think about this. As a young teenager in a foreign nation, Daniel wasn't troubled when he stood before the hot-headed king Nebuchadnezzar who had ordered the death of all of his wise men. Daniel wasn't troubled when he was falsely accused and thrown into a den of lions. But he was greatly troubled by what was revealed to him about this fourth great beast (king or kingdom), which will strike terror in the hearts and minds of those who are here when he arrives.

Prophecy teachers disagree on the identity of the first three great beasts. Some say they are Babylon, the Medes and Persians, and the Greeks. Others say they could be England with the US, Russia with three allies, and a coalition of Arab nations.

Because of this disagreement over the identity of the first three great beasts (kings or kingdoms), and because there is wide agreement that the fourth great beast is the Antichrist and his world government, and because the fourth great beast will be the most important and troubling, this chapter will focus on what Daniel's dream revealed about the Antichrist and his kingdom.

Daniel dreamed that this terrible beast (the coming evil king or kingdom) will crush people and will have ten horns (the same as the ten toes on the statue in Nebuchadnezzar's dream). An eleventh, or "little" horn (a seemingly insignificant king) will come up among them, and will quickly become strong. He will overthrow three of the original ten horns (three of the ten kings or kingdoms), and his speech will be proud and arrogant (Daniel 7:7–8).

Daniel's dream continued until the ten kings were removed from their earthly thrones and God occupied His throne in Heaven. Fire was coming from God's throne. A thousand, thousand angels were standing around Him. Books were opened, and the fourth great beast was cast into a burning flame. One who was like the Son of Man (Jesus, the Rock that struck the ten toes on the statue in Nebuchadnezzar's dream) appeared before God, and was given dominion over everyone on earth (Daniel 7:9–13).

Daniel approached one of the angels he saw near God's throne in Heaven, and asked the angel three questions about the meaning of his dream. The angel responded (Daniel 7:16–25). This chapter will focus on Daniel's three questions first, then we'll consider the angel's response.

Question #1: Will You Explain the Fourth Great Beast and the Ten Horns?

Daniel's dream contained some unusual symbols that he didn't understand. Students of Bible prophecy find them difficult to understand, too. But people don't have to guess what they mean, because God provided an angel to explain them.

Daniel asked the angel to tell him more about the fourth great beast. Daniel specifically wanted to know why the fourth great beast will be so different from the other three great beasts, why it will be so vicious and destructive, why he will crush people on earth, and what the meaning is of the ten horns and of the little horn that overthrew three of the ten horns. Further, he wanted to know more about his penetrating eyes, pompous words, and unusually stout appearance (Daniel 7:19–20).

The reader should know that the angel doesn't use the word "Antichrist" here, but it is clear from the book of Revelation and other Scriptures that this fourth great beast is the coming Antichrist and the one-world government that he will rule over for seven years during the Tribulation Period.

Question #2: Will You Explain What I Dreamed about the Saints?

Daniel told the angel that he saw the little horn (the Antichrist) attacking the saints and prevailing against them (Daniel 7:21). In this case, the word "saints" refers to the Tribulation period saints (Gentiles and Jews who become believers during the Tribulation) because the Church will have been removed by the Rapture.

But the Antichrist, as head of the coming world government, will persecute the unbelieving Jews, because Jesus told those in Judea to flee into the wilderness, and John the Revelator revealed that the Antichrist will attack the sun-clothed woman (Israel) at the middle of the Tribulation period (Matthew 24:16–22; Revelation 12:1–6). The Antichrist and his world government will persecute and kill multitudes of Tribulation period saints (believing Gentiles and Jews) and unbelieving Jews.

Question #3: Will You Tell Me How Long God Intends to Let This Go On?

Daniel told the angel he dreamed that the Antichrist and his world government will persecute the saints until the time comes for the Ancient of

Days (God) to intervene on behalf of the saints and allow them to possess the kingdom (Daniel 7:22). Students of Bible prophecy know that God will allow the Antichrist and his world government to rule for one week of years, which is seven years (Daniel 9:24–27).

The Angel's Response

Daniel had asked the angel for the truth (Daniel 7:16), then he heard the angel's response. It is the Word of God and that is truth (John 17:17). We would be wise to pay close attention to the angel's interpretation of Daniel's dream.

First, the fourth great beast will be a kingdom on earth that will take over and damage the whole earth (Daniel 7:23). The ten horns are ten kings (or leaders) who will rise to power in this global kingdom. The little horn (the eleventh king, who will be the Antichrist) will rise after the ten kings appear and subdue three of them

Second, the little horn (the Antichrist) will speak against (slander) the Most High God. He will persecute God's people and reject existing times and laws (probably the Jewish and Christian calendars and Judeo-Christian values that are based upon the Scriptures; see Daniel 7:25a). He will be anti-Christ, which means he will be against everything that has anything to do with Jesus, the Christ.

Third, the Tribulation period saints will be forced to submit to him for three and one-half years the last three and one-half years of the Tribulation period (Daniel 7:25b). That time will be worse than anything that has ever happened on earth, including the Holocaust, and if Jesus doesn't come back at the end of the Tribulation, everyone will perish (Matthew 24:21–22). But don't be concerned about that. He will come back.

Digging Deeper

The angel's response to Daniel's questions revealed that a one-world government will develop in phases or stages.

Phase 1: A kingdom will devour the whole earth. A one-world government will take over the whole earth. This appears be the UN, which is not a one-world government now (some say "UN" stands for "United Nothing"), but globalists are working to turn it into one.

Phase 2: This one-world government (UN) will be divided into ten regions, with one leader over each region. (It will be a G-10 or a Group of 10). It won't be ten regions in a revived kingdom of iron (the EU) on the statue (Gentile timeline) in Nebuchadnezzar's dream; it will be ten regions in the kingdom of iron plus clay (the EU plus others). Each region will appoint a leader or a king, giving the world ten leaders or ten kings.

Phase 3: After the ten regions and ten kings appear, another king, the eleventh, will appear. This king will be different from the first ten—he will be the Antichrist.

Phase 4: The Antichrist will subdue (take away) the power of three of the first ten leaders. After he does that, the other seven kings will surrender their power to him (Revelation 17:13).

Phase 5: The Antichrist will reshape the world (Revelation 17:12–13), rising to power as a highly respected man of peace. But after he gains control of all ten regions, he will transform them into a satanic, one-world government (Revelation 13:4; 17:11).

Phase 6: The Antichrist will speak against God; he'll be a blasphemer (Revelation 13:6).

Phase 7: During the last three and a half years of the Tribulation period, the Antichrist will persecute and kill the period saints (Revelation 13:5–7).

Phase 8: The Antichrist's dominion will be taken from him. The Rock (Jesus) that struck the statue in Nebuchadnezzar's dream on its toes will strike the Antichrist at Jesus' Second Coming.

Phase 9: God will establish the Millennial Kingdom at the Second Coming of Jesus.

Phase 10: God will turn control of His Kingdom over to the saints; the Church and Tribulation saints will reign with Jesus during the Millennium.

Evidence That the Ten Kings Are Rising

It is amazing, but the European globalists seem to have a demonic (satanic) desire to form a ten-nation group. One of the first indications was in 1955 when ten nations formed the Western European Union (WEU) to coordinate matters of European security. That folded in 1955.

A second indication came in the early 1970s when a powerful group of European globalists called the Club of Rome suggested that the world be divided into ten regions called ten mega territories or ten kingdoms, with a three-step plan to bring in world government.

The first step is to use treaties to create a financial new world order with ten regions or ten trading blocs of nations (called regionalization). The second step is to transform the financial new world order into a political new world order with a constitution and a leader over each group or region of nations. The third step is to merge the political new world order into a one-world government.

In connection with this, the United Nations established the European Union as the political pattern (model) for the other nine trading blocs to follow. The purpose was to organize every trading bloc the same way politically in order to make it easier to merge the ten regions into a one-world government.

A third indication came in the fall of 2018, when President Emmanuel Macron of France called for a ten-nation EU army to deter the growing surge of nationalism in some nations. He said, "We have to protect ourselves against China, Russia and even the United States of America." German Chancellor Angela Merkle backed him.

The US and many of the EU nations have been allies for years, and there is no reason to expect that the EU would have to defend itself from the US. But the EU is clearly beginning to see itself as a group of nations (one of the ten toes) that is different from the US (a different toe).

In addition to the EU, a partial list of other groups already organizing includes the North American Union (NAU), the African Union (AU), the Union of South American States (UNASUR or UNASUL), and the Eurasian Economic

Union (EEU). The fact is, there is no nation on earth that is not being pushed into a regional group of nations.

Concerning the NAU, on November 30, 2018, US President Donald Trump, Mexico's outgoing President Enrique Pena Nieto, and Canada's Prime Minister Justin Trudeau signed the USMCA (the new NAFTA or the NAFTA replacement agreement). Shortly after signing the agreement, Peña Nieto tweeted:

> On my last day as President, I am very honored to have participated in the signing of the new Trade Treaty between Mexico, the United States and Canada. This day concludes a long process of dialogue and negotiation that will consolidate the economic integration of North America. The USMCA is not a step back towards American independence and sovereignty it's a step closer toward greater integration.

On April 30, 2019, the *New American* posted an article by Christian Gomez about the NAU that deserves the attention of every US citizen.[33]

Gomez reported that Mexico recently passed a labor reform bill that the US considers essential before it agrees to merge the United States, Mexico, and Canada economically and politically. According to Gomez, the passage and implementation of the US-Mexico-Canada merger agreement (USMCA) isn't a done deal, because some US officials want an enforcement procedure added to Mexico's new labor reform bill. Anyway, it appears that an enforcement procedure is in the works. So, if the USMCA is going to be stopped, that needs to happen soon because some want it to go into effect by January 1, 2020.

Evidence that Persecution Is Growing

On November 12, 2018, it was reported that UN officials are demanding a worldwide crackdown on those who oppose globalism, LGBT (lesbian, gay, bisexual, transgender) rights, open borders, Islam, and more. These officials believe national populism (what is popular with the people of a nation) is a growing threat to world government and world religion. They want to prosecute the opponents of world government and world religion for violating international laws

International laws are an effort to intimidate and silence enough of the opposition to world government and world religion to meet the UN's goal of a world government by 2030. This is no less than a UN demand for the persecution and prosecution of people, especially those who believe in Jesus. It is a major step toward forcing people to declare support for world government by taking the mark of the Beast.

In addition to calling for the opposition to be prosecuted for violating international laws, the Antichrist and False Prophet will call for the death of those who oppose their newly instituted international laws. Trying to force people all over the world to believe what the UN believes is a major step toward a global ethic (one-world religion), and the UN appears to be getting anxious to bring it in.

Without going into a lot of detail, it should be noted that radical professors are fueling hatred against Christians on college and university campuses. Unbelievers are using their freedom of speech to destroy the freedom of speech of believers. Christians are regularly called hate-mongers, homophobes, racists, etc., and have been sued to force them to violate their beliefs (such as a Christian baker being forced to make a cake for a gay wedding, etc.). They have been threatened in public places (such as Ted Cruz and his family in a restaurant), and Christian websites have been blocked and shadow-banned. Christian groups have been singled out by the IRS (remember Lois Lerner), and individuals have been attacked for wearing MAGA caps, etc.

China has instituted a plan to have every citizen of Beijing in a social credit score system by the end of 2020. Chinese Christians are being punished for not supporting China's anti-Christ policies, and non-Christians are being rewarded for supporting them. Church buildings are being burned, and crosses are being removed and destroyed. Some Christians have been beaten and forced to renounce Jesus. Christians and others are being banned from flying, using trains, etc. Dissidents are being sent to concentration camps, and globalists are being rewarded.

Radical Muslims in Africa seem determined to eradicate Christianity. Muslims are organizing protests against Jews in many EU nations. Anti-Semitism in Canada, France, the United Kingdom, etc., is prompting Jews to consider immigrating to Israel. The Boycott, Divestment, and Sanctions (BDS) movement is trying to destroy Israel.

It is obvious that the persecution of Christians has already gotten bad, but one must realize that the Restrainer (Holy Spirit and Church; see 2 Thessalonians 2:7–12) is hindering its progress or it would be much worse. Nevertheless, the Holy Spirit and Church won't always be here. They will be removed in the Rapture. Then, the Tribulation Period will begin and billions will die. The UN is already openly endorsing a reduction in the earth's population (through such means as abortion, euthanasia, gay marriage, etc.), and it will grow much worse in the future.

Luke 17:22–37

Confusion abounds about the Rapture of the Church and the Second Coming of Jesus. These are two different events. Pretribulation prophecy teachers believe the Rapture will take place before the Tribulation period, and that the Second Coming will take place at the end of it.

The Rapture will occur without any signs or warnings (John 14:1–3). It is imminent, meaning Jesus could come for His Church at any time. He will descend from Heaven with the souls and spirits of deceased Christians, and will remain in the air above the earth while the souls and spirits accompanying Him touch down on the earth. He'll shout with the voice of an archangel, a trumpet will sound, and the souls and spirits of the deceased Christians will receive new immortal, incorruptible, resurrected bodies. The bodies of Christians who are alive when the deceased Christians are raised will be changed, and the entire Church will be caught up (raptured) into Heaven with Jesus (1 Thessalonians 4:13–18; 1 Corinthians 15:53).

Unlike the Rapture that has no signs, the Second Coming of Jesus is preceded by many signs (a covenant for seven years of peace in the Middle East, a rebuilt Temple, a resumption of the animal sacrifices in Israel, a world government under the rule of the Antichrist, the mark of the Beast, the Battle of Armageddon, etc.). Unbelievers will be removed from the earth (Matthew 13:41-42, 49–50), and Jesus will establish His Millennial Kingdom (Matthew 25:31–34).

Confusion also abounds about the interpretation of the days of Lot and the days of Noah mentioned in the Gospel of Luke (Luke 17:26–29). The days of Noah are mentioned in the Gospel of Matthew, but Matthew doesn't mention the days of Lot (Matthew 24:37–39). This writer suggests that the correct interpretation of the days of Lot and the days of Noah may well depend on which Gospel is being referenced.

Luke was probably a Gentile. He wrote the Gospel of Luke and the book of Acts in Greek (Luke 1:3; Acts 1:1). His books appear to be written primarily for the Greeks. He traced Jesus' genealogy back to Adam (the beginning of all mankind, a Gentile), and wrote about what Jesus said in response to a question about the kingdom of God (Luke 17:20--1). It seems reasonable that what Luke said about the days of Lot and the kingdom of God, and about the days of Noah, are about the Rapture of the Church.

Matthew was a Jew who wrote the Gospel of Matthew in Hebrew. His book appears to be written primarily for the Jews (Israel). Much of Matthew 24 is about the Tribulation period (signs of Jesus' Second Coming, the Temple, the Jews in Judea, the fig tree, the literal Second Coming of Jesus, etc.). Matthew traced Jesus' genealogy back to Abraham (the beginning of Israel and the Jews). He wrote about what Jesus said in response to a question about the end of the age and the signs of Jesus' coming. There are no signs of the Rapture, but there are signs of Jesus' Second Coming. Hence, it seems reasonable that what Matthew said about the signs of Jesus' Second Coming and the days of Noah are about the Second Coming of Jesus, not the Rapture.

Concerning the Rapture, Jesus' message to the Church is:

> And as it was in the days of Noe, so shall it be also in the days of the Son of man. They did eat, they drank, they married wives, they were given in marriage, until the day that Noe entered into the ark, and the flood came, and destroyed them all. Likewise also as it was in the days of Lot; they did

eat, they drank, they bought, they sold, they planted, they builded; But the same day that Lot went out of Sodom it rained fire and brimstone from heaven, and destroyed them all. Even thus shall it be in the day when the Son of man is revealed. (Luke 17:26–29)

People will be concerned about material things (not spiritual things) right up until the very moment Jesus removes His people from this earth. Even though Noah preached that the Flood was coming for 120 years, there was no repentance or change in people's lifestyle before Noah entered the Ark and the rain started to fall. It was the same way in the days of Lot, and it will be the same right up to the Rapture.

Concerning the signs of the end of the age and His Second Coming, Jesus' message to Israel is:

But as the days of Noe were, so shall also the coming of the Son of man be. For as in the days that were before the flood they were eating and drinking, marrying and giving in marriage, until the day that Noe entered into the ark, And knew not until the flood came, and took them all away; so shall also the coming of the Son of man be. (Matthew 24:36–37)

There is no question that there will be a great difference in the global situation at the time of the Rapture and the global situation at the time of the Second Coming. Two-thirds to three-fourths of the people on earth will have died from persecution, famine, pestilence, earthquakes, war, etc., between the Rapture and the Second Coming, but even though these signs of His Coming are crystal clear, many still won't repent or change their lifestyle—right up until the instant when Jesus splits the eastern sky. People will be suffering and dying all around them, but many will be like they were in the days of Noah, and Israel should know that it will be the same way right up to the Second Coming (and they should not make the same mistake, but repent, seek forgiveness, and turn to Jesus).

This brings up an interesting question: Why are the days of Lot mentioned to the Church in Luke's account, but not to Israel in Matthew's

judgment will fall upon unbelievers at the Rapture and

ming? The answer may be that God's judgment didn't fall

vers at Sodom and Gomorrah in Lot's day until God had

le. In like manner, the Tribulation period will not fall upon

...evers on earth until God has removed His Church.

The situation will be different with Israel and the Tribulation period saints at the Second Coming. At Sodom and Gomorrah, God's people were removed and the lost were left behind. At the Second Coming, the lost will be removed (Matthew 13:36–43; 47–50), and the saved will be left behind to repopulate the earth during the Millennium. The Rapture will be like the days of Lot, when God's people were removed and the lost were left behind to face God's judgment (the Tribulation). The Second Coming will be like the days of Noah, when God's people got on the Ark and survived to repopulate the earth, and the lost perished.

The is the message: God has appointed a time of judgment for the nations (Zephaniah 3:8). But before His judgment falls, Jesus will remove His people (via the Rapture of the Church) like God did in the days of Lot. At the end of the Tribulation period, Jesus will come back, God's people will repopulate the earth, and the lost will perish like they did in the days of Noah.

Concerning evidence that the Rapture is close, there are no signs. But the event will take place before the Tribulation period, and signs of that are converging right now. Also, society is very much like it was in the days of Lot and Noah. Prophetically speaking, there is every reason to believe that God's Tribulation period judgments are close, but the vast majority of society is going about normal activities and showing little to no interest in repentance or changing lifestyles. Even worse, God doesn't want ignorance of the Rapture in the Church (1 Thessalonians 4:13), but ignorance is widespread because most preachers never mention it.

Revelation 13:1–10

Chapter-and-verse divisions weren't in the original manuscripts of Scripture, and Revelation 12 contains verses that relate to Revelation 13:

> And there appeared another wonder in heaven; and
> behold a great red dragon [Satan; Revelation 12:9], having
> seven heads and ten horns [ten kings; Daniel 7:24], and
> seven crowns upon his heads. And his tail drew the third
> part of the stars of heaven, and did cast them to the earth.
> (Revelation 12:1–3)

Notice that Revelation 12 depicts Satan as a dragon or a beast with seven heads and ten horns. It also describes that something will happen to Satan in the future:

> And the great dragon was cast out [of heaven], that old
> serpent, called the Devil, and Satan, which deceiveth the
> whole world: he was cast out into the earth, and his angels
> were cast out with him. (Revelation 12:7–9)

Satan and his fallen angels will be cast out of Heaven and will come down to the earth at the middle of the Tribulation period, and they'll make war with God's people (Revelation 12:14, 17).

In Daniel 2, we read that the last Gentile world government will be divided into ten groups of nations (ten toes, ten kings, or ten horns) that will be destroyed by the Rock (Jesus at His Second Coming; Psalms 18:2, 31; Daniel 2:44). Daniel 7 pictures this last Gentile world government as the fourth great beast—dreadful and terrible and exceedingly strong, with great iron teeth.

The legs of iron on the statue in Nebuchadnezzar's dream represented the Roman Empire, and the feet with ten toes of iron mixed with clay represented a final Gentile world government dominated by a revived Roman Empire (the EU) with ten leaders at the end of the age (Daniel 2:40–44).

All four great beasts, including the fourth in Daniel 7, will come up out of the sea (Daniel 7:3). The beast in Revelation 13 will come up out of the sea (Revelation 13:1). The Bible interprets the sea as vast multitudes of wicked people (Revelation 17:1, 15; Isaiah 57:20).

The fourth great beast in Daniel 7 will speak great words against the Most High (Daniel 7:25). The beast in Revelation 13 will have blasphemous words on his heads (Revelation 13:1); he'll speak great things against God (Revelation 13:5).

The fourth great beast in Daniel 7 will be given power over God's people for three and a half years (Daniel 7:25). The beast in Revelation 13 will be given power to persecute God's people for three and a half years (Revelation 12:14–17).

The fourth great beast in Daniel 7 will have ten horns (Daniel 7:7, 20, 24), as will Satan (Revelation 12:3) and the beast (Revelation 13:1). These are the ten toes or the ten kings (Revelation 17:12–13).

The first three great beasts in Daniel 7 will be like a lion, a bear, and a leopard (Daniel 7:4–6). The beast in Revelation 13 will be like a leopard, a bear, and a lion (same characteristics, but in reverse order). The beasts in Daniel 7 will be different from the one in Revelation 13, but the evil characteristics (wicked heart, ferocious nature, and swiftness) of the first three will be present in the beast of Revelation 13.

These facts seem to indicate that the great beasts in Daniel 7, especially the fourth, great and terrible and strong exceedingly, are pictures of the great beast in Revelation 13.

But there is more. The great red dragon, Satan, will have seven heads and ten horns (Revelation 12:3), and the beast in Revelation 13 will have seven heads and ten horns (Revelation 13:1). Satan and the beast in Revelation 13 are two different beings, but they're alike in many ways.

For example, the beast in Revelation 13 will get his power, throne, and great authority from the dragon (Satan; Revelation 13:2). The death and destruction that the beast in Revelation 13 will bring upon the earth will be the result of Satan's power.

Nebuchadnezzar's dream in Daniel 2 revealed that this beast will rise to power in the EU. Revelation 13 reveals that this beast will be a man (Revelation 13:18), one whom Paul called the "man of sin" and the "son of perdition" (2 Thessalonians 2:3). John called him "antichrist" (1 John 2:18). For this reason, many prophecy teachers refer to this man as the Antichrist (1 John 2:18), and this chapter will now start referring to him as the Antichrist.

The Antichrist

The Antichrist will appear to receive a deadly wound that will leave him without the use of one arm and his right eye (Zechariah 11:17), but he will survive and this will cause multitudes to marvel and follow him (Revelation 13:3). Many will worship Satan and the Antichrist. Many will ask, "Who is like him?" "Who can make war with him" (Revelation 13:4)?

The nature of the Antichrist will dramatically change after he survives this deadly wound. He'll abandon his pretense of being a godly person and will take on the nature of the fourth great beast, speaking great words and vile blasphemies. This will continue for the next forty-two months of his rule (Daniel 7:8, 11, 20, 25; Revelation 13:5).

Understand that the Tribulation period will be seven years long, and the Antichrist will work with the ten kings during the first forty-two months (three and a half years), but he will subjugate them. At the middle of the Tribulation period, the Antichrist and his ten puppet kings will come under the total domination of Satan; that will last for forty-two months.

Persecution and World Government

Power will be granted to the Antichrist to attack and overcome the Tribulation period believers. This agrees with Daniel 7. The Antichrist will wear out the saints of the Most High (Daniel 7:25) and will attack Jews and those who become believers in Jesus after the Rapture.

Revelation 13 adds that the Antichrist will receive power over all kindreds, tongues, and nations (Revelation 13:7). He'll have absolute power—and anyone, anywhere on earth, who opposes him will be quickly persecuted or killed.

World Religion

Every unsaved person on earth will worship the Antichrist (Revelation 13:8). It is difficult to imagine multitudes worshipping a murdering, lying, deceiving Satan-worshipper, but it will happen. Those who are saved after the Rapture and are still alive won't worship the Antichrist; God has known their names since the foundation of the world.

The Lamb that was slain is Jesus, the omniscient (all-knowing) Son of God. He knows the end from the beginning, and wrote the names of the saved in the Book of Life before the world was created.

The False Prophet and Mark of the Beast

Revelation 13 continues with information about the False Prophet and the mark of the Beast. These things are covered in another chapter.

CHAPTER 6

HARLOT SYSTEM ASTRIDE SATANIC STEED

TOM HUGHES

A CENTURY AGO, WILLIAM BUTLER Yeats wrote a poem called "The Second Coming." But he was no Christian. He was a student of the occult, a spiritualist, and an admirer of Benito Mussolini. His poem was not about the return of Christ, but the return of heathenism. Yeats pictured a new era of pagan bloodlust. He wrote, "Things fall apart.... Mere anarchy is loosed upon the world, the blood-dimmed tide is loosed, and everywhere."

Then he gave us an unforgettable picture of paganism rising from slumber to devour Christianity. He described a sphinxlike "beast" as it "slouches towards Bethlehem." He wrote that the beast had been asleep for "twenty centuries," but now, "the darkness drops again."

The poem is not prophecy. But a hundred years later, it seems prophetic. For centuries, Christianity has been the tentpole holding up the canvas of civilization. It blessed not just the West, but the whole world. A Christian definition of right and wrong came to permeate the earth. Religions and governments try to show themselves good by the measure of Christian principles. It gave the earth its best foundation for human rights and dignity.

Today, that influence is dying. The taproot of Christianity is being chopped away by governments, courts, educational institutions, entertainment, and other societal forces. But the most significant damage is not coming from outside of Christendom. Today, the greatest enemy to the Church is the church.

One-World Religions

Bible prophecy makes it clear that religion will play a key role in the seven-year period leading up to the return of Jesus to the earth. That period is sometimes known by Bible students as "Daniel's seventieth week." It's popularly called "the Tribulation."

The Bible foretells the formation of two last-days, global religions that will come in sequence—first one, then the other. The second is probably the best known among Christians. It will be based on the worship of Antichrist.[34] But before that, there will be another global religion, "Mystery Babylon the Great."[35] This religion will be associated with Antichrist, but he will not lead it. Later, he will destroy it in favor of the religion based on himself. [36]

Revelation 17:1 identifies "Mystery Babylon" as a "great harlot who sits on many waters." Verse 15 says the waters signify that she will be a massive international power:

> The waters which you saw, where the harlot sits, are peoples, multitudes, nations, and tongues.

Verses 4 through 6 describe and identify the harlot:

> The woman was arrayed in purple and scarlet, and adorned with gold and precious stones and pearls, having in her hand a golden cup full of abominations and the filthiness of her fornication. And on her forehead a name was written: Mystery, Babylon the Great, the Mother of Harlots and of the Abominations of the Earth. I saw the woman, drunk with the blood of the saints and with the blood of the martyrs of Jesus. And when I saw her, I marveled with great amazement.

The harlot's clothing indicates great wealth and influence. The beautiful cup filled with abominations is a façade of beauty that covers and contains a core of pure evil. In verse 6, John says he marveled at her. In the next verse, an angel rebukes John for doing that. But his amazement tells us something crucial. She is *religion-spectacular*!

The Bible says she will be "drunk"—smashed! Drunkenness refers to an altered state of mind. She entered this altered state by consuming the blood of saints. She's a serial killer and a mass murderer. And with each murder, she loses a little more lucidity.

She will be spectacular and horrible, shining and grotesque—all at the same time.

Harlot Wife

For a variety of reasons, most premillennial Bible scholars believe the harlot will be an amalgam, a mixture or blend, of the world's religions. I agree with this, but I believe her core will be those who call themselves "Christian."

We already see this—most every day, if not every day, coming from the group of people who call themselves progressive Christians. More and more politicians, religious leaders, entertainers, and leaders of culture fall into this group, yet their words, actions, and lifestyles are what the Bible calls sin. If you challenge them on their "Christian" faith, you will be ridiculed, mocked and labeled a "hater."

The Bible calls this woman a harlot. In Scripture, when God accuses a people of harlotry, He's speaking of extreme unfaithfulness. This indicates a strong association between the new religion and formerly Christian organizations. A group of Hindus cannot be called "unfaithful" the same way unless, at some point, their association pledged allegiance to the God of Abraham, Isaac, and Jacob. But churches, denominations, and parachurch organizations usually began in service to God.

We also see the word "harlot" in the first chapter of Isaiah. At that point in history, the religious system of Judah was in full bloom. The people performed a "multitude of sacrifices," including "burnt offerings of rams...the fat of fed cattle...the blood of bulls."[37] They burned incense and held festivals and feasts. They prayed. But God said He did "not delight" in any of those things. They represented a mere façade of godliness, and that sickened Him. He said, "I have had enough of burnt offerings."[38]

Outward signs of religious devotion were everywhere, but to them, Jehovah had become just another god. For that reason, He called their incense "an abomination." He said they had become "a people laden with iniquity, A brood of evildoers."[39]

Then He compared Israel to a prostitute. Isaiah 1:21 says, "How the faithful city has become a harlot! It was full of justice; Righteousness lodged in it, But now murderers."

The harlotry described is worse than a person on the street selling sex. This is a wife selling herself out—*His wife*. Israel's relationship with God was supposed to be one of faithfulness, like a spouse. In this and other passages, He painted a picture of Himself as a husband watching his wife sell herself into prostitution. It vividly illustrated why He felt so much anger and frustration. It may be hard to imagine the Lord God omnipotent feeling frustrated. But love makes even Him vulnerable. For proof, see Jesus on the cross.

In Jeremiah 3:1, God said to Israel, "You have played the harlot with many lovers." The "many lovers" represent the pantheon of gods Israel had begun to worship and call on in prayer. They still claimed the God of Abraham, but they weren't *exclusive* anymore. Now they were *inclusive*. And "sexual inclusiveness" is not a good thing in a wife or husband.

That's how we know that Mystery Babylon will be more than an amalgam of religions. It will be led by churches and other organizations that once revered God and His Word. Those who should have been faithful will prostitute themselves to "the kings of the earth" in order to gain power and prestige in the world system. [40]

New Flowering of Religion

Mystery Babylon will be a harlot, but not just a harlot. Revelation 17:5 calls her "the mother of harlots." Not only that, she will be the "the mother…of abominations of the earth." That means she will embrace a restoration of ancient paganism with its bloodlust.

The harlot religion will feel no shame over this. It will be seen as a virtue. Inclusiveness and nonjudgmentalism will be the cornerstone of its creed. It will embrace (and even consume) Hindus, Buddhists, Muslims, Satanists, Wiccans, cults of all kinds, and every other vestige of religion on the earth… except one.

Its spine, though, will be composed of the chaff of a post-Rapture, left-behind church.

Before this "church" can arise, the restraining influence of the Holy Spirit working through the real Church must be removed. Second Thessalonians 2:7 says:

> For the mystery of lawlessness is already at work; only
> He who now restrains will do so until He is taken out of the
> way.

The "He" in that verse refers to the Holy Spirit. He won't be "removed" from the earth. He's omnipresent—everywhere. But He will be "taken out of the way." When the Church is raptured, He will cease to work through the Church on earth because it will be gone. In that sense, the Rapture will be Pentecost in reverse.

In the early decades of the twenty-first century, bad things are already happening. "The mystery of lawlessness is already at work." But it will get worse. When the Holy Spirit stops restraining it, evil will break loose like a massive, sudden dam break.

You might expect this "blood-dimmed tide" to bring an end to religion and spirituality. But just the opposite will occur. Humans are religious by nature. Blaise Pascal is usually credited with saying that there is "a God-shaped vacuum in the heart of each man." That longing will not be eliminated by the Rapture. In fact, it will be heightened by the terror of living in a world of unrestrained evil.

The Rapture will mark a new flowering of religion and religiosity around the world. People will turn hard to it. But in religion, as in everything else, evil's restraint will be gone. Religion will become the worst version of itself—viewing people as objects to be used, manipulated, and bilked.

Happening Now!

When the world's people look to the "church," they will find "Christians" without Christ. They will find a church that no longer looks to Jesus and says, "There is no other name under heaven given among men by which we must be saved."[41] In fact, they will hardly mention the real Jesus. Instead, they will honor a "good person" who was wrongfully executed and "died before His time."

It will be a church without the resurrected Christ. And the other religions of the world will like what they see. They will find that their religions and Christianity-as-mere-religion have much in common. The new global faith will be an umbrella for all sorts of religious traditions.

Tradition will give each group a facsimile of their old distinctions. Buddhists, for instance, will still call themselves Buddhists. They will quote Buddhist sources and have a Buddhist outlook on the world. They will follow Buddhist rituals. But in the big picture, they will have become one with the Christ-less church. So it will be with all surviving religions.

In the post-Rapture chaos, some people will reexamine the biblical Jesus. We don't know how many will turn to Him. But this new group of Jesus followers will be large enough to give Mystery Babylon a much-needed enemy. And there will be enough of them to make the new religion drunk on the blood of martyrs.

Mystery Babylon's mantra will be tolerance and inclusion. But it will not apply to believers in Jesus. They'll be depicted as the primary source of evil in the world. As such, they'll be relentlessly persecuted and brutally murdered.

Those who join me in believing that the Rapture of the Church will take place before the beginning of Daniel's seventieth week may say, "What does this have to do with me? I'll be gone."

So…does it have anything to do with you? For the Christian who will be raptured or resurrected, does it matter? Or is it nothing more than an intellectual exercise?

It matters immensely!

Mystery Babylon will not come to full fruition until after the Rapture. But, in yet another sign of Christ's soon return, it is forming now!

The groundwork for Mystery Babylon is being laid. The ideas are being sown, the lessons are being taught, and the brainwashing has begun. It's happening now! The harlot is forming. Her seductions are taking hold!

Don't believe it? Ask a church-going young person if homosexual activity is wrong, or if Islam is a valid means of knowing God. Ask if premarital sex is a sin. Ask if sin is a valid concept. But be warned. You may find the answers deeply unsettling.

Fire in the Cathedral

It was holy week of 2019, the day after Palm Sunday. In Paris at around 6 o'clock in the evening local time, a fire started in one of history's most famous buildings—Notre Dame Cathedral. Images of the fire began to appear on television screens around the world. In the United States, cable news quickly turned their coverage to the fire. Soon, the four major broadcasting networks switched to live feeds from Paris.

Notre Dame Cathedral is one of the most beautiful buildings on earth. Its cornerstone was laid in 1163—an architectural marvel of its day. Innovative use of flying buttresses and rib-vaulted ceilings allowed a massive stone-and-wood structure to rise hundreds of feet into the air.

By 2019, France had long since ceased to be a Catholic nation. But when Notre Dame burned, the country rallied around it—at least briefly. Within five days of the fire, more than a billion dollars had been pledged to its rebuilding. As big as that number sounds, it's probably not enough. Stephane Bern, head of heritage renovation programs in France, estimated that the actual restoration could cost over $2 billion.

And with a building from the twelfth century, you can't just call Angie's List to find the kind of artisans needed for an actual restoration. Such artisans don't exist anymore. Soon after the fire, wealthy donors and government experts came to realize that euros alone could not fix the cathedral.

The outcry at Notre Dame's burning was spurred by more than the potential loss of a magnificent medieval cathedral. Many throughout the world see Notre Dame as a symbol—not so much of Christianity, but of civilization. In 1969, Kenneth Clark began his groundbreaking, thirteen-part documentary, *Civilization*, standing in front of Notre Dame, and asking a profound question. "What is civilization? I don't know. I can't define it in abstract terms. Yet. But I think I can recognize it when I see it. And I'm looking at it now." He then turned to look over his shoulder at Notre Dame.

In 2019, as the great spire of the cathedral toppled over into the flames, for millions of people around the world, it seemed like an omen—as if civilization itself were falling into an inferno.

Saint Augustine defined a sacrament as "an outward and visible sign of an inward and invisible grace." In our evangelical churches, we practice the sacraments of baptism and communion. The burning of Notre Dame was a sad perversion of a sacrament. It was "an outward and visible sign" of an inner fire that is destroying the foundations of civilization.

Horror Picture

In my book, *America's Coming Judgment*, I wrote about the rejection of biblical Christianity in the United States. "The God-things now painted as offensive," I said, "were once the roots that nourished and anchored our republic."

I was talking about America, but I could have been describing almost any nation in the Western world. We're cutting ourselves off from the roots that have long nourished civilization, human rights, and the march toward justice and human dignity.

For those of us who discern what's happening, watching nations reject all mention of Christ and the Bible is like watching a horror film. We see the lead character walking down a dark hall to an ominous door. We're saying, "No! Don't do it! Don't open that door!" But they don't hear us. They open the door and unleash the horror on the other side.

The destroyers gaily rip away the source of our society's love of justice, fairness, human rights, and human dignity. Then they congratulate themselves because they think "the arc of the moral universe…bends toward justice" no matter what. [42] They don't realize that social progress springs from the flow of God's Spirit, and the heeding of His Word.

A few days after the fire, the *Wall Street Journal* ran a story with the headline, "Decades of Neglect Threatened Notre Dame, Well Before It Burned."[43]

The fire at Notre Dame only made it official. Neglect of all things Christian has been going on a long time. A 2010 Eurobarometer study showed that only 27 percent of the French people believe there is a God. Sad as that statistic may be, it gives an overly optimistic impression. Mere belief in God doesn't make you a follower of Christ. God has a remnant in France, but the numbers are small.

Churches in France have not only been neglected, they have been under attack—literally. The day before the Notre Dame fire, Raymond Ibrahim wrote a column for the Gatestone Institute on a phenomenon that started in France and is spreading across Europe. "In France," he wrote, "two churches are desecrated every day on average. According to PI-News, a German news site, 1,063 attacks on Christian churches or symbols (crucifixes, icons, statues) were registered in France in 2018. This represents a 17% increase compared to the previous year (2017), when 878 attacks were registered—meaning that such attacks are only going from bad to worse."[44]

Here's the deal. Continued disrespect for the God of the Bible will not just diminish Western civilization. It will destroy Western civilization—and with it, human rights the world over.

The Down Grade

Sadly, the deadliest culprit in the loss of a strong Christian influence in the world doesn't come from secular universities alone, but also from so-called Christian universities and seminaries. The modern iteration of what Spurgeon called "the Down Grade" did not start on X-rated movie screens, but in pulpits.

Churches, including evangelical churches, pattern themselves after corporations—especially in the area of marketing. That's not altogether bad, but it carries a profound danger. Corporations freely alter their product to maximize sales.

Our "product" is the gospel of Jesus. We can be flexible in our product presentation, but we must not change the product. And yet we do. It's happening all over the world. Pastors are altering messages to make the gospel more palatable to a "postmodern" world.

A Barna Study from April of 2019 found that "half of Christian pastors say they frequently or occasionally feel limited in their ability to speak out on moral and social issues because people will take offense."[45]

This includes hot-button topics like abortion, same-sex marriage, and children being identified as transgender. But I think the real number is much higher than half. It's not just the hot-button topics they're afraid to talk about. For instance, I believe pastors self-censor on the topic of the blood of Christ. It has become politically incorrect.

Church leaders see themselves as marketers—not of the gospel, but of their own particular congregations. Like MacDonald's, they want to make going to their church an easy, fun experience. They don't want to upset people. This often means creating what universities call a "safe zone"—a place where no one challenges you or says anything potentially upsetting to you, and everything is positive.

Don't get me wrong. Christians have good reason to be positive and optimistic. In the end, we win! And in the meantime, God is with us. His provision is miraculous and His love without limits. My life would not be possible if God didn't answer prayer. I believe in physical and emotional healing. Christians have more fun and are generally happier than other people. Going to church should be a positive experience. I pastor 412 Church in San Jacinto, California, and we have a good time there.

But God's message to humanity isn't always completely positive. Read the Bible. Read those passages you didn't underline. They can be hard and challenging. In the long run, they're super optimistic, but not always in the short run. And we need to be honest about God's message.

Fear in the Pulpit

Sometimes pastors are afraid to talk about even the most positive things. For instance, when was the last time you heard a pastor mention Heaven? There's a good chance it was at a funeral or was a specific reference to an individual who is clearly not long for this world. Evangelicals used to talk a lot about Heaven. Look at the old hymns.

I see two things that have made Heaven a forbidden topic. First, we've been sold a bill of goods that says Heaven is a dodge—an excuse to do nothing in this world about poverty, war, or pain. They say it's just pie in the sky. But seeing Heaven as the context for life on earth encourages us. It surrounds us with an atmosphere of hope. It may be possible to be "so heavenly minded that we're of no earthly good," but usually it's the other way around. We're often too earthly minded to be of any good here or there.

Colossians 3:2 says, "Set your mind on things above, not on things on the earth."

Second, we don't like to talk about Heaven because we don't want to think about its earthly door: death. It frightens us. But unless you're alive when the Rapture takes place, death is the door through which you will step into Heaven. Our fear of death is exactly why we need to talk and sing about Heaven.

As Christians, we no longer need to be bound by the fear of death. Hebrews 2:14–15 in the New Living Translation says:

> For only as a human being could He die, and only by dying could He break the power of the devil, who had the power of death. Only in this way could He set free all who have lived their lives as slaves to the fear of dying.

We can be free of that fear, but we need to address it—in part, by setting our minds "on things above."

If some find Heaven a daunting topic, imagine how they feel about Hell. There are now evangelical, Bible-believing pastors who go years without ever saying that word. Yet, Jesus spoke a great deal about it. He warned us. We need to send out the same warning, but it is extraordinarily unpopular.

Perhaps worst of all, many churches no longer mention sin. After all, no one is comfortable being told that he or she is a sinner. In our marketing-oriented churches, making people comfortable and happy can easily become the primary thing.

Imagine a doctor taking that approach. Say, for example, that a patient will die of cancer if he doesn't get treatment. But the doctor doesn't want to offend the patient or hurt his self-image by telling him there's a flaw in his body. So, the doctor tells the patient that all is well. The patient goes home happy, with a good feeling about that doctor. But in reality, such a doctor would be guilty of malpractice.

A church that never mentions sin is also guilty of malpractice.

Galatians 3:24 says that "the law was our tutor to bring us to Christ, that we might be justified by faith." What does a tutor do? Teach. The law teaches us that we are sinners. And because we're sinners, we need a Savior. Of all the possible saviors, only Jesus will do. In that way, the law brings us to Christ.

But if sin is constantly excused or never mentioned, then people have no idea why they need Christ. Some say that people don't need to be reminded of their moral failures. But Jesus reminded people all the time. He spoke to a culture of people who thought they were good enough on their own terms. His teaching showed them that they needed Him.

Church of Gaga

In 2019, Guthrie Graves-Fitzsimmons wrote an opinion piece for CNN titled, "Christianity's Future Looks More Like Lady Gaga Than Mike Pence." Graves-Fitzsimmons and Lady Gaga are both angry at Mike Pence. The vice president's wife teaches art to elementary students twice a week at a Christian school in Virginia. According to the *Christian Post*, school "policy bars teachers from engaging in acts of homosexuality or premarital sex. Meanwhile, the school's parent agreement asks parents to 'acknowledge the importance of a family culture based on biblical principles and embrace biblical family values such as a healthy marriage between one man and one woman.'"[46]

This enraged Lady Gaga. She tweeted to Pence, "You are the worst representation of what it means to be a Christian."

It would be easy here to attack Gaga on a personal level, comparing things she has said and done to biblical standards. But let's focus on the real issue: Where does the belief system underlying Christianity come from? Is the Bible the written Word of God, or not? If not, then how do we know anything about Jesus or what it means to be a Christian?

If we can rely on the Bible, we have another problem. Do we bend *to* God's will as expressed in His Word? Or do we bend His Word to express our will? To be intellectually honest, we must go with the first answer. If you tell me you're a Christian, but you don't believe the Bible, my question is, "Why are you a Christian? How can you know anything substantial about Jesus outside of the Bible?"

The Bible consistently condemns homosexual behavior. It's not my job to defend Vice President Pence. But this is not about him. It's about the reliability of the Bible. David French, a senior writer for *National Review,* said, "Simply put, this is Christianity 101, and if the *New York Times*, the *Washington Post*, and *CNN* find it problematic enough to report that Christians are Christians, then it's rather clear that institutional support for gay marriage under civil law is now veering into institutional hostility against Christian orthodoxy and against the basic free exercise of the Christian faith."[47]

This isn't just the national media being hostile to biblical Christianity. Lady Gaga and Guthrie Graves-Fitzsimmons both claim to represent "real" Christianity. Gaga has millions of fans who claim the name of Christ.

I can imagine someone reading this and thinking that I have elevated Lady Gaga to the level of an "end-time event." But that's exactly what she is. In fact, all of us alive today are elements of the end times. The question is where we stand regarding the Jesus revealed in the Bible.

Blasting the Pillars

Most people on the planet would point to Pope Francis as the world's most famous and visible Christian. Yet, ever since he ascended to the papacy, he has said things that directly contradict both the Bible and traditional Catholic doctrine. Among atheists, agnostics, liberal Protestants, and members of other religious groups, he's the most popular pope in memory. But he's left more traditional Catholics (as well as conservative Protestants) scratching their heads.

Instead of going through a litany of troubling things Pope Francis has said, let's zero in on just one. On several occasions, the Pope seemed to teach that faith is not necessary to salvation or entrance into Heaven. At the very least, Pope Francis has a positive opinion of an atheist's chances for getting into Heaven.

Remember that when the pope said these things, he was not speaking *ex cathedra*, meaning with the full weight of his office. When a pope speaks in that manner, "it means exemption from the possibility of error."[48] But Francis has never invoked papal infallibility. In fact, since that doctrine was made official by a Vatican Council in 1870, only once has a pope invoked *ex cathedra* papal infallibility.[49]

I am also cognizant of the fact that anyone might have a slip of the tongue, or even write something that just didn't come out right. The problem here is that Pope Francis has said it several times. He spoke it in a homily, meaning it was part of a prepared message. Then he wrote it to a newspaper. Later, he said it again in a moment that left reporters in awe of his kindness and open-mindedness.

In a homily presented on May 22, 2013, Pope Francis said:

> The Lord has redeemed all of us, all of us, with the Blood of Christ: all of us, not just Catholics. Everyone! "Father, the atheists?" Even the atheists. Everyone! And this Blood makes us children of God of the first class! We are created children in the likeness of God and the Blood of Christ has redeemed us all! And we all have a duty to do good. And this commandment for everyone to do good, I think, is a beautiful path towards peace.

I have read many Catholic apologists who have tried to explain this away. Many of them are quite technical, whereas the pontiff's words seem simple and clear. I think any fair-minded reader of these words will come away with the idea that this pope believes the "blood of Christ" has redeemed atheists, whether they like it or not.

This seems to be a direct contradiction to the words of Jesus in John 3:17–18:

> For God did not send His Son into the world to condemn the world, but that the world through Him might be saved. He who believes in Him is not condemned; but he who does not believe is condemned already, because he has not believed in the name of the only begotten Son of God.

Later in 2013, Pope Francis wrote an open letter to Eugenio Scalfari, the founder of *La Repubblica* newspaper, and a well-known atheist. Scalfari had written an article in which he laid out some questions for Francis.

Francis decided to answer. His answer included this statement:

> You ask me if the God of the Christians forgives those who don't believe and who don't seek the faith. I start by saying—and this is the fundamental thing—that God's mercy has no limits if you go to him with a sincere and contrite heart. The issue for those who do not believe in God is to obey their conscience.

Once again, it sounds like he's saying that we are saved by following the good works imposed on us by conscience. But according to 1 Timothy 4:2, conscience is fallible. It can be "seared with a hot iron." First Corinthians 8:7 speaks of a "weak conscience" causing confusion over right and wrong.

And the idea that salvation comes as a result of good works, even those assigned by our consciences, is antibiblical. Ephesians 2:8–9:

> For by grace you have been saved through faith, and that not of yourselves; it is the gift of God, not of works, lest anyone should boast.

To say "God's mercy has no limits" sounds beautiful, but God never said it. Second Thessalonians 1:8–9 says that "those who do not obey the gospel of our Lord Jesus Christ…shall be punished with everlasting destruction."

To many, "follow your conscience" means "do what feels right." In fact, that's the message of this world. Every other television show gives the advice, "Follow your heart." The heart is the seat of emotions. Follow your heart means follow your feelings.

In 2018, the pope visited some school children at a parish near Rome. It was an event with the press and was carried on television. A young girl asked the pope a difficult question from the Catholic point of view. He began his answer by asking, "What does your heart say?"

Perhaps it would be better to ask what the Bible says. Here's what it says about the heart. "The heart is deceitful above all things, And desperately wicked; Who can know it?"[50]

I'm sure this answer made most of those present feel warm and cozy. But he was teaching the girl and everyone watching by television to rely on their hearts—on their feelings—for answers to the great theological questions. Feel-good answers are not enough. Twice, the book of Proverbs tells us, "There is a way that seems right to a man, But its end is the way of death."[51]

Atheists in Heaven

Later in that same question-and-answer session, Pope Francis found himself in a heartbreaking situation. A young and grieving boy stepped forward to ask a question.

According to *Huffington Post*:

> The child, whom Francis referred to as Emanuele, met the pope during a papal visit to the St. Paul of the Cross parish on the outskirts of Rome. During a question-and-answer session with children of the parish, Emanuele approached the microphone to ask Francis a question. But the child froze before he could get his words out. He can be seen sobbing into his hands in video recordings of the encounter. Francis encouraged the boy to come forward and whisper the question into his ear.[52]

The boy approached, and the pontiff gave him a hug. The pair conversed quietly for a moment and Emanuele went back to his seat. Francis then said that Emanuele had given him permission to share their conversation. He said the boy's father recently died. The man had wanted his children to be baptized but was himself an atheist.

The boy asked, "Is Dad in Heaven?"

The Pope gave reasons why he believed the father had been a good man, then said:

> God is the one who decides who goes to heaven. But how does God's heart react to a Dad like that? How? What do you think? A father's heart. God has a father's heart. And with a dad who was not a believer, but who baptized his children and gave them that courage, what do you think? Do you think that God would be able to leave a man like that far from Him? Do you think that?

A small reaction can be heard from the crowd in the background, and the pope said, "Louder, with courage!"

This time they could be heard clearly, mostly the voices of children crying out, "No!"

The pope asked, "Does God abandon His children?"

The parish children again cried out, "No!"

He asked, "Does God abandon His children when they are good?"

"No!" the children shouted.

"There, Emanuele, that is the answer," the pope told the boy.

> God surely was proud of your father, because it is easier as a believer to baptize your children than to baptize them when you are not a believer. Surely this pleased God very much. Talk to your dad. Pray for your dad. That is the answer.

It was surely a tough situation, but one that all pastors face in one form or another. Most of them, I hope, can answer the question without lying to the child. In fact, let's take that off the table. If the pontiff had been willfully lying to the child, he would have left their conversation private. He wouldn't have involved all the other children and asked for their participation. No. This is what he believes.

And according to his words that day, if you make sure your children are baptized, you go to Heaven. You don't have to believe in Jesus. In fact, Jesus seems to play no role in salvation at all.

As I studied this story on the Internet, I was struck by the number of positive comments by professing Christians. Many of them thought it was wonderful and amazing. It felt great to them, as it did to the children in the pope's audience that day. But it isn't the truth.

Hebrews 11:6 makes it crystal clear:

> Without faith it is impossible to please Him, for he who comes to God must believe that He is.

The Mirror Church

Churches desperately copy the mindset of the world in order, they rationalize, to win the world. Attempting to "make church relevant," they neuter the Christian message. They remove the very things that make the Church relevant. In other words, to better relate to the world, they have become the world. Instead of showing the world the light of the gospel, they have chosen to become a mirror, reflecting the world back on itself.

Such churches pine for the world's kind of success—fame, numbers, and money. All of that is fine if its purpose is subservient to God. Billy Graham gained worldwide fame and he used it for the gospel. But he didn't get fame by seeking it. He sought ways and means to spread the message of Jesus.

When fame, money, or popularity become the focus, it's almost impossible not change the message.

The Cause

Evangelicals should work for the downtrodden, for the unfairly accused, and even for the rightly accused. But when we focus on being social justice warriors, we begin to see human government as the hand of God. And then we start to see it as God Himself.

In his novel, *The Screwtape Letters*, C. S. Lewis writes from the perspective of a demon mentoring a subordinate. He tells the young tempter how best to make a new Christian's life ineffective. Written during World War II, it takes on the question of whether the demon should push the Christian toward patriotism or pacifism. "Whichever he adopts," Screwtape says, "your main task will be the same. Let him begin by treating the Patriotism or the Pacifism as a part of his religion. Then let him, under the influence of partisan spirit, come to regard it as the most important part. Then quietly and gradually nurse him on to the stage at which the religion becomes merely part of the *cause*, in which Christianity is valued chiefly because of the excellent arguments it can produce in favor of the British war-effort or of Pacifism."

Satan's goal is to make Christ subordinate in our lives—subordinate to anything, even a good cause.

Church should be engaging and encouraging, but never at the expense of truth. The message of Jesus can make you feel great, but it also challenges you in innumerable ways. And, yes, we want people to be comfortable (and I'm not just talking about padded pews and air conditioning). We want a safe environment where people are free to ask questions. We should not be antagonistic or judgmental.

But churches can't be marketed like Disneyland. Those who would diminish the gospel to reach the world should look at how that has gone in the past. Lots of denominations have done it. Some of them are dead, and others are dying.

Wretched, Miserable, Poor, Blind, and Naked

The death of churches often begins when its leaders deny the inerrancy of Scripture. In 2002, John Killinger wrote that once you deny the inerrancy of Scripture, it is "a simple step to denying that Jesus is the only way to God, or that he really had to die for our sins."[53]

Killinger wasn't giving a warning. He was encouraging people to take that step. He wrote, "Any God whose parameters are defined by the Bible alone is too small for the yearnings and understandings of the twenty-first century heart."[54]

Those quotes come from a book called *Ten Things I Learned Wrong from a Conservative Church*. Albert Mohler, president of the Southern Baptist

Theological Seminary, writing about Killinger's book, said, "The lessons Killinger unlearned are   placed in their proper biblical frame—the very lessons the church must relearn in this generation."[55]

Soon, the end justifies the means. Like the church at Laodicea, we cease to be either cold or hot.[56] Our churches become so lukewarm that they are worthy of being vomited out of the mouth of God.[57] Jesus gave Laodicea a harsh rebuke. In Revelation 3:17, He said, "You say, 'I am rich, have become wealthy, and have need of nothing'—and do not know that you are wretched, miserable, poor, blind, and naked."

That describes far too much of the twenty-first century church.

But Jesus didn't just rebuke them. He also gave them the answer. In Revelation 3:18–20, He said:

> I counsel you to buy from Me gold refined in the fire, that you may be rich; and white garments, that you may be clothed, that the shame of your nakedness may not be revealed; and anoint your eyes with eye salve, that you may see. As many as I love, I rebuke and chasten. Therefore be zealous and repent. Behold, I stand at the door and knock. If anyone hears My voice and opens the door, I will come in to him and dine with him, and he with Me.

We have more access to the Word of God than generations before us could even imagine. We can carry dozens of Bible versions on the phone in our pockets. We can access this most precious treasure whenever we choose. But we don't so choose—not very often. We have real wealth, but we leave it in our pockets.

Shadow of Things to Come

Church history hasn't always been glorious. At many times and in many places, it wasn't even Christian. But in the last few centuries, there has been an unprecedented renewal of the New Testament Church. And when you think about it, it makes sense. The great falling away naturally would be preceded by a great in-gathering. This preaching of a purer gospel and the ingathering of souls that accompanied it led to a worldwide surge in human rights and the realization of human dignity.

There are signs that a great awakening to Christ will soon sweep across our world. We may be seeing the first stirrings of it. I hope so. But I also believe that the harlot church of Revelation 17 is lurking near. Earlier I wrote, "The groundwork for Mystery Babylon is being laid. The ideas are being sown, the lessons taught, and the brainwashing has begun. It's happening now! The harlot is forming. Her seductions are taking hold!"

Let's look at Mystery Babylon again and compare it to the present.

Mystery Babylon's mantra will be tolerance and inclusion. But it will not apply to believers in Jesus.

Already happening. The tolerance-and-inclusiveness-at-all-costs people are already at work bringing every wicked thing into the Church, while excluding the actual gospel and those who preach it.

Mystery Babylon will be led by churches and other organizations that once revered God and His Word. Those who should have been faithful will prostitute themselves to "the kings of the earth" in order to gain power and prestige in the world system.

Already happening.

Mystery Babylon "will embrace a restoration of ancient paganism with its bloodlust."

That's happening, too.

Inclusiveness and nonjudgmentalism will be the cornerstone of its creed. It will embrace (and even consume) Hindus, Buddhists, Muslims, Satanists, Wiccans, cults of all kinds, and every other vestige of religion on the earth…except one.

Already happening. The harlot church is forming, and already beginning to stalk its prey.

CHAPTER 7

GOSPEL DISCERNMENT IN THIS EVIL DAY

PHILLIP GOODMAN

JESUS GAVE US REVELATION as the capstone book of prophecy and the Bible. He framed Revelation with the free gospel of grace (1:5; 22:17). He called it the "everlasting gospel" (14:6) and designated it as perhaps the greatest sign of the end time (Matthew 24:14; Mark 13:10).

> And this gospel[58] of the kingdom shall be preached in the whole world for a witness to all the nations, and then the end shall come. (Matthew 24:14)[59]

> And the gospel must first be preached to all the nations. (Mark 13:10)

To preach the whole "gospel of the kingdom" (Matthew 24:14) is to preach the gospel of salvation (Mark 13:10), for you cannot "enter into the kingdom of God" apart from the gospel of salvation (John 3:3–5). Therefore, since the gospel must "be preached in the whole world" **before** "the end shall come," both Matthew 24:14 and Mark 13:10 establish the gospel as a premier sign of end-time prophecy. And since it must be the correct gospel of salvation to be the correct gospel of the kingdom, to preach any other gospel does not fulfill that sign.

Furthermore, the gospel is the ultimate personal prophecy, since it foretells a destiny of Heaven or Hell for every person based on his or her acceptance or rejection of the free gift of salvation in Jesus Christ.[60]

Discernment of the correct gospel is literally a matter of life or death. This makes the gospel the priority sign of Bible prophecy. For example:

1. I may know all about the prophecies of end-time Israel, but if my faith is not in the correct gospel, then I will enter the end-time Tribulation.[61]

2. I may know all about the Rapture prophecies, but if my faith is not in the correct gospel, then I will be left behind at the Rapture.

3. I may know all about the resurrection prophecies, but if my faith is not in the correct gospel, then I will be in the resurrection of judgment.

4. I may know all about the prophecies of the coming kingdom of Christ, but if my faith is not in the correct gospel, then I will be excluded from that kingdom.

Serious indeed! Why? Because there is more than one gospel in Christianity. But there is only one true gospel. The distinguishing mark of the true gospel is that its saving work was "finished" at the cross by Jesus Christ. The distinguishing mark of a "contrary" gospel (Galatians 1:6–9) is that it is "unfinished," requiring the additional work of man.

The true gospel has accurately been described as salvation by grace alone, through faith alone, in Christ alone. The "contrary" gospel seems to agree with the three "alone" statements—until it adds "works"—at which point the "alone" concept is destroyed in all three of its applications ("grace alone," "faith alone," "Christ alone"). The very moment that "works" are introduced, the finished gospel of Christ is replaced by the unfinished gospel— that is, the "different, distorted, contrary" gospel Paul strongly condemned in Galatians 1:6–9.

Discernment of the difference between the finished gospel and the unfinished gospel should be a supreme issue in Bible prophecy.

Unfinished Gospel Being Spread Today

There is an unfinished gospel being spread today. It mixes faith with works.[62] That makes it biblically wrong. In brief, it lays out a path to salvation whereby a man must justify his faith by works so that his faith can justify him.

This is a semantic confusion of faith mixed with works—or, faith plus works.[63] Its likeness to Roman Catholicism is unsettling.[64]

I attribute no motivation to those who push the unfinished gospel, because many could themselves be victims of the semantic fog that presents it in a shroud of righteousness.[65] I consider them Christian brothers and sisters. Yet the unfinished gospel can be an unwitting snare for all of us, as it has been to believers for two thousand years. The book of Galatians is a witness against its mingling of faith and works to gain salvation.[66] That book rolls out the case that the truth of the gospel is a most serious matter.

I pray that the following will help lift the cloud of uncertainty that sidetracks so many of us into pondering the muddled perplexity of the unfinished gospel. I hope we can refocus on the simplicity, clarity, and freeness of the finished gospel, for, according to Jesus, "It is finished."

Where Are We Going in This Study?

We will briefly examine the finished gospel, the two finish lines, my part, the unfinished gospel, the contract gospel, and, finally, the unbiblical nature of the unfinished gospel by shining the light of Scripture on the question, "Could Lot, Samson, or Solomon have been saved by the unfinished gospel?"

What Is the Finished Gospel?

At the end of His sacrifice for sin, Jesus said, "It is finished!"[67] That is the basis for the biblical gospel of free grace.

The repetitive message of the Bible is that salvation is a **free** and **finished** gift to be received by those who simply believe (have faith) in the resurrected Jesus Christ as the Son of God who died for their sins and rose from the dead to give them eternal life.[68]

The payment for sin is finished. I can **have no part** in its accomplishment; it was finished at the cross.[69] But I do have **my part** in receiving it. **My part**—my only part—is to believe in Jesus and His finished gospel of free grace.

This free gift is available.[70] I have **no part** in qualifying for it.[71] As a helpless sinner, I'm already qualified.[72] My part is to simply believe and thereby receive the free gift of salvation.[73]

The gospel of free grace was finished by Jesus at the cross.[74]

What Are the Two Finish Lines in Life?

There are two finish lines in life. The first distinguishes the finished gospel and its free grace salvation from the works orientation of the unfinished gospel, drawing a line that separates grace from works.

1. Christ's finish line

Christ's finish line was accomplished once and for all when Jesus Christ sacrificed Himself to pay for our sins on the Cross.[75] His finish line distinguishes the finished gospel from the unfinished gospel.

> Therefore, when Jesus had received the sour wine, He said, "It is finished!" And He bowed His head and gave up His spirit. (John 19:30)

God offers Christ's payment for our sins as a free gift of grace. Jesus "ran the first race" to secure the free gift of salvation ("the prize") for us. We don't enter that race. We accept by faith His victory for us as our own at the first finish line.

2. Our finish line

The second finish line becomes our finish line in life's race once we accept the gift won for us at Christ's finish line. If we reject the gift of Jesus' victory at the first finish line, then that becomes the only finish line that matters, and we will not see the second finish line.

Why?

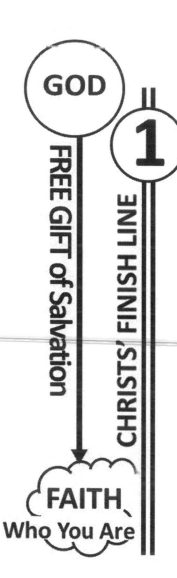

Because the first finish line, already secured for us by Jesus, when personally received by faith, becomes **our** starting line toward the second finish line. Therefore, to reject Christ's finish line is to reject my starting line. And to reject my starting line is to refuse to enter the race.

But if we receive by faith the free gift of the first finish line (salvation), then God will enable us to "run the race" of discipleship (sanctification) toward the "prize" of the second finish line.

But I do not consider my life of any account as dear to myself, so that I may **finish** my course and the ministry which I received from the Lord Jesus, to testify solemnly of the gospel of the grace of God. (Acts 20:24, emphasis added; see Hebrews 12:1)

I have fought the good fight, I have **finished** the course, I have kept the faith. (2 Timothy 4:7, emphasis added)

(Chart-above) God gives you the free gift (grace alone) of salvation, which you receive by faith alone. There can be no human works involved. At the moment of receiving this salvation by faith, one becomes saved. Christ finished the work of salvation at the cross for all who believe (faith). There is no more to be done. Christ died for our sins. He proved His finished payment for our sin by His resurrection. The gospel of salvation was completed at Christ's finish line—the cross.

The first finish line is exclusively for Jesus Christ, for He is the only Way (John 14:6), the only Name (Acts 4:12) to reach that finish line in victory!

But **your finish line** is yours to run toward, in the power of the Holy Spirit, which was secured for you at **Christ's finish line.**

The Finished Gospel

1. *Christ's finish line* decides your destiny of eternal life if you receive His free gift with simple, childlike faith.

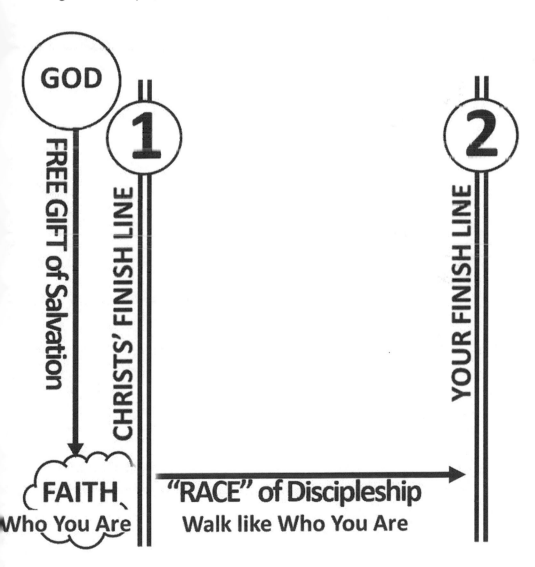

2. *Your finish line* defines the depth of your walk as Christ's disciple over the course of a lifetime.

3. God reaches down with His free gift to helpless sinners who offer nothing but empty hands of faith.

4. God guarantees your salvation changing you into "Who You Are" (in Christ), instantly[76] and irreversibly,[77] based solely on what Jesus accomplished at Christs' finish line.

5. God enables your simple, childlike faith and says, "Now, walk like who you are" to your finish line.

6. Simple, childlike faith will grow to mature faith "working through love" if you "walk like who you are" in life's race to your finish line.

My Part: When and How?

What is my part in the gospel? Do I have any part?

THE KEY: Who you are; now, walk like it!

My part in my salvation is not to pre-pump, pump-up, or post-pump my faith with promises, commitments, pledges, actions, attitudes, holy thoughts, holy goals, good works, deeds and standards, etc. These are meritorious works. Works are the substance of the Ten Commandments, the Law. The Law is holy, and always requires **my part** to **walk** in perfect holy living. As such, the Law cannot save us. It condemns us because it proves that I cannot **do my part**.

That is why Jesus gave us the finished gospel of grace.[78] The gospel of grace is always and totally from the top down.[79] From God to me. That's how Lot, Samson, and Solomon were saved (see below). Totally from the top down.

The unfinished gospel, however, needs some degree of **my part** from the bottom up. But how can I possibly help in my own salvation? I am helpless (Romans 5:6). My only part in my salvation is faith alone, as made clear in Ephesians 2:8–9:

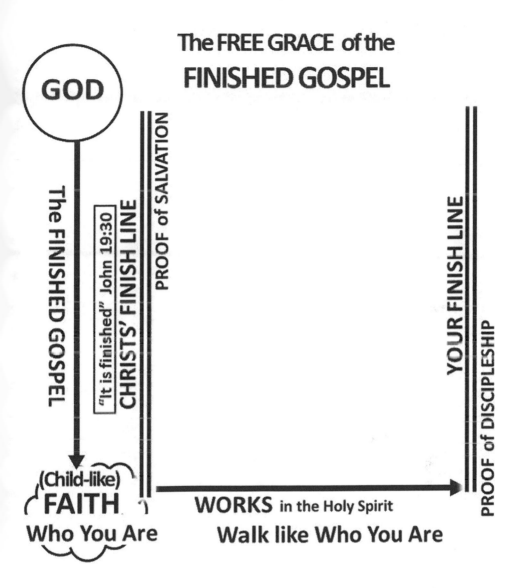

The FREE GRACE of the FINISHED GOSPEL

GOD

The FINISHED GOSPEL

"It is finished" John 19:30 CHRISTS' FINISH LINE

PROOF of SALVATION

YOUR FINISH LINE

PROOF of DISCIPLESHIP

(Child-like) FAITH
Who You Are

WORKS in the Holy Spirit
Walk like Who You Are

For by grace you have been saved through faith; and that not of yourselves, it is the gift of God; not as a result of works, that no one should boast.

But make no mistake: There is a place for **my part** somewhere, sometime. It follows *after* the free gift. It follows *after* belief in Jesus and His finished gospel. And therefore, it follows *after* I am no longer helpless. Here's how that works in the Bible:

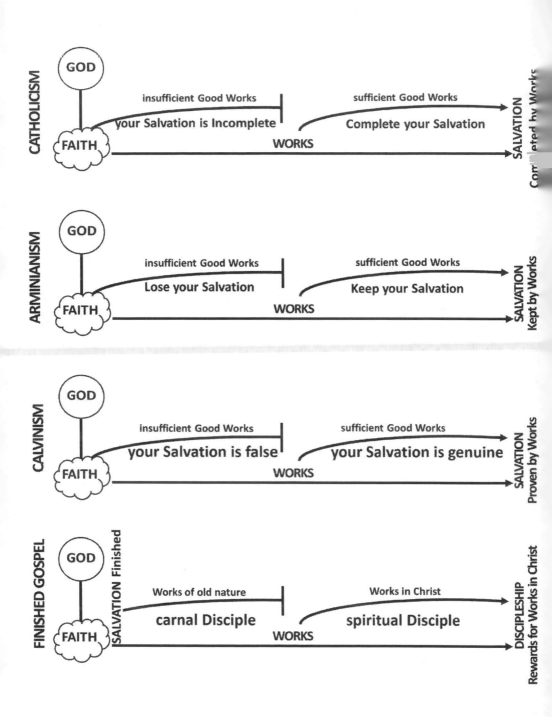

(Chart-opposite) The letter of Paul to the Galatians church served as a warning of the error of mixing faith and works in the gospel of salvation—"Having begun by the Spirit [faith], are you now being perfected by the flesh [works]?" (Galatians 3:3). Note the similarity of this "gospel error" of the Galatians with Catholicism, Armin-ianism, and Calvinism (the three main branches of today's church; each of them an unfinished gospel). All begin with "faith," but salvation must be completed by works. However, the biblical gospel is "finished" by grace alone at the time of faith (justification). Works of the Holy Spirit in the saved person should follow (sanctifi-cation) through the rest of life. But salvation in this finished gospel occurs by faith alone, "not of works, lest any man should boast" (Ephesians 2:8–9).

1. Through my faith in Jesus, the free gift gives me instantaneous salvation that cannot be lost.[80] It makes me a new person in Christ. It assures me: "This is **who you are**—from now on and forever."

2. Then **my part** is made possible. God enables me, and says, "Now, walk like *who you are*." Walk as a "new creation in Christ."[81] Walk as a disciple of Jesus.

We see this truth clearly and succinctly in Ephesians 5:8:

> For you were formerly darkness [previously, this is *who you were*: a lost sinner separated from God], but now you are light in the Lord [now, this is *who you are*: a saved, justified new creation in Christ]; walk as children of light [now, *walk like who you are*: a sanctified disciple of Christ]." (Ephesians 5:8, brackets added)

This is a central message seen throughout the New Testament in almost every epistle. Understanding and spotting this repetitive message will eradicate a ton of confusion!

This biblical distinction between justification (who you are in Christ) and sanctification (walking like who you are) has been seen by some of the greatest Bible teachers, including Lewis Sperry Chafer, Everett Harrison, John Walvoord, Charles Ryrie, Dwight Pentecost, Mal Couch, Thomas Ice, Arnold Fruchtenbaum, Mike Stallard, Andy Woods, Paul Benware, David Anderson, J. B. Hixson, Charles Bing, Joseph Dillow, Dave Hunt, Robert Lightner, Norman Geisler, and many, many more. All don't agree on every particular issue, but all do agree on the paramount issue: The Bible makes a distinction between justification and sanctification, and this distinction is the biblical key to keeping works out of the faith that saves.

That's WHO YOU WERE, but this is WHO YOU ARE! Now...WALK LIKE IT!

Bible passage	WHO YOU WERE	WHO YOU ARE	WALK LIKE Who You Are
Galatians 5:24-25		those who belong to Christ Jesus... live by the Spirit; 24-25	walk by the Spirit; 25
Ephesians 5:8	you were formerly darkness; 8	but now you are light in the Lord; 8	walk as children of light; 8
Colossians 2:6		As you therefore have received Christ Jesus... 6	...walk in Him, 6
Colossians 3:5-12	[evil desires] in them you also once walked; 5-7	[But now] as those who have been chosen of God; 12a	put on a heart of compassion kindness, humility...; 12b
2 Timothy 2:19		The Lord knows those who are His; 19a	Let [those] of the Lord abstain from wickedness; 19b
Titus 3:3-8	we also once were foolish ourselves, disobedient...:3	[But now] those who have believed God; 8a	may be careful to engage in good deeds; 8b

This chart shows a few passages illustrating this truth framed so concisely in a single verse, Ephesians 5:8.

The Unfinished Discipleship: A Special Note

Once we're saved by the finished gospel, apart from works (which are a condition of the unfinished gospel), then works become paramount for the newborn child of God.

The works of discipleship are never finished until life's end (your finish line). Works, meaning good works or fruits of the Holy Spirit, are the fruit of the finished gospel in the believer's life. Every epistle of the New Testament implores believers to walk in good works. As disciples of Jesus Christ, we are to mature in works, glorify God in works, draw near in fellowship with God through works, and bless other believers by our works.

Works are paramount for the believer.

The Unfinished Gospel?

The **unfinished gospel** can be summed up in seven points in this typical Lordship-gospel[82] statement of the "saving faith" required to be saved by the gospel:

A summary of the unfinished gospel:[83]

> [The essence of saving faith is] unconditional surrender, a complete resignation of self and absolute submission... Salvation is for those who are willing to forsake everything.... Saving faith is a commitment to leave sin and follow Jesus Christ at all cost. Jesus takes no one unwilling to come on those terms.... Forsaking oneself for Christ's sake is not an optional step of discipleship subsequent to conversion; it is the *sine qua non* [indispensable and essential action] of saving faith.[84]

This is not the faith of the finished gospel. The finished gospel responds to the question, "What must I do to be saved?" with the grace-laden answer, "believe": "Believe in the Lord Jesus, and you shall be saved" (Acts 16:30–31).

"Believe"—throughout Scripture. Not complex. Not complicated. Simple, childlike. "Believe."[85]

But the unfinished gospel, with its seven points, answers the same question this way:

"Believe in the Lord Jesus, and commit to:

1. unconditional surrender

2. complete resignation of self

3. absolute submission

4. forsaking everything

5. leaving sin

6. following Jesus Christ at all cost

7. coming on those terms

...and you shall be saved" (this is no longer Acts 16:31; it is Acts 16:31 PLUS my part).

As such, Acts 16:31 no longer saves; it judges.[86] It is no longer a gospel; it is a "yoke."

Since you must complete your salvation by obedience to this seven-point works system, which you are unable to do, then you're not saved, but judged, by those seven points (a form of law and works).

Who among the Lordship-gospel proponents can bear the "yoke" of their own seven-point criteria for "saving faith"?

> Now therefore why do you put God to the test by placing upon the neck of the disciples a yoke which neither our fathers nor we have been able to bear? (Acts 15:10)

This is the essence of the unfinished gospel.

The unfinished gospel

1. Your finish line decides your eternal destiny since your possession of real (working) faith is not decided until life's race is over. This focus on your finish line as a salvation process obscures and effectually subordinates Christs' finish line to your finish line

2. God reaches down with His gift for those who are ready to do their part with raised hands of promissory works.

3. God's guarantee that real faith will persevere is proven IF you walk like "who you *can become*" to your finish line.

4. You prove your faith by your race. It must be justified as "real" before it can justify you as "saved." In other words, you must justify your faith so your faith can justify you.

5. Works pave the path to salvation if they add up to real faith at your finish line.[87]

6. This gospel is never finished since no one, even those who promote it, can live up to its "terms." If they say they can, then aren't they **"boasting"** about their justifying-works?

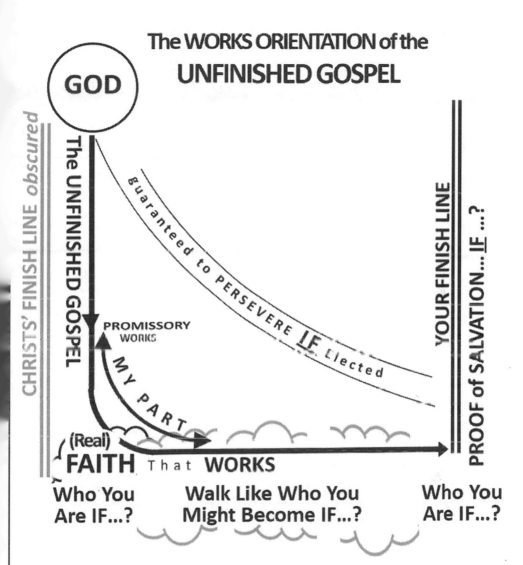

The WORKS ORIENTATION of the UNFINISHED GOSPEL

(Chart) This *"gospel"* is **unfinished** *because faith is not enough. Since faith must be linked to works to make it "real," then I must add **my part** to prove my profession of faith in Christ was "saving faith." I must promise, pledge, and commit myself to a life of "working faith." By faith alone, I cannot be saved. With faith plus promissory works, I can be saved—IF I persevere within some unknown percentile measure of good works throughout life. Salvation is based on a BIG "if." Christ's finish line of finished salvation is at best obscured, at worst, ignored. Therefore, it's your finish line—your life of works—that prove whether you were ever really saved when you believed. Short of some unknown degree of works, your faith will be insufficient to save you. Therefore, this gospel is **unfinished** until your works prove otherwise. No works, no salvation.*

For by grace you have been saved through faith; and that not of yourselves, it is the gift of God; not as a result of works, that **no one should boast.** (Ephesians 2:8–9, emphasis added)

…knowing that a man is not justified by the works of the Law but through faith in Christ Jesus…not by the works of the Law. (Galatians 2:16; note the double repetition for emphasis)

How Can I Do My Part to "Finish" the Unfinished Gospel?

The **unfinished gospel**, as summarized above in seven points, becomes strikingly works oriented when **my part** is identified and inserted into those seven points, below:

[The essence of saving faith is] unconditional surrender [my part], a complete resignation of self [my part], and absolute submission [my part].… Salvation is for those who are willing to forsake everything [my part].… Saving faith is a commitment to leave sin [my part] and follow Jesus Christ at all cost [my part]. Jesus takes no one unwilling to come on those terms [my part].… Forsaking oneself for Christ's sake is not an optional step of discipleship subsequent to conversion; it is the *sine qua non* [indispensable and essential action] of saving faith. (brackets added)[88]

Since I must contribute more to the gospel above than to simply "believe," then it is an **unfinished gospel**.

Since I am expected to "surrender," "resign self," "submit," etc., then I am not "helpless"—a helpless sinner—as Romans 5:6–8 says I must be to be saved. I can and must *do my part*, as shown above. At the point I *do my part*, then the gospel above will be **finished.** Only at that point can I be saved, because "Jesus takes no one unwilling to come on those terms" (point 7). According to the above, this unfinished Lordship-gospel is the "indispensable and essential action of saving faith."

The essence of the **unfinished gospel** is this: It needs my help!

1. But as a helpless sinner, am I not helpless? (Romans 5:6; Ephesians 2:1).

2. Why should I be condemned for being "unwilling" to help with *my part* to gain salvation? As a lost person, I am *unable* to help with *my part* (Romans 8:7–8).

3. Before I become "born again," how can I commit to "walk as children of light" if I am not yet "light in the Lord," as I must be to be able to "walk as children of light"? (Ephesians 5:8).

4. If I am not yet "created in Christ Jesus for good works," how can I promise good works and gain salvation "on those (7) terms"? (Ephesians 2:10).

This "gospel" requires *my part* to truly say "it is finished." That's why I call it the **unfinished gospel**. It has no more power than *my part* has. And I am helpless.

As a helpless sinner, I need outside help with my salvation. I need the **finished gospel**.

The Unfinished Gospel: A "Contract Gospel"

The "saving faith" of the unfinished gospel is not the "empty hands of faith," as Francis Schaeffer correctly terms the faith of the biblical gospel.[89] This is "faith" with hands full of promises and pledges. Helping hands from a "helpless" sinner.[90] Hands with an offering, an offering that amounts to *my part*.

Since the unfinished Lordship-gospel engages only with those willing to "come on those terms" (point 7, quoted above), am I not entering a contract when I insert "terms" into the gospel, terms about which I can "boast"? Paraphrased, "Here is my part, the 'terms' required to finish the gospel and gain salvation." That is, faith plus works. What does this "contract do to the gospel?

Salvation is no longer always and totally from the top down. My hands of faith are no longer empty or helplessly extended to receive the free gift of the finished gospel. The unfinished gospel from the top down meets halfway my helping hands extended from the bottom up. This is my offering,

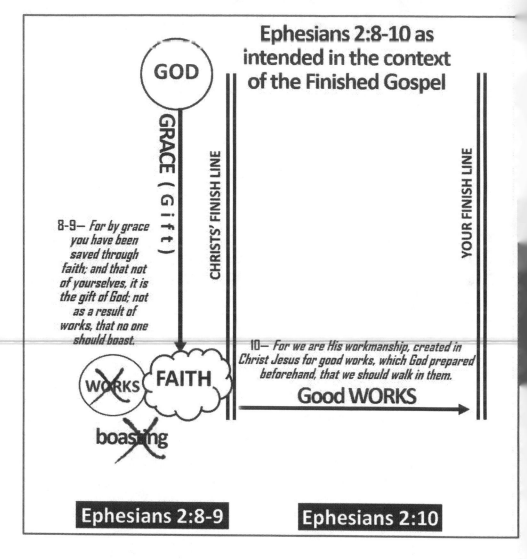

Ephesians 2:8-10 as intended in the context of the Finished Gospel

GOD

GRACE (G i f t)

CHRISTS' FINISH LINE

YOUR FINISH LINE

8-9— *For by grace you have been saved through faith; and that not of yourselves, it is the gift of God; not as a result of works, that no one should boast.*

WORKS FAITH

boasting

10— *For we are His workmanship, created in Christ Jesus for good works, which God prepared beforehand, that we should walk in them.*

Good WORKS

Ephesians 2:8-9   **Ephesians 2:10**

(Charts) Ephesians 2:8–10 (above left), is distorted (above right) by faith PLUS trust in future works to pave the path to salvation. In the distorted version, I can "boast" that "when I believed in Christ, I committed myself to a dedicated life of righteous works." Is this not a boast? When "I believed" (faith), "I committed" (works). Ephesians doesn't permit this. There are to be no works—promises, pledges, commitments, etc., anywhere on the chart that is left of Christ's finish line.

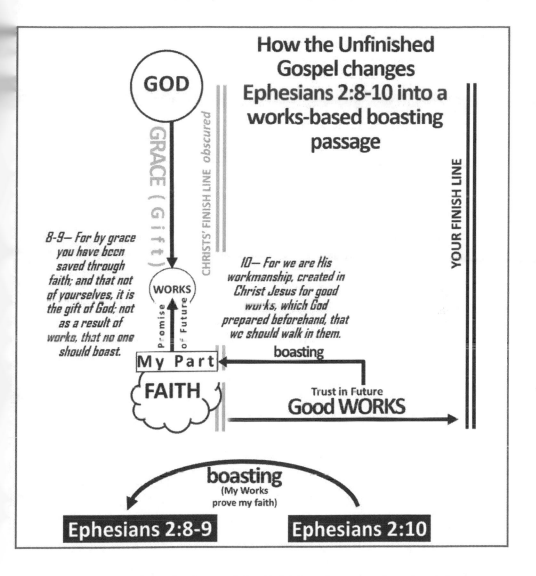

How the Unfinished Gospel changes Ephesians 2:8-10 into a works-based boasting passage

GOD

GRACE (Gift)

CHRIST'S FINISH LINE *obscured*

YOUR FINISH LINE

8-9— For by grace you have been saved through faith; and that not of yourselves, it is the gift of God; not as a result of works, that no one should boast.

WORKS

Promise of Future

10— For we are His workmanship, created in Christ Jesus for good works, which God prepared beforehand, that we should walk in them.

My Part

boasting

FAITH

Trust in Future
Good WORKS

boasting
(My Works
prove my faith)

Ephesians 2:8-9

Ephesians 2:10

my part, to complete the "terms" for finishing the gospel and gaining my salvation. I promised, I pledged, I committed—and I can "boast" about it.

Yet Ephesians 2:8–9 says I cannot gain salvation "as a result of works, that no one should boast." If Ephesians 2:10 is trusted as a future works—an IOU to validate my faith as saving faith, then works are added to Ephesians 2:8–9. Grace is no longer grace, and I can "boast."[91] Ephesians 2:8–9 is unable to save without trusting in my future works (v. 10)—a works IOU—the very opposite of what those verses say.[92]

This unfinished lordship-gospel has no capacity to save anyone. The biblical record of the lives of Lot, Samson, and Solomon are proof that the lordship-gospel is unbiblical.

Can Lot, Samson, and Solomon Be Saved by the Unfinished Gospel?

Here we must remember two things.

1. First, the finished gospel was applied backwards (retro action) to Old Testament and pre-cross believers (Romans 3:25; Hebrews 9:15).[93]

2. Second, these Old Testament believers were saved through childlike faith (simple belief) in the very same way as we who live after the cross are saved (Genesis 15:6; Romans 4:1–5).[94]

Now, let's look at how Lot, Samson, and Solomon would fare under both:

1. The unfinished gospel (using the unfinished Lordship-gospel of MacArthur),

and

2. The finished gospel (Genesis 15:6; John 3:16; Acts 16:31, etc.)

LOT

How would Lot fare under MacArthur's unfinished gospel? Below are the major events of Lot's life according to notes taken directly from John MacArthur's *Study Bible*.

In addition to the previously mentioned seven terms, consider the proof of salvation standard[95] (according to the MacArthur unfinished lordship-gospel).

> Faith obeys. Unbelief rebels. The fruit of one's life reveals whether that person is a believer or an unbeliever. There is no middle ground.[96]

Would not Lot have failed miserably both the proof of salvation standard above as well as the seven-point, unfinished lordship-gospel? Remember, "The fruit of one's life reveals whether that person is a believer or an

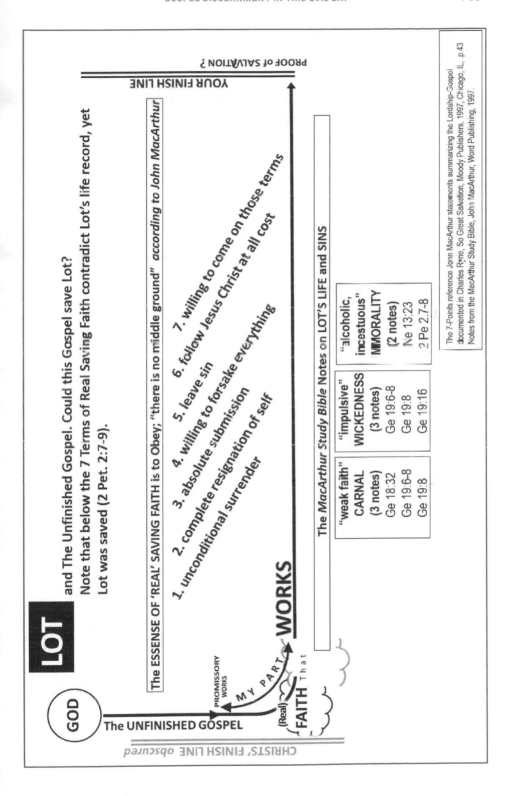

LOT and The Unfinished Gospel. Could this Gospel save Lot?

Note that below the 7 Terms of Real Saving Faith contradict Lot's life record, yet Lot was saved (2 Pet. 2:7-9).

The ESSENCE OF 'REAL' SAVING FAITH is to Obey; "there is no middle ground" *according to John MacArthur*

PROOF of SALVATION?

YOUR FINISH LINE

7. willing to come on those terms
6. follow Jesus Christ at all cost
5. leave sin
4. willing to forsake everything
3. absolute submission
2. complete resignation of self
1. unconditional surrender

The *MacArthur Study Bible* Notes on LOT'S LIFE and SINS

"weak faith" CARNAL (3 notes)	"impulsive" WICKEDNESS (3 notes)	"alcoholic, incestuous" IMMORALITY (2 notes)
Ge 18:32	Ge 19:6-8	Ne 13:23
Ge 19:6-8	Ge 19:8	2 Pe 2.7-8
Ge 19:8	Ge 19:16	

The 7-Points reference John MacArthur statements summarizing the Lordship-Gospel documented in Charles Ryrie, So Great Salvation, Moody Publishers, 1997, Chicago, IL, p.43
Notes from the MacArthur Study Bible, John MacArthur, Word Publishing, 1997.

GOD

The UNFINISHED GOSPEL

PROMISSORY WORKS

MY PART **WORKS**

(Real) **FAITH** That

CHRISTS' FINISH LINE *obscured*

unbeliever. There is no middle ground," according to the MacArthur proof of salvation standard.

In the chart above, MacArthur's own Bible notes at the bottom of the chart on Lot's life show Lot could not be saved by the unfinished gospel. Yet the Bible says Lot was saved. Either MacArthur's Bible notes or his lordship-gospel is wrong!

In his 2 Peter 2:7–9 note, MacArthur admits what he cannot deny: The Bible says that Lot was saved. Yet if MacArthur's gospel is right, then his notes about Lot's life show that Lot did not *do his part* to be saved according to the expectations of MacArthur's unfinished lordship-gospel.

But it is MacArthur's Bible notes on Lot that are right, including the note that Lot was saved. Therefore, his lordship-gospel cannot be right. Lot's life proves the unfinished lordship-gospel is wrong!

SAMSON

As with Lot, how would Samson fare under the unfinished lordship-gospel? At the bottom of the chart are the major events of Samson's life. The notes are taken directly from John MacArthur's *Study Bible*.

In his Judges 16:29–30 Bible note, MacArthur agrees that the Bible says Samson was saved. But the MacArthur Study Bible notes on Samson's life, when compared to MacArthur's proof of salvation standard, condemn Samson as an unbeliever. Therefore, the unfinished lordship-gospel, with its mixture of faith and works, is proven wrong again.

SOLOMON

Would King Solomon have been saved by MacArthur's unfinished lordship-gospel? At the bottom of the chart are the major events of Solomon's life. The notes are taken directly from John MacArthur's *Study Bible*.

Remember again what the Proof of Salvation Standard says, "Faith obeys. Unbelief rebels. The fruit of one's life reveals whether that person is a believer or an unbeliever. There is no middle ground."[97]

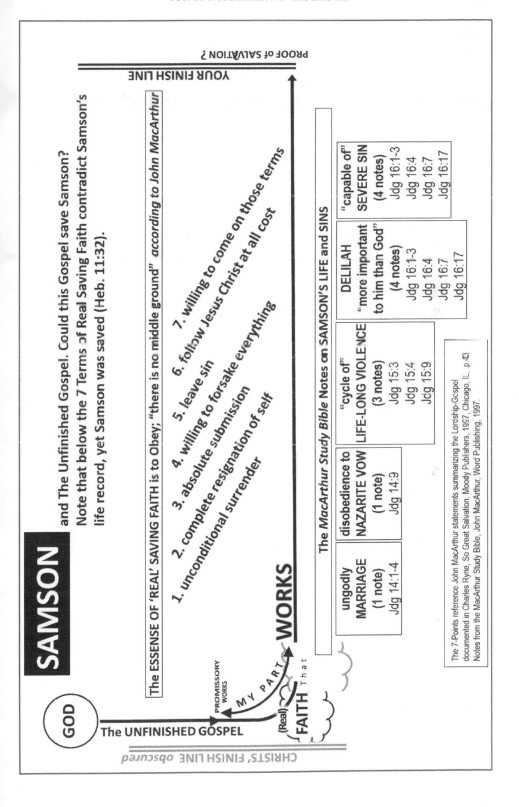

SAMSON

and The Unfinished Gospel. Could this Gospel save Samson?
Note that below the 7 Terms of Real Saving Faith contradict Samson's
life record, yet Samson was saved (Heb. 11:32).

The ESSENSE OF 'REAL' SAVING FAITH is to Obey; "there is no middle ground" *according to John MacArthur*

YOUR FINISH LINE
PROOF of SALVATION?

7. willing to come on those terms
6. follow Jesus Christ at all cost
5. leave sin
4. willing to forsake everything
3. absolute submission
2. complete resignation of self
1. unconditional surrender

GOD

The UNFINISHED GOSPEL

PROMISSORY WORKS
MY PART
(Real) FAITH That
WORKS

CHRIST'S FINISH LINE obscured

The *MacArthur Study Bible* Notes on SAMSON'S LIFE and SINS

ungodly MARRIAGE (1 note)	disobedience to NAZARITE VOW (1 note)	"cycle of" LIFE-LONG VIOLENCE (3 notes)	DELILAH "more important to him than God" (4 notes)	"capable of" SEVERE SIN (4 notes)
Jdg 14:1-4	Jdg 14:9	Jdg 15:3 Jdg 15:4 Jdg 15:9	Jdg 16:1-3 Jdg 16:4 Jdg 16:7 Jdg 16:17	Jdg 16:1-3 Jdg 16:4 Jdg 16:7 Jdg 16:17

The 7-Points reference John MacArthur statements summarizing the Lordship-Gospel
documented in Charles Ryrie, So Great Salvation, Moody Publishers, 1997, Chicago, IL, p.43
Notes from the MacArthur Study Bible, John MacArthur, Word Publishing, 1997.

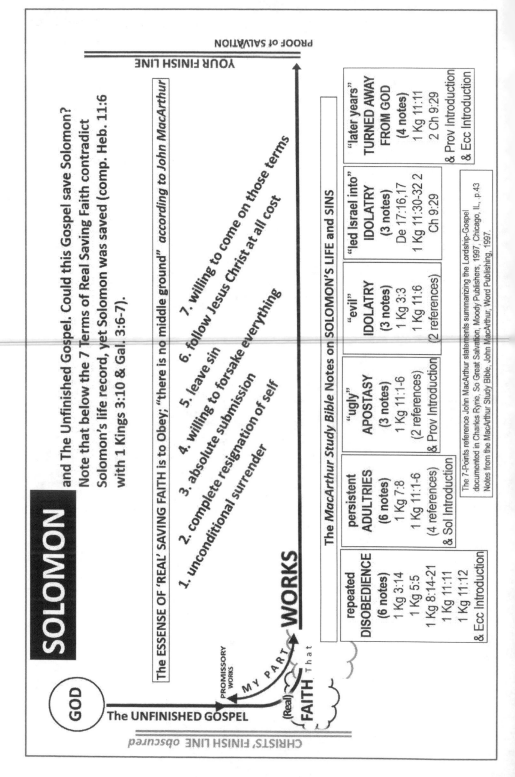

SOLOMON

and The Unfinished Gospel. Could this Gospel save Solomon?
Note that below the 7 Terms of Real Saving Faith contradict
Solomon's life record, yet Solomon was saved (comp. Heb. 11:6
with 1 Kings 3:10 & Gal. 3:6-7).

YOUR FINISH LINE

PROOF of SALVATION

The ESSENSE OF 'REAL' SAVING FAITH is to Obey; "there is no middle ground" *according to John MacArthur*

7. willing to come on those terms

6. follow Jesus Christ at all cost

5. leave sin

4. willing to forsake everything

3. absolute submission

2. complete resignation of self

1. unconditional surrender

The *MacArthur Study Bible* Notes on SOLOMON'S LIFE and SINS

repeated DISOBEDIENCE (6 notes)	persistent ADULTRIES (6 notes)	"ugly" APOSTASY (3 notes)	"evil" IDOLATRY (3 notes)	"led Israel into" IDOLATRY (3 notes)	"later years" TURNED AWAY FROM GOD (4 notes)
1 Kg 3:14	1 Kg 7:8	1 Kg 11:1-6	1 Kg 3:3	De 17:16,17	1 Kg 11:11
1 Kg 5:5	1 Kg 11:1-6	(2 references)	1 Kg 11:6	1 Kg 11:30-32 2	2 Ch 9:29
1 Kg 8:14-21	(4 references)	& Prov Introduction	(2 references)	Ch 9:29	& Prov Introduction
1 Kg 11:11	& Sol Introduction				& Ecc Introduction
1 Kg 11:12					
& Ecc Introduction					

The 7-Points reference John MacArthur statements summarizing the Lordship-Gospel
documented in Charles Ryrie, So Great Salvation, Moody Publishers, 1997, Chicago, IL, p.43
Notes from the MacArthur Study Bible, John MacArthur, Word Publishing, 1997.

GOD

PROMISSORY WORKS

MY PART

WORKS

(Real) **FAITH** That

The **UNFINISHED GOSPEL**

CHRISTS' FINISH LINE obscured

MacArthur's own Bible notes on Solomon's life show the king could not be saved under MacArthur's lordship-gospel, proof of salvation standard. And the seven-point unfinished gospel? Solomon failed miserably.

But in his introduction to Ecclesiastes, MacArthur says the biblical evidence shows that Solomon was saved.

Since Solomon was saved, and since he could not be saved under the lordship-gospel, then MacArthur's unfinished lordship-gospel is wrong!

The Bible says that Lot, Samson, and Solomon were saved. But why couldn't they have been saved by the lordship-gospel? Many verses—but in this case, Genesis 15:6—give us the conclusive answer.

"Abraham believed God, and committed to…

1. unconditional surrender

2. complete resignation of self

3. absolute submission

4. willingness to forsake everything

5. turning away from sin

6. following Jesus Christ at all cost

7. willingness to come on those terms

…and it was 'reckoned to him as righteousness.'"

ONLY the **bold in the chart** is the gospel gifted by God to Abraham as expressed in Genesis 15:6. When you add the additional seven-point requirements of the lordship-gospel, then you have Genesis 15:6 PLUS Abraham's part. True, Abraham was a pillar of faith and faithful works. He would have rated much better than Lot, Samson, or Solomon under the seven points above. But the Bible says at least nine times that Abraham was saved by only the part in bold. Even Abraham could not be saved under the unfinished lordship-gospel. **But praise God for the part in bold—and the finished gospel of free grace.**

Lot, Samson, and Solomon fail miserably the unfinished gospel. By adding *their part*, it doesn't help them. It condemns them. But they weren't condemned; they were saved.[98] So how could these three woefully sinful men have been saved?

Could Lot, Samson, or Solomon Have Been Saved by the Finished Gospel?

Yes. And they were.[99] They each were saved by the finished gospel, and, unlike the lengthy dissertation above on the unfinished gospel, it won't take long to explain how!

1. First, cancel parts 1–7 above.

2. Second, stick with "believed."

3. Third, add nothing to it.

4. Fourth, realize that, at this point, we now have the faith of a child, not a theologian.

5. Finally, I have arrived at *my part*—my ONLY part to receive eternal life—"**Believe** on the Lord Jesus Christ and you shall be saved" (Acts 16:30–31, emphasis added).

The Bible says that Lot (2 Peter 2:7), Samson (Hebrews 11:32–33), and Solomon (1 Kings 3:10 and Hebrews 11:6) were saved. Below, in chart form, is how the simple finished gospel saved them.

#1 (chart-right) Move their salvation to the left of Christs' finish line. This is done by faith alone, in Christ alone, by grace alone—no works allowed—the only possible way of salvation. Christs' finish line is the sole proof of their salvation. Salvation finished, instantaneous, irreversible, "once for all."

#2 (chart-right) Salvation (justification) was finished in #1. Here in #2 are sanctification works (fruits). These were only possible when they walked by the Holy Spirit in their new nature, as "children of light" and not by their old nature, as "children of darkness." Their works determined the maturity of their discipleship and fellowship with their Savior. This is who you are (new nature), now, walk like it (Ephesians 5:8).

#3 (chart-right) Here, their own finish line concluded their works of "gold and silver, or wood and stubble" in their race through life (#2) since they became a child of God (#1). Their works (fruits) are the basis for the heavenly

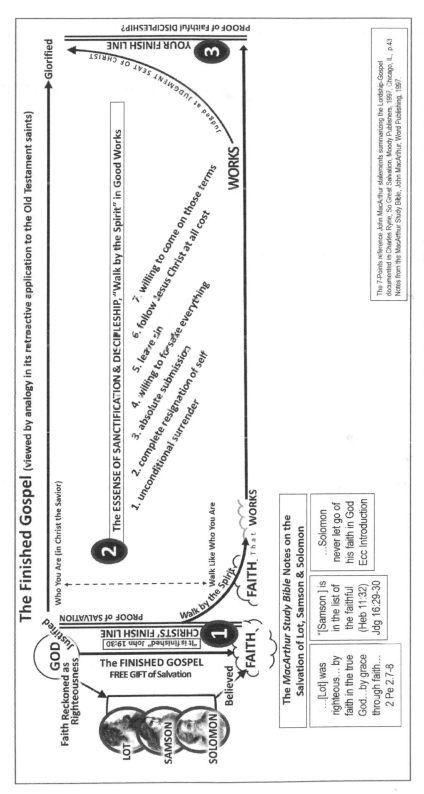

The Finished Gospel (viewed by analogy in its retroactive application to the Old Testament saints)

2 The ESSENSE OF SANCTIFICATION & DISCIPLESHIP, "Walk by the Spirit" in Good Works

Who You Are (in Christ the Savior)

1. unconditional surrender
2. complete resignation of self
3. absolute submission
4. willing to forsake everything
5. leave sin
6. follow Jesus Christ at all cost
7. willing to come on those terms

3 YOUR FINISH LINE

PROOF of FAITHFUL DISCIPLESHIP?

Judged at JUDGMENT SEAT OF CHRIST

Glorified

WORKS

Walk Like Who You Are

Walk by the Spirit

FAITH *That* WORKS

Who You Are (in Christ the Savior)

GOD
Justified

Faith Reckoned as Righteousness

The FINISHED GOSPEL
FREE GIFT of Salvation

Believed

FAITH

1 CHRISTS' FINISH LINE
"It is finished" John 19:30

PROOF of SALVATION

LOT
SAMSON
SOLOMON

The *MacArthur Study Bible* Notes on the Salvation of Lot, Samson & Solomon

| ...[Lot] was righteous... by faith in the true God...by grace through faith... 2 Pe 2.7-8 | "[Samson] is in the list of the faithful (Heb 11:32) Jdg 16:29-30 | ...Solomon never let go of his faith in God Ecc Introduction |

The 7-Points reference John MacArthur statements summarizing the Lordship-Gospel documented in Charles Ryrie, So Great Salvation, Moody Publishers, 1997, Chicago, IL, p.43 Notes from the MacArthur Study Bible, John MacArthur, Word Publishing, 1997.

How Lot, Samson, and Solomon were saved by the finished gospel (#1, #2, and #3 correspond to the paragraph numbers opposite.

bema seat judgment determining their position in their Father's Kingdom. They have had eternal life, with no condemnation, since the instantaneous, irreversible, once-and-for-all, finished gospel of #1 above.[100]

Summary Conclusion

Justification (Finished at Christ's finish line)

1. We are irreversibly saved by grace alone, through faith alone, in Christ alone in a moment of time, apart from any works at any time.

2. No works can rise up subsequent to salvation to retro judge or justify the faith by which we were saved. It has been decided once for all who you are in Christ.

Sanctification (Finished at your finish line)

1. Godly works only become possible when we are saved, whereby as children of God, we should seek to grow and mature in godly works, fellowship, and discipleship. The New Testament letters written to believers implore, teach, and guide: "Now, walk like who you are."

2. Faith that has already saved will always bear fruit (works), but it may not be apparent to man (James 2:18)—the "stubble" works may overshadow and obscure the "gold" works (1 Corinthians 3:12–15). We would not know Lot's faith bore any "gold" fruit if 2 Peter 2:8 hadn't told us.

Glorification (Eternal)

1. We will enter (Matthew 5:20; John 3:5) the eternal life inherited (Hebrew 1:14) at the moment (1 John 5:24) of our justification—for it was "finished."

2. We will receive our inheritance within the heavenly Kingdom—either the "least," the "greatest (Matthew 5:19), or somewhere in between (1 Corinthians 3:12–15) based on the heavenly rewards earned in our walk of sanctification—for our life walk is finished as our eternal life begins.

What Should We Do about the True Gospel in These Last Days?

1. We must proclaim the finished gospel that "through faith you are saved…it is the gift of God, not of works, lest any man should boast" (Ephesians 2:8–9).

2. If it were true that in order to be saved, alongside your faith you must work the works of lordship, then Lot, Samuel, and Solomon would not have been saved. Their lives, dominated more by wood, straw, and stubble than by gold, silver, and precious stones, would have proven they were not saved. Not enough good works.

3. But the Bible says that they were saved—by faith, for by free grace alone, "where sin increased, grace abounded all the more" (Romans 5:20). From the moment of salvation, they HAVE had assurance (1 John 5:13). Amazingly, 1 Corinthians 3:12–15 shows how they will remain securely and assuredly saved apart from their works record.

4. Yet Ephesians 2:10 shows it is God's desire that, once we are saved (vv. 8–9), from day one, we "walk" in good works in the Name of Jesus to His glory. God's unbounded grace given freely to us in our salvation will by the Holy Spirit empower us, and should motivate us to walk as our Savior walked!

5. When sharing the gospel, follow the example of Jesus, with His very personal witness to the Samaritan women on the earth in John 4:10–14, and then repeated by Him in Heaven

almost verbatim sixty-five years later (Revelation 21:6, 22:17): We learn from Jesus' own lips that if we "hear" about "the gift of God," and "know [believe in]" who it is [Jesus Christ, the Son of God] who offers it to us, if we wish, we may come and ask Him, and He will give us to "take without cost" the "living water of eternal life." That is the finished gospel without cost. (Note that the quotations preserve the essence of the passages).[101]

FINALLY, LET'S BE FAIR

Two points need to be said:

1. John MacArthur's Bible notes DO say that Lot (note on 2 Peter 2:7–8), Samson (note on Jude 16:29–30) and Solomon (note on Ecclesiastes introduction) were saved. He must, because the Bible says that. But his own Bible notes are glaringly clear that they could not have been saved by his seven-point "terms" that define his unfinished gospel.

2. John MacArthur's seven-point "terms" are alien to the finished gospel. But they are absolutely biblical if applied to their proper category—your race (sanctification, discipleship) to your finish line. They are the expected fruit ("works," *my part,* enabled by the Holy Spirit) of an already saved person who should strive to walk as a mature disciple in close fellowship with his Savior.

As for Lot, Samson, Solomon—and yes, myself—we are singing God's praises now and forevermore, because by the finished gospel, "where sin increased, grace abounded all the more" (Romans 5:20). Grace only made possible by what Jesus did on the cross that enabled Him to declare: "It is finished" (John 19:30).

CHAPTER 8

THE BELIEVER'S WITNESS WITHIN END-TIMES WICKEDNESS

GRANT PHILLIPS

Satan Attacks the Human Race

> Then the Lord saw that the wickedness of man was great on the earth, and that every intent of the thoughts of his heart was only evil continually. (Genesis 6:5)[102]

I was born in 1947, so I remember much of the '50s, the '60s, the '70s, etc. In the seventy-plus years I've been upon this earth, much has changed. Travel, medical advancements, and electronic gadgets are just a few areas in which our lifestyle has been greatly improved. Without a doubt, we are much better off in many ways due to modern technology. The same cannot be said for us socially, however, and particularly spiritually. So what have we given up?

Crime

Criminal acts have exploded due to a national apostasy from the Christian foundation instituted by our forefathers. This nation, having turned its back on God, listened instead to the left-wing, anti-biblical teachings of Dr. Benjamin Spock in the '50s. Actually, his first book was published in 1946. From there, we began following parenting methods that led us away from the biblical view. Not surprisingly, once we veered off the path God had laid out for parents, "free love" and illicit drug usage moved in, producing a society that rebelled against any and all authority, especially the authority of God.

Criminals are mollycoddled, while victims of crime receive little to no justice.

Police officers are being attacked and murdered by those who were never taught by their parents to respect authority (the results of listening to Dr. Spock). These little angels have become drug-induced, out-of-control hellions.

An increase in the number of serial killings no longer shocks us as it once did. Most of these killers thrive on the publicity. They also know that if they are caught, it is unlikely they will be executed any time soon, and probably not at all. On the contrary, society will provide free room and board, medical care, libraries, gyms, basketball courts and television entertainment for them for the duration of their imprisonment. In the meantime, the victims will remain in their graves while their families continue to mourn the loss of their loved ones.

According to a Pew Research article dated January 3, 2019, serious crimes have actually decreased, so says the FBI.[103] In a *New York Times* article dated September 25, 2017, serious crime is definitely on the rise.[104]

It is odd that a liberal source like the *New York Times* would admit to the rise of crime, but they do just that. On the other hand, it makes me wary when the Pew Research article is obviously relying completely on the integrity of the FBI. (The FBI remarks remind me of 2 Timothy 4:3–4 from a secular viewpoint.) Feel free to read the two articles, use some common sense, and come to your own conclusion. I personally cannot be convinced that crime has not risen dramatically in this country. Even in our own small locale, it is painfully obvious.

> For the time will come when they will not endure sound doctrine; but wanting to have their ears tickled, they will accumulate for themselves teachers in accordance to their own desires, and will turn away their ears from the truth and will turn aside to myths. (2 Timothy 4:3–4)

Morality

What used to be sought after in the back alleys of red-light districts is now publicly displayed via Hollywood movies, television, newsstands, and the "adult" entertainment businesses throughout large cities and even in smaller towns. Yes, the back alleys and red-light districts have now spread their tentacles into our living rooms.

Marriage is frowned upon and ridiculed. Living together is the new norm. If by chance a couple does marry, they can easily undo their bond with a quickie divorce, regardless of the consequences to innocent children.

Children, if they are fortunate enough not to have been aborted, are living in homes without even knowing their father or who he is. Others are raised by two "daddies" or two "mommies." Many are being raised by grandparents because their parents are either in prison or dead as a result of the carnage caused by illicit drugs.

Homosexuality is a curse upon any nation, and we are having it force fed to us in nearly every genre of our lives. If that were not enough, transgenderism has now been added. Our decadence knows no bounds. Will bestiality be the next insanity legalized on the plate of corruption?

Children

In a "civilized" society you would think that at least the children would be off-limits and would be protected from the evil machinations of adults. There was a time when child molesters would be killed in prison by fellow inmates for their vile acts upon the innocent. If that remains true, I am unaware of it. I realize that the violation of the innocent is nothing new in any society, but why is there so much of it in today's modern, "civilized" twenty-first-century society?

Thousands of years ago, the children of Israel were drawn into the practice of sacrificing their own children to Baal. God told them to eliminate the heathen from the land He was giving them, but they did not listen. God knew that Israel would be corrupted by false religions. They disobeyed God, and their children paid the price on the altar of Baal. We today have disobeyed God, and our children are paying the price on the altar of the abortion clinics.

My wife and I live in a small suburban area. The city population is approximately eight thousand, and the county population is approximately sixty thousand, but even here child molestation and abuse are no strangers to our newspapers. On a regular basis, I open our newspaper and read of one or more perverts (male and/or female) committing vile obscenities upon a child or children.

False Religion

Even though we today can wrap ourselves in the robe of material opulence, the stench of the sewers fills our nostrils. Why don't we smell it? Have you ever been around people who do not bathe, but they don't seem to notice the odor? They desperately need a good scrubbing with soap and hot water, but are totally oblivious to their own body odor.

Our many problems today are a result of sin, and this problem has not, for a long time, been properly addressed from most of the pulpits of America. Our sins are even more offensive to God than another person's body odor is to those who bathe. As a populace, our hearts have grown cold toward God and our spiritual noses insensitive to our sin problem.

Churches that believe and proclaim the entirety of God's Word are rapidly declining in number. Satan's message of "Did God say?" is given credence over the truth. Just as Eve, in Genesis chapter 3, listened to the serpent, we also listen and follow that slippery-tongued con artist.

I well remember my teenage years when our church members would go out into the community in pairs and visit our neighbors. Even if they weren't interested in Christ, they were gracious hosts and would politely listen to what we had to say. Many would request prayer. In those days, it was common for those of the world not to use profanity in front of a Christian, especially a pastor. This may be hard to believe for some reading these comments, but it was so. How does that compare with today?

- Today, Christians are called extremists, and many Christian churches and organizations are labeled as hate groups. Christians are mocked and despised. Don't think so? Just notice how Christians are portrayed in movies and television episodes, or how they are laughed at and ridiculed on talk shows.

- Six Virginia State Police chaplains resigned their voluntary positions of chaplain because they were ordered not to use Jesus' name in public prayer.[105]

- Those in the public eye who are devout Christians, such as Sarah Palin, Vice President Mike Pence, and Franklin Graham, have been verbally attacked for just being Christians who stand with God.

- In 2008, the supporters of Proposition 8 in California were verbally and physically assaulted for supporting traditional marriage between a man and woman.[106]

- During Obama's term as president, the Department of Defense was training US troops to regard Catholics, Orthodox Jews, and evangelical Christians as "religious extremists," classifying them along with groups such as the Ku Klux Klan, al-Qaeda, and Hamas.[107]

These are just a few examples out of hundreds that occur more and more each day. Some Christians, particularly those who are more biblically attuned to God's Word, are becoming nervous and gun-shy at the attacks upon Christianity in this country. Christianity has been such a mainstay in the United States of America, who would have ever thought it would come under attack here as it has in other countries?

On December 30, 2018, Michael Brice-Sadler had an article in the *Washington Post* concerning Facebook temporarily blocking Franklin Graham over a post Mr. Graham entered on Facebook in 2016. Mr. Graham states as follows:

Franklin Graham

Well, now we know. Facebook has a secret rulebook for policing speech. I was banned from posting on Facebook last week for 24 hours. Why? Because of a post from back in 2016 about North Carolina's House Bill 2 (the bathroom bill). Facebook said the post went against their "community standards on hate speech." Facebook is trying to define truth. There was a character in a movie a few years back who said, "The truth is what I say it is!" That's what Facebook is trying to do. They're making the rules and changing the rules. Truth is truth. God made the rules and His Word is truth. Actually, Facebook is censoring free speech. The free exchange of ideas is part of our country's DNA. Since Facebook took down the 2016 post last week, I'll copy it here so you can read it for yourself. Do you see any hate speech here?

April 9, 2016—Bruce Springsteen, a long-time gay rights activist, has cancelled his North Carolina concert. He says the NC law #HB2 to prevent men from being able to use women's restrooms and locker rooms is going "backwards instead of forwards." Well, to be honest, we need to go back! Back to God. Back to respecting and honoring His commands. Back to common sense. Mr. Springsteen, a nation embracing sin and bowing at the feet of godless secularism and political correctness is not progress. I'm thankful that as of the time of this writing North Carolina has a governor, Pat McCrory, and a lieutenant governor, Dan Forest, and legislators who put the safety of our women and children first! HB2 protects the safety and privacy of women and children and preserves the human rights of millions of faith-based citizens of this state.

Facebook did reinstate Mr. Graham's Facebook "privileges," but when I read this the first thing that came to my mind was the State of Colorado confirming that a baker illegally discriminated against a gay couple by refusing to bake the couple a wedding cake. Now think about this real hard. Is this any different than Bruce Springsteen cancelling his North Carolina concert because he did not approve of NC law #HB2?

Hear me out. The baker is in the baking business, and Mr. Springste is in the music business. Both men, in their respective businesses, withheld their product because of their beliefs. The baker's decision affected two people. Mr. Springsteen's decision affected thousands. Yet, to my knowledge, no one has sued Mr. Springsteen for not honoring his commitment to the public. No court has taken action against Mr. Springsteen as far as I know for withholding his product. Mr. Springsteen has not had a bullseye painted on his forehead as did the baker.

The truth is neither the baker nor Mr. Springsteen should be sued for how they run their own business enterprise. However, the baker is accused of discriminating, and Mr. Springsteen is not? Why? It certainly sounds like a double standard. And then there is the Facebook standard.

I can almost hear God telling Isaiah to write:

> Woe to those who call evil good, and good evil; Who substitute darkness for light and light for darkness; Who substitute bitter for sweet and sweet for bitter! (Isaiah 5:20)

These words were written about 2,700 years ago, and they describe our society today with the accuracy of a laser. Actually, they are so true today; it is almost scary to think about it.

The Apostle Paul warned us when he told his protégé Timothy that the time would come when people would refuse sound doctrine and replace it with what their itching ears longed to hear—i.e., the syrupy sweet lies of Satan over the truth of Almighty God. We are there.

> For the time will come when they will not endure sound doctrine; but wanting to have their ears tickled, they will accumulate for themselves teachers in accordance to their own desires, and will turn away their ears from the truth and will turn aside to myths. (2 Timothy 4:3–4)

What has caused this growing animosity toward God, His Word, and His people? Again, let's turn to the Apostle Paul. He said to the Ephesians that our struggle is not with people, but the fallen angelic realm of Satan.

>r our struggle is not against flesh and blood, but
1st the rulers, against the powers, against the world
es of this darkness, against the spiritual forces of wick-
1ess in the heavenly places. (Ephesians 6:12)

Christians here in America are being attacked verbally and sometimes physically. Our own courts are attacking most everything Christ related. Employers are attacking Christians by firing them if they stand up for Jesus. Christian children who stand with Christ are being harassed in school by fellow students and even their teachers. All we are seeing is the person attacking us, but in truth they are only an instrument used by Satan to advance his cause. Our real enemy is Satan and his demonic realm. So what do we do about this?

Christians Living in a Fallen World

How does a Christian live as God would have us to in the throes of evil that is all around us? How can we possibly be a witness for our Lord when the world around us hates Jesus, His Word, and His followers? Anyone who has lived very long can readily see the downward slide from the society of the '50s as opposed to today. That which is the norm today would have been unthinkable not too many years ago. So what do we do?

Paul informs us in Ephesians 6:10–11:

> Finally, be strong in the Lord and in the strength of His might. Put on the full armor of God, so that you will be able to stand firm against the schemes of the devil.

Paul went on to say in the following verses that we need to dress for the occasion.

> Therefore, take up the full armor of God, so that you will be able to resist in the evil day, and having done everything, to stand firm. Stand firm therefore, **having girded your loins with the truth**, and **having put on the breastplate of righteousness**, and **having shod your feet with the preparation of the gospel of peace**; in addition to all, taking up the shield of faith with which you will be able to

extinguish all the flaming arrows of the evil one. And **take the helmet of salvation**, and the sword of the Spirit, which is the word of God. With all prayer and petition pray at all times in the Spirit, and with this in view, be on the alert with all perseverance and petition for all the saints. (Ephesians 6:13–18, emphasis added)

Paul said first of all (in verse 10) that we "be strong in Christ and His power."

At some point in our lives, we trusted Jesus to save us, to keep us, and to take us to be with Him. By the same token, we must trust Him now to guide us as a witness for Him while we live in this fallen world. We cannot lean on our own power. We have none.

Unfortunately, most Christians are as spiritually weak as kittens because they are stepping outside the umbrella of God's power. Statements are made such as, "I can't make it." "Life is too hard." "I just don't understand." "Nothing goes right for me." "I feel so empty." All of this is due to living outside of God's power.

Second Corinthians 12:9–10 says:

And He has said to me, "My grace is sufficient for you, for power is perfected in weakness." Most gladly, therefore, I will rather boast about my weaknesses, so that the power of Christ may dwell in me. Therefore I am well content with weaknesses, with insults, with distresses, with persecutions, with difficulties, for Christ's sake; for when I am weak, then I am strong.

We will never be strong in Christ and His power until we freely submit to Him as His bond servant. He is the general. We are the footsoldiers.

Paul went on to say (twice, in verses 10 and 13) that we are to put on the "full armor of God."

That means we put ALL of it on, not just some of it. We don't take faith and leave off prayer. Neither do we stand alert but forsake righteousness. We can't be biblically illiterate and expect to know His will.

Most Christians just dip their toe in the shallow end of the pool and never dive in the deep end. We want just enough of Christ to feel comfortable, but not so much as to be labeled a "religious nut." If that's the case, maybe we need to go back to the beginning and read very carefully the following Scripture passage:

> Test yourselves to see if you are in the faith; examine yourselves! Or do you not recognize this about yourselves, that Jesus Christ is in you—unless indeed you fail the test? (2 Corinthians 13:5)

Now get this, Paul said FOUR times (verses 11, 13 and 14) that we are to "stand."

- Verse 11: "so that you can take your stand."

- Verse 13: "so that…you may be able to stand your ground."

- Verse 13, again: "after you have done everything, to stand."

- Verse 14: "Stand firm then."

My dearly beloved (as Dr. J. Vernon McGee would say), we not only are not standing, but we're falling like autumn leaves. The Church should be introducing a revival of spring upon the souls of man, but the dead of winter remains in the lives of many Christians as far as our witness to the world is concerned.

The remainder of our armor is:

Go with truth, not hypocrisy. As I've already stated, far too many Christians are so biblically illiterate that they are easily duped by teachers who are more than willing to scratch their itching ears (2 Timothy 4:3).

How can we share Jesus Christ with the lost when we can't even explain to them the very basics of Christianity? Are we able to share the plan of salvation to a lost soul? Do we even know the "Roman Road" method of witnessing?

Practice righteousness (or holiness). Jesus has clothed us in His righteousness, but how many prefer to drag out their old clothes from the attic instead? We have the finest apparel from God's closet, but we continue to go to our own attic instead. If we can't find clothing appropriate to our liking in the attic, we just drag out our Singer sewing machine and make our own.

Let us remember that we are children of the King. We have been clothed in the finest. Maybe we just need to remember that and act the part. However, does that now call for us to act "holier than thou?" Let me answer that by asking one question. Was Jesus ever "stuck up" toward anyone on any occasion? The question demands a "NO" answer, of course.

> Whoever then humbles himself as this child, he is the greatest in the kingdom of heaven. (Matthew 18:4)

> Whoever exalts himself shall be humbled; and whoever humbles himself shall be exalted. (Matthew 23:12)

> But He gives a greater grace. Therefore it says, "**God is opposed to the proud, but gives grace to the humble.**" Humble yourselves in the presence of the Lord, and He will exalt you. (James 4:6, 10, emphasis added)

> You younger men, likewise, be subject to your elders; and all of you, clothe yourselves with humility toward one another, for **God is opposed to the proud, but gives grace to the humble.** Therefore humble yourselves under the mighty hand of God, that He may exalt you at the proper time. (1 Peter 5:5–6, emphasis added)

Paul goes on to say that we are to be prepared to serve. I have noticed many Christians vainly attempting to serve Jesus while they floundered like fish out of water simply because they weren't prepared. We must prepare ourselves by ingesting the food of God's Holy Word and being in constant prayer. Again, we must rely on His strength and wisdom, not ours.

Jesus spent much time preparing His disciples to be apostles. For example, He spent forty years training Moses in the desert (Acts 7:30). He spent three training Simon Peter, Andrew, James (son of Zebedee), John, Philip, Bartholomew, Thomas, Matthew, James (son of Alphaeus), Thaddaeus,

Simon the Zealot, and Judas Iscariot (the one who betrayed Him). He spent three years training the Apostle Paul in Arabia (Galatians 1:17).

Is it possible that some may be running ahead of God, bypassing that valuable time in the wilderness alone with Him we all so desperately need? I believe it is. Let us earnestly serve Him, but let us also allow Him to prepare us first for His service.

Then Paul tells us to go with the gospel of peace, faith, assurance of salvation, the Word of God, and prayer.

- **The gospel of peace.** This is the peace we have in Him when He lives in us. We may go with the gospel that declares all is made new in Jesus Christ. The Lord says in Revelation 21:5 that He is making everything new.

  When we rest our faith in Him, we are born again (John 3:3ff). We are a new person by the blood of Jesus that was shed for us. Every sin (past, present, and future) we have committed against Him was laid on the shoulders of God's Son Jesus. Every true born-again child of God can experience the peace only God can give (John 14:27). We have peace, real peace, because we know who walks beside us each day, and we anxiously long to spend eternity with Him. That is the gospel of peace we proclaim.

- **Faith.** Because of the peace only found in Him, we live our life in faith. Our trust in Him is never disappointed. Regardless of the battles in our life brought on by Satan, we are comforted because of our faith in Jesus Christ. The world says it is a blind faith, but we know better. Who are the truly blind?

  But He answered and said, "Every plant which My heavenly Father did not plant shall be uprooted. Let them alone; they are blind guides of the blind. And if a blind man guides a blind man, both will fall into a pit." (Matthew 15:13–14)

- **Assurance of salvation.** Today's true Christian is living at the cusp of Christ's return. The world around us is getting darker and darker, but there is light in the one true God. It is in Jesus Christ that we have assurance of our salvation and His light shines in our heart.

  > This is the will of Him who sent Me, that of all that He has given Me I lose nothing, but raise it up on the last day. (John 6:39)

- **Word of God.** With that assurance, we can proceed in our service for Him with His Word. The Bible is being attacked today from every angle. Satan hates God's Word and the Bible is God's Word. However, our Lord made it clear that His Word will not return to Him void.

  > For as the rain and the snow come down from heaven, And do not return there without watering the earth And making it bear and sprout, And furnishing seed to the sower and bread to the eater; So will My word be which goes forth from My mouth; It will not return to Me empty, Without accomplishing what I desire, And without succeeding in the matter for which I sent it. (Isaiah 55:10–11)

  Living the Christian life and being a witness for God in the twenty-first century really isn't any easier than it was in the first century. In some ways it may be more difficult, but our weapon is the same one used by every first-century Christian—i.e., God's Holy Word. Many today, instead of proclaiming, "Thus saith the Lord" with Bible in hand, prefer to tickle their audiences with their own clever devices. Their words will fail, but His will not.

- **Prayer.** As true Christians live out their days, much prayer is also needed. We lift up our prayers before a holy God, asking His forgiveness for our failures and for His continued guidance in our lives. He comforts us in His response, and that strengthens us in our serving Him as He wills.

I will lift up my eyes to the mountains;

From where shall my help come?

My help comes from the LORD,

Who made heaven and earth.

He will not allow your foot to slip;

He who keeps you will not slumber.

Behold, He who keeps Israel

Will neither slumber nor sleep.

The LORD is your keeper;

The LORD is your shade on your right hand.

The sun will not smite you by day,

Nor the moon by night.

The LORD will protect you from all evil;

He will keep your soul.

The LORD will guard your going out and your coming in

From this time forth and forever. (Psalm 121)

This is just as much a psalm for the Christian as it is for Israel. When we are on our knees (figuratively speaking) before the Lord in prayer, He is listening.

After all is said and done in donning our armor, we must not forget to be alert. The Apostle Peter explains why we should be alert:

Be of sober spirit, be on the alert. Your adversary, the devil, prowls around like a roaring lion, seeking someone to devour. (1 Peter 5:8)

Lastly, but certainly not of least importance, we need to be praying for each other. Our prayers need to lift up others who are fellow Christians, especially as we "see the day approaching" (Hebrews 10:25).

Any Christian who is trying to live for Jesus in this sin-fallen world needs desperately the armor of God the Apostle Paul has proclaimed in

Ephesians 6. The battle will continue to heat up as each day draws closer to our Lord's return.

If we have followed these words, we're on the right road in remaining faithful and standing tall for the Lord Jesus Christ. Now that we're clothed in the spiritual armor that the Apostle Paul has described, we now must go forward in proclaiming Jesus Christ to a fallen world.

To assure that we stand and not fall, let us also glean God's further instructions in Galatians 5:13–26. In short, He tells us to "walk by the Spirit" so we will produce the fruit that comes by walking by the Spirit—i.e., love, joy, peace, forbearance, kindness, goodness, faithfulness, gentleness, and self-control.

Don't feel bad if you are asking the same question I've also asked in the past: "How do I walk in the Spirit?" The greater question is: "How do I walk in the Spirit so that the fruit God mentions is produced in my life?" My abbreviated answer would be: Find what God wants and do it.

In reading the Word, we know where God stands. Since we know where He stands on lying, for example, don't lie. He says we are to forgive. Therefore, let us forgive. He wouldn't want us to listen to dirty jokes, so don't listen to dirty jokes. He would never want us to belittle others, so don't do that. In my opinion, we just simply need to do what He expects of us, and we find what He expects of us in His Word.

Final Days of the Church Age

Jesus said in Revelation 22, "Behold, I am coming quickly" (v. 7), and again, "Behold, I am coming quickly" (v. 12), then lastly, "Yes, I am coming quickly" (v. 20).

When Jesus said "Behold" in verses 7 and 12, He was basically saying "Pay attention! Listen!" When He used the word "Yes" in verse 20, He was basically saying, "I tell you the truth!"

We're at the very cusp of the final days of the Church Age, and only a few seem to be aware of that. Most of the world, even most Christians, live as if there is no tomorrow, but tomorrow is going to come.

The world laughs and ridicules all last-days' prophecy. The removal of millions of Christians from the earth in an instant (Rapture) is a farce in the eyes of those outside the Church, as is the years of Tribulation that follow. Again, many Christians don't believe Jesus is coming first to remove His Bride, then seven years of judgment will follow.

Truthfully, it really doesn't matter what we think. The only thing that matters is what God says, and He has made it abundantly clear in His Word that He is going to return.

Our world today is eerily like the days of Noah, Lot, and even Rome at Jesus' First Advent.

Noah

Jesus said in Matthew 24:37 and Luke 17:26 that when He returns, the days will be like they were in Noah's day. What were they like? He said in verse 38 of Matthew 24 that the "people were eating and drinking, marrying and giving in marriage, up to the day Noah entered the ark."

The Bible even tells us that wickedness prevailed in that day.

> The LORD saw how great the wickedness of the human race had become on the earth, and that every inclination of the thoughts of the human heart was only evil all the time. The LORD regretted that he had made human beings on the earth, and his heart was deeply troubled. So the LORD said, "I will wipe from the face of the earth the human race I have created—and with them the animals, the birds and the creatures that move along the ground—for I regret that I have made them." But Noah found favor in the eyes of the LORD. (Genesis 6:5–8)

Isn't that just how we are today? The world as a whole has no thought or care of Christ's return. Most people today are going about their daily lives without a care in the world concerning their own soul.

Our world today is so disinterested in anything concerning the Lord Jesus Christ that they not only don't care to hear the gospel; they ridicule it and mock any who dare share it. Yet some will be saved. Keep in mind that Noah preached for 120 years with no converts except those in his own household. All we can do is deliver the message, both verbally and by our actions. God will take care of the rest.

Lot

Most of us are familiar with what happened to Sodom and Gomorrah in Lot's day. The account is very clear that their sins were great, as they were in Noah's day. Homosexuality was running rampant. The stench of sin had become so great, just as it had in Noah's day, that God had had enough, and the people were destroyed.

Notice that judgment fell upon those of Noah's day immediately after Noah and his family were safe in the ark. Also, judgment fell upon Sodom and Gomorrah and the surrounding cities as soon as Lot and his family were safely removed. This leads me to say that once Jesus removes His Church from this earth at the Rapture, judgment will fall upon this earth. In my opinion, this earth is quickly approaching the last hour before our Savior and Lord comes to take His Bride home and judge this world.

Rome

There are many ways the United States of America of today resembles the Roman Empire—political corruption, our laws, superior military, and addictions to sports and immorality, to name a few. The particular one I have in mind, though, is that Rome accepted many religions.

Rome didn't care what god their citizens worshipped, as long as they also worshipped Caesar as god. Christianity and the Jews didn't get in trouble for having their own religion. They got in trouble because they would only worship one God, the one and only true God of Heaven.

This is exactly why true Christians in America are being hated more and more in this country. We will only worship Jesus Christ, the one true God, and we actually believe Him when He says, "I am the way, and the truth, and the life; no one comes to the Father but through Me" (John 14:6). We refuse to accept the lie that there are many ways to God, as our society keeps proclaiming.

It's very important for every true born-again Christian to stand up and be counted.

> Now, therefore, fear the LORD and serve Him in sincerity and truth; and put away the gods which your fathers served beyond the River and in Egypt, and serve the LORD. "If it is disagreeable in your sight to serve the LORD, choose for yourselves today whom you will serve: whether the gods which your fathers served which were beyond the River, or the gods of the Amorites in whose land you are living; but as for me and my house, we will serve the LORD." (Joshua 24:14–15)

Apostasy

The Lord God has forewarned us with many signs that will come to life in the final days. He gave no signs for the Rapture, but there are many for the Tribulation that follows. Many events need to be in place for the Tribulation to begin. For example, Israel must again be a nation. Therefore, after 1,900 years, Israel became a nation on May 14, 1948. On June 27, 1967, Israel extended her legal and administrative jurisdiction over Jerusalem. The players are in place for Ezekiel 38–39 to be fulfilled.

In my opinion, Israel becoming a nation after 1,900 years is the second-greatest sign to be fulfilled. Again, in my opinion, the greatest sign is the convergence of all the signs the Bible tells us about for the last days. There are many, many signs and they are all coming together at one time.

Allow me one more thought. I believe that the apostasy of the Church may be the third greatest sign, and I'll tell you why.

If all the churches in America alone were biblically based and Holy Spirit-driven, we would not be anywhere near as close to the final days as we are now. However, this thing the Bible calls "apostasy" has turned most churches into servants of Satan.

Through apostasy, most churches deny the basic doctrines of God's Word, resulting in the following:

- Ordination of homosexuals

- Straying from the true gospel

- Marketing and merchandising God's Word

- Pastors who are more concerned with numbers than with souls

- Pastors who don't pray

- Compromising the truth

- Permissiveness

This isn't to say that there are no churches left that are not apostate. Of course no church is perfect, because no Christian is perfect while clothed in the flesh, but there are, thankfully, some churches remaining that follow Christ and not the world.

None of us know when Jesus will return for His Bride, the Church, but He has given us (I repeat) many, many signs to know that we are close to the end of this age. How close are we? I don't know, but it is most likely very soon.

THE FINISH LINE

When I was a young fellow in school, I loved to run, especially the 100-yard dash or the 220. I'll always remember how sweet that finish line looked, especially if I would be leading the pack.

In horse racing, I think of Secretariat racing to the finish line and my heart pounds. What ball carrier doesn't love to cross the goal line with the football secured in his hands? Consider the baseball player rounding the bases and finally stepping on home plate.

There is one very important thing about the finish line that needs to be noted. No one can cross the finish line unless he or she is in the race. Spectators can't cross the finish line since they aren't in the race.

Spiritually speaking, every true, born-again Christian is in the race. Some will come in first, some second or third or fourth—even some dead last—but they are in the race. Please understand that this race is for servitude only, and has absolutely nothing to do with our salvation, which is guaranteed by God Almighty.

The Apostle Paul had much to say about "the race." Read carefully the next three Scripture passages.

> Do you not know that those who run in a race all run, but only one receives the prize? Run in such a way that you may win. Everyone who competes in the games exercises self-control in all things. They then do it to receive a perishable wreath, but we an imperishable. Therefore I run in such a way, as not without aim; I box in such a way, as not beating the air; but I discipline my body and make it my slave, so that, after I have preached to others, I myself will not be disqualified. (1 Corinthians 9:24–27)

> Therefore, since we have so great a cloud of witnesses surrounding us, let us also lay aside every encumbrance and the sin which so easily entangles us, and let us run with endurance the race that is set before us, fixing our eyes on Jesus, the author and perfecter of faith, who for the joy set before Him endured the cross, despising the shame, and has sat down at the right hand of the throne of God. (Hebrews 12:1–2)

> I have fought the good fight, I have finished the course, I have kept the faith; in the future there is laid up for me the crown of righteousness, which the Lord, the righteous Judge, will award to me on that day; and not only to me, but also to all who have loved His appearing. (2 Timothy 4:7–8)

I again emphasize that Paul isn't talking about running the race and performing works to maintain our salvation. We can no more be unborn as a child of God than we can be unborn from our earthly parents. He is referring to our Christian service for our Lord and Savior Jesus Christ. The next few verses will explain what he was referring to.

> According to the grace of God which was given to me, like a wise master builder I laid a foundation, and another is building on it. But each man must be careful how he builds on it. For no man can lay a foundation other than the one which is laid, which is Jesus Christ. Now if any man builds on the foundation with gold, silver, precious stones, wood, hay, straw, each man's work will become evident; for the day will show it because it is to be revealed with fire, and the fire itself will test the quality of each man's work. If any man's work which he has built on it remains, he will receive a reward. If any man's work is burned up, he will suffer loss; but he himself will be saved, yet so as through fire. (1 Corinthians 3:10–15)

Obviously, Paul is speaking of Jesus rewarding Christians according to their works performed in service for Him. If our works are like gold, silver, and precious stones, it will be evident, because fire only enhances those materials. However, if our works for Him are like wood, hay, and straw, our works will burn up, because they cannot survive the fire. Notice that if our work is burned up, we will suffer loss (rewards), but we are still saved, because Jesus was judged for us and none of His work is wood, hay, or straw.

However, it will not be a happy day for many Christians who may have no works to present to Jesus that are worthy of His praise. Some Christians say it is wrong to seek rewards, but that is not true. It is very biblical to seek rewards, and the next Scripture passage explains why.

> And when the living creatures give glory and honor and thanks to Him who sits on the throne, to Him who lives forever and ever, the twenty-four elders will fall down before Him who sits on the throne, and will worship Him who lives forever and ever, and will cast their crowns before the throne, saying, "Worthy are You, our Lord and our God, to receive glory and honor and power; for You created all

things, and because of Your will they existed, and were created." (Revelation 4:9–11)

The twenty-four elders represent the Church. That means this passage is speaking of you and me standing before our Savior and Lord. What is it we do at that time? The passage above says we will fall down before Him, worship Him, and cast our crowns before the throne where He sits. We will then say, "Worthy are You, our Lord and our God, to receive glory and honor and power; for you created all things, and because of Your will they existed, and were created."

Here's the problem. If our works are burned up, we receive no rewards. If we receive no rewards, we have no crowns. If we have no crowns, what are we going to present to Jesus at that time? All we will have to show for our life on earth in His service are two empty hands. Oh, we are saved (yet, so as through fire), but we will have no rewards.

Now before you hyperventilate, keep this in mind. Only Jesus has the right and the ability to examine our life and determine what will or will not survive His fire of judgment at the finish line. He wants each of us to succeed, and He makes every effort to see to it that we do succeed.

In my humble opinion, I believe there is hope that every Christian may have something in his or her life that Jesus will commend. There are just too many Scriptures referring to the Holy Spirit's work in the Christian life for any Christian to stand before our Lord with nothing. We may not be able to see anything worthwhile in another Christian or even in our own life, but Jesus sees what we cannot.

This passage has been used many times by Christians when going through rough times, but apply it now as a shot in the arm to get busy.

> In the same way the Spirit also helps our weakness; for we do not know how to pray as we should, but the Spirit Himself intercedes for us with groanings too deep for words; and He who searches the hearts knows what the mind of the Spirit is, because He intercedes for the saints according to the will of God. And we know that God causes all things

to work together for good to those who love God, to those
who are called according to His purpose. (Romans 8:26–28)

Even though no one knows the day or hour of Christ's return, we certainly must be getting close to the midnight hour. There can be no doubt that we are at the least in the season of His return.

Do we really prefer to settle for less? If we knew for a fact that Jesus was coming tomorrow morning at 9 o'clock, we would be scampering to make some changes in our lives. We would be warning loved ones and friends who are lost. We would be getting rid of a lot of the trash in our homes and lives. Guess what? He may come tomorrow or perhaps later, but He is coming, and very unexpectedly. That's what He means by "soon" when He says "I am coming soon."

The Roman Road

I mentioned earlier "the Roman Road." It is a very easy method for Christians to use when witnessing to others about the need to be saved. All the Scriptures are found in the book of Romans.

- Romans 3:23: "For all have sinned and fall short of the glory of God."

  The Lord is telling us in this passage that all of us, without exception, are sinners and fall short of God's glory. You're a sinner. I'm a sinner. None of us has any bragging rights when it comes to our sinful lives. We come to Jesus, recognizing that we are sinners and need to be saved.

- Romans 6:23: "For the wages of sin is death, but the free gift of God is eternal life in Christ Jesus our Lord."

  This verse is saying that mankind suffers physical death because of our sin, and those who don't call upon Jesus to be saved will also suffer eternal death. This eternal death, by the way, is an eternity spent in total existence in the Lake of Fire. However, all who call upon Jesus to be saved will receive God's free gift of eternal life in Heaven with Jesus Christ. It is free to us, but it cost Him more than we will ever know.

- Romans 5:8: "But God demonstrates His own love toward us, in that while we were yet sinners, Christ died for us."

  If this verse doesn't melt your heart, I honestly don't know what can. God is letting us know that regardless of our sinful state and how much we may hate Him, He loves us and is eager to save us—if we will just come to Him and ask.

- Romans 10:9: "That if you confess with your mouth Jesus as Lord, and believe in your heart that God raised Him from the dead, you will be saved."

  If we will truly believe down in our heart that God raised His Son Jesus from the dead and ask Him to be the Lord or Master of our lives, He will save us.

- Romans 5:1: "Therefore, having been justified by faith, we have peace with God through our Lord Jesus Christ."

  Once we are saved we are justified, reconciled, and made right with God, we will have peace with God because of being saved by His Son, the Lord Jesus Christ. He accomplished this for us not by anything we have done or how good we may have been, but only through our faith, our trust, solely in Jesus Christ.

- Romans 8:1: "Therefore there is now no condemnation for those who are in Christ Jesus."

  From the moment we are saved and throughout all eternity, we will never be condemned by God, because we have been saved by the blood of Jesus. Jesus took all our condemnation for us...upon Himself.

- Romans 8:38–39: "For I am convinced that neither death, nor life, nor angels, nor principalities, nor things present, nor things to come, nor powers, nor height, nor depth, nor any other created thing, will be able to separate us from the love of God, which is in Christ Jesus our Lord."

Once we are saved, this verse is the icing on the cake. Nothing can be clearer than what this passage proclaims. It simply says that once we are saved, we are always saved (OSAS) and nothing—NOTHING—will ever separate us from Him. That includes even you and me ("nor any other created thing"). It is impossible for a born-again Christian to ever be unborn. We are His from the moment of our new birth throughout all eternity.

Become familiar with these wonderful verses. If you are uncomfortable in having to turn to different books in the Bible, this will help immensely, since they're all in this one book. As you get more familiar with your Bible, you can add other Scriptures later. During your study time, read the verses before and after each of these. It will help you have a better understanding of what God is saying.

As I close this chapter, I must emphasize that the world is running out of time. Obviously, no one knows the date and time of our Lord's return, but to think we are not in the season of His return is dangerously foolish.

We know that Jesus will come in all His glory, with His Bride, seven years after the Tribulation begins, but we don't know when the Tribulation will begin, other than it will start after Jesus removes His Church from this earth in the Rapture.

We don't know when the Rapture will occur, because there are no signs for the Rapture. All of the signs for today are directed toward the Tribulation period. The Tribulation follows the Rapture. So, since we can now see the dark clouds of prophecy moving across the sky in preparation for the Tribulation storm that will fall upon mankind, how close is the Rapture? I don't know, but don't you think it is time to be looking up?

Jesus admonished those of His day for not recognizing the signs of His First Coming. Jesus promised that He would come a second time, and just as He did with His First Coming, He also provided many prophetic signs of this day. Will you be one who saw the storm approaching and was prepared, or will you ignore all the warnings and face His wrath?

CHAPTER 9

END-TIMES HATRED FOR ISRAEL

BY JIM FLETCHER

WHEN QUEEN ISABELLA DECIDED to expel Spain's Jews (yes, the same Isabella who sent Columbus to find the New World), she didn't expect to receive a prophetic word from one of those Jews.

Don Isaac Abravanel was a man of many talents. Diplomat, confidante to royalty, and financier, Abravanel was also something more important than these things.

He was a Bible scholar.

This is how Benzion Netanyahu, in his masterful profile of Abravanel, describes the showdown between the Jew and the queen, as he sought to change her mind about her harsh treatment of Spain's Jews:

> If Isabella thought that, by measures like expulsion, the Jews could be brought to surrender or to extinction, she was greatly mistaken. He pointed out to her the eternity of the Jewish people, that they had outlived all who had attempted to destroy them, that it was beyond human capacity to destroy the Jewish people, and that those who tried to do so only invited upon themselves divine punishment and disaster. Isabella, who had a mystic vein in her soul, could understand such an argument; but her reaction must have been along the same lines. She too invoked the

name of God, but of course to prove the very opposite of Abravanel's conclusions.

"'Do you believe,' she said to the Jewish representatives, 'that this comes upon you from us? *The Lord hath put this thing into the heart of the king.*'"[108]

Ferdinand.

The king.

Isabella was telling Abravanel that it was the king who had issued the edict and would stand behind it. In modern terms, she threw him under the bus.

Yet Isabella will go down in history, along with her king, as another persecutor of the Jews. (The Catholic Church recognized her as a *Servant of God* in 1974.)

What Isabella couldn't know then, but surely does now, is the thing all Jew haters and persecutors eventually learn. They are like the modern Jew haters of the international community who do not yet know what their predecessors now know all too well.

They have no idea what's coming.

Demonic Diplomacy and the Drive to Divide the Land

When President George Herbert Walker Bush decided to use the political capital he'd gained from the spectacular victory in Desert Storm, one of his priorities was to force the Israelis to the negotiating table with the villainous Palestinian Liberation Organization (PLO).

This he and his advisors did beginning in 1991. Operators like James Baker were never the friend of the Jews, and in fact, because Israel rightly pointed out that Yasser Arafat was an unrepentant terrorist and killer of Jews, negotiations would not work. Remember, the US would not consider negotiating with the Axis powers during World War II, with good reason.

Israeli Prime Minister Yitzhak Shamir, however, knew his back was to the wall. The US threatened to withhold badly needed loans to the Jewish state, an unconscionable move that is a permanent stain on the record of Bush.

(As an aside, Bush was never going to be friendly to the Jewish state. Like many Washington operatives, the former congressman, CIA director, and vice president was an Episcopalian—a denomination that has no use for the Old Testament as real history, certainly not the legitimate history of the Jewish people. It simply didn't resonate with him at all.)

It does no good to appeal to such people based on Scripture. They are scoffers. Therefore, Joel 3:2 has no warning for them:

> I will gather all nations and bring them down to the Valley of Jehoshaphat. There I will put them on trial for what they did to my inheritance, my people Israel, because they scattered my people among the nations and divided up my land.

I once talked to a major evangelical figure who advocates for Israel. He smiled a self-assured smile when he told me that the day before, he had visited with Condoleezza Rice in the White House and forcefully told her of God's provision for Israel, and that the land belonged to them due to divine decree.

I walked away dismayed that this man seemingly did not understand that Rice surely thought he was a lunatic. One simply cannot appeal to Washington politicians and media figures by using biblical arguments. I don't mean that one should stop having the conversations, but I do believe it is futile to debate political solutions by using biblical arguments.

Hillary Clinton has contempt for the Bible and the God of the Bible, so appealing to someone like that by using Joel 3:2 is ludicrous.

Now, at the same time, I want to be clear that I believe Joel 3:2 is absolutely an end-times scenario, a serious and lethal warning to Israel's enemies.

Unfortunately, Washington, Paris, London, Moscow, etc., do not.

Beginning at the Beginning

Before we dive into modern anti-Semitism, what would be the origin of Jew hatred? Because, I have to tell you, logically and rationally, it makes no sense.

For millennia, Jews have contributed to society in ways no one else can claim. Financial bailouts for entire nations, technical innovations, medical breakthroughs…the Jews have probably kept humanity from sliding into some terrestrial black hole.

But consider that the Jews have been hunted, harassed, and murdered for four thousand years, by everyone! That makes no sense.

The Turks slaughtered the Armenians a century ago. Stalin murdered his own people in the twentieth century, as did Mao and Pol Pot. Iran today murders people with its global terror network.

Not one of those groups, though, has been despised 24/7 for thousands of years.

I've had many conversations over the years with Jewish and Christian friends, each wondering…why? Why anti-Semitism?

There is only one real, substantive answer, I believe. As usual, it's found in Scripture.

In Genesis 3, we see the sad and tragic outcome of Adam and Eve's sin. Here, the Lord of history tells them—and the serpent—what punishments will befall them.

To the fallen Lucifer, God says:

> Because you have done this, Cursed are you above all livestock and all wild animals!
>
> You will crawl on your belly and you will eat dust all the days of your life. And I will put enmity between you and the woman, and between your offspring and hers; he will crush your head, and you will strike his heel.

There you have it. Enmity. As my good friend, Dr. G. Thomas Sharp of Creation Truth Foundation, has said, this meant war. All-out, total war for the duration. Not a day off, not an era off.

All the time war. Enmity.

This is the source of anti-Semitism. Nothing else really makes sense.

God was telling the enemy, and all of humanity, exactly what was going to happen. The offspring of the woman (Israel) would be Jesus Christ. The Messiah.

Only a seething, burning, supernatural hatred would be a satisfactory reason for four thousand years of Jew hating. It was set from the beginning.

Modern Devilish Diplomacy

From the time PLO negotiator Saeb Erekat wrapped a "Palestinian scarf" around his neck in order to irritate Israeli counterparts in Madrid, Spain, the devil has been in the details and the big picture, as well.

Succeeding American presidents all put pressure on Israel, although George W. Bush's "letter of understanding" with Ariel Sharon in 2002 gave Israel some wiggle room.

Do you remember the treachery of Wye in 1998? Bill Clinton, a rank liar if there ever was one In the White House, lured Israeli Prime Minister Benjamin Netanyahu—then in his first term—to Maryland's Wye Plantation, he intended to lie.

Netanyahu apparently came in part because Clinton promised that if the Israelis would offer substantial concessions (this was five years after Rabin and Arafat signed the so-called Oslo agreement on the White House lawn), the US would release Jonathan Pollard, imprisoned for passing intelligence about Iran on to Israel.

When Netanyahu offered concessions and was packing to leave—assuming Pollard would also be on the plane—Clinton reneged on the deal. The damage was done.

Israel then went through a series of Oslo spinoffs, once it became clear that the PLO's Yassar Arafat was what he always had been—a blood-soaked terrorist. Next it was the Quartet (the United States, Russia, the European Union, and the United Nations) that still exists, attempting to squeeze suicidal concessions from Israel.

We who believe Scripture and have a biblical worldview believe that these things are brought along by the Lord of History. Consider this from Isaiah 28:

> Wherefore hear the word of the Lord, ye scornful men, that rule this people which is in Jerusalem. Because ye have said, We have made a covenant with death, and with hell are we at agreement; when the overflowing scourge shall pass through, it shall not come unto us: for we have made lies our refuge, and under falsehood have we hid ourselves: Therefore thus saith the Lord God, Behold, I lay in Zion for a foundation a stone, a tried stone, a precious corner stone, a sure foundation: he that believeth shall not make haste. (Isaiah 28:14–15)

The Lord goes on to say that He will break the unholy covenants that His people craft and then do his "strange work" (verse 21) to rescue Israel from destruction.

With regard to the holy city of Jerusalem, I am reminded of something I heard Dave Hunt say many years ago (and which he wrote in the seminal work, *A Cup of Trembling*): The sovereignty of Jerusalem would come to be an obsession for the international community, for only one reason—God said so.

Isn't that beautiful?

Of course, Jerusalem is an historic city, beautiful in its way, etc. But in many ways, it is not as strategic as Brussels or New York. Not perhaps as beautiful as Paris. Not as lively as Los Angeles.

But it is the spot that the Lord of History says is His own personal real estate, and the very place where He will bring history to its conclusion.

Jerusalem would become a cup of trembling for the whole world simply and only because God said so.

There are those of us who love the fact that God is in control of literally everything. But not all love the fact.

In the waning days and even hours of Bill Clinton's presidency, the "Boy from Hope (Arkansas)," Clinton, was attempting to handcuff Israel, in hopes the Jewish state would concede a state to the Palestinians, with a shared Jerusalem. It was offered on a silver platter by Ehud Barak, to Arafat, in early 2001.

Arafat walked away!

He didn't even have a counteroffer to the promised concessions. Barak had offered 94 percent of what the Palestinian Authority officially claimed it wanted!

(As an aside, as recently as 2017, while strolling through the Arab Quarter of Jerusalem's Old City, I bought a refrigerator magnet. It was an image of modern Israel, a map, with the word "Palestine" in black lettering covering the entire thing. The Palestinian leadership has always taught its people that it is entitled to "Palestine," *all* the land from the river to the sea.)

Yet Arafat, who never sought to be a statesman or to engage in state building, less than 100 percent was folly.

In fact, I believe it is one fulfillment of biblical passages like Isaiah 28. Do you see it? Men will craft evil pacts, but the Lord tears them in pieces.

The status of Jerusalem, since Israel's lightning victory in the 1967 Six Day War, has irritated international diplomats, from still shell-shocked Arabs in '67 to modern diplomats like Martin Indyk of the US. It began at the beginning:

> When the UN General Assembly voted on July 4, 1967, to support a Pakistani draft resolution condemning the extension of Israeli law to eastern Jerusalem, the U.S. notably abstained along with 19 other countries.[109]

US President Lyndon Johnson, as was his predecessor, was sympathetic to Israel's plight. After his terms in office, though, the US position would be much more uneven, even dangerous, for Israel.

Jimmy Carter's loathing of Israel, particularly Prime Minister Menachem Begin, is legendary. At the same time, Carter was "losing" Iran, much to the continuing suffering of the world. Iran today is Israel's most lethal enemy.

It was Barack Obama, though, who made Carter seem like a Boy Scout.

Obama wasted no time in his promise to fundamentally transform America. His "apology tour" made a notorious stop in Cairo, Egypt, was met with approval by the Muslim Brotherhood audience. There was also a symbolic and very telling gesture after that.

> One encouraging omen was that Obama did not make a stop next door in Israel during his trip to Egypt, but rather left for Europe after being given a tour of the Pyramids and Sphinx. It was an unusual move for an American leader to be in the Middle East without also paying a call on Jerusalem.[110]

Obama showed his contempt for Israel in this way. His malevolent nature was on full display, and his loathing of Netanyahu will long be remembered.

So, we all are aware of the political intrigue and evil being done on behalf of Israel's enemies. What I'd like to do now is turn to another devilish effort to undermine Israel—one largely unknown, since the story is not really being covered.

I speak of the painful reality that exists today within the Church. This is nothing short of a satanic plot to hurt the Jewish state.

The Evangelicals

I grew up in the heyday of Bible prophecy teaching, in the shadow of Hal Lindsey's first efforts to mainstream this teaching.

In those days, we knew that the end times would be characterized by many things, including a one-world religion.

I understood that to mean the Catholic Church and the New Agers combining forces. I still think that's in play.

However, what I never saw coming (and I think I'm glad I didn't) was the American evangelicals turning away from Israel.

I didn't begin researching this heavily until 2010 or so. A few years before, I'd read *Furnace of the Lord*, by the almost mythical figure, Elisabeth Elliot. She was of course the widow of famed missionary martyr Jim Elliot, who was killed by an Indian tribe in Ecuador in the 1950s.

Elisabeth Elliot in the intervening years had carved out her own fame, first for bravely venturing into the same territory that had claimed her husband, then for her writing skills.

But by the late '60s, she had visited Israel just after the Six Day War, and she wrote about it. Unfortunately, only weeks after the war was over, she began her own investigation. I say unfortunately, because she bought into Arab propaganda.

She relates how she visited an Arab attorney in Jerusalem and listened carefully to his version of events.

> "It is very difficult to get the truth through to the outside," the lawyer told me. "There is a blackout of information. But I will tell you what I believe, and I hope you will put it down carefully."
>
> I was very careful. While coffee was brought to us in tiny cups on a brass tray, he talked and I wrote.
>
> "I am optimistic about Jerusalem. An Israeli withdrawal is essential, and internationalization will never work. But Jerusalem must revert to Arab administration."[111]

You see, Elisabeth Elliot had gone there with a preconceived notion about Jews and Israel. Her background as a member of mainline churches, education at Wheaton, and friends from such places as Gordon-Conwell Theological Seminary didn't endear her to the Jewish people.

In the late 1990s, I attempted to interview her about what she wrote in *Furnace of the Lord* (you really should read it to fully understand her animus for Israel and the Jewish people), but she politely declined. That's what the "Christian Palestinianists" usually do.

She would simply be the forerunner of those who would come after her and really ramp up the Israel hate.

In 2010, I became aware of a film titled *Little Town of Bethlehem*, produced by EGM Films. The film claimed to be an even-handed look at the Israel-Palestinian conflict, but it's anything but that. Though the film's producers cleverly point out they interview Arabs and Israelis, all of them are anti-Israel!

I was then flabbergasted to discover that EGM Films was housed and bankrolled by the Green family, of Hobby Lobby fame. Specifically, EGM Films had been given office space at the corporate headquarters in Oklahoma City by Mart Green.

I drove there to interview the director, Jim Hanon. He told me, among other things, that one of his first interviews for the film was with…wait for it…Sheik Nasrallah of Hezbollah.

That's right, Hanon and his team traveled to Lebanon to ask Hezbollah what they thought of the Israeli-Arab conflict. Hanon even told me that he found Nasrallah to be a fairly charming fellow.

This is mind-boggling.

In 2012, Mark Tooley of the Institute on Religion and Democracy shined a spotlight on this:

> **Washington, DC**—Often identified as strong supporters of Israel, Pentecostal Christians are now being targeted by anti-Israel activists from the Evangelical Left.
>
> Meeting March 1–4 in Virginia Beach, Virginia, the Society for Pentecostal Studies is jointly gathering with Empowered 21, a group of Pentecostal ministry leaders. Themed on "peacemaking and social justice/righteousness," this year's gathering will feature presentations by academics with anti-Israel views, as well as a screening of "Little Town of Bethlehem," a film with a subtle anti-Israel message aimed at usually pro-Israel evangelicals.
>
> **IRD President Mark Tooley commented:**
>
> "The Evangelical Left is eager to dissuade Pentecostals, Charismatics and Evangelicals from their traditional support for Israel.

"Although some Pentecostals rely on their end-times teachings to buttress support for Israel, many (including the vast majority of American Evangelicals) support Israel because it is a democratic ally surrounded by hostile dictatorships.

"The inclusion of several speakers to conduct workshops around themes of liberation theology, which emphasizes Jesus Christ as a political revolutionary rather than an atoning savior, is distressing.

"Almost certainly the vast majority of Pentecostals reject these leftist and anti-Israel themes. But just as in the old-line Protestant denominations decades ago, often church academics pursue political fashion at the expense of faithfulness to their own church."[112]

Notice they were at Regent! What has become clear is that the enemy is going right into the heart of evangelicalism. Honestly? It's a smart strategy. With the failed and failing mainline denominations, and the slide of the Catholic Church into cultural irrelevance, it's smart for Jew haters to attack evangelicalism, the one-time bastion of support for Israel.

None of this is an isolated incident. The same year, pro-Palestinian Christians (led by Lynne Hybels, cofounder of Willow Creek) tried to infiltrate the Calvary Chapels with their seminar program that presents alleged Israeli abuses of Palestinians. Fortunately, Chuck Smith slapped that effort down.

But Chuck has now gone on to glory. What will the future bring here for pro-Israel support?

Another attempt by the enemy in this regard came that same year, 2012, when popular author Donald Miller (*Blue Like Jazz*) accused Israel of war crimes in a blog post he wrote. He actually accused Israeli soldiers of murdering Palestinian women and children, and he accused Israel of controlling the daily calorie intake of Gazans!

None of this is proven and in fact is a lie, yet Miller got away with it. To date, he has not retracted the lies. I attempted to interview him, but got the brush-off.

Then we have Russell Moore, now president of the Southern Baptist Convention's (SBC) Ethics & Religious Liberty Commission (ERLC). I did not know of Moore until reading an article by (then) SBC pastor, Randy White. His assessment of Moore taking over the ERLC in 2013 has been spot-on:

> My word to Southern Baptists who may hope for a pow-
> erful pro-Israel denominational stance coming from the
> ERLC: Good luck! There is no hint Moore would allow it. My
> prediction is subtly anti-Israel messages or Israel-phobia.
> Moore is too much the politician to throw Israel under the
> bus, but he is not a supporter of Israel as a modern Jewish
> state unless it serves the purposes of the new Israel's expan-
> sion and well-being.

Now, here is just a snippet of Moore's own thoughts on the subject, from a January 2009 blog post:

> We need not hold to a dispensationalist view of the
> future restoration of Israel (and I don't) to agree that such
> support is a necessary part of a Christian eschatology (and
> I do).

> Novelist Walker Percy pointed to the continuing exis-
> tence of Jewish people as a sign of God's presence in the
> world. There are no Hittites walking about on the streets of
> New York, he remarked.

> There does appear to be a promise of a future conver-
> sion of Jewish people to Christ (Rom 9–11). The current
> secular state of Israel is not the fulfillment of God's promise
> to Abraham; Jesus is.

There you have it. Yet, how can Moore make the connection with Walker Percy and still dispute the prophetic significance of modern Israel?

I believe he and others like him simply have a problem with Jews. I've had many, many conversations with people like this and in all cases in which we've had dialogue, I discover some irritation with Israel, or the Jewish people.

Moore is another evangelical leader who has ducked interview requests from me. Oddly, I happened upon Mart Green in two different airports and in a hotel lobby a few years ago. This was after repeated requests for an interview through his office. He always deflected my questions.

What does that tell you about their views of Israel and Jews? I was specifically going to ask what he thought about each.

Why not just answer?

In a remarkable book, *New Evangelicals*, Paul Smith sheds much light on issues few in the pews are aware of: how we got to this place. Notice his remark about the ministries of some famous evangelicals:

> The second generation sons of fundamentalists and evangelical pastors who have gone astray include: Daniel Fuller, Frank Schaeffer, Rick Warren, and Chuck Smith Jr. In addition to the problem of fully valuing the doctrine of the inerrancy of the Bible, could it also be a problem with how they interpret end-time events?[113]

This is exactly the problem. All of these men do not see Israel for what she is. And think of their influence! Is it any wonder that thousands of churches have fallen under Warren's spell? He is Southern Baptist, by the way.

If you want to know the key to end-times hatred of Israel and the Jewish people, you need to understand the core problem rests within the heart of American Evangelicalism.

That community is shot through with apostate thinking.

Israel is just one unfortunate casualty of that evil worldview.

It began in Genesis.

It will end in Revelation.

CHAPTER 10

PROPHETIC COALITION FORMING: THE END-TIMES PROPHECIES OF EZEKIEL 38 AND 39

BY BILL SALUS

"Russia, Turkey and Iran hold rival conference
to US-backed Warsaw summit."
—Euronews 2/14/2019

AS THIS 2019 EURONEWS headline points out, Russia, Turkey, and Iran appear to be forming an alliance. Russian President Vladimir Putin, Iranian President Hassan Rouhani, and Turkish President Recep Tayyip Erdogan met in Sochi in November of 2017 and renewed their commitment to Syrian sovereignty, independence, territorial integrity, and unity. They reconvened again in Tehran on September 7, 2018, and in Sochi on February 14, 2019, to plot their respective roles in the reshaping of Syria's future in the aftermath of the eight-year Syrian civil war.

Russia, Turkey, and Iran are members of a coalition identified in the prophecies of Ezekiel 38 and 39. According to Ezekiel 38:1–13, an alignment of nine populations come together in the latter days to invade Israel to take a spoil, to carry away silver and gold, to take away livestock and goods, and to take great plunder. This coalition is sometimes referred to as the "Magog Coalition."

The fact that these strange bedfellow countries of Sunni Turkey, Shia Iran, and multifaith Russia are coming together as Syria's "guarantor countries" has some of today's popular Bible prophecy teachers sounding the "Ezekiel 38 is coming soon" alarm!

This chapter will provide an overview of the prophecies presented In Ezekiel 38 and 39. In addition, the potential timing of the fulfillment of these biblical predictions will be explored. Lastly, observations will be made and poignant questions will be asked at various sections of this writing that will be addressed at the end of the chapter. This Q-and-A aspect is intended to provide the reader with a deeper study of these profound Ezekiel 38 and 39 foretellings.

When it comes to studying the prophecies contained in Ezekiel 38 and 39, it's important to recognize that they can all be interpreted literally. At no point is it necessary to allegorize or spiritualize these predictions. The common-sense Golden Rule of Interpretation applies, which says:

> When the plain sense of Scripture makes common sense, seek no other sense; therefore, take every word at its primary, ordinary, usual, literal meaning unless the facts of the immediate context, studied in the light of related passages and axiomatic and fundamental truths, indicate clearly otherwise.
>
> —Dr. David L. Cooper (1886–1965), founder of the Biblical Research Society[114]

Overview of Ezekiel 38 and 39

This section will provide a synopsis of the Ezekiel 38 and 39 prophecies. Open your Bibles to follow along, as this is only a summary rather than a verse-by-verse commentary. This overview will be categorized as follows:

- The identities of the Gog of Magog coalition (Ezekiel 38:1–7)

- The conditions in Israel before the Gog of Magog invasion (Ezekiel 38:8–13)

- The evil plan of Gog and his coalition (Ezekiel 38:10–12)

- The conditions in Israel during the divine defeat of the invasion (Ezekiel 38:14–39:8)

- The conditions in Israel in the aftermath of the invasion (Ezekiel 39:9–21)

The identities of the Gog of Magog coalition (Ezekiel 38:1-7)

Ezekiel 38 and 39 involves at least fifteen primary participants. They are:

- **The Victor**: God.

- **The (intended) victim**: Israel.

- **The nine invaders**: Magog, Rosh, Meshech, Tubal, Persia, Cush, Put, Gomer, and Togarmah.

- **The four protestors**: Sheba, Dedan, the merchants of Tarshish, and their young lions.

Identifying the modern-day equivalents of these nine invaders that Ezekiel listed in the vocabulary of his time has been the task undertaken by several of today's top Bible prophecy experts, such as Dr. Arnold Fruchtenbaum, Joel Rosenberg, Dr. Ron Rhodes, Dr. Andy Woods, Dr. Mark Hitchcock, and yours truly, to name just a few. The general consensus as to which countries these Ezekiel invaders represents is below.

1. **Magog** – Parts of the former Soviet Union and the "-stans," such as Kazakhstan and Afghanistan.

    Dr. Ron Rhodes writes the following:

    > Magog, mentioned in the Table of Nations in Genesis 10:2, probably constitutes the geographical area in the southern portion of the former Soviet Union. Many scholars take Magog to generally refer to an area near the Black Sea or the Caspian Sea.[115]

Dr. Andy Woods inscribes,

> Josephus identifies Magog as the Scythians, saying "Magog founded those that from him were named Magogites, but who are by the Greeks called Scythians." Any encyclopedia will tell you that the Scythians migrated from central Asia to southern Russia around the eighth to the seventh century B.C. So I believe that the Scythians represent the nations of central Asia. These nations would represent the various "stans," such as Kazakhstan and Afghanistan, as well as the Ukraine.[116]

2. **Rosh** – Russia

For several reasons, Rhodes, Hitchcock, Woods, and many others believe that Rosh is Russia. One reason is that Ezekiel 39:2 points out that Rosh invades Israel from the "uttermost parts of the north." Directionally on a map, that favors Russia. Another compelling factor to consider is provided by Dr. Mark Hitchcock, who writes:

> Rosh was apparently a well-known place in Ezekiel's day. In the sixth century B.C., when Ezekiel wrote his prophecy, several bands of the Rosh people lived in an area to the north of the Black Sea. After providing extensive evidence of the origin and early history of the Rosh people, and then tracing them through the centuries, Clyde Billington concludes: "Historical, ethnological, and archaeological evidence all favor the conclusion that the Rosh people of Ezekiel 38–39 were the ancestors of the Rus/Ros people of Europe and Asia…. The Rosh people who are mentioned in Ezekiel 38–39 were well-known to ancient and medieval writers by a variety of names which all derived from the names of Tiras and Rosh…. Those Rosh people who lived to the north of the Black Sea in ancient and medieval times were called the Rus/Ros/Rox/Aorsi from very early times…. From this mixture with Slavs and with the Varangian Rus in

the 9th century, the Rosh people of the area north of the Black Sea formed the people known today as the Russians.[117]

3. **Meshech** - Turkey

4. **Tubal** – Turkey

Hitchcock writes:

> Meshech and Tubal are identified in ancient history with the Mushki and Tabal of the Assyrians, and the Moschi and Tibareni of the Greeks who inhabited territory that is in the modern nation of Turkey.[118]

5. **Persia** – Iran (Persia was renamed Iran in 1935)

6. **Cush** – Ethiopia and Sudan

Dr. Ron Rhodes says.

> Yet another nation that is part of the end-times northern military coalition against Israel is Ethiopia (NASB) or Cush (NIV) (Ezekiel 38:5). These terms refer to the geographical territory just south of Egypt on the Nile River—what is today known as Sudan.[119]

Dr. Andy Woods pens:

> The next nation named by Ezekiel is Cush. In *The Antiquities of the Jews*, Josephus defines Cush as Ethiopia, explaining, "For of the four sons of Ham, time has not at all hurt the name of Cush; for the Ethiopians, over whom he reigned, are even at this day, both by themselves and by all men in Asia, called Cushites."… "The designation, Ethiopia, is misleading for it did not refer to the modern state of Ethiopia…Cush…bordered Egypt on the S[outh]…or modern Sudan. Thus, Cush is most likely modern-day Sudan."[120]

7. **Put** – Libya, Tunisia, Algeria, and maybe Morocco

Joel Rosenberg suggests:

> Put may include "the modern-day countries of Algeria and Tunisia, though it may not have extended as far as Morocco."[121]

8. **Gomer** – Turkey or possibly Germany

Dr. Arnold Fruchtenbaum writes that Gomer:

> …is located in present-day Germany. This too was the rabbinic view. The Midrash calls Gomer Germania, and that is also the way the Talmud refers to Gomer.[122]

9. **Togarmah** – Turkey

Dr. Andy Woods writes:

> Josephus equates Togarmah with Phrygia. He notes, "…Thrugramma the Thrugrammeans, who, as the Greeks resolved, were named Phrygians."… "Phrygia is the area between Galatia and Asia, which would also be modern-day Turkey. Therefore, Togarmah also should be equated with modern-day Turkey.[123]

> Dr. Ron Rhodes summarizes who he believes the Ezekiel 38 coalition is comprised of: "Based on our best information, I believe the coalition will be led by Russia, and will include Iran, Sudan, Turkey, Libya, Kazakhstan, Kyrgyzstan, Uzbekistan, Turkmenistan, Tajikistan, Armenia, and possibly northern Afghanistan.[124]

Observations:

- The Ezekiel invaders form an "Outer Ring" of nations, none of which share common borders with Israel. (Refer to the "Outer Ring Ezekiel 38" image.)

(Outer Ring Ezekiel 38 Image superimposes the Ezekiel 38 invaders by their ancient names over their modern-day equivalents)

- None of these nations has been notorious historical enemies of Israel (excluding perhaps Persia at the time of Esther around 486–468 BC).

- These invaders are mostly non-Arab peoples.

- The coalition is comprised of many Muslim populations.

Question #1: Why does Russia need such a big coalition to invade tiny little Israel, which presently is about the size of the state of New Jersey? Russia, Turkey, Iran, Tunisia, and Libya, not including the other invaders, have populations that currently total over three hundred million. When you compare this to Israel's estimated Jewish population of about 6.5 million, it seems a bit like overkill.

Question #2: Why doesn't Ezekiel include the "Inner Circle" of Arab states that share common borders with Israel among the Gog of Magog invaders? After all, these Arabs have been the notorious enemies of Israel since time immemorial. Ezekiel is familiar with these Arab populations; he lists them by their historic names at least eighty-nine times in his forty-eight chapters, but seemingly intentionally omits them among the lineup of the Ezekiel invaders.

Question #3: If the Ezekiel invasion is poised to happen soon, then why are Iran's proxies not listed in the Ezekiel 38 coalition? Syria, Hezbollah in Lebanon, Hamas in the Gaza, and the Houthis in Yemen are MISSING IN ACTION!

The conditions in Israel before the Gog of Magog invasion (Ezekiel 38:8–13)

Ezekiel 38:8–13 includes the telling verses that describe what Israel looks like geopolitically and socioeconomically prior to the Gog of Magog invasion. In a summary, Ezekiel 38:8–13 informs that, at the time of the Gog of Magog invasion, Israel will be:

1. Regathered from the nations

2. In the "Latter Years"

3. Brought back from the "sword" (of persecution)

4. In the land of "Israel," which will have "long been desolate"

5. Dwelling in the "midst," or center, of the Promised Land

These five conditions have either been met or are currently being met, depending on what exactly Ezekiel meant by the "midst" of the land. The Hebrew word used is *Tabbur*, which also means the "center." Technically speaking, the midst or center of the Promised Land, as per Genesis 15:18, could today include the West Bank, which is mostly under Palestinian control, and perhaps the country of Jordan. Israel is not presently in control of these areas, but according to Obadiah 1:19–20, Jeremiah 49:2, and Zephaniah 2:8–9, someday the Jewish state will expand into these territories. However, the conditions #6 to #9 below have not been fulfilled yet.

6. Israel must be "peaceful people" who are "dwelling securely."

7. The Jewish state must exist without "walls, bars nor gates."

8. The country must possess great wealth comprised of "gold and silver" and have "acquired livestock and goods."

9. Israel must be a very wealthy country possessing "great plunder and booty," because that is what the Ezekiel invaders are coming after.

Observations:

- Presently, Israel IS NOT dwelling without "walls, bars nor gates." Inside the country exists a partition wall that is over four hundred miles long, which at some points is twenty feet tall and filled with concrete. This wall serves to separate Palestinian terror out from Israel proper. There are also security checkpoints at various places inside of Israel. Below are a few telling headlines about Israel's border and security walls.

    ◊   "Israel Completes Lebanon Border Wall around Metulla" – 6/12/2012, *Times of Israel*

    ◊   "Israel Resumes Construction of Wall along Lebanon Border" – 4/10/2018, *Middle East Monitor*

    ◊   "Israel Starts Massive Fence on Southern Border with Jordan" – 1/20/2016, *Times of Israel*

    ◊   "Israel Starts Building Sea Barrier to Defend against Gaza Attacks" – 5/27/2018, *Times of Israel*

    ◊   "Israel Unveils Plans for 40-mile Underground Wall around Gaza" – 1/18/2018, *Telegraph*

    ◊   "Palestinian Protesters Breach Israel-Gaza Border Fence; 3 Killed, Hundreds Injured in Clashes" – 4/27/2018, *Los Angeles Times*

Observe that most of the headline dates above are relatively recent. This suggests that Israel isn't presently dwelling securely. Otherwise, it would not need to construct new walls or extend existing walls. Also, because of the existence of these walls, Hezbollah and Hamas have been reduced to digging tunnels in order to infiltrate Israel in the event of a future ground war.

Moreover, the Jewish state IS NOT "dwelling securely" at this time. It is surrounded by Arab countries and terrorist populations that don't enable them to dwell safely. Ezekiel tells us ten chapters earlier, in Ezekiel 28, what will have to happen for Israel to dwell securely:

> "And there shall no longer be a pricking brier or a painful thorn for the house of Israel from among all who are around them, who despise them. Then they shall know that I am the Lord God." Thus says the Lord God: "When I have gathered the house of Israel from the peoples among whom they are scattered, and am hallowed in them in the sight of the Gentiles, then they will dwell in their own land which I gave to My servant Jacob. And they **will dwell safely** there, build houses, and plant vineyards; yes, they **will dwell securely, when I execute judgmens on all those around them who despise them**. Then they shall know that I am the Lord their God." (Ezekiel 28:14–16; emphasis added)

These verses tell us that Israel will dwell securely when their surrounding Arab neighbors who despise the Jewish state have judgments executed upon them. Ezekiel 38:8, 11 and Ezekiel 28:26 (two times) uses the same Hebrew words, *yashab betach*, to emphasize that Israel will indeed dwell securely.

However, in Ezekiel 28:26, Israel dwells safely after its Arab neighbors are judged, but in Ezekiel 38, Israel dwells safely in advance of the Gog of Magog invasion! Until Israel dwells securely without walls, bars, or gates, Ezekiel 38 will not find final fulfillment.

Question #4: When and how will God execute judgments on Israel's neighbors who despise them so that Israel can dwell securely and eliminate its walls, bars, and gates? And who are these despisers of the Jewish state?

The evil plan of Gog and his coalition (Ezekiel 38:10-12)

> Thus says the Lord God: "On that day it shall come to pass that thoughts will arise in your mind, and you will make an evil plan: You will say, 'I will go up against a land of unwalled villages; I will go to a peaceful people, who dwell safely, all of them dwelling without walls, and having neither bars nor gates'—to take plunder and to take booty, to stretch out your hand against the waste places that are again inhabited, and against a people gathered from the nations, who have acquired livestock and goods, who dwell in the midst of the land. (Ezekiel 38:10-12, NKJV)

We're informed in Ezekiel 38:10 that when the Israelis are a peaceful people who are dwelling securely without walls, bars, or gates, Gog, the title of the leader of the Ezekiel 38 coalition, devises a maniacal plan against Israel.

Gog's "evil plan" is to assemble a formidable strategic coalition in order to invade Israel for the sake of material gain, "to take plunder and to take booty." Although some of the tactical measures to invade Israel are missing in the prophetic details, it is possible that in the initial stages of the evil plan is an attempt to choke off Israel's ability to export its commerce internationally. This can be deduced by considering the geographical locations of the coalition members and a clue provided in Ezekiel 38:13 quoted below.

> Sheba, Dedan, the merchants of Tarshish, and all their young lions will say to you, "Have you come to take plunder? Have you gathered your army to take booty, to carry away silver and gold, to take away livestock and goods, to take great plunder?"

In this verse, the four protestors, Sheba (Yemen), Dedan (Saudi Arabia), Tarshish (probably the United Kingdom), and their young lions (perhaps the USA),[125] are concerned about what they are witnessing in the developmental stages. To these four, it appears that Russia has assembled its formidable coalition and is advancing toward Israel to fill their coffers with Israel's booty and great plunder. The merchants of Tarshish, not the entertainers, athletes, or politicians of Tarshish, are lodging their protest. This implies that at least Tarshish has commercial interests at stake.

What these protestors are observing with bated breath is the advance against Israel of a coalition that borders every strategic waterway and potential pathway that Israel could use to export its commerce to international markets. This alignment of nations can blockade these important water arteries. Turkey, Libya, Tunisia, and Algeria surround the Mediterranean Sea. Iran can blockade the Persian Gulf. Ethiopia and Sudan can hinder shipments passing through the Red Sea.

Observation:

- The following assessment involves some speculation on my part, but perhaps Gog's evil plan has a layered approach. *First*, form a coalition of mostly Muslim countries that dislike Israel. *Second*, make sure they are strategically located geographically to choke off Israel's ability to export its commerce internationally. *Third*, invade Israel to take its booty and great plunder.

Question #5: What is the plunder and booty that the Russian-led coalition will covet? And does Israel possess it?

The Conditions in Israel During the Divine Defeat of the Invasion (Ezekiel 38:14–39:8)

These eighteen Ezekiel 38 and 39 verses explain how God intervenes on behalf of Israel and supernaturally defeats the Magog invaders. The Gog of Magog invasion will be the most massive Mideast invasion of all time. To the onlooker, it will be a spectacle like none they ever heard or seen before.

Just when the hordes of Ezekiel 38 invaders are marching upon the soil of Israel, with all their weapons of warfare locked and loaded, something catches them completely off guard. Television viewers around the world become shocked to see that a massive earthquake rocks the area! The sequence of supernatural catastrophes that follow are explained in Ezekiel 38:14–39:8 and summarized below.

1. A great earthquake occurs in the land of Israel.

2. The mountains are thrown down.

3. The steep places fall, and every wall falls to the ground.

4. The Ezekiel invaders panic and kill one another: "Every man's sword will be against his brother."

5. This brings about pestilence and bloodshed.

6. Then pelting rain pours down on the invading troops.

7. This causes severe flooding.

8. The rain manifests into great hailstones of fire and brimstone.

Ezekiel 38:19–20 says there will be a "great earthquake in the land of Israel." The magnitude of the quake will cause all men upon the face of the whole earth to "shake." Affected *mountains* will crumble and *walls* will fall. When was the last time you saw mountains (plural) topple as the result of an earthquake? Also, who might be killed when the affected mountains are thrown down?

Imagine watching this spectacular scene that interrupts the advance of the Magog invaders on your TV set. What is about to follow is all supernatural. Neither the IDF nor the American military plays any role in what happens next.

Ezekiel 38:21 declares that "every man's sword will be against his brother." This is alluding to the Magog invaders. Apparently, the powerful repercussions from the seismic event cause panic among the troops, who then begin attacking one another. This is much more than "friendly fire." This is an illustration of what similarly happened in Israel's history when Gideon's three-hundred-man army fought against the Midianites. Judges 7:22 says "the LORD set every man's sword against his companion throughout the whole camp." Judges 8:10 says "for one hundred and twenty thousand men who drew the sword had fallen."

Ezekiel 38:22 says, "I will rain down on him, on his troops, and on the many peoples who are with him, flooding rain, great hailstones, fire, and brimstone." As if the earthquake, which will topple mountains, crumble walls, and cause the killing of one another isn't enough, matters go from terrible to horrendous for the invaders. Flooding rains accompanied by stone-sized hail pummels the invaders. Fire and brimstone finish them off. By the time all the supernatural events above conclude:

1. The Magog invaders are destroyed.

2. The television watchers around the world are in shock.

3. Israel is counting their blessings and praising Jehovah the God of Abraham, Isaac, and Jacob.

Ezekiel 39:1–6 provides more graphic details about what happens to the invaders, and Ezekiel 39:7–8 sheds light on the purpose of the experience.

> So I will make My holy name known in the midst of My people Israel, and I will not let them profane My holy name anymore. Then the nations shall know that I am the Lord, the Holy One in Israel. Surely it is coming, and it shall be done," says the Lord God. This is the day of which I have spoken. (Ezekiel 39:7–8)

It will be hard for anyone who watched or experienced this event first-hand to walk away with any conclusion other than what is said in these two verses. After the Magog invaders are divinely defeated, it will be undeniable that the God of the Bible singlehandedly protected His people, Israel, in the land of Israel. The nations of the world will have no other recourse but to recognize this. This is the marquee event the Lord has chosen to notify the nations, including Israel, that He is the one true God, the upholder of the unconditional Abrahamic Covenant, and thus the promise-keeper of all believers.

"My people Israel," "the Holy One," and "in Israel" identify three integral components of the unconditional covenant that God made with Abraham in Genesis 15. Numerous unsuccessful attempts throughout history have been made to annihilate the Jews, "My people Israel," profane the name of God, "the Holy One," and dispossess Jews from the Promised Land "in Israel."

> On the same day the Lord made a covenant with Abram, saying: "To your descendants [My people Israel—the chosen people] I [the Holy One] have given this [Promised] land [of Israel], from the river of Egypt to the great river, the River Euphrates." (Genesis 15:18, NKJV; emphasis added)

Notice that Ezekiel 39:7 reads, "the nations shall know that I am the Lord." Although the supernatural defeat of the Ezekiel invaders makes it evident that the God of the Bible is the Lord, it doesn't mean that mankind at large accepts the Lord. Several predictions that follow Ezekiel 38, like in the seventh bowl judgment of Revelation, point out that many people remain in rebellion against the Lord.

The seventh bowl judgment:

> And great hail from heaven fell upon men, each hailstone about the weight of a talent. Men blasphemed God because of the plague of the hail, since that plague was exceedingly great. (Revelation 16:21)

Some teach that the hailstone attacks from Ezekiel 38 and Revelation 16 are the same, but the great hail from this bowl judgment is not the same as that of Ezekiel 38:22. The Revelation 16:21 hail judgment happens near the end of the seven-year Tribulation, which is sometime after the destruction of the Ezekiel invaders.

Conditions in Israel in the Aftermath of the Invasion (Ezekiel 39:9–21)

Ezekiel 39:9–21 explains what happens in Israel in the aftermath of God's supernatural victory over the Magog invaders.

- **Israel burns the enemy's weapons for seven years.**

  Ezekiel 39:9–10 clues us in to the types of weaponry the invaders possess. The weapons must be of the sort that Israel will be able to convert into fuel. Ezekiel says that "they will make fire with them for seven years." The picture is of energy provision for the entire nation, rather than a few isolated households. Verse 9 says "those who dwell in the cities" utilize this converted weapons-grade fuel.

The use of the pronouns "they" and "those" identify the Israelis. It is the Israelis that are utilizing the leftover weapons of the invaders for civilian purposes. The Magog invaders intended to use the weapons to harm Israel, but the Lord intends to use them for Israel's good.

The widespread use and lengthy, seven-year span suggest that the weapons must be far more sophisticated than wooden bows and arrows, which would undoubtedly only last a short while. I mention this because some expositors today limit the weapons to wooden ones. I doubt that nuclear nonproliferation will reduce Russian arsenals to wood between now and then. In fact, Russia is still building and testing nuclear weapons according to the July 19, 2018, headline from *The Hill* below.

Russia Announces New Nuclear Weapons Tests Days after Trump-Putin Summit

The missiles and rockets that are being converted to fuel in Ezekiel 39:9-10 probably include the ABCs of weaponry—atomic, biological, and chemical. We can presume this because these types of weapons already exist inside the arsenals of Russia and some of their cohorts. Additionally, the dead soldiers appear to require Hazmat (Hazardous Materials) teams to assist with their burial according to Ezekiel 39:14–16. The fascinating fact is that whatever the weapons configuration, Israel will possess the technological know-how to convert them into national energy. Today, whether it is cell phones or irrigation techniques, Israel is on the cutting-edge of technological advances.

- **Israel buries the Magog invaders for seven months.**

Ezekiel 39:11–16 describes the location of the mass burial grounds of the destroyed armies of Gog. A valley east of what is probably the Dead Sea is destined to be named Hamon Gog, which means the "hordes or multitudes" of Gog, in Hebrew. Why I believe it refers to a valley in modern-day Jordan is explained in the chapter called "Greater Israel" of my *Psalm 83: The Missing Prophecy Revealed, How Israel Becomes the Next Mideast Superpower* book.

We also find in Ezekiel 39:11–16 that the Israelis will be burying the dead for seven months in order to cleanse the land. This could imply two things. *One*, the hordes of Gog's dead soldiers are contaminated, which would require a professional quarantined burial. This contamination could come from either the fallout from their atomic, biological and/or chemical weapons, or the deteriorating corpses strewn across the battlefield. *Two*, the Jews are adhering to their ancient levitical law, according to Numbers 19:11–22 and Deuteronomy 21:1–9. These verses set forth specifications about the appropriate handling of dead bodies lying on the land of Israel.

Ezekiel 39:11 points out that Israel gains renown as the world witnesses the burning of the weapons and the burial of the hordes of God.

"Indeed all the people of the land will be burying,
and they will gain renown for it on the day that I am
glorified," says the Lord God. (Ezekiel 39:11)

Ezekiel 39:17–20 is an invitation "to every sort of bird and to every beast of the field" to partake of the sacrificial meal of the "flesh" and "blood" of the invaders. This passage is not for the faint of heart. Some try to connect this feast with the similar sacrificial meal described in Revelation 19:17–18, but there are stark differences.

1. Ezekiel's sacrificial meal involves the death of Gog, a Russian leader, but the Revelation 19 account is dealing with the Antichrist of

European descent—who, according to Daniel 9:26, comes out of the revived Roman Empire.

2. Ezekiel's meal is dealing with the carnage of only the Gog of Magog invaders, but the Revelation scenario includes "the flesh of kings, the flesh of captains, the flesh of mighty men, the flesh of horses and of those who sit on them, and the flesh of all people free and slave, both small and great."

Ezekiel 39:21–29 concludes the chapter with a recap of some Jewish history and a promise to the faithful remnant of Israel whom the Lord will pour His spirit upon in the end. The Holy Spirit will be bestowed to the faithful remnant when they recognize Christ as their Messiah. This is one of the rewards for receiving Jesus Christ as Savior (see John 14:16–17, 26, 15:26, 16:7).

Observation:

- The Ezekiel 39:17 birds of prey appear to be already gathering in Israel. This implies that the Ezekiel 38 invasion, which concludes with the sacrificial meal, draws near. If this is the case, this makes sense because the local birds, rather than those that have to migrate from great distances, would be the immediate benefactors of the sacrificial feast. Some interesting headlines below reference the increased bird populations existing in Israel.[126]

    ◊   May 14, 2007, *Haaretz* – "The Iraqi Bird(s) That Made Aliyah (to Israel)"

    ◊   January 25, 2012, *Haaretz* – "Long-lost Starlings Are Flying Back to Israel"

    ◊   February 26, 2016, *Times of Israel* – "Why Israel Is a Pilgrimage Site for Birds and Bird-Watchers."

    ◊   January 23, 2017, *Haaretz* – "Israel's 500 Million Birds: The World's Eighth Wonder"

◊ April 25, 2017, *Jerusalem Post* – "Bird Makes a Rare Stop in Israel after Wrong Turn"

◊ July 24, 2017, *Jerusalem Post* – "Israeli Vulture Population on the Rise"

Ezekiel 38 and 39 provides some of the most important, well explained, and easy-to-understand prophecies in the Bible. This is because these chapters foretell of the coming marquee event, whereby the Lord upholds His Holy Name before the watchful eyes of humankind. The event is so epic that the Lord achieves the undivided attention of mankind. Israelis continuing to inhabit their homeland of Israel, after the prophetic wars of Psalm 83 and Ezekiel 38, will provide humanity with ample evidence to recognize that the God of the Bible is the one true God!

The timing of Ezekiel 38 is critical. It occurs in the end times when the Promised Land of Israel hosts the chosen people (Israeli Jews). The Rapture of the Church could occur before, during, or after the event. My personal view is that the Ezekiel 38 is a prophecy that occurs after the Rapture, but prior to the seven-year Tribulation period. I non-dogmatically believe that Ezekiel 38 finds fulfillment prior to the implementation of the Antichrist's "mark of the Beast" campaign in Revelation 13:11–18.

The Timing of Ezekiel 38 and 39

Below are a few of my reasons for adopting the post-Rapture, but pretribulation time-gap view for the timing of Ezekiel 38. There exists a mysterious lapse of unspecified time between the Rapture and the seven-year Tribulation period. This is because it's not the Rapture that starts the Tribulation. Rather, this span is initiated by the confirmation of the false covenant described in Isaiah 28:15–18 and Daniel 9:27. I write about this time gap in my book entitled, *The NEXT Prophecies*.

1. *My People Israel* – God calls the Israelis "My people Israel" three times in Ezekiel 38 and 39 (Ezekiel 38:14, 16 and 39:7). This suggests that the true believers within the Church need not be present. This is all

about Israel and the Israelis. This is one reason I believe the Rapture could occur before Ezekiel 38 finds fulfillment.

2. *Upholding His Holy Name* – The fact that the Lord chooses this end-times episode to uphold His Holy Name suggests that timing is important. Demonstrating His holiness by delivering Israel from the most massive Mideast invasion in all of history up to that point gives humanity the opportunity to believe in God before being deceived by the Antichrist.

The Antichrist becomes a central figure throughout the seven-year Tribulation period. He rises to power through great deception, according to 2 Thessalonians 2:8–12. A pre-Tribulation fulfillment of Ezekiel 38 provides people with a clear choice between believing in the holy, promise-keeping God of the Bible or the unholy deceiver, the Antichrist.

If the Rapture happens prior to Ezekiel 38 and Ezekiel 38 finds fulfillment prior to the Tribulation, then the two arguments below could be forwarded:

1. The Lord is a promise keeper - The Lord kept His promises to Christian believers by catching them up into Heaven in the Rapture as per 1 Thessalonians 4:15–18, 1 Corinthians 15:50–52, John 14:1–6, and elsewhere.

2. The Lord is a covenant keeper – The Lord upheld His unconditional covenant with Abraham by protecting the chosen people in their Promised Land as per Genesis 15:18 and elsewhere.

In addition to the reasons above, I hold to the teaching that Ezekiel 39:9 presents another clue to the pretribulation timing of Ezekiel 38 and 39.

> Then those who dwell in the cities of Israel will go out and set on fire and burn the weapons, both the shields and bucklers, the bows and arrows, the javelins and spears; and they will make fires with them for seven years. (Ezekiel 39:9)

These Ezekiel verses say that Israelis, "those who dwell in the cities of Israel," will make fires with the enemy's weapons. Israelis appear to utilize these weapons for energy consumption for seven years. This will be no problem during the peaceful first half of the Tribulation, but not likely during the perilous second half, because Jews will be fleeing for their lives, rather than harnessing this energy.

Concerning the separation point between the first and second halves of the Tribulation period, Christ warned the Israelis in Matthew 24:15–22 that they should flee for their lives when they witness the "abomination of desolation," because that signaled a period of "Great Tribulation" was coming. This abominable event occurs at the midpoint of the Tribulation.

> Therefore when you see the "abomination of desolation," spoken of by Daniel the prophet, standing in the holy place (whoever reads, let him understand), then let those who are in Judea flee to the mountains. Let him who is on the housetop not go down to take anything out of his house. And let him who is in the field not go back to get his clothes. But woe to those who are pregnant and to those who are nursing babies in those days! And pray that your flight may not be in winter or on the Sabbath. For then there will be great tribulation, such as has not been since the beginning of the world until this time, no, nor ever shall be. And unless those days were shortened, no flesh would be saved; but for the elect's sake those days will be shortened. (Matthew 24:15–22)

These Matthew 24 verses are part of the reason the second half of the Tribulation is commonly called the "Great Tribulation." It stands to reason that if Christ instructs Israelis to flee immediately for safety at the midpoint of the Tribulation period, the refugees won't be stopping along the way to convert more of these weapons in the process. If anything, they might pick up a weapon to use it, rather than burn it.

Therefore, some scholars suggest that Ezekiel 38 and 39 must conclude, not commence, no later than three and one-half years before the seven years of Tribulation even begins. This allows the Jews seven full years to burn the weapons before they begin fleeing for their lives.

Ezekiel 38 and 39 Questions and Answers

As promised, this closing section will answer the five questions that were previously asked throughout this chapter. Most all of the answers below are related to the strong possibility that, prior to the fulfillment of Ezekiel 38, several other prophecies will have already happened. I write about these potential pre-Ezekiel 38 foretellings in my book entitled, *The NOW Prophecies*. As the word "NOW" suggests, these are the prophecies that lack any further preconditions. Thus, they could happen at the present time.

The fulfillment of these NOW prophecies will likely result in a future *greater*, *safer*, and *wealthier* Israel, like the one described in Ezekiel 38:8–13. The NOW prophecies include, but are not limited to, the following globally impacting events. They are:

1. Disaster in Iran – (Jeremiah 49:34–39)

2. ~~Destruction of Damascus – (Isaiah 17; Jeremiah 49:23–27)~~

3. Final Arab-Israeli War – (Psalm 83)

4. Toppling of Jordan – (Jeremiah 49:1–6; Zephaniah 2:8–10; Ezekiel 25:14)

5. Terrorization of Egypt – (Isaiah 19:1–18)

6. Emergence of the exceedingly great Israeli army – (Ezekiel 37:10, 25:14; Obadiah 1:18),

7. Expansion of Israel – (Obadiah 1:19–20; Jeremiah 49:2; Zephaniah 2:9; Isaiah 19:18)

8. Vanishing of the Christians – (1 Corinthians 15:51–52; 1 Thessalonians 4:15–18)

9. Emergence of a greater, safer, and wealthier Israel – (Ezekiel 38:8–13)

10. Decline of America (Ezekiel 38:13; the USA could be the "young lions" of Tarshish, which is pointed out in the *NOW Prophecies* book).

Question 1: Why does Russia need such a big coalition to invade tiny little Israel, which presently is about the size of the state of New Jersey?

Answer 1: Russia needs to formulate a big coalition to invade Israel because tiny little Israel no longer exists. It has been replaced by a **greater, safer,** and **wealthier** Israel. This transformation likely results from the following events.

1. The Israeli Defense Forces (IDF) have become an exceedingly great army in fulfillment of Ezekiel 37:10, 25:14; Obadiah 1:18; Zechariah 12:4–6; Isaiah 11:12–14 and elsewhere.

2. The IDF accomplished this by decisively defeating the Arabs in Psalm 83, destroying Damascus in Isaiah 17:1, 9, 14 and toppling Jordan in Jeremiah 49:2 and Zephaniah 2:8–9.

3. Furthermore, the tiny Jewish state of 2019 has become a significantly larger Israel. This resulted from annexing the formerly occupied Arab lands identified in Obadiah 1:19–20; Zephaniah 2:9; Isaiah 19:18; and Jeremiah 49:2.

Question 2: Why doesn't Ezekiel include the "Inner Circle Circle" of Arab states that share common borders with Israel among the Gog of Magog invaders?

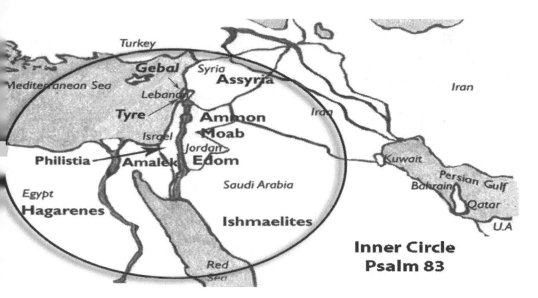

(*Inner Circle Psalm 83 image superimposes the Psalm 83 confederacy by their ancient names over their modern-day equivalents*)

Answer 2: Oddly, Ezekiel doesn't list the Arab states that mostly share common borders with Israel within the nine-member Magog coalition. I call these Arab countries, the "Inner Circle." Ezekiel's seemingly intentional omission is shocking because these Arabs have been Israel's historical enemies and the Magog coalition needs to cross through these Arab states to invade Israel.

The likely reason the Inner Circle is not included is because they will have previously been defeated by the exceedingly great IDF in fulfillment of the Psalm 83 war and the other related NOW prophecies. As such, the Arabs are of no military value to the Ezekiel invaders. These defeated Arabs are either killed, imprisoned (POWs), or exiled as refugees.

In the aftermath of the IDF victory the Jewish state will have expanded territorially, which was previously pointed out in Answer 1. (Refer to the "Inner Circle Psalm 83" image).

Israel has historical precedence for expanding its borders after conquering its enemies. They did this around 3,300 years ago during the conquests of Canaan by Joshua and about 3,000 years ago during the time of Kings David and Solomon. Israel also did this in the aftermath of the Six Day War in June of 1967. The Jews feel justified in annexing neighboring lands because:

1. Victors are not prevented from capturing the plunder, booty, and territories they conquer.

2. Expanded borders offers Israel greater national security.

3. The land in question was promised to their patriarchs Abraham, Isaac, and Jacob for an everlasting possession (Genesis 15:18, 17:7–8, 35:12).

Question 3: If the Ezekiel invasion is poised to happen soon, then why are Iran's proxies not listed in the Ezekiel 38 coalition?

Answer 3: Some of today's prophecy commentators teach that Ezekiel 38 could happen now. If this is the case, then why are Iran's proxies, Syria, Hezbollah in Lebanon, Hamas in Gaza, Shiite sections in Iraq and the Houthis in Yemen, not listed in the Magog Coalition. After all, Ezekiel 39:2

informs that the invaders are coming from directly north of Israel, which is where Lebanon is located.

Lebanon is the host country of Hezbollah. This US-designated terrorist organization is a vowed enemy of Israel and possesses an estimated 150,000 missiles in its arsenal. Since Hezbollah is a proxy of Iran and Iran is in the Magog coalition, then the logical question is why is Lebanon not listed as one of the Ezekiel 38 invaders? Surely, Iran would order Hezbollah to launch its missiles into Israel as part of the invasion.

The likely reason that the Iranian proxies, Syria, Hezbollah, and Hamas are not part of the Magog coalition is because they, like the Inner Circle, have been eliminated as a threat to Israel through the fulfillment of one or more of the NOW prophecies. Observe that all of Iran's present proxies, apart from the Houthis, are geographically located in the Inner Circle Psalm 83 image.

Question 4: When and how will God execute judgments on Israel's neighbors (of the Inner Circle) who despise them so that Israel can dwell securely and eliminate its walls, bars, and gates? And who are these despisers of the Jewish state?

Answer 4: Some of today's Bible prophecy teachers believe that Israel will dwell securely in fulfillment of Ezekiel 38:8–11, after the Daniel 9:27 false covenant is confirmed. They generally tend to dismiss Psalm 83 and often overlook the related peripheral NOW prophecies as the viable means for Israel's ability to dwell securely, without walls, bars, or gates.

The problem with this teaching is that it implies that the false covenant resolves the Arab-Israeli conflict, which is not scripturally supported. Also, it doesn't explain how the judgments upon Israel's Arab neighbors who "despise them" as per Ezekiel 28:24–26 happen.

I explain in my book and DVD, *The NEXT Prophecies*, that the true content of the false covenant has nothing to do with the Palestinians or their Inner Circle Arab cohorts, but appears to enable the Jews to build their Third Temple.

Therefore, in my view, the judgments upon the Arab despisers of Israel in Ezekiel 28:24–26 happen as part of the NOW prophecies, and as a result, the coming **greater, safer,** and **wealthier** Israel in Ezekiel 38:8–13 becomes a reality.

Question 5: What is the plunder and booty that the Russian-led coalition will covet, and does Israel presently possess it?

Answer 5: Ezekiel 38:12–13 inform that the Magog invaders are coming to take from Israel a great spoil, which includes livestock, goods, silver, and gold. The Hebrew words utilized for this great spoil are *shalal gadol shalal*. According to the definitions given in the *New America Hebrew and Greek Dictionaries*, these words can be translated successively to read, "Plunder the great spoil of the despoilers."[127]

"Despoil" means to plunder or deprive someone of something valuable by force. It suggests, at least in part, that the invaders are coming to plunder the spoils Israel previously captured from another. Zechariah 14 may hold a clue in this regard. Apparently, Israel acquires it from the Arab nations round about them.

> And Judah also shall fight at Jerusalem; *and the wealth of all the* (Arab) *nations round about shall be gathered together,* gold, and silver, and apparel, in great abundance. (Zechariah 14:14, ASV; emphasis added)

Presently, Israel is discovering large natural gas deposits and drilling for oil. In addition, its economy is continuing to grow and prosper. As this economic trend in Israel continues, and after the some of the NOW Prophecies happen, Israel will have an even more robust economy that should also include Arab lands and spoils of war. When these things happen, then in my estimation, the Magog coalition will set its sights on invading Israel to take a great spoil.

CHAPTER 11

MEANING OF ISRAEL'S SEVENTIETH FIG TREE ANNIVERSARY

PETE GARCIA

The Budding of the Fig Tree

THROUGHOUT CHURCH HISTORY, THE most pressing question believers have wrestled with has been *when, how,* and even *if* Christ would return. Almost every generation has wondered if it could be in their lifetime. I have to use the word "almost," because Christendom today seems to be entering a phase where interest and enthusiasm for His return is at an all-time low. This is due to several factors, but primarily, the majority of mainline churches today don't study or teach Bible prophecy at all. In light of that theological vacuum, there has been a meteoric explosion of false teachings. Sound teaching has been replaced by inoffensive messages, and discernment has been abandoned for feelings. At a time when prophetic events are literally leaping off the pages of the Bible and into the headlines, the majority of Christendom is either fast asleep or is willfully being led astray.

> Nevertheless, when the Son of Man comes, will He really find faith on the earth? (Luke 18:7–8)

It has been nearly two thousand years since Christ ascended, and the Christian today has to reconcile with two *seemingly* paradoxical positions regarding His return. The first is that we cannot know the time, nor should we even bother trying (see Mark 13:32; Acts 1:7; and 2 Peter 3:10). The second idea is that we can and should know when Jesus will return (see Matthew 24:42; 1 Thessalonians 5:1–9; Hebrews 10:27; Revelation 3:2–3, etc.).

So, which is it?

Like every other major and minor doctrine found in Scripture, the Bible only teaches one position regarding Bible prophecy. Therefore, the idea that there are two contrasting positions regarding Christ's return is simply not biblical. It may *seem* that way due to the myriad false teachings out there these days, but God is not the author of confusion (1 Corinthians 14:33). Just as Scripture only teaches one doctrine on soteriology (the study of salvation) and one doctrine on ecclesiology (the study of the Church), the Bible only has one doctrine regarding eschatology (the study of last-time things). Nor is the Bible double-minded regarding the most important event on our horizon. The only biblical eschatological position regarding the Rapture (Greek, *harpazo*) of the Church is that it takes place before the seventieth week of Daniel.

The Bible is upwards of 30 percent prophetic in nature, with two events among that portion truly standing out as being *signless*. The first is the rebirth of the nation of Israel, and the second is the Rapture of the Church. What makes the return of Israel a signless event is that her rebirth was a miracle. A miracle, then, is defined as that which defies natural or human abilities or understanding. What makes Israel's rebirth so miraculous is that no other nation has ever come back after being displaced for more than a generation. National Israel had been displaced for almost two thousand years.

This is why no one thought Israel *could* even come back as a nation again, because it had never been done before. Regrettably, most of us alive since 1948 have simply come to take Israel's existence for granted, and we miss the miraculous nature of her return. We miss the fact that no other nation has ever recovered its culture, language, religion, economic prosperity, and military might as Israel has done. We miss the fact that for the 1,878 years leading up to 1948, national Israel existed only in the history books.

> Surely, the Lord God does nothing, unless He reveals His
> secret to His servants the prophets. (Amos 3:7)

Israel's national rebirth should be considered a signless event—not in that no one saw it coming, because there were a few who did (primarily nineteenth-century dispensationalists), but that the world at large did not see it coming. These early dispensationalists believed it would happen, because they understood that according to Scripture, Israel **must** become a nation again (Isaiah 11:11, 66; Ezekiel 37–39; Daniel 9; Amos 9; Zechariah 12; Luke 21; Romans 11:25; etc.). Because the Scriptures are so clear and adamant about it happening a second time, these few could boldly proclaim it as a future certainty without pause or hesitation.

They just did not know *when* or *how* it was going to happen.

We know historically that there were steps (or processes) in Israel becoming a nation again, but those signs were largely overshadowed by the events of those days. Events like World War I, the Great Depression, the Third Reich, World War II, and the Holocaust held everyone's attention. One would have had to have a decent understanding of Bible prophecy and a keen eye on current events to see the prophetic winds changing to have noticed Israel's stirring. Fortunately, God had already placed men in certain positions of power who would carry out His plan, men like British Foreign Secretary Lord James Balfour and United States President Harry Truman, who knew and understood the prophetic significance of the political processes they came to support. Again, for the few who were watching the dry bones rattling (Ezekiel 37), these were exciting times, and they were not taken by surprise. Nevertheless, the world was largely caught unawares until events began to unfold in front of their very eyes.

> But concerning the times and the seasons, brethren, you have no need that I should write to you. For you yourselves know perfectly that the day of the Lord so comes as a thief in the night. For when they say, "Peace and safety!" then sudden destruction comes upon them, as labor pains upon a pregnant woman. And they shall not escape. But you, brethren, are not in darkness, so that this Day should overtake you as a thief. (1 Thessalonians 5:1–4)

Going back to the original question, we find in Scripture that there is a way through the predicament of knowing versus not knowing. The Scripture that supports and connects these two seemingly paradoxical positions (as well as being signless events) is none other than the Lord's parable of the fig tree. This is how you can both know the season, but not know when the Lord will return specifically. It also connects the two seemingly unrelated events (the rebirth of Israel and the Rapture) in a way only God could do. It means we would not even know the season of His return until national Israel came back to life in her ancient homeland. That is why for nearly seventeen hundred years, the Christian Church could not understand where they were on God's prophetic calendar.

Unfortunately, in the ignorance of the theological Dark Ages (AD 200–1700), the religionists of Christianity began creating stifling and toxic doctrines meant to discourage the study of Bible prophecy. They also created false doctrines that made the church the Kingdom, and replaced national Israel with the Church (replacement theology or supercessionism). Even worse, these *doctrines of demons* were later used as theological justifications to carry out some of the most heinous acts in human history: the Crusades, the Inquisitions, and the Third Reich's Final Solution, the latter of which resulted in the death of some six million Jews in the Holocaust.

However, the Scriptures are clear: Once the first event occurred (the rebirth of Israel), the second (the Rapture) would soon follow suit. In fact, no one would know who the last generation was until Israel was brought back again as a nation. Moreover, because no nation had ever done that before (come back after diaspora), the likelihood of it happening seemed impossible. And this doesn't mean a symbolic or figurative nation, but a real nation with real borders, a real government, and real Jews living back in her land. This is why the Lord's parable of the fig tree (capping off the Olivet Discourse) is so significant. For your edification, I would like to present four main arguments that can be made from this parable. These are categorized simply as symbolic, historic, prophetic, and numerical.

> Now learn this parable from the fig tree: When its branch
> has already become tender and puts forth leaves, you know

that summer *is* near. So you also, when you see all these things, know that it is near—at the doors! Assuredly, I say to you, this generation will by no means pass away till all these things take place. Heaven and earth will pass away, but My words will by no means pass away. (Matthew 24:32–35)

Symbolic

We know that all manner of symbols, types, foreshadows, and examples are used throughout the Old and New Testaments. Although Scripture is chock full of their usage, these varying forms of symbolism are not to be taken as arbitrary or nonsensical. All scriptural symbolism has meaning and relevance; thus, it must be interpreted by using Scripture. For example, Noah's ark was a type of Christ. Not only can we draw this reference from the fact that it saved Noah and his family, but that is how the apostle Peter used it as a type (Genesis 6:14; 1 Peter 3:19–21).

The halted sacrifice of the *son of promise,* Isaac, on Mount Moriah (this later becomes the Temple Mount) was meant to portray what God would later allow with Jesus (another son of promise) some two thousand years after Abraham (Genesis 22:1–19; Galatians 3:16). Isaac had to carry his own wood up the mountain, as Christ carried His own cross to His death. God told Abraham that He Himself would provide the sacrifice, which we later see is the literal fulfillment of this with Christ's sacrificial death on Mount Calvary. Abraham agreed to sacrifice "his only son" (Genesis 22:2) because he believed that God would raise him from the dead again (Genesis 22:5; Hebrews 11:17–18). Of course, we know that Christ rose again on the third day (Matthew 16:21, 28:5–7; 1 Corinthian 15:4–5).

The multi-metal statue that Nebuchadnezzar saw in his dream and the series of beasts later shown to Daniel in a dream (Daniel 2, 7–8), represented actual kingdoms. We know they are actual kingdoms because the Bible says they were (Daniel 2:44, 7:23, and 8:22). Israel was also portrayed as a valley of bones (Ezekiel 37:1–13) who would, in dramatic fashion, come back to life in the latter times. Likewise, the same is true regarding the usage of trees as nations. Judges 9, Hosea 9:10, and Ezekiel 31 are just a few places where trees were used symbolically to convey the status of nations.

In the Gospels, Jesus almost exclusively taught publicly by using parables, especially toward the end of His ministry on earth. What is interesting about the parable of the fig tree is that Jesus neither is asked, nor explains, the meaning of it. Previous to this, in Matthew 13, Jesus gives the famous seven parables in which He later explains why He teaches in parable form when queried by His disciples (13:11–15):

> He answered and said to them, "Because it has been given to you to know the mysteries of the kingdom of heaven, but to them it has not been given. For whoever has, to him more will be given, and he will have abundance; but whoever does not have, even what he has will be taken away from him. Therefore I speak to them in parables, because seeing they do not see, and hearing they do not hear, nor do they understand. And in them the prophecy of Isaiah is fulfilled, which says:

> 'Hearing you will hear and shall not understand,
>
> And seeing you will see and not perceive;
>
> For the hearts of this people have grown dull.
>
> Their ears are hard of hearing,
>
> And their eyes they have closed,
>
> Lest they should see with their eyes and hear with their ears,
>
> Lest they should understand with their hearts and turn,
>
> So that I should heal them.'"

Of note, Jesus uses the fig tree in two separate parables and in one actual object lesson to convey the status of Israel. Notice the subtle differences and what is in focus:

[Fruit]—The parable of the barren fig tree (Luke 13:6–9)

[Fruit]—The lesson of the fig tree (Mark 11:12–14, 20–21)

[Leaves]—The parable of the fig tree (Matthew 24:32–35; Mark 13:28–29; Luke 21:29–31)

Regarding the fig tree, the leaves would represent their national status, while the fruit represented their spiritual status. Jesus' predecessor and forerunner, John the Baptist, foretells the coming evil of that generation by saying, "Even now the ax is laid to the root of the trees. Therefore every tree **which does not bear good fruit** is cut down and thrown into the fire" (Luke 3:7–9, emphasis added). Given how history played out, this prophecy was fulfilled literally by that generation who rejected and crucified their own Messiah, thus bringing upon themselves (and their children) His blood and their cursing (Matthew 27:25).

Historical

Old Testament

A second case can be made for the validity of Israel as the fig tree, using historical means. The story begins roughly four thousand years ago in the heart of the ancient Middle East. There, in the land of Ur, God began the process of separating humanity and narrowing down the path for which the Messiah would one day come. This came by way of a promise made to a man named Abram. The promise was that God would make him a great nation, and that his descendants would be as countless as the stars in heaven. Packed inside of that unconditional promise (what we call the *Abrahamic Covenant*), were the promises of land, seed, and blessing. Encapsulating that blessing into a singular statement, God said, "I will bless those who bless you, and curse those who curse you," and so it was. Any nation that helped the Hebrews (or later the Israelites and Jews), were themselves blessed. Any nation since who attempted to destroy them were themselves destroyed. This same promise of land, seed, and blessings were later conveyed to Abram's (now Abraham's) son Isaac, and grandson Jacob (Genesis 12, 15).

Over time, however, that promise became a source of great consternation to the Jewish people. Either their Gentile neighbors were busy trying to steal the title of "the chosen ones" or they were continually attempting to destroy them because they were chosen and special in the sight of God. Not even four centuries after the time of Abraham, the Hebrew people

(Abraham's descendants) found themselves in bondage to the Egyptians, who were the regional powerhouse of the day (Genesis 15:13–16).

Around this time, God raised up a man named Moses who would lead the Israelites out of bondage and into the Promised Land. However, because of their disobedience and disbelief in the wilderness, that entrance was delayed by forty years. It was here in the wilderness that God intentionally tied their national identity and sovereignty to their obedience to the Law He gave Moses at Mount Sinai. This Mosaic Covenant was different from the unconditional covenant God made with Abraham, Isaac, and Jacob, in that this latter one was conditional, with the primary difference being that the former promise (Abrahamic) was bound by God's honor, while the other (Mosaic) was bound by their obedience.

The Law (actually 613 laws) was the one the Israelites willingly bound themselves to as a nation (Exodus 19:7–9). Thus, their obedience and reward, or disobedience and punishment, would in fact, become a bellwether for God's interaction with humanity as a whole. When they were in good standing with God through obedience to the Law, God's timeline marched forward. When they were in rebellion against Him, God used their enemies to put them into bondage and the prophetic clock was paused. We see this pattern repeated throughout the Old Testament when their enemies were allowed to overtake them temporarily (Egyptians, Philistines, Assyrians, Babylonians, Persians, Greeks, etc.). Consequently, God's divine calendar was inextricably connected to whether Israel as a nation was in relation with God. As has been often repeated today, Israel is God's timepiece. Jerusalem is the minute hand, and the Temple Mount its second hand.

New Testament

By the turn of the first millennium, the moment had come that Scriptures call "the fullness of time" (Galatians 4:4–5). This was the time for the arrival of the Jewish Messiah in fulfillment of Old Testament prophecies such as Micah 5, Isaiah 7, and Daniel 9. Jesus' earthly arrival was at a point when the Roman Empire was just beginning to flex its geopolitical muscles and exert greater control over its expanding empire. *Pax Romana* (Roman peace) ruled the empire, and *koine* Greek (common Greek) was spoken throughout the lands. And to the Romans, Judea was nothing more than a backwater province of little strategic importance. It was, however, frequently problematic, which meant that things in this particular area could flare up very quickly.

It was also here when John the Baptist's ministry was about to decrease (John 3:30) so that Christ's ministry could increase. Upon seeing Jesus of Nazareth (now of age) approach him on the bank of the Jordan River, John said, "Behold, the Lamb of God who takes away the sins of the world" (John 1:29). For three and a half years, God walked the earth in the form of a man, providing divine insight and wisdom to all, encouragement to the downtrodden, and chastisement for the religiously blind. He spoke of things past and things to come with equal authority. In particular, and of interest to this discussion, was what He had to say about the future of Israel. Upon His arrival to Jerusalem on His appointed day (the 173,880th day)[128] and a week prior to His crucifixion, Christ warned His disciples that He would be killed but would rise again on the third day, and that Jerusalem's days were numbered.

> Now as He drew near, He saw the city and wept over it, saying, "If you had known, even you, especially in this your day, the things *that make* for your peace! But now they **are hidden** from your eyes. For days will come upon you when your enemies will build an embankment around you, surround you and close you in on every side, and level you, and your children within you, to the ground; and they will not leave in you one stone upon another, because you did not know the time of your visitation." (Luke 19:41–44, emphasis added)

Not only that, but the Temple itself (the centerpiece of Jewishness and Judaism) would be torn down and not one stone left atop the other. Furthermore, the entire city would be destroyed and the peoples scattered. Matthew's Gospel records that Jesus' statement about this greatly troubled His disciples (Matthew 23:37–24:2), so they approached Him privately and inquired what that meant in the form of three questions:

- When will this be?

- What will be the sign of His Coming?

- What is the sign of the end of the age?

Echoing Moses' warnings in Deuteronomy 4 and 30, Jesus stated that because of their national rejection of His Messiahship, they were about to undergo a lengthy and undefined period of hostilities and homeless wandering (see again Matthew 27:25; Mark 11:12–14, 20–21). They would, in effect, become nomads who would not find rest in this world. This age would be marked by religious deception, wars, rumors of wars, earthquakes, pestilence, signs in the sun, moon, and stars, and lawlessness. He likened all these signs to birth pangs, in that they would increase in both frequency and intensity as the end drew closer. However, before all these, their temple and city would be utterly destroyed, "and they will fall by the edge of the sword, and be led away captive into all nations. And Jerusalem will be trampled by Gentiles until the times of the Gentiles are fulfilled" (Luke 21:24).

Ante-Nicene Era

And so it was. By the mid '60s AD, the Romans had begun turning their militaristic attention toward the troublesome city of Jerusalem due to a recent number of revolts and unrest that was increasingly occurring there. By AD 70, the Roman legions, under General Titus, laid siege to Jerusalem and ultimately destroyed the city and the temple. According to the eyewitness Josephus, the revolt, which began in AD 66, culminated with the Romans unleashing their fury in a savage act of bloodlust.

> As the legions charged in, neither persuasion nor threat could check their impetuosity: passion alone was in command. Crowded together around the entrances many were trampled by their friends, many fell among the still hot and smoking ruins of the colonnades and died as miserably as the defeated. As they neared the Sanctuary they pretended not even to hear Caesar's commands and urged the men in front to throw in more firebrands. The partisans were no longer in a position to help; everywhere was slaughter and

flight. Most of the victims were peaceful citizens, weak and unarmed, butchered wherever they were caught. Round the Altar the heaps of corpses grew higher and higher, while down the Sanctuary steps poured a river of blood and the bodies of those killed at the top slithered to the bottom.[129]

In the aftermath, just as Jesus predicted, not one stone was left atop the other.

> Now as soon as the army had no more people to slay or to plunder, because there remained none to be the objects of their fury (for they would not have spared any, had there remained any other work to be done), [Titus] Caesar gave orders that they should now demolish the entire city and Temple, but should leave as many of the towers standing as they were of the greatest eminence; that is, Phasaelus, and Hippicus, and Mariamne; and so much of the wall enclosed the city on the west side.[130]

Even the vegetation was laid to waste, of which, most notably, was the fig tree.

> And truly, the very view itself was a melancholy thing; for those places, which were adorned with trees and pleasant gardens, were now become desolate country every way, and its trees were all cut down. Nor could any foreigner that had formerly seen Judaea and the most beautiful suburbs of the city, and now saw it as a desert, but lament and mourn sadly at so great a change. For the war had laid all signs of beauty quite waste. Nor had anyone who had known the place before, had come on a sudden to it now, would he have known it again. But though he [a foreigner] were at the city itself, yet would he have inquired for it.[131]

Post-Nicene Era

For the next eighteen centuries, numerous foreign powers would come in and dominate the land for succeeding periods of time. This included the

Catholic Byzantines, the Muslim Umayyad, Abbasid, and Fatimid sects, the Roman Catholic Crusaders, the Mamelukes, the Ottoman Turks, and finally the British after World War I. Famed American author Mark Twain had this to say when he visited the Holy Lands in 1867:

> A desolate country whose soil is rich enough, but is given over wholly to weeds-a silent mournful expanse.... A desolation is here that not even imagination can grace with the pomp of life and action.... We never saw a human being on the whole route.... There was hardly a tree or a shrub anywhere. Even the olive and the cactus, those fast friends of the worthless soil, had almost deserted the country.[132]

Seeing how Christ's predictions about the coming desolation of Israel would be literally carried out, so too should Christians look toward its restoration as also being fulfilled literally. God told the prophet Ezekiel to look upon the valley of dry bones and breathe on them, and they would grow back sinew and flesh and would one day be brought back "as the whole house of Israel" (both Israel and Judah) (Ezekiel 37:1–13). However, in keeping consistent with the symbolism of the fruit and leaf, they would be brought back in unbelief, meaning that although they would bear the leaves, they would not yet bear the fruit of the budding fig tree (Ezekiel 37:11).

Numerical

> We are a commonwealth. In form it is new, but in purpose very ancient. Our aim is mentioned in the First Book of Kings: "Judah and Israel shall dwell securely, each man under his own vine and fig tree, from Dan to Beersheba."— Theodor Herzl[133] (citing 1 Kings 4:25; Micah 4:4)

In 1897, an Austrian Jew named Theodor Herzl chaired the world's first Zionist Congress in Basel, Switzerland. Recognizing a rise in anti-Semitism in Europe at the time, Mr. Herzl began looking back at where they had come from, and where things were heading, and decided to act. He sought out other like-minded Jews who would start working toward establishing a permanent Jewish state back in the land of their forefathers. Part of their established agenda was creating a homeland for the dispersed Jews who were still scattered about the world.

> Zionism seeks to establish a home for the Jewish people in Eretz-Israel secured under public law. The Congress contemplates the following means to the attainment of this end:
>
> 1.   The promotion by appropriate means of the settlement in Eretz-Israel of Jewish farmers, artisans, and manufacturers.
>
> 2.   The organization and uniting of the whole of Jewry by means of appropriate institutions, both local and international, in accordance with the laws of each country.
>
> 3.   The strengthening and fostering of Jewish national sentiment and national consciousness.
>
> 4.   Preparatory steps toward obtaining the consent of governments, where necessary, in order to reach the goals of Zionism.[134]

What Herzl did not know, nor did anyone else at the time, was that to achieve this reborn Jewish state would cost mankind two world wars. Therefore, it is here at the turn of the twentieth century that the world entered the most unlikely of wars. One writer noted the sheer absurdity of its cause:

> In early 1914, though, it seemed almost impossible that Britain and France would go to war with Germany to defend Russia against Austria-Hungary over a dispute with Serbia. Yet by June 28, war moved straight from impossible to inevitable — without ever passing through improbable. Four years later, 10 million people had died.[135]

World War I (the Great War) began in 1914 with the assassination of the Austrian-Hungarian Archduke Franz Ferdinand. It pitted the Allied Powers (British, French, Russians, and Americans) against the Central Powers (Germany, Austro-Hungary, and the Ottoman-Turks). Toward the middle of the war, the British and French had already begun drafting plans for carving up what remained of the Ottoman Empire. Part of this restructuring included the Sykes-Picot Agreement (Asia Minor Agreement of 1916), which would define the *spheres of influence* in Asia Minor post World War I. The other major initiative was the 1917 Balfour Declaration, which would, in effect, legalize Zionist repatriation to Palestine. This was carried out in the abolition of the Ottoman Sultanate, which officially occurred from 1918–1922 after the war's end.

What is of interest to this topic is how the timeline has played out since 1897 and what those numbers mean in relation to Bible prophecy. While numbers certainly figure significantly throughout Scripture (for example, 3, 7, and 40), we should exercise a certain degree of caution lest we read too much into their meanings. At the same time, numbers and what they might mean should not be ignored, either, because their significance to the steps (or processes) we see are playing out over time...especially when certain numbers keep showing up in a similar context (as relating to Israel). So, take the following as something "of interest" to the larger discussion at hand, while keeping in mind 2 Peter 3:8–9.

Timeline

1. From 1897 to 2017: **120 years**

    > And the Lord said, My Spirit shall not strive with man forever, for he is indeed flesh; yet his days shall be **one hundred and twenty years**. (Genesis 6:3, emphasis added)

This could mean either that man's life would be no longer than 120 years (but Noah, Shem, Job, and Abraham are all apparent violations of that) or that, in 120 years, judgment would come upon all mankind. I believe the latter explanation fits better with what actually transpired as a converging of events occurred: Methuselah died at the age of 969 the same year that Noah turned 600, which was the same year that the Flood (judgment) came.

2. From 1917 to 2017: **100 years** (concerning future Israel)

    > Now when the sun was going down, a deep sleep fell upon Abram; and behold, horror and great darkness fell

upon him. Then He said to Abram: Know certainly that your descendants will be strangers in a land that is not theirs, and will serve them, and they will afflict them **four hundred years**. And also the nation whom they serve I will judge; afterward they shall come out with great possessions. Now as for you, you shall go to your fathers in peace; you shall be buried at a good old age. **But in the fourth generation** they shall return here, for the iniquity of the Amorites is not yet complete. (Genesis 15:12–16, concerning future Israel; emphasis added)

Here we have God prophesying over an unconscious Abraham, stating that for 400 years (four generations), his descendants would be in bondage. But in the fourth generation, they would be delivered. This is where we are dealing with a generation being as long as 100 years in length.

3. From 1947 to 2017: **70 years** (in relation to the Jews in Judaea; from the United Nations legal vote [Resolution 181, November 29, 1947] to allow for the reconstitution of a Jewish State [70 represents both judgment and fulfillment])

   And this whole land shall be a desolation and an astonishment, and these nations shall serve the king of Babylon **seventy** years. "Then it will come to pass, when **seventy** years are completed, that I will punish the king of Babylon and that nation, the land of the Chaldeans, for their iniquity," says the Lord; "and I will make it a perpetual desolation." (Jeremiah 25:11–12, emphasis added)

Israel's enslavement by the Babylonians for exactly 70 years was punishment and payment for idolatry and the seventy Sabbath years they had violated in the land of Israel. (Leviticus 25:1–19; 2 Chronicles 36:20–21; Jeremiah 25:8–12)

Also (to the Jewish people and Jerusalem):

   Seventy weeks are determined for **your people** and for **your holy city** (Daniel 9:24–27, emphasis added)

We know that the 70 weeks are weeks of years. Genesis 29:18–28 validates the use of this as a means of measurement, as does Leviticus 25 for a measurement of time (70 x 7 = 490 years). We know that God deals with Israel in the form of heptads (groupings of seven), similar to how the Gentile world deals in decades (groupings of ten). We also know that 483 of those years were completed with Christ's death on the cross (Daniel 9:26). His triumphal entry into Jerusalem on Palm Sunday marked the 173,880th day from the commandment given to Nehemiah by the Persian King Artaxerxes in 445 BC (Nehemiah 2).[136]

This leaves one final week (seven years) to be completed. This final week does not begin at the Rapture, but at the confirmation of a covenant between Israel, the Antichrist, and the many nations around her (Daniel 9:27). This further develops the idea that the Antichrist comes with a deceptive initiative that he fully plans to violate at the midpoint of that final week (Matthew 24:15). This Antichrist is Revelation 6's "rider on the white horse," Daniel 7's "small horn," Daniel 8's "little horn," and Daniel 11's "willful king."

4.   From May 14, 1948 to 2018: **70 years**

We are living through a second set of 70 years from the actual proclamation of the birth of the nation of Israel (the birth pangs after the birth):

> Before she was in labor, she gave birth; Before her pain came, She delivered a male child. Who has heard such a thing? Who has seen such things? Shall the earth be made to give birth in one day? Or shall a nation be born at once? For as soon as Zion was in labor, She gave birth to her children. (Isaiah 66:7–8, emphasis added).

5.   From 1967 to 2017: **50 years** (fifty equals a jubilee)

> And you shall count seven sabbaths of years for yourself, seven times seven years; and the time of the seven sabbaths of years shall be to you forty-nine years. Then you shall cause the trumpet of the Jubilee to sound on the tenth day of the seventh month; on the Day of Atonement you shall make the trumpet to sound throughout all your land.

And you shall **consecrate the fiftieth year**, and proclaim liberty throughout all the land to all its inhabitants. It shall be a Jubilee for you; and each of you shall return to his possession, and each of you shall return to his family. (Leviticus 25:8–12, emphasis added)

6. From 1977 to 2017: **40 years**

> For after seven more days I will cause it to rain on the earth forty days and forty nights, and I will destroy from the face of the earth all living things that I have made. (Genesis 7:4)

See also: Exodus 16:35 (Israelites wandered in the desert forty years); 1 Samuel 17:16 (Goliath taunts Israel for forty days); 1 Kings 19:8 (Elijah fasted forty days); Luke 4:1–13 (Jesus' temptation for forty days and nights), etc.

1977 is a unique year that saw the genesis of what would become a 40-year period of testing known as the "Land for Peace" initiatives, which officially began at Camp David after the election of US President Jimmy Carter, Israeli Prime Minister Menachem Begin, and Egyptian President Anwar Sadat.[137]

7. From 1987 to 2017: **30 years**

Thirty years is most commonly associated with the Jewish Temple in terms of age and of measurements (cubits). One could not enter into his ministerial duties until he was of age (30 years), which speaks as to why Christ waited until He was "about 30" before He began His own ministry (Numbers 4; Luke 3:23). In 1987, the Temple Mount Institute was established in Jerusalem. Its sole purpose is raising funds, resources, and people to serve in a newly rebuilt third Jewish Temple.

8. December 6, 2017: **0 years**

The leader of the most powerful nation on earth, United States President Donald Trump, officially recognizes Jerusalem as the undivided capital of the state of Israel while in the office of president, and instructs his administration to begin preparations to move the US Embassy from Tel Aviv to Jerusalem.

In 1995, Congress adopted the Jerusalem Embassy Act, urging the federal government to relocate the American embassy to Jerusalem and to recognize that that city—and so importantly—is Israel's capital. This act passed Congress by an overwhelming bipartisan majority and was reaffirmed by a unanimous vote of the Senate only six months ago.

Yet, for over 20 years, every previous American president has exercised the law's waiver, refusing to move the U.S. embassy to Jerusalem or to recognize Jerusalem as Israel's capital city.

Presidents issued these waivers under the belief that delaying the recognition of Jerusalem would advance the cause of peace. Some say they lacked courage, but they made their best judgments based on facts as they understood them at the time. Nevertheless, the record is in. After more than two decades of waivers, we are no closer to a lasting peace agreement between Israel and the Palestinians. It would be folly to assume that repeating the exact same formula would now produce a different or better result.

Therefore, I have determined that it is time to officially recognize Jerusalem as the capital of Israel.

While previous presidents have made this a major campaign promise, they failed to deliver. Today, I am delivering.[138]

9. May 14, 2018: more than 5 months

The US moves its embassy from Tel Aviv, to Jerusalem. Other nations begin to follow suit.

In summary, we see the countdown from the first stirrings of the Jewish people to the final recognition of Jerusalem as Israel's capital. Let us add in the biblical implications.

1897–2017= 120 years (time-span limits)

1917–2017= 100 years (outer limits of a generation)

1947–2017= 70 years (judgment, testing, heptad)

1948–2018= 70 years (judgment, testing, heptad)

1967–2017= 50 years (jubilee, liberation, freedom)

1977–2017= 40 years (testing)

1987–2017= 30 years (related to the Temple)

2017= Year 0

2018–2028=10 years (Psalm 90:10; 2 Peter 3:8–9)

Prophetic

A sure sign of summer is the leafing of the fig tree; a sure sign of the end of the world is that "all these things" (of Matthew 24) are taking place. Those who are on the earth then will have only a short time left.[139]

Jesus gives the parable of the fig tree at the end of His objective narrative (the Olivet Discourse) regarding all the signs that would accompany the end of the age: wars, rumors of wars, earthquakes, famines, pestilences, and the lawlessness that would accompany them. Not only that, but all these individual signs would begin converging with both frequency and intensity just as birth pangs come upon a woman in pregnancy. Capping all of these signs off as a summation was His parable of the fig tree. Jesus stated that "this generation" (the generation that sees the rebirth of national Israel and all of the aforementioned signs) would not pass away before they saw His return.

Moses (who lived to be 120 years) wrote that a man's life span would be limited to between 70 and 80 years, and *not* the wide variance of ages we see throughout the Old Testament (Psalm 90:10). Throughout history, most people died well short of 70 or 80 years, and very few managed to have lived beyond it…until this generation. In other words, exceeding 80 years of age wasn't much of an issue in the generations before 1948. However, this generation (our generation since 1948) has seen mankind's lifespan increase due to the rapid advancements in healthcare, medicine, and genetics. Experts believe that within the next few decades, humanity will have cracked the genetic code, which will extend life back into the range of centuries. We know, according to Scripture, that man (our physical bodies) has the capacity to live for centuries and see this demonstrated—even after the Fall, when sin and death entered the world.

- Noah lived to be 950 years old

- Shem lived to be 600 years old

- Job lived to be at least 210 years old

- Abraham lived to be 175 years old

- Isaac lived to be 180 years old

- Jacob lived to be 147 years old

- Joseph lived to be 110 years old

By adding the phrase "this generation **will not pass away**," God is limiting how far mankind will progress into the future. So if, as the experts believe, in the years to come, average life spans will be extend far beyond the national average (79 years), we can be resolutely confident that Christ will have returned long before that happens.

> And all the trees of the field shall know that I, the Lord,
> have brought down the high tree and exalted the low tree,
> dried up the green tree and made the dry tree flourish; I, the
> Lord, have spoken and have done it. (Ezekiel 17:24)

Author Michael Neutzling most aptly summarized the rise, fall, and rebirth of Israel in his 2014 book, *The Fig Tree Parable*. Most notably, the trees here have played out prophetically (from Ezekiel's perspective) and align historically (from our perspective) regarding the history of Israel. He has this explanation concerning the passage above:

> -Bring low the high tree (Davidic kingdom) thru Nebuchadnezzar

-Exalt the low tree (under the Persians, Greeks, and Romans)

-Dry up the green tree (Romans thru the Diaspora)

-Make the dry tree flourish (rebirth of Israel in 1948) (p. 88)[140]

All the Trees

In Luke's version of the Olivet Discourse, he adds an additional, interesting comment:

> Then He spoke to them a parable: "Look at the fig tree, **and all the trees**. When they are already budding, you see and know for yourselves that summer is now near. So you also, when you see these things happening, know that the kingdom of God is near. Assuredly, I say to you, this generation will by no means pass away till all things take place. Heaven and earth will pass away, but My words will by no means pass away. (Luke 21:29–33, emphasis added)

Hearkening back to Judges 9 where nations are symbolized as trees, we see along with the rebirth of the nation of Israel the explosion in the total number of nations come about after the two world wars. Prior to World War I, the Middle East lay primarily under the thumb of just one empire, the Ottoman Turks. The rest of the world lay largely colonialized under varying aging European powers like the Portuguese, French, Spanish, Dutch, Germans, and British (who had the saying that "the sun never sets on the British Empire"). Nevertheless, as destructive as the two world wars were regarding the loss of human life and property, so, too, was the destruction of these large, cumbersome empires. *Is it a coincidence* that Israel is brought back to life, just as all these other nations (in the hundreds) are broken up and given their independence?

Conversely, we see the rebirth of another empire coming back shortly after Israel's 1948 return on the global stage...this being the revived Roman Empire. Before World War II ended, European leaders such as Winston

Churchill believed that the ultimate cure for these European conflicts was to unite all of Europe into a single, sovereign, super-state.

> Hard as it is to say now...I look forward to a United States of Europe, in which the barriers between the nations will be greatly minimized and unrestricted travel will be possible.—Winston Churchill, in an October 21, 1942, letter to his Foreign Secretary Anthony Eden.[141]

Shortly after the war, we see the early stages of a world ripe for globalism begin to take shape with the founding of the United Nations in June of 1945. Soon after, we start to see the coalescing of a fractured Europe begin to take its first baby steps into unification through mutual military and economic agreements. From there, things begin to quicken.

1945 – The end of World War II

1949 – The formation of NATO [North Atlantic Treaty Organization]

1951 – Treaty of Paris creates Coal and Steel Community

1957 – Treaty of Rome creates EEC [European Economic Community]

1963 – Ankara Agreement initiated a three-step process toward creating a Customs Union, which would help secure Turkey's full membership in the EEC.

1967 – ECSC [European Coal and Steel Community], EEC, and EURATOM [European Atomic Energy Community] merged

1973 – Accession of Denmark, Ireland, and the UK [United Kingdom]

1981 – Accession of Greece

1985 – Delors Commission, Greenland leaves Community.

1986 – Single European Act; Accession of Portugal and Spain; flag adopted

1989 – The fall of the Iron Curtain in Eastern Europe

1992 – Maastricht Treaty: The European Union is born and the euro was introduced as the fellow currency

1993 – Copenhagen Criteria defined

1995 – Accession of Austria, Finland, and Sweden

2002 – The euro replaces twelve national currencies

2004 – Accession of ten countries (Cyprus, Czech Republic, Estonia, Hungary, Latvia, Lithuania, Malta, Poland, Slovakia, Slovenia); signing of Constitution

2007 – Accession of Bulgaria and Romania

2009 – Lisbon Treaty abolishes the three pillars of the European Union

2013 – Accession of Croatia

2016 – UK holds a Membership Referendum and votes to leave the European Union

2017 – Start of Brexit: On 29 March 2017, the government of the United Kingdom invoked Article 50 of the Treaty on European Union. The UK is due to leave the EU on 29 March 2019 at 11 p.m. UK time

2017 – Negotiations between UK and the EU officially started in June 2017, aiming to complete the withdrawal agreement by October 2018[142]

As we can see today, the United Kingdom's attempts to extrapolate itself from the EU has proven far more difficult than just letting citizens vote themselves out. Though it is sometimes difficult to see the forest through the trees, a revived Roman Empire must be reborn. Although we look at it today and cannot really make out the shape, the systems and processes (the infrastructure) is quietly being laid. However, the European Union is not the only one making waves in the confederation pool. The Union of the Mediterranean (UfM) started out as the Barcelona Process (1995) and culminated with its foundation in 2008 as the UfM. Taking in the nations of the southern EU, as well as the North African nations and Mediterranean partners (to include Israel), and combined with the EU, this truly looks like the Roman Empire 2.0.

I caution that we have not yet seen the final outline of the coming Antichrist's kingdom. It is highly likely that the EU and/or UfM will ultimately make up either part or the whole of this final, ten-kingdom alignment that is recorded in Scripture (Daniel 2:41–43, 7:7, 8:24–25; Revelation 13:1). In Scripture, we get two separate images projected in the book of Daniel and Revelation of this final kingdom. In Daniel 2, we see the feet and toes of the multi-metallic statue representing the ten-nation confederacy. In Daniel 7–8 and Revelation 13, we see the image of the terrible beast. ***Is it a coincidence*** that the empire that twice destroyed Israel (AD 70 and AD 135) is rising again at the exact same time as Israel comes back onto the global stage?

Conclusion

> What we want is a man of sufficient stature to hold the alliances of all people and to lift us out of the economic morass into which we are sinking. Send us such a man, and be he god or devil, we will receive him.—Attributed to Paul Henri Spaak, first chairman of the UN General Assembly and secretary-general of NATO (1957–1961)

Given the miraculous nature of Israel's return, the subsequent explosion of nations upon the planet, and the revival of a new Roman Empire, we can clearly see, hear, and feel the prophetic winds picking up into a furious tempest. Unlike our predecessors of the nineteenth and twentieth centuries who watched earnestly as Israel came back into the land, we are today witnessing another revival. We are watching the processes for a Revived Roman Empire come into being. We are witnessing the processes coalescing now, setting the stage for that final human kingdom of the last seven years. For those who are now watching and understand Scripture, we know with 100 percent certainty (as did those early Dispensationalists) that Christ is near, even at the door.

Just as those living in the days leading up to the rebirth of Israel could not know the exact time of Israel's reconstitution, so, too, are we witnessing the formation of another rebirth, the revived Roman Empire. While we can see the processes coming together, we cannot know the day or hour of its true rebirth because it is dependent upon the second signless event, the Rapture of the Church. It is likely that the Rapture will provide the globalists in the world the proper catalyst for standing up to this final kingdom, of which the EU seems to be the center.

So not only has the rebirth of Israel been significant in regards to validating the authenticity of the Bible, but it has also largely shaped the geopolitics of the last days. Just consider the old saying that "World War I prepared the land for the people, and World War II prepared the people for the land" as evidentiary. Since Jerusalem has the stamp of ownership placed upon it (2 Chronicles 6:6), it makes absolute sense that a world given over to Satan (Luke 4:5–6; 1 John 5:19) would have such animosity directed toward her (Amos 3:2; Revelation 16:16).

One final thought regarding the miraculous rebirth of the nation of Israel. According to many of the most respected and talented theological scholars of the past two centuries, Abraham was born in the year 2056 AM (Anno-Mundi = the year of the world). This was 1,948 years after Adam's creation in the Garden of Eden. Since Abraham is considered the senior patriarch and father of the Jewish peoples, it is either again extremely ironic or divine providence that Israel was reborn as a nation in the year AD 1948 (Anno Domini = the year of the Lord). In other words, Abraham was born 1,948 years since the first Adam, and the nation of Israel was reborn 1,948 years since the last Adam, Jesus Christ (1 Corinthians 15:45).

Israel's rebirth onto the global stage (the budding of the fig tree), the explosion of nations (all the trees), the rush toward globalism (distress of nations), and the revival of the Roman Empire (the beast rising out of the sea) are all major signs pointing to the nearness of the return of our Lord, Jesus Christ.

This generation shall not pass away…even so, *Maranatha*!

CHAPTER 12

THE RELIGION CALLED SOCIALISM

BY GARY STEARMAN

IN THE HISTORY OF the world, wealth has a mystifying way of being accumulated, then dispersed and re-circulated…again and again. Like a slithering serpent, currency swirls along the routes of trade and power, growing from thousands into millions, billions, and trillions before falling back to earth and finding its way into new hands and stronger vaults. Where money is concerned, centuries of lawless greed have made it easy to become cynical and to long for a new way of handling wealth. Many have theorized revolutionary methods, designed to counter human avarice.

In the early twentieth century, Marx, Lenin, and their followers launched a new economic system dedicated to "fairness." Their scheme has since appeared under various names—Marxism, Maoism, communism, socialism, progressivism, or whatever becomes fashionable. By taking money out of the hands of the common man, the state could distribute wealth equitably. Or so they thought. (And so they think.)

Actually, their new system was a replacement for what they saw as the failure of religion to fairly disburse blessing and prosperity. To them, worship was perceived as either the delusion of the impoverished or the controlling hierarchy of various corrupt priesthoods. Without explicitly saying so, they had invented a new religion. The old religion, Christianity was, as Marx put it, "the opiate of the people." His new "religion," envisioned the secular state and its administrators as the new medium of blessing.

Their "moral cause" led to a series of revolutions and wars. Communism claimed that it would redistribute wealth equitably throughout society, launching a series of upheavals, built on the flimsy scaffolding that held high the dreams of socialist perfection and what has come to be called "social justice." In their way of thinking, they had blessed the multitudes. But by the time Stalin and Chairman Mao and others of their ilk had finished their ghastly reigns of terror, uncounted millions of their victims had died horrific deaths.

In the big picture, a transition from a free-market economy to one dictated by central planning has long been the dream of the surreptitious socialists in our midst. In the process, our economy has purposely been driven toward insolvency.

By way of contrast, free-market capitalism, which depends upon agreements made by participants in a transaction, is socialism's enemy. The freedom to personally manage wealth is always threatened on every side by those who favor some form of government administration, which is generally cruel and dictatorial, viewing Christians as its enemy. The Bible states the situation quite succinctly:

> Now the Lord is that Spirit: and where the Spirit of the
> Lord is, there is liberty. (2 Corinthians 3:17).

The battle for economic freedom is still tilted in favor of the Western powers. There is a remnant of Bible-believing Christians, through whom the liberty of Christ still holds forth, though in diminished fashion.

Across the Atlantic, the once-vaunted common currency of the euro has fallen from grace. Not too long ago, many hoped that it was destined to become the West's regulating currency. They said that the world would soon quote the price of oil in euros. Now, Europe has discovered a simple truth: When rich countries support poor ones, there is never enough money to go around. Economic "fairness" in the form of pensions, strong unions, and socialized medicine soon uses up the money supply. Panicked central planners are in the process of crafting a new Europe. A while back, in a move that was whimsically labeled "Brexit," (British exit from the European Economic

Community), the United Kingdom pulled away from the bondage of the euro. In Parliament, the debate continues.

In the post-Soviet world, Russia is now headed by a group of oligarchs—wealthy capitalists who play fast and loose in the markets of the world. One man has risen to the top of the heap: Raised as a communist, who obtained his credentials in the KGB, Vladimir Putin has, beginning in the year 2000, been in various leadership positions of the Russian Federation.

He claims to be a Russian Orthodox believer, a moral and beneficent leader with his people's interest at heart. In reality, he's a dictator and a communist. Many have said that when all is said and done, he's probably the richest man in the world, with access to the spoils of the old Soviet Union, in league with his billionaire confederates. What will he do with all that money? Simple: He plans to expand Russian control and extend Russian power.

China's finance ministers have dominated foreign trade for the specific purpose of expanding the value of their "people's currency," and its basic unit, the yuan. Daily, they increase its action in foreign trade. They would like to see it emerge as the world's reserve currency—the standard for foreign exchange.

All the while, their exploding technology and military systems are being directed toward higher and higher states of readiness, should a war evolve. But since they rely on the wealth of other countries to sell their goods, the collapsing wealth of free-market capitalist countries has them worried.

Progressives and the Economy

The socialists are on the march. And socialism, having such an appalling past, has forced them to adopt a new name. Calling themselves "progressives," they still pursue the Marxist/socialist dream: a managed global economy in the near future. They envision it under the control of a few powerful men. Interestingly, this is just what the Bible has prophesied for the last days.

To global planners, progress would be the collapse of the free-market economy and its replacement by a managed, global economy.

Clearly, we're headed toward a financial change of historic (some would say biblical) proportions. The Dow-Jones and NASDAQ economic indicators are exploding. Buying, selling, investing, employment, saving, and earning are at the top of every news cycle. Behind it all, a new picture is coming into view. It reveals a cabal of power-mad economic revolutionaries who believe that their time to control the financial system has arrived at last.

The term "economy" has its source in the New Testament Greek word, *oikonomia*. It means "stewardship" or "management of the household." Though the Bible is not an economics textbook, as such, it has much to say on the subject of money and finance. Properly understood, the subject of economics has a vital connection to spiritual life in general. Scripture tells us that there is a way to handle money in this world and a way to view it from the proper perspective.

It is safe to say that money is a global obsession. In the last couple of decades, it was routine for fortunes to be made overnight. The traditional preoccupation was to make as much money as possible, as quickly as possible. And, as the old saying goes, "It's easy to be a financial genius in a bull market."

But finance is like the sea, with waves and tides…even tsunamis…that are heralded by a sudden, radical drop in the tide, followed by a swift, disastrous inundation. When the waters are normal, life goes swimmingly. But in the words of another old financial maxim, "It's easy to see who's swimming naked when the tide goes out." Those who played fast and loose with the economy for the last decade would stand fully exposed in a crisis. Then, their current preoccupation becomes rescuing what's left.

When there is a stable medium of financial exchange, all is well. When the medium becomes unstable, there is anguish and uncertainty. The questions burn. Will we continue to be able to earn…to buy…to sell? Some might say that we are on the verge of a cataclysmic economic collapse; others insist that it's already here.

In many ways, the Bible speaks to the current events that are unfolding before our eyes. There are massive changes sweeping around the world. We are among those who would say that they were forecast in prophecy. And in fact, economic conditions look exactly as they are seen in biblical descriptions of the last days.

After years of attempting to shift power from private investors into the public sector, creating a socialist economy, a new US president has reignited nationalism and strength in the global marketplace. His success depends upon the support he gets here and around the world.

Nuclear weapons proliferate, making it virtually inevitable that, at some point, they will be detonated in an all-out war.

In spite of this threat, the attention of the world is now focused upon the global economy. In this game of rulership, the United States is trillions of dollars in debt, but so are others. Rulers of the East watch for their chance to control the economy.

Gold, Silver, and Prophecy

Uncertainty can be marketed: There are always the ubiquitous gold and silver salesmen, constantly present on video screens around the world. They continually predict an economic crash of historic proportions, at the same time preaching that the only way to survive this calamity is to own hard (metallic) currency. (They've been promoting this idea for a long time.)

What does Bible prophecy have to say about the global economy? Actually, it's quite clear on the matter: At some point in the future, the global economy—including hard currency—will become worthless:

> Go to now, ye rich men, weep and howl for your miseries that shall come upon you. Your riches are corrupted, and your garments are motheaten. Your gold and silver is cankered; and the rust of them shall be a witness against you, and shall eat your flesh as it were fire. Ye have heaped treasure together for the last days. Behold, the hire of the labourers who have reaped down your fields, which is of you kept back by fraud, crieth: and the cries of them which have reaped are entered into the ears of the Lord of sabaoth. Ye have lived in pleasure on the earth, and been wanton; ye have nourished your hearts, as in a day of slaughter. Ye have

condemned and killed the just; and he doth not resist you. Be patient therefore, brethren, unto the coming of the Lord. Behold, the husbandman waiteth for the precious fruit of the earth, and hath long patience for it, until he receive the early and latter rain. Be ye also patient; stablish your hearts: for the coming of the Lord draweth nigh. (James 5:1–8)

In passionate terms, James summons the wealthy to their judgment. James' words seem more suited to the Tribulation than to the period just before it. One can easily see James' proclamation as harbinger of the third seal of Revelation, chapter 6:

And when he had opened the third seal, I heard the third beast say, Come and see. And I beheld, and lo a black horse; and he that sat on him had a pair of balances in his hand. And I heard a voice in the midst of the four beasts say, A measure of wheat for a penny, and three measures of barley for a penny; and see thou hurt not the oil and the wine. (Revelation 6:5, 6)

With the passion of an Old Testament prophet, James addresses the "rich men" who will be alive during the Tribulation…those who have carefully planned a world they can control with absolute power.

One immediately thinks of the days of Daniel's prophecy of the "fourth beast" with "ten horns," that rises up in the last days to establish a global dictatorship. (Then, the Antichrist rises to take it all for himself.) In fact, the fulfillment of Daniel's seventieth week (the seven years of the Tribulation), depends upon the dictatorial management of the world's wealth.

How Do You Handle Mammon?

Today, print and video commercials are replete with offers to buy gold and silver in order to be safe during a coming financial collapse. But as James prophesies, it is "the just," not the rich, who are vindicated.

What got us where we are today? Quite simply: greed, corruption, and incompetence. Honesty and ethics were thrown overboard for the greenback. There is nothing new about behavior of this sort. Jesus spoke to a society riddled with exactly such practices.

Early in His public ministry, He spoke on the subject of "mammon." This word comes from an Aramaic term denoting wealth or property in general. In the New Testament, "mammon" is encountered only on the lips of Jesus. It simply means "property" or "worldly goods." It refers to material goods and land, with its buildings. Today, we would most often call it "money," with all its attributes, good and evil. Jesus made a clear and well-known statement to the effect that money, as a redemptive force, is totally in opposition to God:

> No man can serve two masters: for either he will hate
> the one, and love the other; or else he will hold to the one,
> and despise the other. **Ye cannot serve God and mam-
> mon.** (Matthew 6:24)

Jesus knew that mankind instinctively views money as the remedy for the ills of humanity and society. Thought of in this way, it becomes a god. Redistribution of money is often presented as the solution to longstanding social problems. It is even vaunted as the cure for health problems, as in "universal health care." Jesus draws the line between the worship of money on the one hand and God on the other.

But He also recognized that while they reside in the world, people must realize that there is a proper way to handle monetary affairs. In Luke's Gospel, Jesus delved deeply into the details about how money should be viewed and handled.

Many of His parables were about money. For example, the parable of the unjust steward speaks eloquently of the need to understand steward-ship…saving and investment.

The sixteenth chapter of Luke relates this fascinating story. Its central theme is about shady business practices so familiar that it has our current culture written all over it. It tells of a rich businessman whose steward (busi-ness manager) is a crook. The employer calls the steward forward and ac-cuses him of wasting his possessions. In other words, he is charged with having squandered the capital of the business. We're not told exactly how

he abused his authority, but the context makes it clear that
skimming off much of the profit for himself.

The steward was ordered to produce a record of his de
more, he was told that he would no longer be retained as bus

The steward, rightly reasoning that he would soon be ou ⸻ the street
with no prospects for gainful employment, concocted a wicked scheme to
make friends in the business world: He would quickly short-sell his master's goods so that others in the business community would owe him favors.
Once out on his own, he could call in the favors and be back in business
once again. This was his devious plan for future employment.

One of his clients owed the business a hundred measures (six hundred
gallons!) of oil. In quick fashion, the steward called him in and said, "Pay me
for fifty measures, and you're off the hook!" Another owed for a hundred
measures (sixty-five bushels) of wheat. The steward told him, "Pay me for
eighty measures and we'll consider the debt paid."

And when his employer found out what was happening, how did he
view the steward's actions? Amazingly, he complimented him! Talking as
one shrewd businessman to another, he recognized that the steward was
using the same shady dealings as he, himself, would have used. He recognized the effectiveness of worldly wisdom:

> And the lord commended the unjust steward, because
> he had done wisely: for the children of this world are in
> their generation wiser than the children of light. And I say
> unto you, Make to yourselves friends of the mammon of
> unrighteousness; that, when ye fail, they may receive you
> into everlasting habitations. He that is faithful in that which
> is least is faithful also in much: and he that is unjust in the
> least is unjust also in much. If therefore ye have not been
> faithful in the unrighteous mammon, who will commit to
> your trust the true riches? And if ye have not been faithful in
> that which is another man's, who shall give you that which
> is your own? No servant can serve two masters: for either
> he will hate the one, and love the other; or else he will hold

> to the one, and despise the other. **Ye cannot serve God
> and mammon.** And the Pharisees also, who were covetous,
> heard all these things: and they derided him. (Luke 16:8–14)

Here, as Luke repeats Jesus' statement in Matthew, we are led to a re-markable conclusion. The lord (employer) of the steward must have en-gaged in the very same shady principles as his steward when he first made his own fortune; he recognized good business when he saw it. It was not *moral* business, but it was *good* business.

Jesus then commented that worldly people use their money more wisely (albeit unethically) than many of the righteous. He also urged His righteous listeners to use the "mammon of unrighteousness" wisely, so that when they came to the end of their lives, they would be well received in heaven.

Money and Love

In and of itself, money is not an evil thing. It is the *love* of it that brings ruin. Worshiping it as redemptive in value creates a false god. Paul's words to Timothy ring out with this truth:

> And having food and raiment let us be therewith content. But they that will be rich fall into temptation and a snare, and into many foolish and hurtful lusts, which drown men in destruction and perdition. For the **love of money** is the root of all evil: which while some coveted after, they have erred from the faith, and pierced themselves through with many sorrows. But thou, O man of God, flee these things; and follow after righteousness, godliness, faith, love, patience, meekness. (1 Timothy 6:8–11, emphasis added)

At the present historical moment, the entire world is an exhibit of this fundamental truth. The love of money has driven us all into an insane mer-ry-go-round of financial pursuit. Shipping and receiving, import and ex-port, electronic funds transfers, gimmicks, gadgets, new products, and new forms of entertainment have created an unstable superstructure that is now threatened with total collapse.

The economy is moving at an insane speed, as artificially intelligent marketing and delivery methods compete for "instant" billing and fulfillment. Based on the latest computer technology, they deliver instant gratification.

For some time, world leaders have called for a centrally controlled global government, which Bible prophecy tells us, won't come until the Antichrist commands its inception.

This, of course, would require a world currency and central control of the economy. Up to the present moment, this isn't happening. The old global Group of Eight (G8), whose summits once directed global economic policy, met in 1997, 2004, and 2017. That meeting witnessed the Russian withdrawal from the group. But nothing is permanent in global financial interaction. Now, as the Group of 20 (G20), they meet, but never quite reach their heralded function—to bring economic sense and stability to global trade.

Still, Scripture predicts that they will arrive at some sort of influence. As the global financial picture wobbles into ever-increasing instability, they will soon achieve great power. Their method of control will be a Byzantine forest of regulations that direct the actions of every human being on earth. The Bible refers to their composite power as a "beast." But a major disruption—war or power-grid failure, a complete stop—would bring financial catastrophe.

The Global Merchants

Briefly stated, it's not love that makes the world go around; it's the power of money.

Man's ages-long spiritual struggle has fought many incarnations of this beast. It is the final incarnation of commercial Babylon, the global merchant trade that is destroyed once and for all in the events of Revelation 18.

But its origins are seen in the Old Testament, where they are most clearly described in Ezekiel 27 and its "lamentation for Tyrus." Tyrus, or Tyre, is the Bible's denotation of the ancient Phoenician culture. It rose to power in the centuries that led up to the kingdom of David and Solomon. It was part of the Canaanite civilization that finally concentrated its power at the northeast shores of the Mediterranean Sea, in the territory known today as Lebanon. It also extended northward to the land later known as Syria.

The ships of Tyre literally plied the seven seas, carrying trade goods around the world. In the process, it developed the precedents that have come down to the present age. Its wealth and business acumen were legendary. It was the king of Tyre who brought the materials and architects that built Solomon's great empire and the First Temple. From approximately 1550 BC until about 330 BC (in the great siege of Alexander the Great), Tyre was unequalled in world trade.

From the merchants of Tyre, the principles of international law and credit were formed. They were fully realized in the days of the Dutch East Indies company and the global trade of the British Empire. Out of that system came the law of the sea and the foundations of today's march toward global government.

The merchants of this system become the symbols of a world that values finance and trade above faith in God. Put another way, the merchant trade becomes a god, and merchandise (money) is its spirit.

> The word of the Lord came again unto me, saying, Now, thou son of man, take up a lamentation for Tyrus; And say unto Tyrus, O thou that art situate at the entry of the sea, which art a merchant of the people for many isles, Thus saith the Lord God; O Tyrus, thou hast said, I am of perfect beauty. (Ezekiel 27:1–3)

Here, in the opening of his prophecy against Tyre, Ezekiel describes the dynasty of the Phoenicians as international merchants, who traffic among the "isles," or continents. Further, the king of Tyre sees himself as exemplary of perfection. Later, Ezekiel identifies this dynasty as the earthly expression of the anointed cherub...the fallen one...Satan.

We won't quote the entire twenty-seventh chapter of Ezekiel, in which the prophet describes in detail the range of Tyre's merchant trade, identified under the title "merchants of Tarshish."

> Tarshish was thy merchant by reason of the multitude
> of all kind of riches; with silver, iron, tin, and lead, they
> traded in thy fairs. Javan, Tubal, and Meshech, they were
> thy merchants: they traded the persons of men and ves-
> sels of brass in thy market. They of the house of Togarmah
> traded in thy fairs with horses and horsemen and mules.
> The men of Dedan were thy merchants; many isles were the
> merchandise of thine hand: they brought thee for a present
> horns of ivory and ebony. (Ezekiel 27:12–15)

Here, at the beginning of the roll call of nations, Ezekiel describes the merchants of Tarshish as trading with Greece, the regions of the Caucasus and the Arabians. As he continues, his text also includes Syria, Arabia, Assyria, Damascus, and others. All of them received goods brought from the continents of the world. Even the gold of Solomon's Temple came via their world trade.

But the prophecy moves forward to the latter days in words that foreshadow the book of Revelation, which speaks of the ultimate destruction of the merchants' global trade:

> The ships of Tarshish did sing of thee in thy market: and
> thou wast replenished, and made very glorious in the midst
> of the seas. Thy rowers have brought thee into great waters:
> the east wind hath broken thee in the midst of the seas. Thy
> riches, and thy fairs, thy merchandise, thy mariners, and thy
> pilots, thy calkers, and the occupiers of thy merchandise,
> and all thy men of war, that are in thee, and in all thy com-
> pany which is in the midst of thee, **shall fall into the midst
> of the seas in the day of thy ruin.** The suburbs shall shake
> at the sound of the cry of thy pilots. And all that handle the
> oar, the mariners, and all the pilots of the sea, shall come
> down from their ships, they shall stand upon the land; And
> shall cause their voice to be heard against thee, and shall
> cry bitterly, and shall cast up dust upon their heads, they

shall wallow themselves in the ashes: (Ezekiel 27:25–30, emphasis added).

The final phrase in the passage above is repeated in John's description of the same event. Though his perspective is different and his details more numerous, it is clearly the same event that is being described:

> And they cast dust on their heads, and cried, weeping and wailing, saying, Alas, alas, that great city, wherein were made rich all that had ships in the sea by reason of her costliness! for in one hour is she made desolate. (Revelation 18:19)

Clearly, Scripture foretells the absolute destruction of a future global government, supported by worldwide merchant traffic. Today, in voices urgently crying for the salvation of a collapsing world market, the world's leaders are calling for the formation of just such a government.

Even a few months ago, such an alignment might have been thought impossible, since America was considered the world's single global super-power. Now, with trillions of dollars evaporating like water in the desert, any resistance to joining a world government may simply disappear.

Greek Philosophy and Socialism

We hear the rising cry: We must use the current economic crisis as an opportunity to repair the failed monetary systems of the world. It is unfair that some are rich and others so miserably poor. Now, after centuries of the rich lording it over the poor, we have a chance to create a system that brings *fairness*.

Since the days of Plato and his publication of *The Republic,* men have dreamed of creating a utopia. Devoid of the knowledge of God, they end-lessly devise schemes to bring some equitable system to the masses.

In his famous dialogue, Plato proposes ways to bring justice—fair-ness—to society. He sees cities as being founded to bring social, political, and educational order. He envisions a society being led by philosophically superior men and women who reside in communistic residences, which he calls "guardhouses." They enforce social order, which they regulate to bring the best to mankind. They make certain that everyone gets an equal share of the community property.

On the basis of 2,500 years of experience, we now know that such a system cannot work, because man is basically sinful and unable to regulate his own behavior, much less bring loving order to a community. In a socialist society, powerful men will invariably rise to control, take a growing share of power and money, ruling by executive fiat.

Still, in spite of its history of invariable failure, socialism rises again and again to assert its claim to superiority.

Socialism Seems Good

Socialism is so pervasive and so subtle that it can insinuate itself into even the most moral and ethical of settings. Wherever there is the prospect of taking power, it is always there, masked in benevolence and philanthropy, but ever waiting to leap to power when it sees the opportunity. Like the old serpent, it never sleeps. It is constantly on the prowl, probing for weak spots, and launching endless streams of propaganda.

Socialism, or state control of the means of production and distribution, offers "fairness," on the basis that the underdogs of society are being cheated. In exchange for power and control, it offers to bring blessing to everyone in society. It masquerades as the great provider.

Amazingly, socialism even made its way into the inner council of Christ! Among the disciples of Jesus, one was a socialist. This is best illustrated by looking at an incident recorded by three of the four Gospels. It concerns Mary of Bethany and her act of love toward the Lord.

Notice the reaction of the disciples and the response of Jesus:

> Now when Jesus was in Bethany, in the house of Simon
> the leper, There came unto him a woman having an ala-
> baster box of very precious ointment, and poured it on his
> head, as he sat at meat. But when his disciples saw it, they
> had indignation, saying, To what purpose is this waste? For

this ointment might have been sold for much, and given to the poor. When Jesus understood it, he said unto them, Why trouble ye the woman? for she hath wrought a good work upon me. **For ye have the poor always with you**; but me ye have not always. For in that she hath poured this ointment on my body, she did it for my burial. Verily I say unto you, Wheresoever this gospel shall be preached in the whole world, there shall also this, that this woman hath done, be told for a memorial of her. (Matthew 26:6–13, emphasis added).

Why were Jesus' friends and disciples so angry at such an obvious and sacrificial act of love? Her action showed a willingness to spend a great deal on Christ, which she would never recover. She gave it away. Still, the disciples saw the act as a waste of resources that could be better used elsewhere…probably to cover their "ministry expenses."

Jesus rebuked them, saying in effect that she was directed by the Spirit of God. She gave all to bless Him in the light of the sacrifice that He was about to make, in giving Himself for the sin of mankind.

Furthermore, He uttered those famous words, "For ye have the poor always with you." With profound clarity, He pronounced the truth of a great principle—namely, that the problem of human poverty can never be solved with the mere application of money, as the socialist ideology wrongly insists.

A Year's Wages

Mark's Gospel relates the same episode, with slight variations, naming the ointment and giving an estimate of its price. Spikenard, an appealing perfume, was derived from the plant called "nard" in the Greek language, its Latin designation being *nardostachys jatamansi*. Then and now, it grows in India, in the vicinity of the Himalayan mountain range.

The roots of the plant are fragrant and spicy, and they are harvested and processed with great effort. In Jesus' day, the ointment was a product produced, expensively packaged in carved alabaster, and imported from India.

Before shipping, it was hermetically sealed to avoid any evaporation before it was used.

> And being in Bethany in the house of Simon the leper, as he sat at meat, there came a woman having an alabaster box of ointment of spikenard very precious; and she brake the box, and poured it on his head. And there were some that had indignation within themselves, and said, Why was this waste of the ointment made? For it might have been sold for more than three hundred pence, and have been given to the poor. And they murmured against her. And Jesus said, Let her alone; why trouble ye her? she hath wrought a good work on me. **For ye have the poor with you always**, and whensoever ye will ye may do them good: but me ye have not always. She hath done what she could: she is come aforehand to anoint my body to the burying. Verily I say unto you, Wheresoever this gospel shall be preached throughout the whole world, this also that she hath done shall be spoken of for a memorial of her. (Mark 14:3–9, emphasis added)

The "three hundred pence" mentioned here are in fact, three hundred *denarii*. About the size of a modern dime, the *denarius* is always called a "penny" in the New Testament. In the first century, it was considered *a day's wages* for the common man. In Mark, the amount of the "waste" is given, at over three hundred days' wages—making it approximately a year's income!

The anger of the disciples now becomes somewhat understandable. This was a great extravagance! Still, Jesus puts her actions into the perspective of His upcoming sentence of death. Compared with that, the sacrifice of the ointment is nothing. Only He has the perspective to see that.

John's account of the occasion tells us that His crucifixion is only six days away. As they ate supper, the miracle called Lazarus is seated in their midst, no doubt basking in the good fellowship. We also learn that when Mary unseals the ointment, it is no small quantity. Here it is called "a pound." As given in the original text, it is a Roman *litra* of about 12 ounces—somewhat less than a modern pound, yet a very large amount of a substance so expensive.

Now, in John's Gospel, we discover that it is Judas who leads the objection:

> Then Jesus six days before the passover came to Bethany, where Lazarus was which had been dead, whom he raised from the dead. There they made him a supper; and Martha served: but Lazarus was one of them that sat at the table with him. Then took Mary a pound of ointment of spikenard, very costly, and anointed the feet of Jesus, and wiped his feet with her hair: and the house was filled with the odour of the ointment. Then saith one of his disciples, Judas Iscariot, Simon's son, which should betray him, Why was not this ointment sold for three hundred pence, and given to the poor? This he said, **not that he cared for the poor**; but because he was a thief, and had the bag, and bare what was put therein. (John 12:1–6, emphasis added)

Judas, the Socialist

Here, the words of Judas give us the full explanation of this incident, and its importance, relative to Scripture in general.

Now, we discover that as treasurer (the keeper of the bag), Judas' real motive was the status of the bank account. John tells us that his central concern was his own personal enrichment. But when his role in Christ's inner council is examined, he is the perfect example of socialism.

Think of it: He must have had visions of himself as the secretary of the Messiah's treasury! When the Lord came into His Kingdom, which in his mind was only a short time away, Judas would have had access to millions—even billions—in the coin of the realm.

But publicly, his outcry was for the "poor." It is ever so. The bureaucrats in socialist schemes always couch their motives in the language of saving the underprivileged. They do what they do "for the children," "for the sick," or for the "downtrodden."

Judas is quite simply the perfect illustration of socialism in action. Secretly, he saw himself as an administrator of wealth. He saw nothing wrong with feathering his own nest with the funds intended for Jesus' own public ministry. In retrospect, it is astounding that he believed that the Lord didn't know of his sin.

And remember, Judas is one of two men in Scripture who are called "the son of perdition." The other man is the Antichrist! Significantly, he too, is at the center of a scheme involving the redistribution of wealth.

Financial Ruin

At the beginning of the Tribulation, four horses ride forth to ravage a world gone mad. The first horse, a white one, is commonly thought to represent the initial advance of the Antichrist. The second is a red horse, representing war…a global war. The third horse represents the collapse of the global economic system. Its dark, black color is foreboding, indeed. Finally, there is the pale horse of death.

As they bolt forth, the Tribulation is unveiled to a world that has no inkling of the devastation about to fall upon them. The black horse speaks of what we, today, call commodities. It speaks of wheat, barley, oil, and wine, and their limited quantity, at a high price. A measure (*choenix*, about a quart) of wheat costs a denarius—a day's wages. Three *choenixes* of barley (a less nutritious grain) for a day's wages.

> And when he had opened the third seal, I heard the third beast say, Come and see. And I beheld, and lo a black horse; and he that sat on him had a pair of balances in his hand. And I heard a voice in the midst of the four beasts say, A measure of wheat for a penny, and three measures of barley for a penny; and see thou hurt not the oil and the wine. (Revelation 6:5, 6)

Many have commented on this horse, saying that it represents the global famine that is to come upon the earth. Historians say that the *choenix* of grain was one soldier's daily ration, usually in barley. This means that in that day, a working man won't be able to support his family.

Wealth and "Sudden Destruction"

James, the brother of our Lord, authored a prophecy that presents an uncanny description of events now coming to pass in our contemporary world. It speaks of the plutocrats of the latter day. They are the vastly wealthy managers of banking, commodities, energy, and construction. Their empires have for some time set the tone of the modern world.

But the day is coming when all their complex interactions will completely break down. Earlier, we quoted the opening verses of James, chapter 5. Its first three verses are worth repeating:

> Go to now, ye rich men, weep and howl for your miseries that shall come upon you. Your riches are corrupted, and your garments are motheaten. Your gold and silver is cankered; and the rust of them shall be a witness against you, and shall eat your flesh as it were fire. Ye have heaped treasure together for the **last days**. (emphasis added)

Notice that James' prophecy is focused upon the "last days." This is the period leading up to the global takeover of the economy by the Antichrist.

The vast wealth of the global trading consortium is literally incalculable. It can be expressed only in astronomical figures and unfathomable equations. But it harnesses the real producers of wealth into virtual slavery, so that its power can rise to greater and greater heights. Their palaces and lavish headquarters are alive with electronic trading, but they float upon a sludge pit of global poverty.

Pretending to bring wealth to the masses, they have instead taxed them nearly to death. They have taken the fruits of their work to fashion a thousand worthless programs, proposed to engineer a better society. Their idealist proposals invariably divert profits into their own coffers…all in the name of social idealism. But the real inheritor of their riches will be the Antichrist.

They will suddenly become impoverished and fall into a state of mourning and anguish unprecedented in world history:

> But of the times and the seasons, brethren, ye have no need that I write unto you. For yourselves know perfectly

that the day of the Lord so cometh as a thief in the night. For when they shall say, Peace and safety; then **sudden destruction** cometh upon them, as travail upon a woman with child; and they shall not escape. But ye, brethren, are not in darkness, that that day should overtake you as a thief. Ye are all the children of light, and the children of the day: we are not of the night, nor of darkness. (1 Thessalonians 5:1–5, emphasis added)

The Antichrist's Solution

The Tribulation will be marked by the radical collapse of all the world's infrastructures. One catastrophe after another will befall the world's rapidly diminishing population. War, famine, disease, and natural disaster will reduce the census by half.

As in past wars, the economy will run out of control. Midnight trading, hoarding, an active black market, and the desperation of the starving will set the tone of horror. Criminal activities of all sorts will be the norm. Desperate men will take desperate measures.

Then will arise a man with a solution to the unequal distribution of goods and services. With the aid of the false prophet, the beast will take control of the situation:

> And he had power to give life unto the image of the beast, that the image of the beast should both speak, and cause that as many as would not worship the image of the beast should be killed.
>
> And he causeth all, both small and great, rich and poor, free and bond, to receive a mark in their right hand, or in their foreheads:
>
> And that no man might buy or sell, save he that had the mark, or the name of the beast, or the number of his name. (Revelation 13:15–17)

The Antichrist will become a ubiquitous presence. Probably by means of global video, he will appear on every street corner and in every storefront and home. With the power of life and death, he will enforce a socialist economic system that promises to give every man his "fair" share.

Of course, his definition of "fair" will be entirely self-serving. It will require supplicants to recognize him as a god before receiving their share. The millions who died under the collectivist decrees of Hitler, Stalin, Chairman Mao, or Pol Pot would instantly recognize this routine.

Under Antichrist's regime, believers in Jesus will be required to acknowledge the deity of the Antichrist. Then and only then will they be allowed access to the global market…the ultimate expression of socialism. The oft-mentioned "mark of the Beast" is nothing more than a control mechanism that links access to the wealth with enforced behavior.

Moreover, his system works! During the Tribulation the markets apparently function as usual. But in the end, the system crashes. Revelation brings the prophecies of the "merchants of Tarshish" to a conclusion. At the termination of the seven years, they meet with total destruction:

> For in one hour so great riches is come to nought. And every shipmaster, and all the company in ships, and sailors, and as many as trade by sea, stood afar off, And cried when they saw the smoke of her burning, saying, What city is like unto this great city! And they cast dust on their heads, and cried, weeping and wailing, saying, Alas, alas, that great city, wherein were made rich all that had ships in the sea by reason of her costliness! for in one hour is she made desolate. (Revelation 18:17–19)

The religion of "business as usual" is now being inflated into a colossus, unstoppable in its authority. We live in the time of its formation. Its sudden destruction can't be far behind.

One day soon, in the coming age of Christ's Kingdom, personal freedom and private ownership will characterize the blessed world at last ruled by the Lord:

And they shall build houses, and inhabit them; and they shall plant vineyards, and eat the fruit of them. They shall not build, and another inhabit; they shall not plant, and another eat: for as the days of a tree are the days of my people, and mine elect shall long enjoy the work of their hands. They shall not labour in vain, nor bring forth for trouble; for they are the seed of the blessed of the LORD, and their offspring with them. (Isaiah 65:21–23)

Under Christ's rule, men will live in their own homes and eat the fruits of their own work. They will enjoy the profits of their own labor, and the beauty of their own creative work. Mere human beings have dreamed of a society in which life, liberty, and the pursuit of happiness were living realities. Only under the Lord's administration will this dream become a functioning reality.

CHAPTER 13

DAYS OF NOAH, DAYS OF LOT LUNACY

RYAN PITTERSON

TWO THOUSAND YEARS AGO, the disciples of Jesus Christ asked the Lord when the events of the end-times Great Tribulation would come to pass or what would be the signs of the return of the Savior. In response, the Messiah pointed to two distinct eras that would be indicators of the final years before his Second Coming: the Days of Noah and the Days of Lot.

> And as it was in the days of Noe, so shall it be also in the days of the Son of man. They did eat, they drank, they married wives, they were given in marriage, until the day that Noah entered into the ark, and the flood came, and destroyed them all. Likewise also as it was in the days of Lot; they did eat, they drank, they bought, they sold, they planted, they builded; But the same day that Lot went out of Sodom it rained fire and brimstone from heaven, and destroyed them all. Even thus shall it be in the day when the Son of man is revealed. (Luke 17:26–30)

What was it about both periods of history that moved Jesus to say the days before His return would be identical? The prophets of God preached and warned the people of both eras of the cataclysmic judgment coming and they were ignored. This chapter will explore the distinguishing traits of the world in those days:

- The constant focus on self, the mundane, and the cares of the world with no reverence for God or His Word.

- The obsession with wealth, material success, and industry.

- The stunning increase in violence and moral depravity

- The open presence of angels and humanity's sinful attempts to interact with them. This led to disastrous consequences in both of those eras and foreshadowed the return of the rebel angels to the human realm in the end times. To fully grasp how the world fell into such deep depravity and will once again in the final days before the return of the Lord Jesus Christ, it is where this study must begin.

1. Attempting to Access the Fallen Angelic and Demonic Realm Led to Society's Destruction

> For It God spared not the angels that sinned, but cast them down to hell, and delivered them into chains of darkness, to be reserved unto judgment; And spared not the old world, but saved Noah the eighth person, a preacher of righteousness, bringing in the flood upon the world of the ungodly; And turning the cities of Sodom and Gomorrah into ashes condemned them with an overthrow, making them an ensample unto those that after should live ungodly. (2 Peter 2:4–6)

In this passage, the Apostle Peter, like the Lord Jesus Christ, connects the days of Noah and Lot. But it also links those eras to "the angels that sinned." These rebel spirits were a faction of the fallen angels in Scripture. Unlike Satan and most apostate angelic beings who roam to and fro in the earth, this subgroup has already been "cast down to hell," imprisoned in chains under darkness. Why? Because they had sinful relations with humanity and helped usher the world to epic ruin.

The Descendants of Cain Had Forbidden Relations with Fallen Angels

> Hast thou marked the old way which wicked men have trodden? Which were cut down out of time, whose foundation was overflown with a flood: Which said unto God, Depart from us: and what can the Almighty do for them? (Job 22:15–18)

The days of Noah and Lot were both marked by blatant rejection of God and His Word. This was no doubt started by Cain, the wicked son of Adam and Eve and the first murderer in human history. Scripture is clear that his heart was filled with sinful rebellion:

> In this the children of God are manifest, and the children of the devil: whosoever doeth not righteousness is not of God, neither he that loveth not his brother. For this is the message that ye heard from the beginning, that we should love one another. Not as Cain, who was of that wicked one, and slew his brother. And wherefore slew he him? Because his own works were evil, and his brother's righteous. (1 John 3:10–12)

Cain was "of that wicked one," meaning spiritually, he was a child of Satan. He lied to God's face after murdering his brother with casual indifference. After being banished, his descendants carried on that sad, sinful legacy. However, interestingly, in the seventh generation of Cain's lineage, an intellectual explosion took place.

In *Judgment of the Nephilim,* I detailed how Cain's lineage became the perfect target for the devil's scheme. Through sinful temptation, Satan enticed angels to rebel against God and take human women as wives for fornication. In exchange, the fallen angels offered humanity knowledge and technology. This illicit transaction originated in the family of Lamech, the patriarch of the seventh generation of Adam through Cain:

> And Lamech took unto him two wives: the name of the one was Adah, and the name of the other Zillah. And Adah bare Jabal: he was the father of such as dwell in tents, and

of such as have cattle. And his brother's name was Jubal: he was the father of all such as handle the harp and organ. And Zillah, she also bare Tubal Cain, an instructer of every artificer in brass and iron: and the sister of tubacin was Naamah. (Genesis 4:19–22)

The "sons of God," apostate angels who invaded the human realm, entered a transaction with this family, exchanging knowledge and technology for human wives. In this initial instance, it was Naamah, the daughter, who became infamous for alluring the fallen angels. A nineteenth-century treatise on the fallen angels supports this conclusion:

> The Hebrew Doctors…say of this Naamah that all the world wandered in love after her yea even the Sons of God as in [Genesis 6:2] and that of her there were born evil spirits into the world. It may be remarked that Naamah, as sixth in descent from Cain, whose birth took place many years before that of Seth, would have been in the world, while Jared, Enoch, and Methuselah, were all living: that is in other words about the time at which we suppose the angels to have formed alliances with the daughters of men.[143]

The resulting knowledge and skill acquired by this family was unprecedented. In one generation, Jabal was the father of animal husbandry and tentmaking. Jubal became inventor of musical instruments (the jubilee, a semicentennial celebration on the Hebrew calendar marked by a blowing of trumpets, derives its root from his name). Tubal-Cain was the forefather of blacksmithing and metallurgy, crafting iron and brass into tools and weapons of war. The Roman god Vulcan was the mythic take on the real Tubal Cain from biblical history. A renowned biblical expositor confirms this:

> Tubal Cain, a member of the same family, was "an instructer of every artificer in brass and iron." He is supposed to be the Vulcan of the ancients, one of their fictitious deities often mentioned. It is the same name, simply shortened; and the occupations of both were the same.... As Tubal Cain was a descendant of Cain, living among his followers,

and the earth becoming filled with violence, we may well suppose that he introduced their manufacture and excelled in making them.[144]

Instigated by Satan's temptation and sexual lust, these angels would change the course of human history with their egregious sin:

> And it came to pass, when men began to multiply on the face of the earth, and daughters were born unto them, That the sons of God saw the daughters of men that they were fair; and they took them wives of all which they chose. And the LORD said, My spirit shall not always strive with man, for that he also is flesh: yet his days shall be an hundred and twenty years.
>
> There were giants [Nephilim] in the earth in those days; and also after that, when the sons of God came in unto the daughters of men, and they bare children to them, the same became mighty men which were of old, men of renown. And God saw that the wickedness of man was great in the earth, and that every imagination of the thoughts of his heart was only evil continually. And it repented the LORD that he had made man on the earth, and it grieved him at his heart. (Genesis 6:1–5)

The Nephilim, the offspring of this illicit union between angels and human women, were the hybrid supermen, wholly wicked and extremely violent. They triggered a genetic and moral corruption that led the Lord to bring the flood judgment that wiped out all of humanity save for Noah and his family.

Why did they do this? In addition to satisfying their sinful lust, it was an attempt to thwart God's plan of salvation through a human Messiah who would be born from a woman:

> And the LORD God said unto the serpent, Because thou hast done this, thou art cursed above all cattle, and above every beast of the field; upon thy belly shalt thou go, and dust shalt thou eat all the days of thy life: And I will put

enmity between thee and the woman, and between thy seed and her seed; it shall bruise thy head, and thou shalt bruise his heel. (Genesis 3:15)

Theologian A. W. Pink succinctly summed up the plan of Satan for his rebel angels:

> The reference in Jude 6 to the angels leaving their own habitation, appears to point to and correspond with these "sons of God" (angels) coming in unto the daughters of men. Apparently, by this means, Satan hoped to destroy humanity (the channel through which the woman's Seed was to come) by producing a race of monstrosities. How nearly he succeeded is evident from the fact, that except for one family, "all flesh had corrupted his way upon the earth" (Gen. 6:12). That monstrosities were produced as the result of this unnatural union between the "sons of God" (angels) and the daughters of men, is evident from the words of Genesis 6:4: "There were giants in the earth in those days."[145]

In addition to polluting the genetics of humanity, the Nephilim and their fallen angelic fathers also posed a spiritual threat to the human race. They took on the roles of the pagan gods, fostered false religions, and led nations into idolatry. The demons, spirits of the deceased Nephilim, were instigators of false religion in the Old Testament. When it came to engaging the demonic realm (the *owb* in Hebrew), the Lord instituted harsh prohibitions:

> Regard not them that have familiar spirits [*owb*], neither seek after wizards, to be defiled by them: I am the LORD your God. (Leviticus 19:31)

> A man also or woman that hath a familiar spirit [*owb*], or that is a wizard, shall surely be put to death: they shall stone them with stones: their blood shall be upon them. (Leviticus 20:27)

Demons are real. Knowing the dangers the spirits of the Nephilim posed, God had zero tolerance for their presence among His people. The post-Flood giants, who descended from Canaan (a biblical fact I detail extensively in *Judgment of the Nephilim*), the cursed grandson of Noah, settled in the Promised Land (also called "the land of Canaan"). What is not as well known is that Canaan's offspring were the original settlers of Sodom and Gomorrah:

> And the border of the Canaanites was from Sidon, as thou comest to Gerar, unto Gaza; as thou goest, unto Sodom, and Gomorrah, and Admah, and Zeboim, even unto Lasha. (Genesis 10:19)

Thus, there is a direct connection from Noah's era to Lot's. And God was just as concerned about the pagan and occult practices of the Canaanites:

> When thou art come into the land which the LORD thy God giveth thee, thou shalt not learn to do after the abominations of those nations. There shall not be found among you any one that maketh his son or his daughter to pass through the fire, or that useth divination, or an observer of times, or an enchanter, or a witch. Or a charmer, or a consulter with familiar spirits, or a wizard, or a necromancer. For all that do these things are an abomination unto the LORD: and because of these abominations the LORD thy God doth drive them out from before thee." (Deuteronomy 18:9–12)

Wherever you found giants, you found idolatry and demonic interaction. In the New Testament, we're told explicitly that the gods of the false religions are "devils," or *daimonion*:

> What say I then? that the idol is any thing, or that which is offered in sacrifice to idols is any thing? ***But I say, that the things which the Gentiles sacrifice, they sacrifice to devils***, and not to God: and I would not that ye should have fellowship with devils. Ye cannot drink the cup of the Lord, and the cup of devils: ye cannot be partakers of the Lord's table, and of the table of devils. (1 Corinthians 10:19–21, emphasis added)

Even within the church, the Nephilim spirits play a role in beguiling unsuspecting pastors and congregations away from sound, biblical teaching:

> Now the Spirit speaketh expressly, that in the latter times some shall depart from the faith, giving heed to seducing spirits, and **doctrines of devils.** (1 Timothy 4:1, emphasis added)

Like their fallen angelic forefathers who bribed the family of Lamech and his sons with special knowledge, demons also teach false religious worship to the unwitting souls of the lost. And just as in the days of Noah, today New Age, pagan, and occult religious practices are flourishing. Consider these staggering facts:

- Worldwide, Islam is the fastest growing religion, with 1.8 billion adherents. The Pew Research Center estimates that by 2060, it will replace Christianity as the most followed religion in the world.[146]

- Hinduism, which has one billion followers, boasts thirty-three million different gods and goddesses to worship.

- Every year, thousands of tourists flock to Peru and Colombia for ayahuasca tours—where under the guidance of an indigenous shaman, they spend days taking the hallucinogenic drug that is used by shamans to access the spiritual realm.[147]

- According to extensive surveying done by Trinity College, in 1990, approximately eight thousand adults in America identified as Wiccan. By 2018 that number has reached approximately 1.5 million.[148]

- In the United States, yoga and meditation have experienced a surge in popularity over the past decade. Approximately 15 percent of Americans regularly practices yoga while 14 percent use some form of meditation. Many public schools are not only teaching yoga and meditation to children but even boast of its power to improve student behavior.[149]

In the United States, New Age practices like shamanism and energy crystals are exploding in popularity as celebrities and businesspeople alike proclaim the power of harnessing the mystical forces of crystals to heal their body and soul. It is estimated that the crystal industry has already eclipsed

$1 billion in sales.[150] American society, in short, is increasingly giving itself over to "doctrines of devils" as it immerses itself in spiritualism and the New Age movement.

A quick search of "angels and spirit guides" on Amazon.com will bring up dozens of books with specific steps to contacting the spirit realm and channeling your personal spirit guide or guardian angel. What was once considered "fringe" practice has become completely on trend.

All of this is preparation for the "strong delusion" of the end times: the worship of the Antichrist. Just as Christians plant seeds of the gospel, the enemy sows seeds of the many false gospels luring unbelievers away from the Savior and back to the fallen angels and their demon brood. Even the term "New Age" is a reference to returning to the Old Age, when angels openly manifested and interacted with humanity—the Days of Noah.

During destructive trumpet judgments detailed in Revelation, the unsaved world will continue just like the antediluvians, ignoring God. Instead, they will continue to worship idols:

> And the rest of the men which were not killed by these plagues yet repented not of the works of their hands, ***that they should not worship devils, and idols of gold, and silver, and brass, and stone, and of wood***: which neither can see, nor hear, nor walk: Neither repented they of their murders, ***nor of their sorceries***, nor of their fornication, nor of their thefts. (Revelation 9:20–21, emphasis added)

In the days of Noah and Lot, the abominations of the Nephilim-infested nations led to rampant spiritual idolatry. Today, society is headed down that same dark spiritual path.

2. Vanity Of Vanities: Society Is Obsessed with the Cares of the World And the Mundane

> They did eat, they drank. (Jesus Christ, Luke 17:28)

> Vanity of vanities, saith the Preacher, vanity of vanities; all is vanity. (Ecclesiastes 1:2)

The Lord Jesus Christ instructed us to: "look up, for your redemption draweth nigh" when the signs of His return are coming to pass (Luke 21:28). Instead of looking up, most of society is *looking down* at their mobile devices, distracted by media that is more accessible than ever on the numerous digital platforms. This hyper focus on mundane, worldly matters is a repeat of the Days of Lot:

> Behold, this was the iniquity of thy sister Sodom, pride, fulness of bread, ***and abundance of idleness was in her*** and in her daughters. (Ezekiel 16:49, emphasis added)

This "abundance of idleness" is a tragic sin that takes the world's eyes, hearts, and minds away from God. A pastor preaching in the nineteenth century agreed that this was a grievous iniquity of Sodom:

> But we may well observe that our attention is first drawn to their abundant and luxurious living. So likewise in the days of the Son of Man; our Saviour promises us that in those days of awful trial He shall not "find faith on the earth" but on the other hand, He will find men, as He has expressly told us, engaged as the Antediluvians and Sodomites were, in enjoying their home comforts taking their fill of worldly pleasures, with hearts entirely set on worldly business, and forgetting their Lord, who left them with a solemn warning that they were to watch for His return.[151]

Social media has completely changed global culture, as people spend countless hours peering into the lives of others, posting photos of themselves, their meals, their pets, and their exotic vacations and making sure every moment of their day is broadcast on the Internet. Consider some of these startling statistics:

- According to the first-quarter 2018 Nielsen Total Audience Report, American adults spend over eleven hours per day listening to, watching, reading, or generally interacting with media.[152]

- There are **3.196 billion people** actively using these networks. The Internet user of today spends an average of **two hours and**

twenty-two minutes socializing online, and most of it happens on the six most popular platforms.[153]

- Facebook now has over 2.2 billion users who spend an average of one hour per day using just that platform.

- Instagram, which is owned by Facebook, boasts one billion users who spend an average of fifty-three minutes per day on that platform.[154]

- Ninety-five million photos are shared on Instagram per day.[155]

- YouTube (which is owned by Google) now has 1.9 billion active users. Five hundred hours of videos are uploaded to YouTube **every minute**.[156]

- Five billion videos are watched on YouTube **per day**.[157]

These are just a sample of statistics from the largest social media platforms. It is clear evidence of the pride of life. Social media is the essence of vanity. People have become obsessed with taking thousands of the "perfect" pictures of themselves, their family, their food, dogs, cars, homes, vacations, or even gruesome injuries—to blast onto their social media networks. Families now dine out with each individual member glued to screens while they eat. All this distraction moves the heart from God and onto "self."

This is not a condemnation of moderate or occasional use of any of these platforms. I am referring to the entire religion of self-exultation, self-promotion, branding, and self-idolatry that has been spawned by social media. The apostle prophesied this in 2 Timothy:

> This know also, that in the last days perilous times shall come. For men shall be **lovers of their own selves, covetous, boasters, proud**, blasphemers. (2 Timothy 3:1–2, emphasis added)

Paul accurately captured the essence of much of social media use today.

The Vanity of the World Leads to a Rejection of God's Word

> And Lot went out, and spoke to his sons-in-law who had
> married his daughters, and said, Rise up, and depart out of
> this place, for the Lord is about to destroy the city; but he
> seemed to be speaking absurdly before his sons-in-law.
> (Genesis 19:14, LXX)

Lot tried to warn his sons-in-law about the devastating judgment God was bringing upon the city, and they didn't even take him seriously—which led to their deaths. With all their focus on their day-to-day lives, they rejected God's warning. Did these sons study God's Word? Were they in prayer daily or seeking forgiveness? Of course not. The idle, worldly heart has no time for God.

In Noah's Day, the World Rejected God's Dire Warnings

Noah was indeed a child of prophecy. His great-grandfather Enoch was the first recorded prophet in Scripture. A cousin and contemporary of the wicked Lamech and his fallen angelic-assisted family, Enoch "walked with God" amid a world that was rapidly descending beyond redemption. His warning to humanity, recorded in the book of Jude, was a picture of Jesus Christ at His Second Coming, judging the world that denied His Holy Name and Word:

> And Enoch also, the seventh from Adam, prophesied of
> these, saying, Behold, the Lord cometh with ten thousands
> of his saints, To execute judgment upon all, and to convince
> all that are ungodly among them of all their ungodly deeds
> which they have ungodly committed, and of all their hard
> speeches which ungodly sinners have spoken against him.
> (Jude 1:14–15)

The words from Enoch's lips could not have been more foreboding. God was going to come to the world to execute judgment. The people wouldn't just be judged for their unbelief or for their sin in general, but for the "hard speeches"—the words of hatred and mockery they have specifically uttered against Him. This, beloved, is the inevitable path of a society that no longer has use for God's Word—descending into outright animosity towards the Lord and anyone who dares to adhere to the Bible.

The Prophecy of Methuselah: Countdown to the End of the World

Enoch of course, started to walk with God after the birth of his son Methuselah:

> And Enoch lived sixty and five years, and begat Methuselah: And Enoch walked with God after he begat Methuselah three hundred years, and begat sons and daughters: And all the days of Enoch were three hundred sixty and five years: And Enoch walked with God: and he was not; for God took him. (Genesis 5:21–24)

It was **only after Methuselah's birth** that Enoch started to live for God in a way the Bible honored forever. Methuselah's name itself was a prophecy; its translation ("when he dies, it shall come") signaled a coming judgment from God. A nineteenth-century biblical commentary confirms this:

> [Methuselah], whose name is thought by some learned men to contain a prophecy of the flood, which was to come a thousand years after; for it signifies, *He dies and the dart or arrow of* God's vengeance comes; or *He dies and the sending forth of the waters comes.*[158]

Through divine revelation, Enoch was warned that when his son died, the flood judgment would come upon the whole world. What stunning news to receive at the birth of your first child! Enoch took it to heart, walking with God from that day on. Not only did he walk with God, he warned the world through prophecy that, lest they repent, they would be swept up in the coming global judgment. And yet the antediluvians—captivated by the fallen angels, Nephilim, and the luxuries of their era—did not listen.

Methuselah was a walking doomsday clock to the end of the world. His every breath was another few moments that God gifted the earth to repent. Methuselah's own son, Lamech, would also give a prophecy—but this time one of hope:

> And Lamech lived an hundred eighty and two years,
> and begat a son: And he called his name Noah, saying, This
> same shall comfort us concerning our work and toil of our
> hands, because of the ground which the LORD hath cursed.
> (Genesis 5:28–29)

Catastrophe was coming upon the earth, but it would not wipe out humanity altogether. There was going to be comfort and rest for those who trusted in God and rejected the agenda of the world:

> The name "Noah" signifies "Rest," and the connec-
> tion thought of rest and that of comfort is obvious…. He
> expresses a hope, that Noah would be a comfort to his
> parents and the bringer of rest; whether the mere natural
> hope of a father that his son should be a support and
> comfort to him, or a hope looking to the promise made of
> old to Eve, or a hope inspired by prophetic vision that Noah
> should become the second founder of a race, the head of a
> regenerated world.[159]

Once he was divinely commissioned to build the ark, Noah also shared God's Word. Second Peter 2 reveals that Noah was a "preacher of righteousness." Like his ancestors before him, Noah attempted to win souls for Christ—warning of the flood and preaching repentance that leads to true righteousness, the righteousness of Christ that is freely given to those who believe in His Name.

Generation after generation warned of impending doom. But who listened? Only Noah's wife, sons, and daughters-in law made it onto the ark. The rest of the world mocked and ignored Noah's impassioned pleas. As he constructed the ark, the nonbelievers around him kept on living as if nothing would ever change or that God would ever visit them. Consumed with day-to-day activities of no eternal value, they missed every sign of their coming destruction. A nineteenth-century pastor confirmed this notion:

> The antediluvians, or those that were in the days of
> Noah, when the flood came, were eating and drinking
> marrying and giving in marriage. This is not stated as a sin;

there is no sin in eating, but in eating to excess; there is no sin in drinking it is only in drinking to excess.... Then where lay the sin? In this: these things were their all; they did not look above them; their whole hearts, and sympathies, and hopes, were confined to this present scene and beyond the interests of the present they had no stirring and joyous hope for the future.[160]

3. The Love of Money: Material Success Turned the World away from God

The love of money is one of the most powerful sinful temptations in human history:

> But they that will be rich fall into temptation and a snare, and into many foolish and hurtful lusts, **which drown men in destruction** and perdition. For the love of money is the root of all evil: which while some coveted after, they have erred from the faith. (1 Timothy 6:9–10, emphasis added)

> They bought, they sold, they planted, they builded; "But the same day that Lot went out of Sodom it rained fire and brimstone from heaven, and destroyed them all." (Luke 17:28)

Judgment of the Nephilim explained that Lamech and his brood, with fallen angelic assistance, grew more emboldened in their worship of "self" over God. The prosperity of a society and reliance on its own might, intellect and will, rather than God, will always lead to a rejection of the Creator. The book of Job captures the sentiment of the days of Noah aptly:

> Wherefore do the wicked live, become old, yea, are mighty in power? Their seed is established in their sight with them, and their offspring before their eyes. Their houses are safe from fear, neither is the rod of God upon them. Their bull gendereth, and faileth not; their cow calveth, and casteth not her calf.

They send forth their little ones like a flock, and their children dance. They take the timbrel and harp, and rejoice at the sound of the organ. They spend their days in wealth, and in a moment go down to the grave. Therefore they say unto God, **Depart from us; for we desire not the knowledge of thy ways. What is the Almighty, that we should serve him? and what profit should we have, if we pray unto him?** (Job 21:7–15, emphasis added)

Note that the passage captures all the advances "achieved" by Lamech's family: successful mass animal husbandry, playing instruments for song and dance, and the wealth that can be gained from forging metals for tools and swords. The arrogance of sinful society in the days of Noah was based on their reliance on their own worldly wealth and knowledge.

Sodom and Gomorrah Were Some of the Wealthiest Cities of Their Day

When Abraham and Lot were dividing their land to resolve a dispute among their servants, Lot was captivated by the luxury and splendor of the cities of Sodom and Gomorrah:

And Lot lifted up his eyes, and beheld all the plain of Jordan, that it was well watered every where, before the LORD destroyed Sodom and Gomorrah, even as the garden of the LORD, like the land of Egypt, as thou comest unto Zoar. Then Lot chose him all the plain of Jordan; and Lot journeyed east: and they separated themselves the one from the other. Abram dwelled in the land of Canaan, and Lot dwelled in the cities of the plain, and pitched his tent toward Sodom. But the men of Sodom were wicked and sinners before the LORD exceedingly. (Genesis 13:8–13)

The plains of Sodom and Gomorrah were so lush and bountiful, Scripture compares them to the Garden of Eden! The riches of Sodom were well known. In Genesis 14, Cherdorlaomer launched a war against Sodom after they stopped paying him tribute. And in addition to taking hostages, he took their goods back with him to his homeland. Josephus, the renowned first century Jewish historian, wrote:

> About this time the Sodomites grew proud, on account of their riches and great wealth; they became unjust towards men and impious towards God.[161]

Even a believer like Lot was still drawn to the prospect of financial success within the walls of Sodom. The city was a bustling commercial center, where people bought, sold, planted and built. He ignored the exceeding sin and pitched his tent towards the infamous metropolis. Indeed, theologian John Butler arrived at the same conclusion:

> We shall find Lot's experience a prototype…we wonder that good men often forget religion while they hurry on to make money?[162]

Society Today Is Experiencing Unprecedented Wealth

The lure of riches and its accompanying luxuries and recreation has filled the hearts and minds of society more than any other time in history. There are now more millionaires than ever in the United States:

> As of the end of 2016, there were a record 10.8 million millionaires nationwide, according to a new study from Spectrem Group's Market Insights Report. That's more than ever before and marks a 400,000 person increase from the previous year.… "The record levels of households reflect the significantly higher values of all asset classes, post-recession…and the recent record level of the United States markets following the presidential election has added demonstrably to the asset level of most affluent investors."[163]

Worldwide, the number of billionaires is rapidly growing as well:

> A record 2,208 billionaires made *Forbes'* 32nd annual ranking of the world's billionaires, as featured in the March 31, 2018 issue of *Forbes* magazine. "The superrich continue to get richer, widening the gap between them and everyone else."[164]

While wealth is at an all-time high, so is the gap between rich and poor:

- The top 1 percent of earners in the US make twenty-five times more than the remaining 99 percent and control 36.8 percent of the nation's wealth. The bottom 90 percent of the country controls 22.8 percent.[165]

- Globally, the top twenty-six wealthiest people own $1.4 trillion, or as much as the 3.8 billion poorest people.[166]

Nearly half of the world's population lives on less than $2.50 per day. One billion children live in poverty, and 805 million people do not have enough to eat daily.[167] While God implores His people to "defend the poor and fatherless: do justice to the afflicted and needy" (Psalm 82:3), the poor are suffering more than any time in world history.

Obsession with Wealth Leads Society away from God's Word

To no one's surprise, the great global wealth and excess leads to a rejection of God's Word. Consider some of these statistics:

- Between six thousand and ten thousand churches in the US are dying each year with one hundred to two hundred churches closing each week.[168]

- In a Gallup poll, fewer than one in four Americans (24 percent) reported believing that the Bible is "the actual word of God, and is to be taken literally, word for word."

- Just 26 percent viewed the Bible as "a book of fables, legends, history and moral precepts recorded by man." This is the first time in Gallup's four-decade trend that biblical literalism has not surpassed biblical skepticism.

- Of those who identified as Christians, 50 percent stated the Bible is the inspired Word of God, but that not all of it should be taken literally.[169]

- Although some 80 percent of Americans say they believe in God, only a slim majority of the nation's approximately 327 million people believe in God as described in the Bible, according to results of a new study released by the Pew Research Center. And among those younger than fifty, belief in the God of the Bible drops lower than 50 percent.

- The findings from the survey of more than 4,700 adults conducted nationwide between December 4–18, 2017, reveal that one-third of Americans say they do not believe in the God of the Bible, but believe there is some other higher power or spiritual force in the universe.

- Only 14 percent of Millennials believe the Bible is the actual Word of God, with 33 percent categorizing the Bible as "just another book."[170]

- A LifeWay Research study found that only 45 percent of those who regularly attend church read the Bible more than once a week. More than 40 percent of the people attending read their Bible occasionally, maybe once or twice a month. Almost one in five churchgoers say they *never* read the Bible—essentially the same number of people who say they do read it every day.[171]

Rather than even give a moment to listen to God's Word, much of society lives as if the warnings of Bible prophecy about the Great Tribulation and the Second Coming are the stuff of fairy tales and not to be taken seriously.

In the days of Noah, who attended the altar with the patriarch to worship God and seek forgiveness of sins, aside from his family? Did anyone pray with Noah or seek the gospel during those 120 years? The United States is trending in the same sinful direction.

When it came to Sodom, Gomorrah, and the three surrounding cities, Abraham bargained with God for mercy upon their residents:

> And Abraham drew near, and said, Wilt thou also destroy the righteous with the wicked? Peradventure there be fifty righteous within the city: wilt thou also destroy and

not spare the place for the fifty righteous that are therein? That be far from thee to do after this manner, to slay the righteous with the wicked: and that the righteous should be as the wicked, that be far from thee: Shall not the Judge of all the earth do right?

And the LORD said, If I find in Sodom fifty righteous within the city, then I will spare all the place for their sakes.… And he said, Oh let not the LORD be angry, and I will speak yet but this once: Peradventure ten shall be found there. And he said, I will not destroy it for ten's sake. And the LORD went his way, as soon as he had left communing with Abraham: and Abraham returned unto his place. (Genesis 18:23-33)

There weren't even ten believers left in a city with an estimated population of three hundred thousand! As churches close and more and more pastors move into false, apostate teachings, it's no surprise that society has little concern for the Second Coming of Jesus Christ or fear of His righteous judgment?

4. The Earth Was Filled with Violence: The Celebration of Violence and Moral Depravity

And God saw that the wickedness of man was great in the earth, *and that every imagination of the thoughts of his heart was only evil continually*. And it repented the LORD that he had made man on the earth, and it grieved him at his heart. (Genesis 6:5–6, emphasis added)

While extolling all the great achievements of their society, the people in the days of Noah largely ignored or couldn't care less about their own egregious sins before God. The testimony of Genesis makes it clear that evil and iniquity were at all-time highs. Similarly, the Lord found an extreme level of sin in the streets of Sodom and Gomorrah and their sister cities:

And the LORD said, Because the cry of Sodom and Gomorrah is great, and because their sin is very grievous; I will go down now, and see whether *they have done altogether*

according to the cry of it, which is come unto me; and if
not, I will know. And the men turned their faces from thence
and went toward Sodom: but Abraham stood yet before the
Lord. (Genesis 18:20–22, emphasis added)

Like the blood of Abel, the first martyr of God's faithful, the destructive, perverse sin of Sodom and Gomorrah cried out to the heavens—so much so that the Lord came personally to earth to verify that the evil within the city walls could be so atrocious.

Declining Morality: Minds on Evil Continually

The earth also was corrupt before God, and the earth
was filled with violence. (Genesis 6:11)

Perusing the most popular entertainment for children and adults alike provides stark insight into just how depraved society is becoming as we approach the end times:

- *American Horror Story: Coven* follows a boarding school that secretly is a witch's coven. It features graphic depictions of perversion and violence, including beheadings, a woman using the blood of infants as makeup, real witchcraft rituals, and a mother incestuously assaulting her handicapped son.

- *Game of Thrones*, the most-watched show in HBO history and one of the most popular TV shows of all time, has so much graphic violence, nudity, and sexual scenes that pornography sites have complained that they experience a lull in traffic when it is on air.

- Netflix, the streaming service that is now watched more than traditional TV, reported that two of its most binge-watched shows are *You,* a show about a stalker, as well as documentary, *Making of a Murderer.*

- The Netflix hit, *13 Reasons*, in which a young girl who commits suicide sends thirteen letters to people she blames for driving her to take her own life, has been credited with causing a spike in the number of teen suicides.

- TV shows that make Satan look heroic: *Lucifer*, a show in which the devil works alongside a police officer to help solve crimes, paints Satan as a charming, sympathetic figure who is seeking redemption from God. Similarly, *Supernatural*, now in its thirteenth season, depicts Satan as a disgruntled angel who is merely acting out because God is too cold and mean to him.

- *Fortnite* has become one of the most popular video games of all time, with many players so addicted that they boast of spending thousands of hours online in game play. The entire premise of the game pits two teams of one hundred online players against each other during a competition in which they obtain weapons to kill each other and the winner is the last player alive.

And "evil continually" isn't only a product of Hollywood. The real-world facts are even more frightening:

- In a survey of eleven to sixteen-year-old children, 53 percent admitted to watching pornography, including 25 percent who were eleven years old.[172]

- There are an estimated thirty million sex trafficking slaves in the world in 2019, with six hundred thousand to eight hundred thousand of those in the United States alone.

- The FBI reported that hate crimes have increased by 10 percent in the past year, and are at their highest rate in a decade.

- The years from 2014 through 2016 saw a 10 percent increase in the number of reported sexual assaults in the United States.[173]

- One in four women in the United States will be sexually assaulted by the time they finish college.

- One in four women will have an abortion.

The violence also extends to the church:

- Christian persecution worldwide is at "near genocide levels."

- The Christian population in Iraq has been reduced from 1.5 million in 2003 to less than 120,000 in 2019.[174]

- Every month, on average, 345 Christians are killed for faith-related reasons; 105 churches and Christian buildings are burned or attacked; and 219 Christians are detained without trial, arrested, sentenced, and imprisoned.

- One in nine Christians experience high levels of persecution worldwide.

- On average, eleven Christians are killed for their faith daily.[175]

In nations not experiencing violent persecution, there are still measures being taken to drive out the Christian faith. Public schools repeatedly remove any reference to Christianity. Students are told that papers and projects honoring Jesus are not acceptable. At universities, Christian student organizations that require belief in the Bible for leadership are being defunded or banned altogether.

Sodom's Entire Population Was Given over to Sexual Sin

And there came two angels to Sodom at even; and Lot sat in the gate of Sodom: and Lot seeing them rose up to meet them; and he bowed himself with his face toward the ground; And he said, Behold now, my lords, turn in, I pray you, into your servant's house, and tarry all night, and wash your feet, and ye shall rise up early, and go on your ways. And they said, Nay; but we will abide in the street all night.

And he pressed upon them greatly; and they turned in unto him and entered into his house; and he made them a feast, and did bake unleavened bread, and they did eat. But before they lay down, the men of the city, even the men of

Sodom, compassed the house round, **both old and young, all the people from every quarter**:

> And they called unto Lot, and said unto him, Where are the men which came in to thee this night? bring them out unto us, that we may know them. And Lot went out at the door unto them, and shut the door after him, And said, I pray you, brethren, do not so wickedly. (Genesis 19:1–7, emphasis added)

The entire male population surrounded Lot's home, demanding that the two male angels come out into the street so they could publicly sexually assault them. This was shockingly similar to the very sin of Genesis 6: fornication between angels and humanity. Scripture describes the burning in lust by the same sex as the product of rejecting God (Romans 1:16). In this modern era, there has been no greater dividing line in the Church than the issue of homosexuality. Note that this author is referring to the Church and what God's Word says on sexuality—*not a political movement or legislation*. The government has nothing to do with the Church and will pass whatever measures it sees fit. That should have no impact on a Christian's faith in God's Word.

Bible-believing Christians increasingly find themselves as targets of scorn for believing God's Word on the biblical definition of marriage and sexual relations.

The Modern Quest for Immortality: Being As Gods

The desire to "be as gods" was first offered by Satan to Eve in the Garden of Eden:

> Now the serpent was more subtil than any beast of the field which the Lord God had made. And he said unto the woman, Yea, hath God said, Ye shall not eat of every tree of the garden? And the woman said unto the serpent, We may eat of the fruit of the trees of the garden: But of the fruit of the tree which is in the midst of the garden, God hath said, Ye shall not eat of it, neither shall ye touch it, lest ye die. And

> the serpent said unto the woman, **Ye shall not surely die**: For God doth know that in the day ye eat thereof, then your eyes shall be opened, **and ye shall be as gods**, knowing good and evil. (Genesis 3:1–5, emphasis added)

"Ye shall not surely die" is the first recorded lie in history. And since that time, humanity hasn't been able to resist its allure, despite the disastrous consequences for Adam, Eve, and the entire race. The notion of achieving eternal life absent God has persisted for millennia. In the days of Noah, the fallen angels who interacted with humanity opened the possibility of becoming something "other than human" with the birth of the Nephilim hybrids. Scripture calls them the "men of renown"—the legendary heroes, titans, and figures from the mythologies of pagan cultures all over the world.

At the tower of Babel, the world once again united under Nimrod, who "became a giant" and was a "giant hunter before the Lord" to construct a city and tower that could reach Heaven:

> And the whole earth was of one language, and of one speech. And it came to pass, as they journeyed from the east, that they found a plain in the land of Shinar; and they dwelt there. And they said one to another, Go to, let us make brick, and burn them thoroughly. And they had brick for stone, and slime had they for morter. And they said, Go to, let us build us a city and a tower, whose top may reach unto heaven; and let us make us a name, lest we be scattered abroad upon the face of the whole earth.
>
> And the Lord came down to see the city and the tower, which the children of men builded. And the Lord said, Behold, the people is one, and they have all one language; and this they begin to do: and now nothing will be restrained from them, which they have imagined to do. (Genesis 11:1–6)

Today, the elite of the earth are seeking "nothing restrained from them" in their question to achieve immortality itself:

> Would you like to live forever? Some billionaires, already invincible in every other way, have decided that they also

deserve not to die. Today several biotech companies, fueled by Silicon Valley fortunes, are devoted to "life extension"— or as some put it, to solving "the problem of death."

It's a cause championed by the tech billionaire Peter Thiel, the TED Talk darling Aubrey de Gray, Google's billion-dollar Calico longevity lab and investment by Amazon's Jeff Bezos. The National Academy of Medicine, an independent group, recently dedicated funding to "end aging forever."

As the longevity entrepreneur Arram Sabeti told the *New Yorker*: "The proposition that we can live forever is obvious. It doesn't violate the laws of physics, so we can achieve it."[176]

Google founders Sergey Brin and Larry Page have spent millions on Calico, a secretive health venture which aims to "solve death." Amazon founder Jeff Bezos and the billionaire Peter Thiel are backers of Unity Biotechnology, which hopes to combat the effects of aging. Sierra Sciences is another company racing to cheat death. Its focus is on treatments that can lengthen telomeres—the "caps" at the end of each strand of DNA. Telomeres get shorter each time a cell copies itself. As cells copy themselves throughout our lives, the telomeres eventually get shorter leading to the aging process.[177]

BioViva, whose CEO, Elizabeth Parrish, is so committed to the cause that she became one of the first humans to undergo telomere therapy in 2015. Writing in 2018, she claimed a measurement of her telomeres showed they had "grown younger" by roughly thirty years since she received the treatment—her body was reverse-aging.[178]

The most popular methods of "life extension technology" involve some level of tampering with human DNA. Just as in the days of Noah, when the fallen angels corrupted the genetics of humanity, the billionaires of today are seeking to once again transform humanity into something other than being image bearers of God.

Even in the nineteenth century, Christians were aware of how the increasing reliance on science as the answer to all the world's problems was a troubling sign of the end times. An early twentieth-century commentary came to a similar observation:

> The science, discoveries, culture; the energy and achievements of our modern era—are they all to terminate in worldwide godlessness and the Man of Sin? A forbidding outlook; one utterly repugnant to all our anticipations and our hopes. One whose love for man is deathless, whose power is matchless, has said: "As it was in the days of Noah so shall it be in the days of the Son of man" (Luke 27:26). How was it in the days of Noah? The whole world in revolt against God, and piety reduced to a family of eight souls! "Likewise, also as it was in the days of Lot"; and how was it then? Corruption had culminated, godlessness was at the flood. (Luke 27:28–30)
>
> "There are principles and tendencies at work in our modern society which if left unchecked will ere long make the advent of the Antichrist not only possible but certain."[179]

With such prideful aspirations as achieving immortality via science and intellect, how easily will this world be prepped for a false messiah who blasphemes the God of the Bible and tells humanity they are "as gods"? Revelation predicts that the False Prophet—the cohort of the Antichrist—will lead the world in constructing the image of the Beast, literally artificial intelligence that will be "given life" and order execution of those who resist the worship of the Beast. Clearly the wealth and technology of the future will assist the enemy in spreading the strong delusion.

While the world is pointing to its own wealth, power, and scientific achievement, Christians must remain steadfast in showing the one and only way to immortality: Jesus Christ.

The End-times Flood: God Is Going to Supernaturally Punish the World Once Again

> The great day of the LORD is near, it is near, and hasteth greatly, even the voice of the day of the LORD: the mighty

man shall cry there bitterly. That day is a day of wrath, a day of trouble and distress, a day of wasteness and desolation, a day of darkness and gloominess, a day of clouds and thick darkness, A day of the trumpet and alarm against the fenced cities, and against the high towers. And I will bring distress upon men, that they shall walk like blind men, because they have sinned against the LORD: and their blood shall be poured out as dust, and their flesh as the dung.

Neither their silver nor their gold shall be able to deliver them in the day of the LORD's wrath; but the whole land shall be devoured by the fire of his jealousy: for he shall make even a speedy riddance of all them that dwell in the land. (Zephaniah 1:14–18)

As the world grows emboldened in rejecting the Christian faith, the scene is set for end-times deception. The Bible warns of the Day of the Lord (also referred to as the Great Tribulation): the final years before the Second Coming of Jesus Christ when supernatural punishments are unleashed onto earth. There will be global earthquakes, plagues, and wars across the nations of the earth. One-third of trees will burn up. Many rivers, lakes, and streams will turn to blood. And, just as in the days of Noah, the fallen angels of Genesis 6 will make a return.

At the fifth trumpet of Revelation chapter 9, the bottomless pit, or the abyss—the exact location in which the Genesis 6 rebels were imprisoned—will be opened. And from the pit, grotesque, hybrid beings described as "locusts" will return to earth:

And the fifth angel sounded, and I saw a star fall from heaven unto the earth: and to him was given the key of the bottomless pit. And he opened the bottomless pit; and there arose a smoke out of the pit, as the smoke of a great furnace; and the sun and the air were darkened by reason of the smoke of the pit. And there came out of the smoke locusts upon the earth: and unto them was given power, as the scorpions of the earth have power. And it was

commanded them that they should not hurt the grass of
the earth, neither any green thing, neither any tree; but only
those men which have not the seal of God in their foreheads.

And to them it was given that they should not kill them,
but that they should be tormented five months: and their
torment was as the torment of a scorpion, when he striketh
a man. And in those days shall men seek death, and shall
not find it; and shall desire to die, and death shall flee from
them. (Revelation 9:1–6)

In Revelation 12, Satan and his fallen angels are evicted from Heaven:

And there was war in heaven: Michael and his angels
fought against the dragon; and the dragon fought and his
angels, And prevailed not; neither was their place found any
more in heaven. And the great dragon was cast out, that old
serpent, called the Devil, and Satan, which deceiveth the
whole world: he was cast out into the earth, and his angels
were cast out with him…. Therefore rejoice, ye heavens, and
ye that dwell in them. *Woe to the inhabiters of the earth
and of the sea! for the devil is come down unto you, having great wrath*, because he knoweth that he hath but a
short time. (Revelation 12:7–12, emphasis added)

In the days of Noah, the waters of judgment came from "the fountains
of the deep" and "the windows of Heaven." In the Great Tribulation, the deep
will once again open to release fallen angels, and Heaven will open to send
fallen angels from above to torment humanity.

But how would average unbelievers react to hearing these predictions?
Would they not scoff—water turning to blood and locusts with scorpion
tails and hair like women? The Scriptures sound like a sci-fi tale to the unsaved of today. The notion of a global Antichrist being a real, literal person
is laughable. Christians who believe in a literal interpretation of end-time
prophecy are seen as fringe, bizarre people making ludicrous proclama-
tions. And this will be history repeating itself.

Make Sure You Are on the Ark: Jesus Christ

> Behold, I come quickly: blessed is he that keepeth the sayings of the prophecy of this book. (Revelation 22:7)

> This is not a mere history; but also a solemn prophecy. Thousands will be just as incredulous when the lightning strikes, and preternatural signs are portrayed in the sky; when the earth begins to groan, and crack, and heave as if with yearning expectancy of deliverance; when all things indicate that this great drama is to be wound up; the world will be as incredulous as ever; and like the five foolish virgins they will ask oil for their lamps when it is too late to buy it, and they have none to spare; and theirs must be the blackness of darkness for ever.

> Just as the ark was the only safety in the days of Noah, so the only safety for us this very day is Christ, the living the glorious, the indestructible ark. There is none other name, however magnificent, or brilliant from its historic associations, in which or by which we can be saved from the coming judgments of heaven except the name of the Lord Jesus Christ.[180]

Now more than ever, Bible-believing Christians need to heed the Great Commission: teaching all the gospel of free forgiveness of sin through the atoning work of Jesus Christ on the cross. The ark was a foreshadow of Jesus Christ. When believers are "in Christ," they are protected from God's wrath. This is a time to make disciples and teach the value of reading and studying the Word of God daily. Churches need to proclaim the Second Coming of Christ as the signs of the Savior's return increase in number, frequency, and intensity.

God provided 120 years before the Flood, because He is longsuffering. His patience and common grace allowed time for humanity to repent and seek Him. The lost souls in the days of Noah and Lot didn't know their fate until it was far too late. We need to share the reality of Jesus Christ before the world encounters Him as conqueror and Judge of the wicked.

Noah and Lot Being Spared Judgment: A Foreshadow of the Rapture

Enoch was raptured and translated before the judgment of God. Noah was told to enter the ark seven days before the Flood started in earnest, then God Himself closed the door. Similarly, faithful believers in Christ will be removed from the earth before the supernatural judgments of the Great Tribulation are unleashed upon the world. Lot was similarly spared from experiencing any of the horrors of the fire and brimstone that rained on Sodom and Gomorrah:

> And [the angel] said unto [Lot], See, I have accepted thee concerning this thing also, that I will not overthrow this city, for the which thou hast spoken. Haste thee, escape thither; **for I cannot do anything till thou be come thither**. Therefore the name of the city was called Zoar. The sun was risen upon the earth when Lot entered into Zoar. Then the Lord rained upon Sodom and upon Gomorrah brimstone and fire from the Lord out of heaven; And he overthrew those cities, and all the plain, and all the inhabitants of the cities, and that which grew upon the ground. (Genesis 19:21–25)

The angels dispatched to destroy Sodom couldn't take any action until Lot was removed. This was yet another example of God removing His believers before unleashing supernatural judgment.

When the Lord Jesus Christ detailed the end-times judgments to His disciples in Luke 21, He ended the message with a promise of escape:

> And take heed to yourselves, lest at any time your hearts be overcharged with surfeiting, and drunkenness, and cares of this life, and so that day come upon you unawares. For as a snare shall it come on all them that dwell on the face of the whole earth. Watch ye therefore, and pray always, **that ye may be accounted worthy to escape all these things that shall come to pass**, and to stand before the Son of man. (Luke 21:34–36, emphasis added)

Note that Jesus commands us to watch and pray for His return. Noah and Lot experienced a pretribulation rescue by God because they were watching and trusting in God's promises. Christians need to watch as the signs of the end times increase. And we need to share the signs. A judgment is coming that is going to "be great tribulation, such as was not since the beginning of the world to this time, no, nor ever shall be" (Matthew 24:21).

Let us build our arks and shout for the world to join us. It may fall on deaf ears. It may lead to scoffing, mockery, or even persecution. But if one more soul can join us before God closes the door, it will be more than worth it. God's supernatural wrath is coming upon the earth. As Enoch prophesied, the Lord will return with thousands of His saints to execute judgment upon the ungodly. But amid this warning, there is comfort. There is forgiveness. There is love. Let us continue to urge and plead with the world to accept God's free offer of forgiveness that they may be safely in the loving arms of the Savior—eternally protected from the judgment to come.

CHAPTER 14

RAPTURE REASSURANCE IN MOCKERS' LAST-DAYS SCOFFING

JAN MARKELL

W E'VE ALL READ THE verses on last-days' mocking and scoffing of the glorious good news of Jesus Christ's return. It's another thing to actually come under those words and have to absorb them and deal with the feelings they unleash.

In 2002, I began conducting national prophecy conferences. A year earlier, I had begun a national radio outreach as well. The radio topics covered a plethora of topics, but eschatology was my favorite, because email and letter response told me that the churches had dropped this topic as far back as the 1990s. Bible prophecy wouldn't likely fill the pews. The "seeker-sensitive" approach had been introduced, and that was the "new way of doing church."

Both the conference activity and the radio outreach were fairly high profile. *In other words, the mockers and the scoffers would be able to easily find me!* I wouldn't be able to hide in the bushes and claim anonymity, because both outreaches were going to get significant attention. And both radio and conference activity were very popular, thus jealousy could enter the picture.

But there is a dimension here I didn't expect. The worst of the bashing was going to come *from within the church*. It was from those who either hated the topic of eschatology or from those who didn't hold to dispensationalism or a pre-Tribulation view of the timing of the Rapture.

And I wasn't prepared for their wrath.

Sure, a lot of damage has been done by those who represent Bible prophecy in a fringy manner. Way back in the 1980s, a man by the name of Edgar Whisenant was sure he had the formula for the end of the Church Age. He came up with eighty-eight reasons Christ was returning in 1988. When his date-setting scheme failed, he came up with plan B: Eighty-nine reasons Jesus was returning in 1989.

What an embarrassment. It's why date-setting is not just antibiblical; it is foolish and counterproductive.

That didn't stop broadcaster Harold Camping from trying the same thing in 2011. Since his first date option of May 21, 2011, failed, he went back to the drawing board and concluded it would be five months later. Foiled again, he seemed to fade from the spotlight, although the scoffers never forgot him! They picked up on one angle where their condemnation was justified. A few of Camping's followers committed suicide when both of his dates failed and Christ did not return.

Men like these opened the door to some justified criticism. The Bible is pretty clear that only God the Father knows these kinds of details. No human is privileged to have the inside scoop.

In 2005, I invited Hal Lindsey to the Twin Cities for my conference activity. I asked him about these people. As we talked privately, he told me that some of the most contentious people within the church were those who either did not appreciate eschatology or those who would question Rapture timing. Later that evening in my conference Q & A, he repeated that comment to my audience.

Hal said that those questioning such issues would lean towards being "nasty." I had already experienced them, so this wasn't new news to me, but over the next few years, I would see a growing intensity to his statement's fulfillment.

Hal had suggested that 1988 was significant as well, but he had just advised folks to keep an eye on it, as that would be Israel's fortieth anniversary. He didn't make any statement that he was sure that was the date of the Rapture. *Nonetheless, that accusation was pinned on him.*

Some of the heaviest cannon fire came from fellow premillennial dispensationalists who should have gone to Hal rather than spend many years trying to tarnish his reputation. He told me that his speculation concerning the
year 1988 was a huge mistake, and if there was anything he could take back,
it would have been that comment.

Once again, the mockers had fuel to bash, and they have never limited
their accusations to just one person. No, they've lumped almost all who believe in the theology known as dispensationalism—particularly the doctrine
of the pre-Tribulation Rapture of the Church—into their gunsights and have
fired away for years! I suspect it will go on until we hear the shout and the
trumpet.

Certainly, the Internet has fueled a lot of contention. By the early 2000s,
hundreds had blogs and podcasts, and they used the new bully pulpit to criti-
cize just about anything and call everyone including their mother off-base!

The biggest online presence would soon become the "discerners." Don't
get me wrong. *We need discernment!* The book of Jude tells us to contend for
the faith. But some discerners were picking apart just about everything. And
they seemed to have a special affinity for going after those who were excited
that the King is coming! I think the story behind the story was that they didn't
understand eschatology at all, and it seemed even silly to them, thus, they
said, "Let's take pot-shots at it and the leaders of the movement."

My annual Understanding the Times conference became one of the largest in North America, and that made it an even greater target. Invariably,
someone in the discernment community would conclude that one or more
of my speakers was a heretic, and that person, my overall conference, and I
would be slammed for six months prior to the event. *One person was even
honest enough to tell me that his criticism was an effort to keep people away
from my event!* Imagine a fellow Christian wanting people to stay away from
an event where the gospel of salvation would be presented! You can't make
up things like this.

But ultimately, it gets down to the scoffing and mocking predicted.

Then there are those with aberrant theology. I can honestly say that I
have never known attack—and scoffing—like that coming from preterists.

This theology teaches that all prophecy happened in AD 70. The Tribulation was the destruction of Jerusalem. *Who knew, but we missed all prophecy!* A partial preterist might still believe in the Second Coming.

But, oh, how they come against the truth. Here's what Gary DeMar wrote in 2013:

> For centuries Bible prophecy pundits have predicted that the end was near. They appealed to the same types of signs: wars and rumors of wars, earthquakes, famines, and false religions. They all had one thing in common. They've all been wrong.
>
> None of this has stopped contemporary prophecy writers and speakers from claiming the end is near. My library is filled with their books. I've debated dozens of them over the years.
>
> Prophetic predictions wouldn't be much of a problem, except that millions of people fall for the claims and the effect on our nation's social, political, and moral landscape has been devastating.
>
> Once again the usual suspects are gathering at Grace Church in Eden Prairie, Minnesota, in October of this year to tell an eager and naïve audience that all the signs are aligned for an inevitable end-time event.
>
> Anybody familiar with the history of Bible prophecy knows all of this has been done before. In fact, there is a nearly two thousand-year history of predicting some type of prophetic event based on wars and rumors of wars, earthquakes, famines, and apostasy.
>
> People like Hal Lindsey and Chuck Smith, both popular prophecy authors who have sold tens of millions of prophecy books, assured us that the prophetic excrement would hit the fan by 1988.

I suspect that the majority of attendees who will sit under Mark Hitchcock, Ron Rhodes, Erwin Lutzer, among others, won't realize that only the names, events, and dates have changed. They'll be hearing regurgitated prophetic speculation in the name of the Bible.

But it gets worse! In 2017, the "Bible Answerman," Hank Hanegraaff, who is also a preterist, went on a tirade on his radio program. I had no idea I was on his radar, but we air on some of the same networks, so he was obviously paying some attention. *And he was dismayed!*

Hank fired away once the caller asked him his opinion of Olive Tree Ministries and Jan Markell. Without hesitation, he said I am "reprehensible," "unreliable," "sensational," "a blight on our times," "leading the gullible," and engage in "Script-torture." How thankful I am for Matthew 5:11: "Blessed are you when people insult you, persecute you, and falsely say all kinds of evil against you."

All of these accusations were brought upon me because I represent dispensationalism, which in his mind was invented by John Nelson Darby. What a fool I am. What station manager in his or her right mind would let someone like me on the air? Yet, on his daily program, he regularly bashes Israel, Hal Lindsey, Tim LaHaye, the Rapture, the Jewish people, and more.

Hanegraaff is passionate that God has only one "chosen people": Christians. He keeps saying that God is not a "land broker" based on genetics. *And he has a following of millions though his conversion to Eastern Orthodoxy drove many away!*

On a weekly basis, Hanegraaff laments that dispensationalism is the primary teaching in today's church. *I wish that were the case, but clearly it is not. This wonderful teaching left the building twenty-five years ago.*

He closes his 2016 message at Christ at the Checkpoint by making an appeal that with nonessential theology, we behave with charity so we can debate in a cordial fashion. *I don't think the mud-slinging he did toward this ministry was done in a cordial manner.* His voice was firm and angry as he addressed the earlier-mentioned caller's questions about this ministry. "Olive Tree Ministries is a blight on our times," he stated.

Hearing the anger in the voices of people like this—professed evangelical Christians—is staggering. *How did the glorious message that the King is coming become so divisive?* Why are we raising our voices, scowling, and denigrating others over the wonderful news that Christ is returning to rescue us from a perishing, broken world?

About the same time, another teacher, this time a man who differed with me on Rapture timing, began to rant and rave against me on YouTube. He decided to get two for one, so he often dragged in Pastor J. D. Farag into the controversy. Pastor J. D. is a very good friend of mine, and there is no more mild-mannered person on earth! But we are strong proponents of the pre-Tribulation Rapture of the Church, so Jacob Prasch decided to drag us both through the mud because we reject his pre-Wrath theology.

The insults were legion, and I will not waste time listing them. But this man's loathing for the truth—that the Church is spared from the wrath of God to come—is obviously his passion night and day. Week after week, he pounded away with the assertion that J. D. Farag and I should step down from ministry due to our pre-Trib theology! *I never thought I would see the day!* But those in the discernment world seem to want to contend contentiously, and this is a prime illustration and further fulfillment of what Hal Lindsey told me in 2005.

But you would think I was coming against the virgin birth or other essentials of the faith. Eventually, this man told me that I should retire; I needed to step down now into a forced retirement—one forced by him! *He was judge and jury, and knew better than God when my time was up.* And he accused J. D. Farag of being poorly trained in theology, thanks to his Calvary Chapel association.

We have now moved even beyond the mocking and scoffing to being just plain insulting to win a theological point. If you can't win in a debate, discredit, mock and scorn, and cause people to lose all confidence in you! If you can get away with it, *call them a heretic, too, so people will never believe a word you write or teach!*

It would be one thing if I were espousing false theology such as "kingdom now/dominionism" or "latter rain" theology. Domionism teaches that the

Church will make the world perfect and only then can the Lord return. I think I would warrant some attack and even harsh words if I were propagating a false narrative.

But I represent what major sections of the Church have believed for centuries: Premillennial dispensationalism and the pretribulation timing of the Rapture of the Church. How is this deemed dangerous or heretical? Why can't someone believe this and not come under the rampant mocking and scoffing? *Tim LaHaye actually predicted years ago that someday the "blessed hope" would become the "blasted hope."* He was so right.

But the Bible must fulfill itself, and the verses in 2 Peter 3 had to come to pass in a last generation! *And so they have.*

In 2016, filmmaker Joe Schimmel made a four-hour film titled *Left Behind or Led Astray: Examining the Origins of the Secret Pre-Tribulation Rapture.* Of course, the thrust of the production was to put down the pre-Tribulation Rapture of the Church—*which isn't a secret!* It's a prominent biblical theme! Other participants were aforementioned Jacob Prasch and Joel Richardson.

I have actually worked with Joel on occasion. I admire his passion to win Muslims to Christ. He goes into war zones to witness to them and encourage the brethren in those areas. He is kind and gracious, and never goes on any attack.

But I was stunned to hear him in this film production as he, in essence, said that any pastor who is not preparing his flock to face the Antichrist is failing in his role as a pastor.

The four-hour film went on to hammer away at the theology of the pre-Trib Rapture created in the 1800s by John Nelson Darby. This can be refuted with little effort, but it is an attack that will not go away! Darby may have brought dispensationalism to modern-day prominence, but he hardly invented it! *Why did the early Church anticipate the Lord's return in their day and greet one another with "Maranatha"?*

In one teaching I have, I take a look at another scoffer—Rick Wiles. I have no doubt that Rick loves the Lord. But he is a scoffer and a mocker of the highest degree, and his "Tru News" attracts many who wish to have a deeper understanding of current events.

Wiles calls the "secret pretrib Rapture and Zionism a two-headed freak monster." Give me a break! He goes on to say that Christian Zionism could not be justified without the pre-Trib Rapture theology. He insists that the evangelical church is no longer of any use to God because it has sold out to Zionism and the pretrib Rapture.

Wiles then goes on to call America "Babylon" and a "pagan nation," thanks to people who believe as I do. He insists, with passion, that we are the cause of America's decline. *Really??*

He concludes his rant by saying that people who believe as I do took Jesus off the cross and replaced the cross with a star of David. We put all our focus on a piece of land in the Middle East. Dispensationalists have taken over and have taken our eyes off the prize—Jesus.

I wish we had that kind of influence, and maybe we did forty years ago, but no longer! How do I know that? Because almost every third email my ministry receives tells me they have looked everywhere in their town for a prophecy-preaching, prophecy-loving, prophecy-defending church, and they cannot find it!

Additionally, at my annual conference, almost everyone I speak with says the same thing. They come from around the world, not just my neighborhood! And they attend the few events like mine and travel great distances to be with the likeminded people and to escape the scoffers who have overtaken their church.

In 2016 and 2017, the church I rent in suburban Minneapolis was unprepared for the enthusiasm of my audience that came from everywhere. The church seats forty-three hundred. Those two years, our attendance was more than six thousand. I am told that our freeways were backed up as folks attempted to get there from the various hotels to join the crowds of local and regional attendees.

The church was overwhelmed, and the mega parking lot was filled beyond capacity. People were sitting on the floor and stairs. They were straining at monitors in the foyer to hear the good news that Jesus is coming soon.

The church insisted we ticket the event in 2018 and 2019 to limit the attendance and prevent wear and tear on the church.

Eat your heart out you mockers and scoffers!

Rick Wiles, I wish it were true. I wish the theology I love, grew up with, and teach today was the primary mover and shaker in the Western world. Sadly, it is not. It is the object of scorn other than by a remnant of people who cherish it as I do. This remnant will literally drive across nations, states, and Canadian provinces to be together and rejoice that the King is coming any day.

Here are just a few emails that speak to the alienation people feel that drives their interest:

> Jan, I feel the remnant is getting smaller every day as the time approaches for the Lord's return. The world seems to be getting darker and more evil. I know I am not alone as a member of the Body of Christ, but at times it is easy to feel isolated. And I am mocked.—Benjamin

> My husband and I are visiting churches and have not found one that addresses these issues. Some in these churches have gotten angry and asked that I not come back. I feel like crying when I leave. I try to sit there but wonder why they never talk about what is going on, what's happening in Israel, or the intensifying birth pangs.—Patrice

> And one more: "My church has no excitement about prophetic fulfillment applicable for today. When I bring up what I learn on your broadcast, I am put down, mocked and scoffed. I am so lonely for like-minded believers."—Carolyn

I call these "remnant believers." Remnant believers often feel isolated and misunderstood even though they have the truth and the naysayers are clueless!

Members of the remnant church see our times darkening, but remain enthusiastic that this is but a herald of His coming—not signs of doom and gloom.

When a remnant believer finds someone who is a kindred spirit, it is like discovering a gold mine! They are friends for life. The mockers seem almost silenced!

Keep in mind that people who make quilts use a wide variety of mismatched remnants. Some sections of fabric are from garments that are no longer usable, but they're then sewn into unbelievably elegant quilts! *The tossed aside remnant became an object of creativity and beauty!*

This is today's remnant church that is watching, waiting, and looking up expectantly! The scoffers will not dissuade us. We feel badly for them, for they are missing out on the only hope there is today—the hope of Christ's any-minute return in the Rapture of the church. We want them to share our expectancy and hope.

Perhaps in eternity, none of this will matter, and we'll all be in one accord! Won't that be a glorious day? It may be sooner than we think. *For sure, it will be sooner than the mockers and the scoffers think!*

A little plaque in my office says "Perhaps Today." I look at it daily and am comforted that, indeed, His return could be today. It could be this minute. Yes, I wish every church were excited and had at least one message a year titled "Perhaps Today."

I wish every pastor would set aside his fear that his message of hope—the blessed hope—would offend, scare, and keep people away. I wish he wouldn't cave to the scoffers, and I wish he would set aside the memory of Harold Camping and Edgar Whisenhunt. Yes, they did damage.

But it is far more important to equip the flock to be ready—to be ready, waiting, and watching, and in the meantime, to occupy until He comes.

He is coming: Any day. Any hour. Any minute.

Perhaps today.

CHAPTER 15

AGONIZING AFTERMATH OF SAINTS' ASCENSION

TIM CAMERON

A prudent man foresees evil and hides himself, but the simple pass on and are punished. (Proverbs 22:3)

ONE STORMY SPRING NIGHT at 2:30 a.m. in the Ozarks of Missouri, I was stirred awake by a loud crack of thunder. Looking out from the bedroom window; I could see the rain was moving sideways. I ran and turned on the TV to see that our area was under a tornado warning. My heart raced; I had slept through any warnings that might have been given.

The next morning, when I was talking with other local friends, we all asked the same question: "Did you hear the sirens?"

In the Ozarks, in tornado alley, we take tornado season seriously.

Eight years ago this May, Joplin, Missouri, was hit with the deadliest tornado to hit the USA since 1947: 158 people died in the EF-5 Multiple Vortex Tornado.

On May 22, 2011, I stood outside getting ready to go to a friend's house for dinner, and said, "I better call my parents and ask if it's okay for the kids to stay at their house, just in case."

The reason? My parents have a storm shelter and the clouds in the sky to the west of us looked OMINOUS. It was 4:30 in the afternoon when my wife and I had dropped off our three kids and headed to a friend's house.

We were all eating and talking when I quickly glanced at the radar on my phone and my friend saw my countenance. "Is something wrong?"

"You should see the radar," I replied. "It looks TERRIBLE, and man, it's right on top of Joplin!"

My friend's wife hurried and turned on the TV in the other room, and all of our phones were buzzing with texts: "Home Depot in Joplin got hit, Walmart too!" It was sobering; all of our "watching and praying" eyes were lifted up. We all prayed, then my wife and I made a mad dash to my parents' house to be with our kids.

In the next few hours after watching the storm lift and pass over our area, we learned that one of the deadliest storms in recent American history had just taken place. Many lives were lost and countless others would NEVER be the same.

Many stories came from those who heard the warnings, believed them, and ran for shelter. At the same time we heard stories of those who turned a deaf ear. "Heard them all my life," they said, and just kept grilling burgers. "I heard the sirens, but they go off a lot around here this time of year."

Of course, we also heard devastating stories about those who lost their lives because, even though they heard the warnings, they weren't in a safe place to weather the storm. Still others were even snatched out of loved ones' arms. It was gut wrenching. I pray that, as you continue to read, this disaster will serve as a wake-up call to those who have been blinded to something coming that is much more ominous.

You see, many people died during that storm, but some were prepared for death. They had taken shelter from an eternal storm by placing their faith in Jesus Christ, and even though their physical bodies perished, they did NOT truly die. In an instant, the moment their bodies were struck by that devastating F-5 tornado, because they belonged to God, their souls were transported into His very presence in their eternal home, a place they would never want to leave.

On the other hand, many were not prepared for that tornado. More importantly, they weren't prepared for what would come after the storm. The Bible says all people will die once, then later, at the Great White Throne judgment, they will stand before God, who is Judge.

During the horrendous Joplin tornado, a local doctor reported hearing people "wail and scream" inside the twister and how those sounds haunted him. Even more daunting is that there are those who are even now wailing and screaming from a storm that will NEVER STOP, because, after being propelled through that tornado—out of a Home Depot or Walmart—they arrived in Hell.

After the thousand-year Millennium, they will stand in God's courtroom because they refused to believe in Him and take shelter in Him. They will hear a terrible decree: "Depart from Me; I know you not."

Those who have died after rejecting the free gift of salvation offered through Jesus Christ are now in HELL with NO HOPE—no chance to escape. When they stand before the Lord at the great white throne judgment, they will be sentenced to eternity in the Lake of Fire.

But if you are reading this, you still have hope.

Here is the deal: A storm of biblical proportions is brewing—it's even at the door. You have to have eyes to see and ears to hear.

The radar is screaming for you to PLEASE TAKE SHELTER!

In God's Word, He foretold of a time such as this, and said when we see certain things, we should "take shelter!" What are those things? Here are just a few:

1.   Israel being pressured on every side to "divide her land."

2.   Love growing cold, when the love of pleasure (self-gratification) becomes greater than love for God.

3.   Wars and rumors of wars occurring.

4. Global economies shaking, knowledge increasing, and people traveling rapidly "to and fro."

Okay, everyone would surely concede that there has been a significant increase in "wars and rumors of wars," right? (North Korea, Syria, Russia, China, the USA, Iran in recent days and weeks is taking significant steps towards showing a war footing.)

Would everyone also agree that Israel's existence and its claim upon a certain parcel of land as its capital (Jerusalem) are growing in prominence as a global talking point?

Would anyone disagree that debt is a global epidemic that continues to spiral out of control? The USA's debt alone is has passed $22 trillion!

Anyone over the age of forty can argue that homosexuality was in the closet for most of our lives. NOW it is in our faces demanding not only be accepted, but normalized, and those who oppose it are being marginalized.

What about the prophesied increase of travel and knowledge by the prophet Daniel?

> But thou, O Daniel, shut up the words, and seal the book, even to the time of the end: many shall run to and fro, and knowledge shall be increased. (Daniel 12:4)

For thousands of years, mankind traveled by horse, but in the last century, we've reached a point that we can ship anything worldwide within three days (via Federal Express). We can talk instantaneously to others anywhere via text, instant message, and email, and we can download songs from anywhere in the world within seconds on iTunes.

Just as Daniel forewarned, when we see these things, it's like we're seeing an ominous storm warning shouting something very terrifying: "The Day of the Lord is at hand!"

> Look! The Lord's anger bursts out like a storm, a whirlwind that swirls down on the heads of the wicked. The anger of the Lord will not diminish until it has finished all he has planned. In the days to come you will understand all this very clearly. (Jeremiah 23:19–20)

We're approaching a time of God's undeniable wrath being poured out upon this place we've called home. He, in His mercy, is warning all who will listen.

The jihadists—including the Muslim Brotherhood—are screaming, "Americans MUST die." Even now, these enemies are working around the clock to see that this is accomplished through their planning of tremendous violence and demanding Sharia law (slavery).

We have entire nations to reference for what looks like the ravages of radical Islamists, demanding submission as they train little kids to strap bombs to themselves, walk into crowds, and blow themselves up. Even now they're planning massive attacks on the place we call home—America. They do this believing they're under a "divine" mandate to usher in their "messiah" by way of horror and chaos.

Please hear the heart of this message.

It is not to condemn, but to stir an urgency to sound the alarm to your friends and family while there is still time.

I tell you, the storm clouds are ominous.

Are you prepared? Have you taken shelter with Jesus?

Hatred has replaced love. The love of self has replaced God. "Whatever makes you feel good, just do it." Run up credit cards—who cares that the debtor is enslaved to the lender? Even now, our nation in America is selling its individual citizens into debt slavery by destroying our national sovereignty through spending not billions, but trillions. Yet the masses of Kool-Aid drinkers are trusting that these blind "leaders" know where they are going.

Pope Francis has been lobbying Israel to give up land for peace, referring to the 1967 borders as the starting point of negotiations striving for a "Two-State Solution." The pope is asking for all faiths to unite so we can COEXIST. That is ominous, I tell you!

PLEASE TAKE SHELTER.

In Joplin, the warnings went out, and many heard and believed. They ran and hid in safe places. That is what I'm asking you to do.

You see, you can scoff and say, "I've heard this all my life." And, as one woman testified in Joplin, you can say, "I've heard these warnings all my life."

Thousands of people mocked Noah to the very end, and you can mock the warnings of this time, too. You can say, "Ah, the government will fix it," or "we've seen this before." Or, you can take a serious and sober look at the many things that have taken place in recent days, months, and years, and say, "Maybe I need to wake up to what is really happening and TAKE SHELTER."

Did you know the great damage a tsunami can cause before you saw and heard the news reports following the Asian Pacific tsunami that struck ten years ago? More than 250,000 people died in that catastrophe. That storm will pale in comparison to a time about which the Bible warns, "unless God shortens the days, no flesh will survive."

What must you do to be safe from the wrath to come? What is the wrath to come? It is the time of the seven-year Tribulation when God pours out his judgment upon an unbelieving world.

In a storm warning for that time, if we turned on our televisions, we might expect to see a scrolling message stating the following: "Strong winds in excess of 100 mph, golf-ball sized hail, dangerous lightning."

When the "Storm of the Lord" that Jeremiah 23 describes is unleashed, however, we might instead see the following in a scrolling message:

- "Ninety to one hundred-pound hailstones will fall" (Revelation 16:16–20).

- "A great earthquake will occur, leaving NO ISLANDS and taking down every mountain on earth."

- "A third of all the earth, trees, and grass across the earth will be burned up" (Revelation 8:7).

- "A third of the sea will be turned into blood" (Revelation 8:8–9).

- "The abyss (bottomless pit) will open, releasing locust-like scorpion creatures" (Revelation 9:2–3).

- "Evil angels will be released to kill one-third of the population of mankind" (Revelation 9).

- "Painful sores will break out on people who have taken the mark of the Beast" (Revelation 16).

- "The sun will scorch people with fire" (Revelation 16).

Even worse, we will see that lost souls who die without Christ will be cast into Hell and later into the Lake of Fire for all eternity.

Stop and think. Please! Just look at that list of events the Bible tells us is coming! As the Alan Jackson song goes, do you remember where you were on 9/11/2001? Do you remember how shaken up everyone was who witnessed that awful day?

What took place then was regionalized, but what is coming will make that event look like a picnic. Yet it will encompass the globe.

Jesus described the mindset of those who will be alive when this happens as being like the mindset of those who were living during the days of Noah, when people were carrying on daily business as usual: They were eating, drinking, and marrying. Then the Flood came. One moment it was calm and quiet, then sudden destruction began to fall. Can you imagine the people's fear as the rain began to fall and the ark's doors were closed? Can you imagine the wails and screams of a mom holding her child's hand? "NOAH...please let us in!" Can you see her? Can you hear her?

There will be parents sitting in living rooms in total anxiety watching story after story and event after event. Imagine driving in a car as ninety or one hundred-pound hailstones began to fall! You'd say that everyone would be fleeing to get to safety, when in fact the Bible tells us in Revelation 6 that people will be begging for the rocks to fall upon them to hide them from the Wrath of the Lamb!

Again, Scripture tells us that "unless God shortens the days, no flesh will survive" and that "people will seek death but find it not."

Let's imagine some scenarios.

**

A man sits on a living room couch with a 9 MM handgun, listening to news reports describing how millions of people have been reported missing. In his other hand, he holds a photo of his wife, who is among those said to have been taken away by a shout of Jesus Christ to "Come up here!" He remembers her describing this time, and saying how the Bible said that BEFORE this awful and terrible time, Jesus would remove faithful believers before unleashing wrath upon the earth.

She had begged time and time for her husband to "flee the wrath to come." But now all he has is a photo, memories, and dread—the dread of knowing that since the promise of the removal of believers has come true, all the other things the Bible says will happen must be true.

Overcome with fear and anxiety, the man pulls the gun to his head and pulls the trigger. Despite a bullet piercing his skull, he remains alive, blood pouring out, but he's still fully aware of all the pain he's trying to hide from. He pulls the trigger once again…but he's still alive! The holes in his head throb with ruthless pain alongside each and every haunting thought of what is coming.

***

A husband and wife are driving down the interstate, and the woman begins to scream as the pavement begins to violently divide, shaken so severely that every bridge in sight is collapsing. The severity of the tremors propels the car off the roadway and into trees along with hundreds of others who are now stranded.

Car alarms are reverberating everywhere. The couple is stranded with no food or water, and there is no safe place to walk, as all the people around, with depraved minds, are scratching and clawing, murdering, and stealing every resource they can find. Emergency drones have been put to flight above their heads—not offering any help, just surveilling the survivors and taking inventory. The wife reaches out for her husband seeking help, but, his love having grown cold, he shoves her away, saying, "You're on your own now."

That won't be an isolated case; scenarios like these will be taking place across the globe.

Failed suicide survivors will walk along with zombie-like states of mind. The darkest of depression will invade countless souls with nightmares turned reality.

No, this is not the hallucination it seems; it's an F-5 storm blasting the earth on every side. One 9/11-type of event after another will occur on a global scale, with no relief in sight. Again, unless God shortens the days, "no flesh will survive."

Parents with kids who have gone missing will sit engulfed with loss and sorrow.

Haters and mockers of God will shout to the sky, "Screw you, God!" as awful sores break out all across their bodies, like acid burning, yet no medicine will be available to comfort or soothe.

Nightmarish scenarios of every kind will have gone global, including epidemics. Think of the viral movie *Bird Box,* but on steroids.

War: epidemic.

Violence: epidemic.

Depression: epidemic.

Attempted suicides: epidemic.

Flakka and other mind-altering drug use: epidemic. (Zombie Apocalypse, anybody?)

In the midst of the onset of this horrible time:

World leaders will be giving speeches saying the reason for the missing millions is likely due to a cosmic cleansing by "mother earth" of those detrimental to the collective good of all.

One World Leader will arise over all of the others with urgent, yet calming answers. Global economies will have crashed, having been decimated by the weight of debt and calamity, but this leader will offer a time of debt forgiveness: "It's the year of Jubilee!" he will proclaim. "All debts are now gone and we will be implementing a global reset by electronically assigning each individual a numbered account and a guaranteed monthly income starting immediately."

The masses will love this offer of security. News from Israel will begin to tout this leader as "messianic" in his appeal.

COEXIST will no longer be a bumper sticker, but will become the global mission statement, with adherence encouraged at first, but then demanded. Those who hedge or try to stay off the grid will be hunted by video game experts-turned-drone pilots, gaming away and herding all into compliance but those who rebel, who are shot on site by the Drone Force. Did you see *Schindler's List* and how the evil men shot the Jews in cold blood simply for being Jews? It'll be like that GLOBALLY, but with drones.

Wars won't be rumors anymore, as restraint will have been replaced by depravity. Lust for power and for control for money will have escalated beyond anything earth has ever seen. Darkness and even gross darkness will cover the earth. Hiroshima will have become a global experience.

Some will turn to God and cry out for His rescue, but most will turn inward and self-medicate themselves with humanistic acts of the worst kinds.

Bestiality, rape, incest, murder, violence of every kind will now be unrestrained and licensed by COEXIST, "live YOUR truth"—"whatever will be will be."

Voices calling for righteousness and for the end of the madness will be instant targets of the Drone Police. Yet Heaven will NOT stomach this for long before the wrath of the Lamb will begin to be unveiled for all to see.

Knowing the terror of the Lord, I beg of you to hear this warning.

Right now, if a tornado warning was sounding and you believed it, you would run to find shelter. How can we do that in relation to the choices we must make in this life? We either repent or perish.

Repentance is simply a change of mind; it means to "stop and think" differently than you are now. In its simplest application: In order to be saved, one must BELIEVE upon the Lord Jesus Christ.

Get on your knees and humbly place your faith/trust in the death, burial, and resurrection of Jesus Christ. Believe that He is your only hope, that He is your Lord and Savior, and that He is your Storm Shelter…and He will be your Refuge. If you do that, I have great news: You will NOT die, but will have everlasting life

Will you hurry up and take shelter with the Lord? Don't you hear the warnings?

GOD'S WRATH: MYTH OR REALITY? THE EFFORT TO CONVERT GOD INTO A COSMIC TEDDY BEAR

DR. DAVID R. REAGAN

BACK IN THE MID 1990s, a popular radio talk show host on an Oklahoma City secular station interviewed me live on the air via telephone. He had seen an article I had written about the financial accountability of Christian ministries, and he had liked it.

He began the interview by graciously giving me the opportunity to talk nonstop for about ten minutes about the way God had transformed my life and called me into the ministry. We then moved on to a discussion of the scandals that had recently rocked the Christian community nationwide.

The Unmentionable Word

Everything went well until the host asked me to summarize the fundamental message of my ministry. I responded by saying that God had called me to proclaim "the soon return of Jesus." I then explained that this reality was like a two-edged sword, with a message for both believers and unbelievers. I pointed out that the message for believers is to commit themselves to holiness and evangelism. I then added, "The message for unbelievers is to flee from the wrath that is to come, by fleeing into the loving arms of Jesus now."

Before I could proceed with my explanation, the program host cut me short. "What do you mean when you refer to 'wrath'?" he asked.

"I mean that Jesus is going to return very soon to pour out the wrath of God upon those who have rejected God's love and grace and mercy."

"Your God is a monster!" he snapped. He then added, "I happen to be a Christian, I go to church every Sunday, and I have never heard anything about God 'pouring out wrath.' My God is Jesus, and He wouldn't hurt a fly!"

That was the end of the interview. He hung up on me. I was not given an opportunity to respond to his misrepresentation of our Creator.

An Enraged Pastor

Ten years later, in 2005, I was invited to speak to a large church in the Dallas area where I had spoken several times before. The date of my presentation fell on a Sunday about three weeks after hurricane Katrina had devastated New Orleans.

I decided I would speak about the hurricane, with the intention of pointing out that I believed it to be a remedial judgment of God upon this nation for two reasons. The first reason I mentioned was our nation's strong-arming of Israel to surrender the Gaza Strip to its enemies. I noted that the hurricane had started forming very suddenly near the Bahamas on the last day of the Israeli withdrawal.

The second reason I gave was the immorality of our nation and particularly the city of New Orleans, a city that calls itself "Sin City USA." The hurricane hit the city just as it was preparing to conduct its annual festival called "Gay Mardi Gras." The 2005 theme of this sexual perversion event was "Jazz and Jezebels." In 2004, the event had attracted 125,000 revelers who proudly flaunted their perversion publicly in a garish parade. The event was sponsored by a group called "Southern Decadence."

The sermon was a hard hitting, sobering one. But it seemed to be well received. The church had two services that morning. I preached the same sermon at both. To my surprise, several people stayed over to hear the sermon again at the second service, including some people who were victims of the hurricane. All the comments afterwards were positive—again, much to my surprise, since I was speaking about the wrath of God.

But all hell broke loose during the following week. You see, the pastor had been out of town when I delivered the message. When he returned home and watched a video of the message, he went ballistic! He even checked my speaking schedule on our website and called the next church where I was to speak and warned them about allowing me to present my sermon.

What was he so mad about? Two things. First, he felt it was wrong for me to attribute a disaster to God when it should have been assigned to Satan. Second, he objected to my characterization of the hurricane as being a manifestation of the wrath of God. He insisted that the "God of Wrath" was the Old Testament God, whereas the God of the New Testament is a "God of Grace." The idea of God pouring out His wrath was entirely foreign to him.

These are only two examples of many experiences I have had where Christians have reacted with revulsion against any mention of God's wrath.

Satan's Grand Deception

The fact of the matter is that Satan has sold the world a bill of goods concerning the nature of God. Most people, both Christian and non-Christian, tend to view God as being a sort of Cosmic Teddy Bear.

They see Him as big, warm, and soft, full of infinite love and forgiveness. He couldn't hurt a fly, and He certainly wouldn't be so cruel as to condemn or harm any beings created in His own image. On the Day of Judgment, God will simply give everyone a big hug and wink at their sins.

The only problem with this wonderfully comforting image is that it is a lie straight from the pit of Hell.

Yes, the Bible teaches that God is loving, patient, caring, and forgiving (Psalm 86:15 and John 3:16). As the apostle John put it, "God is love" (1 John 4:8).

Two of my favorite passages in the Bible emphasize the personal, loving nature of God. One was penned by the Apostle Peter. In 1 Peter 5:6–7 he says that we are to cast all our anxieties upon God "because He cares for you."

That is a very comforting thought. Our God is a personal God who desires a personal relationship with us.

The other passage that I love to read over and over consists of words spoken by the prophet Jeremiah in Lamentations 3:22–24 (RSV):

> The steadfast love of the LORD never ceases, His mercies never come to an end; they are new every morning; great is Thy faithfulness. "The LORD is my portion," says my soul, "therefore I will hope in Him."

But the Bible also clearly teaches that another aspect of God's character is equally important. It is the aspect that Satan wants us to ignore, and he has been very successful in prompting ministers to overlook it. After all, it doesn't produce popular sermons! I'm speaking, of course, of the holiness of God (Leviticus 11:44, Isaiah 6:3, and 1 Peter 1:16).

Grace or Wrath?

The Bible teaches that God is perfectly holy. Because of this attribute of His character, He cannot tolerate sin (Numbers 14:18). The Bible says God must deal with sin, and He does so in one of two ways.

All of us seem to know John 3:16—a very comforting verse about God loving us so much that He sent His only begotten Son to die for our sins. But few of us seem to be aware of the words recorded a few verses later in John 3:36—words taken from a sermon by John the Baptist: "He who believes in the Son has eternal life, but he who does not obey the Son shall not see life, but the wrath of God abides on him."

Because God is Holy, He must deal with sin, and according to this verse, God does that in one of two ways—either grace or wrath. That means every person on planet earth is currently living under either the grace or wrath of God. It is a glorious thing to be abiding in His grace, and it is terrible to be living with the wrath of God hovering over your head.

Paul emphasized this point in his preaching and teaching. In Ephesians 5, he warns against immorality, covetousness, and idolatry, and then adds this observation:

> Let no one deceive you with empty words, for because of these things, the wrath of God comes upon the sons of disobedience. (Ephesians 5:6)

We come under God's grace by placing our faith in Jesus and appropriating His atoning sacrifice for our lives (1 John 1:7). There is no salvation apart from Jesus (Acts 4:10–12). Those who have rejected God's free gift of grace in Jesus are under God's wrath (John 3:36), and they have no one to blame but themselves.

The Unchangeable God

Despite the Bible's clear teaching that our Creator is a God of both love and wrath, I never cease to be amazed at the number of pastors I run across who argue that the God of wrath is the Old Testament God and not the God of the New Testament. In the process they ignore another clear teaching of the Bible that is found in Malachi 3:6, where God, speaking of Himself, says, "I, the LORD do not change." In other words, our Creator is immutable—He never changes. There is no such thing as an Old Testament God versus a New Testament God.

The New Testament confirms this important point in Hebrews 13:8, which says, "Jesus Christ is the same yesterday and today, yes and forever."

Nonetheless, Jesus seems always to be presented in sermons as the meek and gentle Savior who is full of grace and forgiveness. That statement is true, but it is not the full picture. Jesus castigated the Pharisees, calling them "hypocrites," "serpents," and a "brood of vipers."

Likewise, in His letters to the seven churches of Asia Minor, Jesus condemned the church at Thyatira for tolerating a false prophetess. He called upon the church to repent, then warned that if they refused to repent of their immorality, He would cast the offenders "upon a bed of sickness," killing them with pestilence" (Revelation 2:22–23). This verse alone destroys the false notion of a "Jesus who would never hurt a fly."

The Sovereign God

Another aspect of God's nature that must be emphasized is His sovereignty. He is on His throne; He is in control. Psalm 2 says he laughs at all the plots and schemes of the world's political leaders. He is not laughing because He doesn't care; His laughter is provoked by the fact that He has the wisdom and power to orchestrate all the evil of Satan and mankind to the triumph of His Son.

People like to attribute all bad things to Satan. But the interesting thing is that the Bible never does that, because the writers believed in the sovereignty of God. They therefore understood that even when bad things happen, God allows them either to discipline us, to refine us in righteousness, or to fulfill purposes known only to Him.

Satan is not free to do as he pleases. The book of Job makes this clear. Satan could not touch Job, his household, or his possessions without God's permission, and even when that permission was granted, Satan was told he could not take Job's life. Even during the Great Tribulation, when Satan and the Antichrist will be rampaging around the world, they will do so under the sovereignty of God. They will be used by God as instruments of His wrath, just as the Babylonians were used by God to pour out His wrath on Judah (Habakkuk 1:5–11).

Types of Wrath

The Bible reveals several different aspects of the wrath of God:

- **Consequential Wrath** — This might be called "sowing and reaping wrath." It is the wrath we bring upon ourselves when we reap what we sow through sinful living. Thus, a smoker might be afflicted with lung cancer and a drunkard may lose his job and family.

- **Cataclysmic Wrath** — This is wrath as evidenced in disasters, either natural or man-made, like the 9/11 attacks. God allows these as a way of calling people and nations to repentance. They are usually referred to as "remedial judgments."

- **Abandonment Wrath** — This is the wrath exhibited by God when He turns His back on a person or a society, allowing self-destruction.

- **Eschatological Wrath** — This is the wrath God unleashed on all the world with the Noahic Flood, and the wrath He has promised to pour out on the world during the Great Tribulation that is yet to come.

- **Eternal Wrath** — This is the ultimate punishment God will inflict upon those who are consigned to Hell.

Abandonment Wrath

God's wrath of abandonment is what the United States and other nations are experiencing today. Again, this type of wrath can fall on an individual as well as a society.

A biblical example of it in the life of an individual can be found in the story of Samson. Although he was mightily anointed by God to protect Israel from the Philistines, he persisted in sexual sin to the point that the Scriptures say that "the Lord departed from him" (Judges 16:20). As a result, he was captured by the Philistines and ended up committing suicide.

In Romans 1, the apostle Paul strongly warns of God's wrath of abandonment concerning nations. He asserts that "the wrath of God is revealed from heaven against all ungodliness and unrighteousness of men, who suppress the truth in unrighteousness" (Romans 1:18). He then proceeds to tell how God does this when dealing with a nation that is in rebellion against Him.

First, God steps back and lowers the hedge of protection around the nation, allowing evil to multiply. The result is an outbreak of sexual sin (Romans 1:24–25), which is what happened in our nation in the 1960s.

If the nation refuses to repent, God takes a second step back and lowers the hedge even further (Romans 1:26–27), producing a plague of homosexuality. Again, this nation has experienced this second phase ever since the 1990s, but it gained momentum after 2003 when our Supreme Court struck down all sodomy laws.

If the nation persists in its rebellion, God will take a third step back and abandon the nation to "a depraved mind" (Romans 1:28). This depravity was manifested in this nation when our Supreme Court sanctioned same-sex marriage in June of 2015, and when our president celebrated the decision by having the White House lit up in the rainbow colors of the sexual perversion movement.

The Coming Wrath

God's eschatological wrath will fall on all the world when Jesus returns (Jude 1:14–15). The passage in Revelation that pictures the return of Jesus says that He will return in righteousness to "judge and wage war" (Revelation 19:11).

The first time Jesus came, He came in loving compassion with eyes filled with tears. But when He returns, He will come in vengeance (Revelation 6:12–17), with eyes like a flame of fire (Revelation 19:12). He will come to destroy the enemies of God (Revelation 19:11).

The presidents, kings, and prime ministers of the world will get on their knees and cry out for the rocks and mountains to fall upon them, so great will be the terror of the Lord (Revelation 6:15–17). The unrighteous will stumble about like blind men, and their blood will be poured out like dust (Zephaniah 1:17).

The Meaning of Wrath

Does this make God a "monster"? No! On the contrary, it proves His goodness, for how could a good God ignore the evil of sin and allow it to go unpunished? His wrath against evil will demonstrate His righteousness.

The prophet Nahum summed it up best. Writing of the love of God, he said, "The LORD is good, a stronghold in the day of trouble, and He knows those who take refuge in Him" (Nahum 1:7). But a few verses earlier (Nahum 1:2–3), Nahum had also spoken of the holiness and wrath of God:

> A jealous and avenging God is the LORD; The LORD is avenging and wrathful. The LORD takes vengeance on His adversaries, And He reserves wrath for His enemies. The LORD is slow to anger and great in power, And the LORD will by no means leave the guilty unpunished.

God's wrath is never motivated primarily by a desire to punish. Rather, it is designed to bring people to repentance so that they might be saved. Isaiah made this point when he wrote: "When the earth experiences Your judgments, the inhabitants of the world learn righteousness." Even in His wrath, God remembers mercy.

God demonstrates His mercy in wrath by never pouring out His wrath without warning. He tried to warn Sodom and Gomorrah through Abraham. He warned Noah's world through the preaching of Noah for 120 years. He sent both Jonah and Nahum to warn the pagan city of Nineveh.

Consider, too, how He sent prophet after prophet to call the nation of Judah to repentance (2 Chronicles 36:15–16):

> The LORD, the God of their fathers, sent word to them again and again by His messengers, because He had compassion on His people and on His dwelling place;

> but they continually mocked the messengers of God, despised His words and scoffed at His prophets, until the wrath of the LORD arose against His people, until there was no remedy.

God's mercy in wrath is also manifested in the fact that He always leads up to His final outpouring of wrath through a series of progressive judgments. These remedial judgments are outlined in detail in Deuteronomy 28:15–57. They include such things as the rebellion of youth, an epidemic of divorce, crop failures, rampant disease, defeat in wars, and foreign domination. This characteristic of God's wrath is demonstrated in the prophecies concerning the Tribulation. Rather than simply pouring out His wrath on the rebellious nations of the world, destroying them in one instant of overwhelming catastrophe, He is going to subject the world to a series of judgments that sequentially increase in scope and intensity (Revelation 6:8–9, 16).

Although most people will refuse to repent in response to these judgments (Revelation 9:20–21), there is "a great multitude, which no one could count, from every nation and all tribes and peoples and tongues" that will repent and respond to Jesus in faith (Revelation 7:9).

These radically different responses to the wrath of God illustrate the point that was often made by Billy Graham. "The same sun that melts the butter also hardens the clay." The wrath of God melts some hearts in repentance, but it has the effect of hardening the hearts of many others.

Wrath and the Redeemed

Many Christians respond negatively to Bible prophecy. It's not at all unusual to hear a Christian say something like this: "I don't want to hear anything about prophecy because it's too full of gloom and doom."

Well, there is a lot of gloom and doom for those who refuse to respond to God's gift of love in Jesus. But there is only good news for the redeemed.

The Old Testament ends with a passage that presents both the gloom and the joy of end-time prophecy. Malachi says that when the Lord returns, the day will be "like a furnace; and all the arrogant and every evildoer will be chaff" (Malachi 4:1). That's the bad news.

But consider the good news:

> But for you who fear My name, the sun of righteousness
> will rise with healing in its wings; and you will go forth and
> skip about like calves from the stall. (Malachi 4:2)

There is no reason for any child of God to fear the wrath of God. Paul wrote that since we have been justified by the blood of Christ, "we shall be saved from the wrath of God through Him" (Romans 5:9). And in a most comforting verse, Paul told the Thessalonians that Jesus will "deliver" the redeemed "from the wrath to come" (1 Thessalonians 1:10). The reason, Paul explained, is that "God has not destined us for wrath, but for obtaining salvation through our Lord Jesus Christ" (1 Thessalonians 5:9).

That wonderful deliverance will take the form of the Rapture of the Church, which Paul describes in detail in 1 Thessalonians 4:13–18. This is the promise that the believing Church, both the living and dead, will be taken out of this world in a great miracle of deliverance before the Great Tribulation begins. It is no wonder that Paul concludes his description of this event by saying, "Therefore, comfort one another with these words."

A Plea

Are you under grace or wrath? The choice is yours. Jesus is coming soon. When He appears, will He be your Blessed Hope or your Holy Terror? Will you cry for the mountains to fall upon you? Or, will you go forth leaping with joy like a calf released from a stall?

Do not be deceived by those who tell you that God is going to wink at your sins. This is a promise of God's wrath for you.

God loves you and He wants you to accept His Son as your Savior so that you will come under grace and can participate in an event that will occur when Jesus returns to this earth to reign for a thousand years (Isaiah: 35:10):

> And the ransomed of the LORD will return And come with joyful shouting to Zion, With everlasting joy upon their heads. They will find gladness and joy,
>
> And sorrow and sighing will flee away.

CONCLUSION

TERRY JAMES

OUR WEEKLY COLUMN ON the raptureready.com website is called "Nearing Midnight," named so because we discern that planet earth has almost reached the midnight hour of the Church Age, or Age of Grace.

Whereas the geopolitical humanist powers that frame their view of human history's closing minutes within their "Doomsday Clock," we observe these fleeting times before Christ's call to the Church by placing the template of Bible prophecy over the converging of prophetic stage-setting.

The political scientists and other scientists can only guess at what will happen to the human race. Most all believe that humankind will meet its end from nuclear holocaust or by climate-change disasters.

We who give total credence to what God's Word has to say about the consummation of the age can know for certain, through a detailed preview by God, Himself, how the end of all things will unfold. We don't know precisely *when* the end will come. We can know, however, the *general time* when it will begin to manifest.

We can know for certain when the mdnight hour of God's prophetic timeline is approaching.

The Lord Jesus gave His family (born-again believers) explicit instruction about how and when to discern the nearing midnight hour.

> And when you see all these things begin to come to pass, then look up, and lift up your head, for your redemption draws near. (Luke 21:28)

Note that Jesus didn't say to watch for when these things "come to pass." He said "when these things **begin** to come to pass," we are to "look up and lift up our heads, for our redemption is drawing near." At that time, He will be on His way to rescue His Bride, the Church, from the carnage that is about to take place on earth.

The blackness of the midnight hour will descend following that rescue of Christ's Bride, the Church. Seven years into the Tribulation, complete evil will have engulfed the planet with satanic darkness. The first bright gleaming that pierces that most horrendous time of all of human history will then burst through the billowing storm clouds of Armageddon. Brilliant light will part the heavens, and Christ and His army will appear.

So, discerning the times in which we find ourselves is all-important to the believer. If it wasn't possible to discern the times, Jesus wouldn't have told us: "What I say unto one, I say unto all. Watch" (Mark 13:37).

He promises in Revelation 3:10 that we're not appointed to God's wrath and will be kept out of the very hour of that wrath.

So, what are the things the Lord forewarned would be taking place—*beginning to come to pass*—that we see happening at this very moment? Exactly *what* are the *things* for which we are to *look?*

Remember, the whole Bible is the Word of God. And, Jesus is that Word (John 1:1).

Every prophecy, whether already accomplished or yet to come, is attributable to Him. God, the Holy Spirit, inspired the Old and New Testament prophets to give the prophecies. So, we don't have to consider just what the Lord Jesus, Himself, said by way of prophecy to discern the times in which we live. We can and must consider every prophecy yet to be fulfilled, presented in the Bible by all Bible prophets, as part of the process.

I am of the camp that believes we're seeing stage-setting for fulfillment of prophecy yet future rather than fulfillment itself. The one caveat concerns the nation Israel. My view is that Israel again being a nation after millennia of dispersion across the world is fulfilled prophecy.

That said, however, everything we see happening around us at this very hour has prophetic significance. Some things involved are profoundly significant.

One such profound sign of stage-setting for prophetic fulfillment, as has been expertly presented by Bill Salus in his chapter, is the coalition of nations forming to Israel's north.

Russia (land of Magog), Iran (much of ancient Persia), and Turkey (the land of Torgomah) coming together in a coalescing alliance is a spectacular example of God's foreknowledge of things to come. These, of course, are exactly the central actors prophetically scheduled to come against God's chosen nation, Israel, according to Ezekiel chapters 38 and 39.

Each author in *Discerners: Analyzing Converging Prophetic Signs for the End of Days* has presented, I believe, Holy Spirit-directed insights into these closing hours of the Age of Grace (Church Age). Each topic they accepted to address covered the stage-setting for Bible prophecy that is on the very verge of being fulfilled.

It must be agreed that much of the stage-setting itself is likened to fulfilled prophecy in some ways. For example, the Apostle Paul's "perilous times," presented in 2 Timothy 3, is almost a vivid snapshot of these spiritually darkening days. Dr. Larry Spargimino, radio host of Southwest Radio Church, presents a tremendous chapter on these times. While prophecy yet future, for the most part, seems reserved for the Tribulation (Daniel's seventieth week), developments in our nation and world today are becoming ever more like those given in God's Word for that last seven years immediately preceding Christ's Second Advent.

Luciferic darkening has so infected this generation in America and throughout the world that we who "watch" in order to discern the times are brought face to face with end-times insanity born of greatly increased rebellion against God. Other than the fact that Israel itself is what most discerners view as the most dramatic sign of where this generation stands on God's prophetic timeline, there runs a deadly septicemia throughout humankind that marks this as a generation at the end of its prophetic rope. The infection proves we're in the terminal stage of rebellion.

The Apostle Paul explains very clearly that infection, satanically injected into humanity's collective bloodstream.

> For the wrath of God is revealed from heaven against all ungodliness and unrighteousness of men, who hold the truth in unrighteousness; Because that which may be known of God is manifest in them; for God hath shewed it unto them. For the invisible things of him from the creation of the world are clearly seen, being understood by the things that are made, even his eternal power and Godhead; so that they are without excuse: Because that, when they knew God, they glorified him not as God, neither were thankful; but became vain in their imaginations, and their foolish heart was darkened. Professing themselves to be wise, they became fools, And changed the glory of the uncorruptible God into an image made like to corruptible man, and to birds, and fourfooted beasts, and creeping things.

> Wherefore God also gave them up to uncleanness through the lusts of their own hearts, to dishonour their own bodies between themselves: Who changed the truth of God into a lie, and worshipped and served the creature more than the Creator, who is blessed for ever. Amen. For this cause God gave them up unto vile affections: for even their women did change the natural use into that which is against nature: And likewise also the men, leaving the natural use of the woman, burned in their lust one toward another; men with men working that which is unseemly, and receiving in themselves that recompence of their error which was meet. And even as they did not like to retain God in their knowledge, God gave them over to a reprobate mind, to do those things which are not convenient; Being filled with all unrighteousness, fornication, wickedness, covetousness, maliciousness; full of envy, murder, debate, deceit, malignity; whisperers, Backbiters, haters of God, despiteful, proud, boasters, inventors of evil things,

disobedient to parents, Without understanding, covenant-breakers, without natural affection, implacable, unmerciful: Who knowing the judgment of God, that they which commit such things are worthy of death, not only do the same, but have pleasure in them that do them. (Romans 1:18–32)

Carefully reread the above block of prophecy. It is astonishing how much it says about the human condition at the time of Christ's next catastrophic intervention into mankind's rebellion.

In my view, no descriptive could be more vivid or accurate of what has taken place in America over the past decade. This nation, despite its founding as a Christian nation—and it was so founded regardless of whether anyone wants to dispute the fact—has served as the prototype for the human condition and comportment given here by the Apostle Paul.

The most recent presidential election and the era surrounding it encapsulates practically every nuance of condemnable points about rebellious man herein characterized by the great apostle. It shows where we currently must stand on God's prophetic timeline.

Paul points out that the culmination of all the rebellion against the God of Heaven results in the Lord turning the rebels over to a "reprobate" mind. This is where this generation, as a collective, stands.

A reprobate mind is one that cannot think clearly. These rebels turn everything upside down. Good is called evil and evil is called good in their convoluted world.

Even Christendom—all religious entities that claim Christianity as their base—has become terminally infected with this end-times lunacy. These are false-teaching, apostate wolves in sheep's clothing who cannot (and do not even want to know) truth. They're of the totally reprobate mind Paul described.

An example of this religious septicemia during our time is provided by my close friend and colleague, Daymond Duck. Daymond writes the following:

On June 16, 2019, the building caretaker at Mount Auburn Presbyterian Church in Cincinnati, Ohio, Dan Davidson, dressed up as a drag queen called Sparke Leigh.

Sparke wore a purple dress, make up and high heels.

Sparke stood at the door of the church to greet people as they entered. (It seems to me that Auburn is a church in name only.)

During the children's portion of the worship service, Sparke went on stage and read "The Story of Harvey Milk and The Rainbow Flag" (possibly the opposite of training up children in the way that they should go).

Sparke could have read Scripture and shared a Bible Story with the children (such as what happened to Sodom and Gomorrah), but Sparke preferred to talk about Harvey Milk and the rainbow flag (days of Lot, departing from the faith, even worse, turning evil into good and flaunting it at church, etc.).

Literal events like this are why I believe the Master of the House is coming (and soon). (The Master of the House is Coming, Daymond R. Duck, https://www.raptureready.com/2019/07/07/master-house-coming-daymond-r-duck/.)

Indeed, in consideration of a worldwide cultural and societal 180-degree turn away from God, the spirit-filled discerner of these prophetic end times cannot but conclude that the moment of Heaven's judgment must be very near at hand.

Even so, come, Lord Jesus!

Looking for that blessed hope, and the glorious appearing of the great God and our Savior Jesus Christ. (Titus 2:13)

AUTHOR BIOGRAPHIES

Terry James

Terry James is author, general editor, and/or coauthor of more than thirty books on Bible prophecy and geopolitics, hundreds of thousands of which have been sold worldwide. He has also written fiction and nonfiction books on a number of other topics.

Essays in Apocalypse (New Leaf Publishing Group, 2018) is his latest book release.

He has also had books published by houses such as the Penguin Group (E.P. Dutton), Harvest House, and others.

James is a frequent lecturer on the study of end-time phenomena and interviews often with national and international media on topics involving world issues and events as they might relate to Bible prophecy. He is partner with Todd Strandberg and general editor in the www.raptureready.com website, which was recently rated as the number-one Bible prophecy website on the Internet. The website has more than twenty-five thousand articles and much more material for those who visit the site.

He writes a weekly commentary for the website in which he looks at current issues and events in light of Bible prophecy. James speaks often at prophecy conferences. He is a member of the Pre-Trib Research Center, founded by Dr. Tim LaHaye. His personal blog is terryjamesprophecyline.com. He lives with his wife, Margaret, near Little Rock, Arkansas.

Todd Strandberg

Todd Strandberg is the founder of www.raptureready.com, the most highly visited prophecy website on the Internet. He is a partner in the site with Terry James. The site has been written about in practically every major news outlet in the nation and around the world. Founded in 1987 when few websites existed, Rapture Ready now commands the attention of a quarter million visitors per month, with more than thirteen million hits registered during most thirty-day periods.

Strandberg is president of Rapture Ready and coauthor of *Are You Rapture Ready?*—a Penguin Group book under the E P Dutton imprint. He has written hundreds of major articles for the site, which have been distributed in major publications and websites around the nation and the world. He writes a highly read column under the site's "Nearing Midnight" section. Strandberg created "The Rapture Index"—a Dow Jones-like system of prophetic indicators—that continues to draw the attention of most major news outlets.

Tim Cameron

Tim Cameron has been an avid student of Scripture, having attended four Bible schools to study theology and eschatology, most notably the School of Berean in Kansas City under Dr. George Westlake of Sheffield Family Life Center.

He has spoken at several Bible conferences across the country, held numerous revival services, and served as a leader of missions teams to Mardi Gras during the mid '90s. Experiencing anxiety over public speaking, however, turned his attention in another direction: He realized he was not called to speak, but rather, to write. Since that time, he has had several articles featured in online publications and blogs, including Rapture Ready and Prophecy Today.

Daymond Duck

By God's grace, Daymond Duck is a graduate of the University of Tennessee in Knoxville, Tennessee, the founder and president of Prophecy Plus Ministries, the best-selling author of a shelf full of books (three have been published in foreign languages), a member of the prestigious Pre-Trib Study Group, a conference speaker, and a writer for raptureready.com

He is a retired United Methodist pastor, has made more than three hundred television appearances, and has been a member of the Baptist church in his home town since 2006.

He can be contacted at duck_daymond@yahoo.com.

Jim Fletcher

Jim Fletcher has a BA in journalism, and spent many years as a book editor in the Christian publishing industry. Since 2007, he has been a freelance writer and editor, authoring several books and writing columns and op-eds. A frequent visitor to Israel, Jim has cultivated rich contacts over the years, and loves to teach Bible prophecy as an evangelism tool. He lives in a pastoral setting in the Ozark Mountains of northwest Arkansas.

Pete Garcia

Pete Garcia is a writer, speaker, and teacher of Bible prophecy and apologetics. He is also a twenty-year Army veteran, with numerous deployments to the Middle East and overseas tours to Europe and Asia. He holds a bachelor of arts in international relations, with a focus in Russian and military history.

Pete began his writing career with *The Omega Letter* (2011–2018) and has since branched out to create his own website, www.rev310.com. To date, he has written more than 350 articles carried on numerous websites and platforms. Pete is a happily married father to five wonderful children. Most importantly, he is a believer in our Lord Jesus Christ.

Phillip Goodman

Phillip Goodman is the founder and president of Bible Prophecy as Written, a ministry dedicated to encouraging and strengthening faith in Jesus Christ and His soon coming. Phillip is also the Bible teacher on the television program with the same name as his ministry and at twenty-four annual prophecy retreats.

Phillip's first book was *The Assyrian Connection*, which develops the outlines of the final world empire and the origins of the Antichrist. Other books include *The Sequence of End Time Events* and *When Your Loved One Goes to Heaven*, as well as many booklets and DVD programs on Bible prophecy. He has shared space with some of the world's best prophecy experts as a contributing author to the books *Piercing the Future, Prophecy at Ground Zero, Revelation Hoofbeats, One World, Frightening Issues, The Departure, The Lawless One, Living On Borrowed Time,* and *Deceivers*.

Phillip is a regular guest on radio and television programs, and he sponsors the annual Mid America Prophecy Conference, one of America's premier Bible prophecy conferences. He and his wife, Mary, who was born and raised in Bethlehem, Israel, have four sons.

Tom Hughes

Tom Hughes serves as lead pastor of 412 Church in San Jacinto, California. He has been teaching Bible prophecy for over twenty-five years and is the founder of Hope For Our Times. He regularly appears on a variety of TV, radio, and Internet programs.

Nathan Jones

Nathan Jones serves as the Internet evangelist for Lamb & Lion Ministries. He can be found cohosting the ministry's television program *Christ in Prophecy*, growing and developing the web ministry at christinprophecy.org, authoring books such as *12 Faith Journeys of the Minor Prophets*, blogging daily on the Christ in Prophecy Journal, discussing current events on the Christ in Prophecy Facebook group, producing video Q & As such as *The Inbox*, being interviewed on radio programs, speaking at conferences and churches, and answering Bible-related questions sent in from all over the world.

A lifelong student of the Bible and an ordained minister, Nathan graduated from Cairn University with a bachelor's degree in Bible. He attended Southern Baptist Theological Seminary and received his master's degree in management and leadership at Liberty University.

Jeff Kinley

Jeff Kinley is a former pastor who has authored more than thirty books. He travels the country and internationally, speaking about Bible prophecy. His weekly Vintage Truth podcast is heard in more than 60 countries worldwide. His website is jeffkinley.com.

Jan Markell

Jan Markell is founder and director of Olive Tree Ministries, headquartered in Minneapolis, Minnesota. The author of eight books and producer of a dozen DVD teachings, Markell is a conference speaker and radio host. Her *Understanding the Times Radio* program airs on 850 radio stations across North America. She hosts the largest prophecy conference in North America and can be reached through www.olivetreeviews.org.

Don McGee

Don McGee, founder and director of CSM, is a Vietnam War veteran and retired Louisiana state trooper. He was a pastor for twelve years, and since 2002 has been an evangelist whose focus is exclusively on Bible prophecy. He and his wife, Valerie, live in a rural area near Amite, Louisiana. They have two grown children and three grandchildren.

Grant Phillips

Grant Phillips has pastored six small churches over the years, served the Lord as Bible teacher, and ministered at retirement centers and nursing facilities via music from 2007 thru 2011. Since September of 2010, he has been writing Christian articles, all of which are available at www.raptureready.com.

Being saved at a young age and having Christian parents instilled in him a love for God's Word. The Bible has always been his guide and the Holy Spirit his teacher. His message is that Jesus saves all those who come to Him and Jesus keeps His own. That same Jesus is coming soon for all who are His. In short; Jesus saves, Jesus keeps, Jesus will return.

He and his wife Debbie live in southeastern Kentucky.

Ryan Pitterson

Ryan Pitterson is a biblical researcher and writer with an emphasis on ancient Hebrew thought and theology.

Ryan is the author of Amazon #1 best-seller *Judgment of the Nephilim*—a comprehensive biblical study of the Nephilim giants and the account of Genesis 6.

The book has received critical acclaim from highly respected biblical scholars, including Gary Stearman of Prophecy Watchers, who declared it "the most comprehensive, well-researched book ever written on the fallen angels." Ryan has appeared on the *Prophecy Watchers* TV program, *Coast to Coast AM, Acceleration Radio* with L. A. Marzulli, Josh Peck *Underground Church,* and many other programs.

Currently, Ryan is completing a study guide and audio book for *Judgment of the Nephilim*. A DVD documentary is scheduled for winter 2019 release, and the sequel to *Judgment of the Nephilim*, which will focus on the Nephilim and fallen angels in the end times, will be released in 2020. Ryan received his bachelor of arts degree in political science from the University of Rochester and his juris doctor from Columbia University Law School.

David Reagan

Dr. David R. Reagan, senior evangelist for Lamb & Lion Ministries, an interdenomination-al, evangelical ministry devoted to proclaiming the soon return of Jesus, is a native Texan who resides in a suburb of Dallas with his wife of fifty-nine years.

A lifelong Bible student, teacher, and preach-er, Dr. Reagan is the author of many religious es-says published in a wide variety of journals and magazines. He has authored eighteen books, all of which are related to Bible prophecy, and serves as the editor of the ministry's bimonthly *Lamplighter* magazine. His sermons have been distributed worldwide in both audio and video formats, and his books have been translated into many different languages.

Dr. Reagan has conducted prophecy conferences all over the world, and he has led more than forty-five pilgrimages to Israel that focus on the pro-phetic significance of the sites visited. For twenty-two years, Dr. Reagan was the spokesman on Lamb & Lion's daily, nationally broadcast radio program, "Christ in Prophecy." The ministry's website can be found at www.lamblion. com.

Bill Salus

Bill Salus, founder of Prophecy Depot Minis-tries, is a bestselling author, researcher, confer-ence speaker, and media personality who has appeared on Fox TV and most major Christian TV shows, like TBN's *Praise the Lord*, Daystar's *Marcus and Jon, Sid Roth, Jim Bakker, Jewish Voice*,

Prophecy Watchers, and more. His articles have been published worldwide over the Internet on sites like Rapture Ready, World Net Daily, and the Christian Post.

Bill is an expert at explaining the prophetic relevance of current Middle East and world events. Readers appreciate his unique insights, and sensible—rather than sensational—approach to understanding the Bible. He allows prophecy to speak for itself, rather than modernizing it into newspaper exegesis.

Several of Bill's books became instant best-sellers in Bible prophecy on Amazon. His books include: *Psalm 83: The Missing Prophecy Revealed; How Israel Becomes the Next Mideast Superpower; Nuclear Showdown in Iran; Revealing the Prophecy of Elam; The NOW Prophecies; The NEXT Prophecies; The Apocalypse Revelations Novel; and Isralestine: The Ancient Blueprints of the Future Middle East.*

Readers may contact Bill by emailing him at prophecydepotministries@gmail.com or by visiting his website at www.prophecydepot.com.

Larry Spargimino

Pastor Larry Spargimino has been with Southwest Radio Church since 1998. A graduate of Southwestern Seminary in Ft. Worth with a PhD, he is regularly heard on the *Watchman on the Wall* broadcast of Southwest Radio Church. He has been a pastor for many years and is currently pastoring in Oklahoma City. He also had the privilege of starting a church and a Christian school in Pakistan. Larry has a heart for missions and works with overseas students in the US. He is currently working on a book titled *Power Life: How Grace Is Overcoming in A Hostile World.*

Gary Stearman

Gary Stearman has pastored Grace Fellowship, a Bible church in Oklahoma City, since 1983. He also serves as director of Prophecy Watchers, a television and Internet video prophetic ministry. Over the years, he has been devoted to the deep investigation and application of God's prophetic truth, as fully expressed in His divinely ordained Scripture. He has also written counseling manuals and hundreds of articles on prophetic interpretation, edited two books, and authored a third called *Time Travelers of the Bible*.

1   Greg Laurie and Ellen Vaughn, *Jesus Revolution: How God Transformed An Unlikely Generation and How He Can Do It Again Today* (Grand Rapids: Baker Books, 2018), 137.

2   https://raystedman.org/daily-devotions/timothy/dangerous-times.

3   https://qz.com/871815/sex-robots-experts-predict-human-robot-marriage-will-be-legal-by-2050.

4   .https://qz.com/1246712/im-building-a-robot-boyfriend-and-you-can-too.

5   https://finance-yahoo.com/news/robot-thinks-itself-scratch-brings-190000563.h.

6   .https://www.charismanews.com/opinion/in-the-line-of-fire/75039-the-governor-of-virginia-lets-be-civil-about-killing-newborns.

7   https://www.foxnews.com/politics/colorado-bill-would-ban-teaching-abstinence-only-sex-ed-in-public-schools.print.

8   www.cnsnews.com/commentary/john-stonestreet/new-york-times-reveals-serious-problems-with-trans-ideology.

9   https://www.wnd.com/2018/10/forget-your-gender-now-pick-your-race-age-species.

10 https://www.foxnews.com/entertainment/the-view-star-joy-behar-mocks-mike-pences-christian-faith.

11 https://www.newyorker.com/culture/jia-tolentino/mike-pences-marriage-and-beliefs-keeps-women-from-power.

12 https://www.theblaze.com/news/karen-pence-lgbt-school.

13 www.foxnews.com/entertainment/neal-mcdonough-recalls-reportedly-being-fired-from-abcs-scoundrels-for-refusing-sex-scenes.

14 https://news4sanantoio.com/news/local/teen-attacked-for-wearing-maga-hat.

15 R. T. Kendall, *More of God* (Lake Mary, FL: Charisma Media, 2019), 1–2.

16 Ron Rhodes, *End Times Super Trends: A Political, Economic, and Cultural Forecast of the Prophetic Future* (Eugene, OR: Harvest House, 2018), 25–27.

17 Tom Doyle, *Standing in the Fire: Courageous Christians Living in Frightening Times* (Nashville: W. Publishing Group, 2017). Tom Doyle, *Killing Christians: Living the Faith Where It's Not Safe to Believe* (Nashville: W. Publishing Group, 2015). Tom Doyle, *Dreams and Visions: Is Jesus Awakening the Muslim World?* (Nashville: Thomas Nelson, 2012). Charles Morris & Craig Borlase, *Fleeing ISIS, Finding Jesus* (Colorado Springs, David C. Cook, 2017). David Garrison, *A Wind in the House of Islam: How God Is Drawing Muslims around the World to Faith in Jesus Christ* (Gloucester, UK. WIGTake Resources, 2014).

18 www.christianpost.com/news/black-lesbian-activist-turned-evangelist. "Pulse survivor says he is no longer gay, has found Christ, nbcnews.com/feature/nbc-out/pulse-survivor…May 1, 2018. www.lifesitenews.com/news/ex-gays-and-ex-trans/rally-against-california-lgbt/theology. www1.cbn.com/cbnnews/2018/November/jesus-can-change-anyone.

19 https://www.foxnews.com/tech/amazon-pulls-out-of-plan-to-build-new-york-city-headquarters.print.

20   Robert Jeffress, *Outrageous Truth…7 Absolutes You Can Still Believe* (Colorado Springs: WaterBrook Press, 2004), 2.

21   Rick Scarborough, *Enough Is Enough: A Practical Guide to Political Action* (Lake Mary, FL: Frontline, 2008), 185–192.

22   Lee Strobel, *The Case for Miracles* (Grand Rapids: Zondervan, 2018), 18–19.

23   Paul Hattaway, *Shandong: The Revival Province* (London: SPCK, 2018), 257.

24   Ibid., 174.

25   https://www.independent.co.uk/news/world/asia/china-social-credit-system-blacklists-millions-of-people-from-booking-flights.

26   https://www.sciencedirect.com/science/article/abs/pii/S0301462297000501.

27   https://www.vanityfair.com/culture/2012/07/lsd-drugs-summer-of-love-sixties.

28   https://www.stuff.co.nz/sport/other-sports/99434993/professor-of-physiology-says-trans-athlete-has-advantage-in-speed-and-power.

29   https://www.washingtonpost.com/opinions/europes-morality-crisis-euthanizing-the-mentally-ill/2016/10/19/c75faaca-961c-11e6-bc79-af1cd3d2984b_story.html?noredirect=on&utm_term=.c0e9aece9fa6.

30   https://www.jewishvirtuallibrary.org/joseph-goebbels-on-the-quot-big-lie-quot.

31   https://www.pewforum.org/fact-sheet/public-opinion-on-abortion/.

32   https://www.str.org/articles/the-trouble-with-the-elephant#.XNr7pS.MzOR.

33   See the article at https://www.thenewamerican.com/world-news/north-america/item/32160-mexico-s-collective-bargaining-law-paves-way-for-usmca-passage-north-american-union?vsmaid=4463&vcid=1356.

34   Revelation 13:4, 8, 15.

35   Revelation 17:4.

36   Revelation 17:16.

37   Isaiah 1:11 NKJV.

38   Isaiah 1:11 NKJV.

39   Isaiah 1:4 NKJV

40   Revelation 17:2.

41   Acts 4:12, NKJV.

42   With apologies to Theodore Parker, Martin Luther King Jr, Barack Obama, and others who have championed this idea that is hopeful, but unsubstantiated outside of Bible prophecy.

43   Valentina Pop, Drew Hinshaw, and Nick Kostov, "Decades of Neglect Threatened Notre Dame, Well Before It Burned," *Wall Street Journal*, April 18, 2019.

44   Raymond Ibrahim, "European Churches: Vandalized, Defecated On, and Torched 'Every Day,'" *Gatestone Institute*, April 14, 2019.

45   "Pastors Face Communication Challenges in a Divided Culture," Barna Group, 2019.

46   Samuel Smith, "DC School Boycotting Sports at Karen Pence's Christian School over LGBT Policy," *Christian Post*, February 5, 2019.

47   David French, "Karen Pence, Are You Now, or Have You Ever Been, Part of a Christian Ministry?" *National Review*, January 17, 2019.

48   Patrick Toner, "Infallibility," *Catholic Encyclopedia*, Vol. 7, 1910.

49   Pope Pius XII invoked papal infallibility in 1950 on the Catholic doctrine of the "Assumption of Mary."

50   Jeremiah 17:9.

51   Proverbs 14:12 and Proverbs 16:25.

52   Carol Kuruvilla, "Heartsick Boy Asks if Atheist Dad Is in Heaven. Pope Francis Reveals the Answer with a Hug," *Huffington Post*, November 28, 2018.

53   John Killinger, *Ten Things I Learned Wrong from a Conservative Church* (Crossroad Publishing Company, 2002).

54   Ibid.

55   Dr. Albert Mohler Jr., "How to Abandon Historic Christianity in Ten Easy Lessons," July 16, 2004.

56   Revelation 3:15.

57   Revelation 3:16.

58   **NOTES:** For an extended version of the Notes, to include full quotations, see "The Finished Gospel" at bibleprophecyaswritten.com. This permits a quicker ready reference and deeper study. All references to the "gospel" refer to the gospel of salvation, unless otherwise noted.

59   The "gospel of the kingdom" refers to the Messianic Kingdom to be inaugurated at the Second Coming of Jesus. But to "see" or "enter" that kingdom, one must be saved through the gospel of salvation. Jesus said, "Truly, truly, I say to you, unless one is born again, he cannot see…he cannot enter into the kingdom of God" (John 3:3–5). So, to truly preach the gospel of the kingdom necessarily requires preaching the gospel of salvation. The gospel (good news) of the kingdom (Matthew 24:14) isn't good news unless one has accepted the gospel of salvation (Mark 13:10). This explains these parallel verses.

60   We have been "released-freed-washed" from all of our sins forever. This is made indisputable by Hebrews 10: "But He, having offered one sacrifice for sins for all time" (v. 12). David Anderson explains the significance of this powerful passage, "'one sacrifice for sins forever.' Christ's death is God's one and only provision for man's sin and it sufficiently pays for all his sins. No time distinction is made. When Christ ascended into heaven, He sat down at the right hand of His Father, signifying His finished work. No further provision would be made. *Ephapax* [the Greek word used]. Once for all. All sins—past, present, or future; black, gray, or white (of course, all sins are black in reality); confessed, unconfessed; known, and unknown—all sins have been paid for." —(David R. Anderson, *Free Grace Soteriology*, [Grace Theology Press, 2012]188)

      This great truth of grace is contrasted with the pre-cross, Old Testament animal sacrifices that had to be repeated perpetually until the "once-for-all" sacrifice of Christ covered all sins for all time for all people in every age who have believed in Christ.

61   To have "faith in the correct gospel" means to have faith in Jesus Christ, the Son of God, who died for my sins and was resurrected to life that I might have eternal life by believing in Him.

62   There are three main strands of formally recognized Christianity that share a faith-works, mixed path to salvation. They are Roman Catholicism and two (2) Protestant branches: Reformed (Calvinism; many) and Arminian-based churches. The primary focus of this look at the unfinished gospel (faith-works mix) will be on its more commonly used designation in Reformed churches, namely, the "Lordship-Gospel" as advocated and articulated by John MacArthur.

      In an email exchange (December 19, 2018) with Andy Woods, author of *Ever Reforming* (Dispensational Publishing House, 2018), he points out that the Lordship-Gospel (unfinished gospel) was not the product of the original Reformers: "It was the second generation reformers (TULIP authors) that really brought in Lordship salvation out of fear that if they taught grace soteriology openly then believers [might abuse their freedom in Christ]. Consequently, today's reformed movement is not grace oriented by and large. However, the original reformers were much more so.

63 "Protestant theology is for the most part thoroughly Galatianized, in that neither law nor grace is given its distinct and separate place as in the counsel of God, but they are mingled together in one incoherent system." (David R. Anderson, quoting C. I. Scofield, *Bewitched—The Rise of Neo-Galatianism*, [Grace Theology Press, 2015]. 322).

64 "In [Galatians] 5:1, Paul says Christ has freed these people. But because they have confused sanctification and justification, many of them who are justified are trying to maintain their justification by their works or trying to prove they are justified by their works. There you have it—Neo[modern]-Galatianism…[Today] Arminians think they must have good works until they die or they lose their salvation; the Calvinists think they must have good works until they die or they never had salvation. And the Roman Catholics have always taught they must have good works (until death) in order to complete their justification." (David R. Anderson, *Bewitched—The Rise of Neo-Galatianism*, [Grace Theology Press, 2015] 162).

"When [John] MacArthur speaks of works being worked in us, his doctrine of justification differs not a whit from Catholicism's idea of justification making us righteous [i.e., Faith = Faith plus Works]." (Joseph Dillow, *Reign of the Servant Kings*, as quoted by David R. Anderson, *Free Grace Soteriology*, [Grace Theology Press, 2012] 172).

Norman Geisler's subtitles in his discussion of the relationship between faith and works reveal the sobering similarity between Catholicism and what we have herein termed "the unfinished gospel" ("Lordship Salvation"). For instance, "The Catholic View Is Similar to the Error of Galatianism" and "The Catholic View Loads Works into Its Concept of Faith." (Norman Geisler, *Systematic Theology*, Vol. 3, Sin-Salvation [Bloomington, MN: Bethany House Publishers, 2004] 270–71.

Those who import works into the faith that saves (justifies) say that "the true test of faith is this: does it produce obedience? If not, it is not saving faith." Charlie Bing is among many who have picked up on the fact that this "view is similar to that of Roman Catholicism which teaches that faith **plus** works obtains salvation. Lordship [Salvation] simply formulates it differently: Faith **that** works obtains salvation. But in both systems works are essential to salvation. **No works, no salvation**" [emphasis his]. Bing elaborates on why a "faith THAT works" is no different than "faith PLUS works" in salvation. "The emphasis on a faith that works conflicts with the grace of salvation that depends on Christ's work. It essentially says that what Jesus Christ did for people was not sufficient to SECURE [emphasis mine] their salvation. One must contribute by commitment, surrender, and obedience. However, the work of Christ is totally sufficient. His one work did all that human beings could not do (Romans 3:24–25; 5:15–21)." (Charlie Bing, *Freely By Grace*, J. B. Hixson, Rick Whitmire, and Roy B. Zuck, eds., [Duluth, MN: Grace Gospel Press, 2012] 103–4.

Joseph Dillow, commenting on a "salvation that is achieved by a synergism of human and divine works [God's supernatural injection into human activity of non-meritorious works]," notes that "it is difficult to distinguish this viewpoint from classical Arminianism or Rome [Catholicism], which also say that final arrival to heaven is conditional [on works]." (Joseph Dillow, *Final Destiny, The Future Reign of the Servant Kings*, Second Revised Edition, [Grace Theology Press, 2015], 582.

Those who espouse the unfinished gospel "fall into the cross hairs of the canon fire that Calvin launched at the [Roman Catholic] Council of Trent: 'according to [the Catholics], man is justified by faith as well as by work, provided these are not his own works, but gifts of Christ and fruits of regeneration.'" (Joseph Dillow, *Final Destiny, The Future Reign of the Servant Kings*, Second Revised Edition, [Grace Theology Press, 2015] 600). (In the above, "his own work" = faith PLUS man's work; "fruits of regeneration =Faith THAT works, with God's help. The point is that either way, without works connected to faith, there is no salvation. The Bible excludes works from any connection to faith in the plan of salvation—emphatically and repetitively!)

Dave Hunt did significant research on the Catholic-Calvinism (Lordship) connection, "the truth discovered by Augustine and passed on to Calvin" (Dave Hunt, *What Love Is This?*, [Sisters, OR: Loyal Publishing, 2002] 390.

"But this was the God of Augustine, the premier 'saint' of Roman Catholicism to whom not only Calvin...looked as [his] mentor but whom so many leading evangelicals praised highly." (Dave Hunt, *What Love Is This?*, [Sisters, OR: Loyal Publishing, 2002] 392.

"Augustine, the greatest of Roman Catholics" [p. 393] was the founder of Calvinism and, indeed, of "evangelical Christianity." (Dave Hunt, *What Love Is This?*, [Sisters, OR: Loyal Publishing, 2002] 392–393. "Sadly, much Roman Catholicism was carried over by Calvin...into Reformed churches, where it remains to this day." (Dave Hunt, *What Love Is This?*, [Sisters, OR: Loyal Publishing, 2002] 51.

"It seems that the Reformers and their creeds are infected with ideas that came from the greatest Roman Catholic, Augustine himself." (Dave Hunt, *What Love Is This?*, [Sisters, OR: Loyal Publishing, 2002] 52.

"Calvin really taught and practiced [according to] Augustine, from whom he obtained most of his beliefs." (Dave Hunt, *What Love Is This?*, [Sisters, OR: Loyal Publishing, 2002] 56.

"Augustine, whom the entire world recognizes as the premier Roman Catholic, who gave that Church so many of its basic doctrines that he is among the most highly honored of its 'saints' [all the way until today]." (Dave Hunt, *What Love Is This?*, [Sisters, OR: Loyal Publishing, 2002] 56.

"How could Augustine, and Calvin who embraced and passed on many of his major errors, be so wrong on so much and yet be inspired of the Holy Spirit as regards predestination, election, sovereignty, etc.?" (Dave Hunt, *What Love Is This?*, [Sisters, OR: Loyal Publishing, 2002] 56.

"[Calvin] viewed the church of Christ through Roman Catholic eyes...[and developed] a **system** [emphasis his] of Christianity based upon an extreme view of God's sovereignty." (Dave Hunt, *What Love Is This?*, [Sisters, OR: Loyal Publishing, 2002] 61..

"[Lordship Salvation] has returned to Roman Catholicism—we will find out if we have enough righteousness in our lives to be accepted only after we die." (David R. Anderson, *A Defense of Free Grace Theology*, p. 80).

Like Catholicism, "The lordship view adds to the Gospel of the grace of God what Scripture does not." (Robert P. Lightner, *Sin, the Savior, and Salvation*, [Nashville, TN: Thomas Nelson, 1991] 213).

"In spite of the Reformation revival of the gospel of grace, much of Protestantism today is working its way back to Rome with a gospel that makes works necessary and justification a process." (Charlie Bing, *Grace Notes*, Number 77, [Burleson, TX: Grace Life Ministries]).

"Many Reformed churches are Protestant in some ways, but continue to be Roman Catholic in others. Here is the key: The weakness of Reformed theology is that people took the progress made by the Reformers and presumed that there was no further progress to be made. They took that progress and froze it into creeds and confessions, such as the Westminster Confession, which became the authority." (Andy Woods, *Ever Reforming*, [Taos, NM: Dispensational Publishing House, 2018] 87).

"What you have in Reformed thought is a hybrid, a mixture, of Protestantism and Roman Catholicism." (Andy Woods, *Ever Reforming*, [Taos, NM: Dispensational Publishing House, 2018] 88).

"The Reformers also dragged other vestiges of Roman Catholicism with them into their new Protestant and Reformed churches. People have been taught that the Reformers made a clean break with Roman Catholicism. But it would be naive to think that way. They brought much errant baggage with them." (Andy Woods, *Ever Reforming*, [Taos, NM: Dispensational Publishing House, 2018] 109).

"Roman Catholicism continued to live on in the minds of the Reformers and their spiritual descendants...it is not shocking at all that these men dragged much of Roman Catholicism along with them into their newfound Protestantism." (Andy Woods, *Ever Reforming*, [Taos, NM: Dispensational Publishing House, 2018] 110–111).

"Roman Catholicism teaches that faith is just the beginning of salvation, so the believer must constantly work throughout his life to complete the process." (Fritz Ridenour, *So What's the Difference?*, [Glendale, CA: Regal Books, 1967] 44. [Lordship Salvation says essentially the same.]

"When you ask Roman Catholics about what is required for salvation, they will mention Christ and His death on the cross, they will mention faith, and they will mention the need for grace. But they will also throw into the mix a life of meritorious works and participation in the various sacramental rituals of the Roman Catholic Church." (Ron Rhodes, *The 10 Most Important Things You Can Say to a Catholic*, [Eugene, OR: Harvest House 2002] 65). [Lordship Salvation also says salvation requires "Christ," the "cross," "faith," "grace," and "a life of meritorious works."]

"[In Roman Catholicism] Justification is obtained by doing meritorious works that cooperate with God's grace, with focus upon the seven sacraments." (John Ankerberg & Dillon Burroughs, *What's the Big Deal About Other Religions?*, [Eugene, OR: Harvest House, 2008], 45). [Apart from the sacraments, a Lordship-Gospel look-a-like]

65   These "word games" are subtle and tricky, but real, just as they were for the Galatians ("You foolish Galatians, who has bewitched you" (Galatians 3:1). Dave Anderson writes, "Thus, sanctification became a justification issue. No sanctification? No justification. After escaping the RCC [Roman Catholic Church in the Reformation], the pressure was on once again for believers to perform... any attempt to deny this is simply playing word games." [Quoting Zane Hodges:] 'Some indeed would claim that discipleship [sanctification] is not a condition for eternal life, but an inevitable result of possessing it. But those who so speak are playing a word-game. Whatever is necessary to achieve a goal is also a condition for reaching it. To call anything an inevitable result is to call it a necessary result and thus to make it a condition. Candor is lacking in those who fail to admit this. Let's put it plainly. If on-going good works are necessary for reaching heaven, they are also a condition for reaching heaven. Thus, on this view, final salvation is based on faith plus works!'" (David R. Anderson, *Bewitched—The Rise of Neo-Galatianism*, [Grace Theology Press, 2015] 66–67).

"It is not that God cannot use an unclear message; doubtless He does this more often than He would prefer to. But why should He have to? Why don't we sharpen our understanding of what the Gospel is about so that we can present it as clearly as possible, using the right words to herald the Good News correctly?" (Charles Ryrie, *So Great Salvation*, Chicago, IL: Moody 1997] 24).

66   "Is not [Modern Galatianism] a subtle way of adding something to the gospel either on the front end (Arminians) or the back end (Calvinists) or for the duration (Roman Catholic Church)? We can see that the basic struggle Paul fights in Galatians rages on in the twenty-first century with Neo-Galatianism." (David R. Anderson, *Bewitched—The Rise of Neo-Galatianism*, [Grace Theology Press, 2015] 60).

"Requiring good works at the end of one's life is no different from requiring them at the initial reception of the gospel. In either position, the sufficiency of Christ's substitutionary atonement and His propitiation for our sins is denied...it makes works an essential part of salvation." (Charles C. Bing, *Grace, Salvation, and Discipleship*, [Grace Theology Press, 2015] 158–159).

"According to Galatians 1:6–9 there is one and only one gospel that saves, not two." (Michael D. Halsey, *Freely by Grace*, J. B. Hixson, Rick Whitmire, and Roy B. Zuck, eds., (Duluth, MN: Grace Gospel Press] 8).

"Christians today need the same zeal for the purity and simplicity of the gospel [that Paul had in Galatians 1:8]..... The apostle Paul is adamant that the gospel he and his colleagues are proclaiming is complete, absolute, and final." (John Witmer & Mal Couch, *The Books of Galatians & Ephesians, Unlocking the Future*, Twenty-First Century Biblical Commentary Series, Mal Couch & Ed Hindson, eds., [AMG Publishers, 2002] 18).

"The same gospel as is always declared in the New Testament [referencing Galatians 1:8]...to attempt to call it something else or something other than the 'good news' of salvation is both tragic and heretical!" (Ed Hindson, *The Book of Revelation, Unlocking the Future*, Twenty-First Century Biblical Commentary Series, Mal Couch & Ed Hindson, eds., [AMG Publishers, 2002] 155.

"If heaven really cannot be attained apart from obedience to God—and this is what lordship salvation teaches—then, logically, that obedience is a condition for getting there." (David R. Anderson, *A Defense of Free Grace Theology*, p. 109).

[Often with "pure motives,"] "Brethren in Christ embrace the lordship view but that is no guarantee that what they hold is not another gospel. The gospel of God's saving grace must not be adulterated, not even by evangelicals." (Robert P. Lightner, *Sin, the Savior, and Salvation*, Nashville, TN: Thomas Nelson, 1991] 213).

"This [free grace gospel vs Lordship Gospel] debate strikes at the very heart of the orthodox Christian faith. It is not simply a fight over words and technicalities. The theological and practical ramifications are indeed far-reaching." (Robert P. Lightner, *Sin, the Savior, and Salvation*, [Nashville, TN: Thomas Nelson, 1991] 201).

67   John 19:30 ("it is finished"); Hebrews 12:2 ("Jesus the author and finisher of our faith," KJV)

68   Romans 4:24–25, 5:8. A person must believe THAT these things about Jesus are true; but he is saved when he believes IN (trusts) Jesus. Note this simple but true to the Bible gospel statement: "The Lord Jesus Himself in the gospel of John chapter 6, verse 47, tells us the very simple fact that if we believe in Him, we HAVE [emphasis hers] eternal life!" (Pat Franklin of London, England, of the Internet news site, The Free Press, in "Does Matthew's Gospel Disqualify Jesus as the Messiah?," *Lamplighter Magazine*, Lion & Lamb Ministries, Nov.–Dec. 2018, p. 7.

69   Romans 6:10.

70   Revelation 22:17.

71   Ephesians 2:8–9.

"[*Sola fide*] is the idea that you are saved through the power of Christ on the basis of one condition—which is faith alone in Christ alone. The Bible teaches this more than 160 times." (Andy Woods, *Ever Reforming*, [Taos, NM: Dispensational Publishing House, 2018] 73).

Ephesians 2:8–9 and its simple, clear statement, "not of works," governs our understanding of all salvation passages. Lightner quotes Everett F. Harrison, objecting to the "subtle form of legalism" of Lordship Salvation (unfinished gospel) advocates: "We reject the teaching that we can be saved by works. The Word of God is emphatic on this (Eph. 2:9; Titus 3:5). Why then bring works in by the side door by asserting that, because we do whatever is necessary to the acknowledging of the lordship of Christ in our lives, we are not saved?" (Robert P. Lightner, *Sin, the Savior, and Salvation*, [Nashville, TN: Thomas Nelson, 1991] 211).

Charles Ryrie points out the error of injecting human effort (works) into salvation passages such as John 3:16 when he says, "The lordship/discipleship/mastery position declares that…'Real faith results in obedience.' No one will debate that, because believers will bear fruit. But to inject the issue of mastery over one's life into John 3:16 as a condition for 'real faith' rather than a consequence is to add something the verse does not say." (Charles Ryrie, *So Great Salvation*, [Chicago, IL: Moody, 1997] 99].

Norm Geisler makes the point that works become meritorious when we can "boast": "If our works had even a small part in obtaining salvation, we **would** have grounds to boast and, hence would still come under condemnation" [emphasis his]. (Norman Geisler, *Systematic Theology*, Vol. 3, [Bloomington, MN: Bethany House, 2004] 269).

72   Romans 5:6.

73   John 3:16; Acts 16:31.

74   John 19:30, "It is finished." Christ died for the sins of humanity "once for all" (Romans 6:10) for all who believe.

75   Hebrews 9:12; 10:12–14.

76   John 5:24 says that at salvation the new believer "has passed out of death into life." This is a past-tense statement, an accomplished fact, instantaneous. Many Bible scholars affirm that salvation is not only instantaneous, but irreversible. We quote a few of them below:

Charles Ryrie: "Further, regeneration is instantaneous—either one is dead in sin or alive in Christ." (*So Great Salvation*, [Chicago, IL: Moody 1997] 128).

R. C. H. Lenski: "Pisteuson [Greek word 'believe'] is properly the aorist, for the moment one believes, salvation is his…. To believe is to accept the divine gift of salvation and at once to have it." (As quoted by Charles Ryrie, *So Great Salvation*, [Chicago, IL: Moody, 1997] 131).

John MacArthur: "We teach that regeneration…is instantaneous…. We teach that every believer is sanctified…by justification…. This sanctification is positional [Salvation] and instantaneous…. We teach that all the redeemed once saved are kept by God's power and are thus secure in Christ forever…it is the privilege of believers to rejoice in the assurance of their salvation." (*MacArthur Study Bible*, [Nashville, TN: Word, 1997] 2194–95).

James G. McCarthy: "Salvation from the eternal consequences of sin is an instantaneous and secure act of God coinciding with justification (Rom 5:9)." (*Roman Catholicism: What You Need to Know*, Quick Reference Guide, [Eugene, OR: Harvest House, 1995] panel 2, point 8.

Mike Gendron: "All Christians have been saved (past tense) from the penalty of sin (Eph 2:8–9)… At the moment of faith, the sinner is justified and has a right standing before God that is permanent (Heb 10:14). He cannot be condemned again (Rom 8:1)." (*Preparing Catholics for Eternity*, [Springfield, MO: 21st Century Press, 2002] 128).

David R. Anderson: "But if justification means 'to declare righteous,' then this legal declaration of righteousness occurred in God's courtroom at a single moment in time…. At a moment in time all one's sins (past, present, future) are wiped away. They were already paid for by Christ's work." (*Bewitched—The Rise of Neo-Galatianism*, [Grace Theology Press, 2015] 50, 52).

Norman Geisler: "Scripture guarantees eternal life as a present possession of those who believe. Jesus said: 'Truly, truly, I say to you, he who hears My word, and believes Him who sent Me, has [present-tense] eternal life, and does not come into judgment, but has [present-tense] passed out of death into life.' (John 5:24; John 3:36; 1 John 5:13)." (*Systematic Theology*, Vol.3, Sin-Salvation, [Bloomington, MN: Bethany House, 2004] 265–66).

Paul Enns: "[Regeneration] is instantaneous. Just as a child is born at a specific moment in the physical birth, so the spiritual birth occurs instantaneously when the Holy Spirit imparts new life. [Note says] The Greek aorist tense in John 1:13 and 3:5 would indicate the new birth is an instantaneous act…[faith and regeneration are] set side by side in John 1:12–13…at the moment of receiving Christ (believing), the person becomes a child of God…at that very moment the persons have been born of God." (*Moody Handbook of Theology*, [Chicago, IL: Moody, 1989], 339–40.

Robert Lightner: "A person who is justified by God's grace is sanctified positionally [saved], set apart to God at the moment of salvation." (*Sin, the Savior, and Salvation*, [Nashville, TN: Thomas Nelson, 1991] 212).

Charlie Bing: "A person [is] declared righteous at the moment of faith in Christ, instead of only beginning a process of becoming righteous. God's righteousness is imputed immediately, not infused over a lifetime." (*Grace Notes*, Number 77, [Burleson, TX: Grace Life Ministries,]).

Andy Woods: "The sinner's unrighteousness is exchanged for Christ's righteousness in a single instant." (*Ever Reforming*, [Taos, NM: Dispensational Publishing House, 2018] 74).

NOTE: If salvation is received through faith alone, is instantaneous, is irreversible, and is purely of grace, then where is there a place for works? Ephesians says there is not (Ephesians 2:8–9) until AFTER justification, DURING sanctification in verse 10.

77 A few simple proofs of irreversible salvation, or eternal security, are found in John 6, where Jesus says that those who believe (v. 29, 35) in Him "shall never thirst" (v. 35); He "will certainly not cast out" any believer (v. 37), He will "lose" none (v.39), and He "will raise him up on the last day" (v.40). In John 10, Jesus promises "eternal life," which is defined as "they shall never perish" and that "no one [not even the believer himself, who is 'someone']…shall snatch them out of my hand…[or] the Father's hand" (vv. 28–29). The New Testament is full of these assurances of eternal security.

78 Galatians 2:16.

79   Ryrie points out the simple truth that the gospel is vertical—always from God, from the top down. When man tinkers with the gospel, he always inserts his contribution (promissory works, pledges, commitments) from the bottom up (the "unfinished gospel"). Ryrie writes, "The Direction of the Gospel: We also must keep the direction of the Gospel clear.... The direction is from Christ to me. It is never from me to Him. I do not offer Him anything. How could I?... In salvation I am always the recipient; the donee, never the donor. It I try to donate anything with respect to becoming a Christian, then I have added a work, and salvation is no longer solely and purely of grace. Keep the direction straight, and keep His grace unmixed with any work." (*So Great Salvation*, [Chicago, IL: Moody, 1989] 39).

"To add commitment of life to God's free salvation is to add human works.... Salvation is either by God's grace or by human effort, commitment, or work. It cannot be by both, anymore than law and grace were both means of salvation in Paul's day. A promise to live for God and obey His Word is doing something more than receiving God's salvation, and to that degree, it is a human work, no matter how vociferously it is said not to be…promising Him complete surrender and dedication of one's entire life…involves human effort or work.... Salvation is hardly a gift if the recipient must promise to surrender every area of his life as long as he lives to get it. Doesn't that involve doing something to at least partially deserve the "gift"? The Bible does not add surrender or obedience to the one condition of faith for salvation." (Robert P. Lightner, *Sin, the Savior, and Salvation*, [Nashville, TN: Thomas Nelson, 1991] 201, 203, 204, 211).

"Eternal salvation is not about what man gives to God; it is about what God gives to man…(Rom 3:24)." (J. B. Hixson, *Freely by Grace*, J. B. Hixson, Rick Whitmire, and Roy B. Zuck, eds., [Duluth, MN: Grace Gospel Press, 2012] 187–88).

"[God] justifies the sinner who does no more than believe in Jesus." (Lewis Sperry Chafer and John F. Walvoord, *Major Bible Themes*, Revised Ed., [Grand Rapids, MI: Zondervan, 1974] 183).

"Salvation in every dispensation and in every situation must be by faith and not by works.... Not only works in general, but any meritorious work that humans may perform, is automatically eliminated as a basis for salvation. The grace of God depends on the work of Christ, not on the merit a person might achieve by doing something worthwhile. Those who come to Christ for salvation come without any redeeming feature, and even faith is not regarded as a meritorious work but is a channel through which the grace of God can flow." (John F. Walvoord, *Major Bible Prophecies*, [Grand Rapids, MI: Zondervan, 1991] 190–91).

80   John 6:37; 6:39; 10:28–29.

81   God sets us apart instantly into His family when we are saved as a "new creation" in Christ (2 Corinthians 5:17), "created in Christ Jesus for good works, that we should walk in them" (Ephesians 2:10). Notice that FIRST we become saved "in Christ" (justification), and SECOND we walk in "good works" (sanctification). The importance of works in the life of a believer is not misplaced as an "aid" to saving faith, it is biblically placed as a walk of discipleship. "Good works in the life of the believer are terribly important, not to be saved, or to stay saved, but as a natural expression of gratitude to God for his great salvation." (Robert P. Lightner, *Evangelical Theology*, [Grand Rapids, MI: Baker Book House, 1986] 213).

82   "Lordship Gospel" refers not only to believing in Christ as the Son of God who died for our sins for salvation, but insists on adding the requirement of works bearing witness to the Lordship of Jesus in order to be saved. As previously mentioned, the commonly used term for this teaching is the "Lordship Gospel," as advocated and articulated by John MacArthur and many others in the Reformed Church. Lordship-Sanctification would be accurate, but never Lordship-Salvation (gospel), since that mixes works with faith/grace.

83   Ryrie uses a number of different quotes (what we herein term "7 Points") from John MacArthur's writings. They are documented in Charles Ryrie, *So Great Salvation* (Chicago, IL: Moody, 1997) 43.

Lightner quotes Everett F. Harrison on the importance of not confusing justification (Christ's finish line) with sanctification (my finish line). This mixing of the two is fundamental to the problem of the unfinished gospel.

"True, a person who is justified by God's grace Is sanctified positionally [saved], set apart to God at the moment of salvation. But that is when the Holy Spirit **begins** His work of ongoing sanctification, not **finishes** it. [emphasis his] One follows the other. Discipleship starts at rebirth and should continue on after it. Regeneration pertains to one's relationship to Christ as Savior from sin. Sanctification on the other hand pertains to one's relationship to Christ as his Lord and Master. In the new birth a person is made a new creation in Christ. In sanctification, he grows in that relationship." (Everett F. Harrison, as quoted by Robert P. Lightner, *Sin, the Savior, and Salvation,* [Nashville, TN: Thomas Nelson, 1991] 212).

"This Lordship teaching fails to distinguish salvation from discipleship and makes requirements for discipleship prerequisites for salvation. Our Lord distinguished the two (Luke 14:16–33)." (Charles C. Ryrie, *Basic Theology*, [Wheaton, IL: Victor, 1986] 339).

"We do works **as a result of** being saved, not **in order to become** saved" [emphasis his]. (Norman Geisler, *Systematic Theology*, Vol. 3, [Bloomington, MN: Bethany House, 2004] 271.

"We do not work in order to obtain salvation; we work because we have already been given it. God works salvation **in** us by His justification, and we work **out** our salvation through sanctification by His grace (Phil. 2:12–13)" [emphasis his]. (Norman Geisler, *Systematic Theology*, Vol. 3, [Bloomington, MN: Bethany House, 2004] 267.

"Obedience leading to good works is a natural result of saving faith but not a qualification for being saved." (Norman Geisler, *Systematic Theology*, Vol. 3, [Bloominigton, MN: Bethany House, 2004] 520).

Dillow refers to a typical statement of self-salvation by works promoted by unfinished gospel advocates: "We are to use all the resources at our disposal in order to be saved on the last day. We must obey, pray, resist the flesh and yield to the Spirit to inherit salvation. No theology is acceptable that diminishes this call to work out our salvation." Pointing out the error, Dillow observes: "Thus, one needs to make his actual obedience the necessary ingredient for obtaining heaven." (Joseph Dillow, *Defense of Free Grace Theology*, Fred Chay, ed., [Grace Theology Press, 2017] 127–30.

"The TULIP Calvinists have misled many down a path that compromises the free grace of God by requiring obedient faith and evident works [works giving evidence that their 'saving-faith' was real] as proof of saving grace. These works must be demonstrated over a lifetime and until the end of life. While they declare that salvation is by grace alone through faith alone, they also insist that faith is never alone—it always includes evident works making works necessary for salvation." (Charlie Bing, *Grace Notes*, Number 77, [Burleson, TX: Grace Life Ministries]).

84   John MacArthur, as quoted by Charles Ryrie, *So Great Salvation* (Chicago, I: Moody 1997] 43).

85   "What does it mean to believe? Are there different kinds of faith—genuine faith, spurious faith, saving faith, sign faith, head faith, heart faith? Can I believe in Jesus and still not go to heaven?... There are different quantities of faith in the Bible, but not different qualities. Faith is faith...to say I must believe in Jesus and then wait around to look at the fruit in my life to see if I had enough faith or the right kind of faith...is not found in the Bible.... It can get to the point that people spend so much time examining their faith to see if it was of the right quality or the right quantity that they wind up putting faith in their faith." Anderson makes the point that biblical faith has an object, and that object is not faith—it is "Jesus as God who will take away my sins," and to believe that biblical fact and promise "will open the gates of heaven." (David R. Anderson, *Bewitched—The Rise of Neo-Galatianism*, [Grace Theology Press, 2015] 98–99).

"Saving faith is a simple equation—simple enough for a child to understand (cf. Mat18:3–5; Luke 18:15–17)." (J. B. Hixson, *Freely by Grace*, J. B. Hixson, Rick Whitmire, and Roy B. Zuck, eds., [Duluth, MN: Grace Gospel Press, 2012] 159.

"We have no conclusive evidence in the NT for different categories of faith. Different levels, yes; different categories, no. Faith is faith, real faith, genuine faith, through and through. It is true that not all faith in the NT is saving faith.... Saving faith obviously needs to be tethered to the person and work of Jesus Christ. So we are not taking issue with the assertion that some faith in the NT is not saving faith. We are taking issue with the notion that some faith in Jesus as Savior in the NT is not saving faith. The NT knows of no sub level or insufficient faith in Christ as Savior that does not save." (David R. Anderson, *Free Grace Soteriology*, [Grace Theology Press, 2012] 183–4.

J .B. Hixson reminds us that it was Jesus who taught the concept of "childlike faith." Hixson says, "Saving faith is actually quite simple. Jesus likened it to the faith of a child (Matt. 18:3–4; 19:14).… Remember, saving faith must be exclusively in Christ alone." Then, Hixson quotes Charles Ryrie to make the important point that "works" continues to find its illicit partnership with faith: "Salvation is a free gift.… Period. And yet the heretical doctrine of works goes on all around the world and always will…because the pride of men and women is so strong." (J. B. Hixson, *Freely by His Grace*, Classical Free Grace Theology, , J .B. Hixson, Rick Whitmire, Roy B. Zuck, eds. [Grace Gospel Press., 2012] 36,159–60).

86   This is not the faith of a child. The unfinished gospel saves a person this way: "**Believe in the Lord Jesus**, and commit to...

1. unconditional surrender

2. complete resignation of self

3. absolute submission

4. forsaking everything

5. leaving sin

6. following Jesus Christ at all costs

7. to come on those terms

...**and you shall be saved, you and your household." (Acts 16:31**—PLUS—7 "terms," i.e., legalisms. Obviously, only the **bold** part above is the actual biblical part). These 7 "terms" are emblematic of the Lordship Gospel, and are a selection of those used by Lordship proponent John MacArthur (as quoted by Charles Ryrie, *So Great Salvation*, [Chicago, IL: Moody, 1997], 43).

In regard to the 7-point terms above, there is one point that destroys them all. Ryrie writes, "Salvation is a free gift, therefore, any statement of the terms must carefully avoid implying that we give God something. He gives it all; we receive that gift through faith (1 John 1:12)." (*Survey Of Bible Doctrine*, [Chicago, IL: Moody, 1972] 134).

CONTRADICTION: John MacArthur contradicts his own 7-point "Believe-PLUS" list above in his well-stated and correct comment on Matthew 18:3 about the childlike faith that saves a person. This is revealing, since MacArthur's 7 points above bear no resemblance to this MacArthur Study Bible note: "This is how Jesus characterized conversion. Like the Beatitudes, it pictures faith as the simple, helpless, trusting dependence of those who have no resources of their own. Like children, they have no achievements and no accomplishment to offer or commend themselves with." (*MacArthur Study Bible*, [Nashville, TN: Word, 1997] 2195).

Here is the Scripture: "Truly I say to you, unless you are converted and become like children, you shall not enter the kingdom of heaven." "Whoever then humbles himself as this child, he is the greatest in the kingdom of heaven." "And whoever receives one such child in My name receives Me…one of these little ones who believe [*pisteuo*] in Me" (Matthew 18:3–6).

Note that the same Greek word used for the Matthew 18:6 childlike "believe" [*pisteuo*], is used in salvation passages such as John 3:16 and Acts 16:31. Check out the concordance.

"For God so loved the world, that He gave His only begotten Son, that whoever believes [*pisteuo*] in Him should not perish, but have eternal life" (John 3:16).

"Believe [*pisteuo*] in the Lord Jesus, and you shall be saved, you and your household" (Acts 16:31).

87   In this system, you have absolutely no assurance of salvation until you have reached life's conclusion. But the Bible has no such system and doesn't saddle us with that burden: "The objective

proof and assurance of salvation comes from God's promise of eternal life through Christ and the fact that a person believes in Christ according to that promise." (Charlie Bing, *Grace Notes*, Number 77, [Burleson, TX: Grace Life Ministries]).

88 John MacArthur, as quoted by Charles Ryrie (*So Great Salvation*, [Chicago, IL: Moody 1997] 43). Insertions mine.

89 *Complete Works of Francis Schaeffer*, Vol. 3, (Crossway, 1982) 279–281.

"There are many commands to be obeyed by Christians, but to become a Christian only requires receiving the gift of eternal life from our Lord." (Charles Ryrie, *So Great Salvation*, [Chicago, IL: Moody, 1997] 101.

"[God] justifies the sinner who does no more than **believe in Jesus**" [emphasis his]. (John F. Walvoord, *Lewis Sperry Chafer's Major Bible Themes*, Rev. Ed., (Grand Rapids, MI: Zondervan, 1974) 183.

"He brings life to sinners who are totally dead spiritually. He does this in response to and at the same time that the condition He prescribes for salvation is met—faith in His Son as substitute for sin." (Robert P. Lightner, *Sin, the Savior, and Salvation*, [Nashville, TN: Thomas Nelson, 1991] 213).

"That assurance, according to [1 John 5:13] and many others, is for all those who simply believe in Christ." (Dave Hunt, *What Love Is This?*, [Sisters, OR: Loyal Publishing, 2002] 382.

"The gospel was God's means of saving souls and all he had to do was believe." (Dave Hunt, *What Love Is This?*, (Sisters, OR: Loyal, 2002) 387.

90 The Bible teaches that an unbeliever cannot perform any truly good work before he is saved (Romans 8:7–8; John 15:5). "But lordship or progressive sanctification can be committed to and experienced only by believers" (i.e., only in life's race to "my finish line") (Robert P. Lightner, *Sin, the Savior, and Salvation*, [Nashville, TN: Thomas Nelson, 1991] 213.

91 Works can be added to faith as a future IOU to help faith "save"—still this is faith (as a deposit) PLUS works (as a promissory note). Works may be trusted as future fruit to validate one's faith as saving faith—still, this is faith (incomplete) PLUS works (now complete). Even thoughts and intentions are often "works"—i.e., "I promise not to think adulterous thoughts," Matthew 5:21, in the same legal category as "I promise not to break the Seventh Commandment," or the Lordship-Salvation 7-Point "terms," such as, "I promise to leave sin and forsake everything."

92 Ephesians 2:8–9 is emphatic: no works "that no one should boast." One may boast that he has never had an adulterous affair, but as we've seen, even thoughts can be "works"; i.e., "I promise not to think adulterous thoughts," Matthew 5:21. Law-keeping is not just ceremonial ritual, but also promises and pledges. In the Lordship-Gospel, one may boast that "when I believed in Jesus, I promised Him that from now on I would leave sin and forsake everything." How is this different from the Catholic boasting that "when I believed in Jesus, I promised Him that from now on I would keep the Seven Sacraments"? Or how does this differ from the Galatian believers making this boast: "When I believed in Jesus I promised Him that from now on I would obey the Jewish Law"? The Galatians were warned that this would constitute a false gospel; a gospel they were trying to finish by the addition of works (Galatians 1–3). The unfinished Lordship Gospel, Catholic Sacramental Gospel, and Galatians Judaizer Gospel all share this fact: They take present faith and insert future works by promises, pledges, and commitments. A works IOU. Thus, contradicting Ephesians 2:8–9, one can "boast" about "my part" in my salvation.

"The principle of salvation by grace through faith apart from works pervades the New Testament (John 3:16, 4:10, 20:31; Romans 3:21–24; Ephesians 2:8–9; Titus 3:4–5; Revelation 22:17)." (Charlie Bing, *Grace Notes* #82, [Burleson, TX: Grace Life Ministries]).

The logical necessity of Calvinism is that works must prove salvation: "The Calvinist's assurance is in God having predestined him to eternal life as one of the elect—and his performance [works] plays a large part in helping him to know whether or not he is among that select group." (Dave Hunt, *What Love Is This?*, [Sisters, OR: Loyal Publishing, 2002] 377).

"Since…the genuineness of a man's faith can only be determined by the life that follows it, assurance of salvation becomes impossible at the moment of conversion." (Zane Hodges, as quoted by Dave Hunt, *What Love Is This?*, [Sisters, OR: Loyal Publishing, 2002] 378).

"Neither salvation nor the assurance thereof is by works, nor can works be a sign of the reality of one's salvation or the means of providing assurance." (Dave Hunt, *What Love Is This?*, [Sisters, OR: Loyal Publishing, 2002] 411–12.

"Our final salvation is made contingent upon the subsequent obedience which comes from faith," as per Lordship advocate John Piper. (Quoted by Dave Hunt, *What Love Is This?*, [Sisters, OR: Loyal Publishing, 2002] 378).

"Many Calvinists believe that the only way to make one's 'calling and election sure' (2 Peter 1:10) is not through faith but through good works." (Dave Hunt, *What Love Is This?*, (Sisters, OR: Loyal Publishing, 2002] 381).

Hunt points out that Calvinists consider they are among the elect if they have the works to prove it. (Dave Hunt, *What Love Is This?*, [Sisters, OR: Loyal Publishing, 2002] 405).

"Neither salvation nor the assurance thereof is by works, nor can works be a sign of the reality of one's salvation or the means of providing assurance." (Dave Hunt, *What Love Is This?*, [Sisters, OR: Loyal Publishing, 2002] 411–12).

(In the vein of a "works IOU," "James Montgomery Boice proposes the following salvation prayer for the prospective convert, modeled after a wedding ceremony: "I, sinner, take thee, Jesus, to be my Savior and Lord; and I do promise and covenant **["my part," works]** before God and these witnesses, to be thy loving and faithful disciple." (Michael D. Halsey, *Freely by Grace*, J. B. Hixson, Rick Whitmire, and Roy B. Zuck, eds.,[Duluth, MN: Grace Gospel Press, 2012] 4).

Dillow says, "But, if anything is plain from the New Testament, works have NOTHING to do with a person's arrival in heaven either as a cause or a condition." [Note: emphasis his; "cause" = faith PLUS works;""condition" = faith THAT works.] Dillow then quotes these Scriptures—Romans 11:6, 4:5; Ephesians 2:8–9; Titus 3:5–7), and notes that "these passages make clear, one cannot mix faith and works in the plan of salvation and be faithful to the New Testament. If works are introduced, grace is no long grace." (Joseph Dillow, *Final Destiny, The Future Reign of the Servant Kings,* Second Revised Edition, [Grace Theology Press, 2015] 593).

A saving faith THAT works, no matter how it is framed, does not equal faith without works, because still, "these works cause"'something' related to our final destiny." (Joseph Dillow, *Final Destiny, The Future Reign of the Servant Kings*, Second Revised Edition, [Grace Theology Press, 2015] 600).

"Salvation is hardly a gift if the recipient must promise to surrender every area of his life as long as he lives to get it. Doesn't that involve doing something to at least partially deserve the 'gift'? The Bible does not add surrender or obedience to the one condition of faith for salvation." (Robert P. Lightner, *Sin, the Savior, and Salvation,* [Nashville, TN: Thomas Nelson, 1991] 211).

Works are not simply a prescribed legal-religious system: "[Works] is extended beyond the actual writings of the Mosaic system…[and] includes any human action which is attempted (whether in conformity to a precept of the Scriptures or not) with a view to securing favor with God…. Therefore, whatever is undertaken in the energy of the flesh is legal in its nature, whether it be the whole revealed will of God, the actual written commandments contained in the law, the exhortations of grace, or any spiritual activity whatsoever." (John F. Walvoord, *Lewis Sperry Chafer's Major Bible Themes*, Revised Edition, [Grand Rapids, MI: Zondervan, 1974] 191).

"Paul's statements against works for salvation cannot be limited only to works of the [Mosaic] law…they extend equally to all kinds of meritorious good works…[in the famous "works" referenced passage of Ephesians 2:8–9], Paul explicitly addresses alienated Gentiles (Eph. 2:11–12), and the Titus text (3:5–7) does not point to 'works of the law' but rather 'works of righteousness.'…all moral works are 'works of the law'…. The simple truth is that no works of any kind merit salvation: Eternal life is a gift received only by faith (cf. John 3:16, 36; 5:24: Rom 6:23)." (Norman Geisler, *Systematic Theology*, Vol.3, Sin-Salvation, [Bloomington, IL: Bethany House, 2004] 268–70.

93   Anderson writes that "all the Old Testament saints, Tribulation saints, millennial saints—all must enter the gates of heaven through the blood of Christ. His death was retroactive for all who lived before the cross and forward acting for all those who have lived or live or will live after the cross." (David R. Anderson, *Bewitched—The Rise of Neo-Galatianism*, [Grace Theology Press, 2015] 162).

"Salvation has always been by grace through faith in God's promised Savior. The essential content of the gospel has not changed, but it has been expanded as more information became known in the progress of revelation. In Old Testament times, people were saved by believing in God's provision of the coming divine Savior...by looking forward to the good news [Gospel]." (Charlie Bing, *Grace Notes* #82, [Burleson, TX: Grace Life Ministries]).

94   The Greek word "believe" (*pisteuo*) that is used in "saving faith" passages like John 3:16 and Acts 16:31 and in the "child-like faith" passage of Matthew 18:6, is also the same unembellished word used for the Romans 4:1–5 Greek rendering of Genesis 15:6 and the faith ("believed") that saved Abraham.

95   This is my descriptive term to identify the standard of belief MacArthur applies to a faith that saves.

96   John MacArthur, as quoted in J. B. Hixson, *Getting the Gospel Wrong*, Rev. Ed., (Duluth, MN: Grace Gospel Press, 2013) 230.

97   Ibid.

98   Genesis 15:6; Psalm 106:31; Romans 4:3, 4:5, 4:9, 4:11, 4:22; Galatians 3:6; James 2:23.

99   For proof of Solomon's salvation, see http://www.bibleprophecyaswritten.com/salvationbygrace/gracetothekings.html.

Consider this:

Since Solomon's answer to the Lord's question in 1 Kings 3:5–10 "was pleasing in the sight of the Lord" (v. 10),

and, since "without faith it is impossible to please" the Lord (Hebrews 11:6),

then Solomon's faith was "real," saving faith.

However, many (Calvinistic, reformed theologies) would claim that Solomon's late-life sins proved his faith could not be "real" faith, and thus Solomon was never really saved.

But how could Solomon's faith be found "pleasing in the sight of the Lord" without "real" faith, when Hebrews 11:6 says that "without faith it is impossible to please Him"?

Wayne House refers to Solomon along with Noah, Job, Abraham, Joseph, and Moses as "these believers." (H. Wayne House, *Charts of Christian Theology and Doctrine*, [Grand Rapids, MI: Zondervan, 1992, Chart 55] 93).

Also, many of Israel's kings who had very imperfect lives were saved because the Finished Gospel is by grace alone, through faith alone, in Christ alone; see bibleprophecyaswritten.com/Salvation by Grace/Grace to the Kings.

Ryrie adds the Ephesian believers (*So Great Salvation*, [Chicago, IL: Moody, 1997] 101–102; Benware adds David and Peter and others (Paul Benware, *The Believer's Payday*, [Chattanooga, TN: AMG, 2002] 103–115; Dillow has a comprehensive list of very carnal biblical people saved and kept secure by the grace of God (1 Corinthians 3:1–3 establishes this reality when it describes the existence of "carnal believers"); (Joseph Dillow, *Defense of Free Grace Theology*, Fred Chay, ed., [Grace Theology Press, 2017] chapter 10).

100   Lot, Samson, and Solomon believed God, and "it was reckoned to them as righteousness," instantly and irreversibly. Christ's finish line (His sacrifice on the cross) was applied "backwards" to them. So, in Christian-era terms, they were saved instantly and irreversibly at Christ's finish line. At

that moment they became "who you are" in Christ, forever in God's Family. That is what "finished" means. "It is finished" (John 19:30).

1. They couldn't "fail" at salvation, because Christ can't fail, and it was His "race" and His "finish" that He gave to them as a free gift (Revelation 21:6; 22:17) through their unaided, simple belief. They became "who you are"—children of God in the family of God—forever.

2. But they could fail to always "walk like who you are." They failed at times miserably, sometimes over extended periods of time. When they reached their own "finish line," they were received into Heaven. There, at the judgment seat of Christ, they stand glorified and secure in their salvation forever. Their works completed at their finish line during their race of life are judged. Solomon, for example, will receive heavenly rewards for his works of gold, silver, and precious stones during the early, Temple-building phase of his life. But he will receive loss of rewards for his works of worthless wood, straw, and stubble during the extended latter period of his life when he tread on God's commandments, worshipped idols, and multiplied his adulteries in a massive sinfest. Those many, many works of wood, straw, and stubble will burn in deepest of ember and blackest of smoke, and Solomon "shall suffer loss; but he himself shall be saved, yet so as through fire" (1 Corinthians 3:15).

3. In the Bible, works are not excluded—never for a moment—except at the moment of salvation. Charlie Bing writes, "Romans 4:1–5 states that justification [salvation] is apart from works altogether, but Scripture teaches that sanctification depends on good works. Works are not a requirement for salvation, but should be a result. Works are not a condition for faith, but should be a consequence. Justification should lead to sanctification just as faith should lead to works, but the distinctions must be maintained. One should and might lead to the other, but they are not the same. Only faith alone upholds grace as a free gift of God (Rom. 4:16; Eph. 2:8-9)." (*Freely By Grace*, (J. B. Hixson, Rick Whitmire, and Roy B. Zuck, eds., [Duluth, MN: Grace Gospel Press, 2012] 104).

"There could be in the life of a particular person not one good work to indicate the reality of salvation, yet that person could be truly saved…. All of one's works could be consumed in the fire of God's testing of motives and deeds; yet that person not be lost, according to [1 Corinthians 3:11–15], in spite of no outward evidence of salvation." (Dave Hunt, *What Love Is This?*, [Sisters, OR: Loyal Publishing, 2002] 412).

101   The gospel of salvation (the finished gospel) is given in many New Testament passages, in various parts. A helpful summary to the simplicity of the gospel is Jesus' own delivery of it to the Samaritan woman at Jacobs' well in John 4:10–14. The last mention of the Gospel occurs in Heaven sixty-five years later and uses the same language, again from the very lips of Jesus, in Revelation 22:17. Note how other passages add information, or emphasis, to the John 4 passage. The phrases "If you knew the gift of God," "ask Him," and "He would give you" are highlighted in Ephesians 2:8–9, emphasizing grace alone and faith alone. The phrase "who it is" focuses on the person of Jesus (as seen in Gospel passages such as John 3:16 and Acts 16:30–31) and the saving work of Jesus (1 Corinthians 15:1–4; Romans 4:25). We learn from these and other passages the essentials and simplicity of the Gospel: If we believe in Jesus Christ, the Son of God, who died for our sins and was resurrected to life, our sins are forgiven and we have eternal life. This is the gospel. Finally, in a personal email exchange May 3, 2019, Bible scholar J. B. Hixson sent me this helpful insight given by Charles Ryrie: "The basis of salvation in every age is the death of Christ; the requirement of salvation in every age is faith; the object of faith in every age is God; the content of faith changes in the various dispensations." (*Dispensationalism Today* [Chicago: Moody, 1965], p. 123).

102   Unless otherwise noted, all Scripture from this chapter is from the New American Standard Bible (NASB).

103   John Gramlich, "Pew Research: 5 Facts about Crime in the U.S.," January 3, 2019, http://www.pewresearch.org/fact-tank/2019/01/03/5-facts-about-crime-in-the-u-s/.

104   Timothy Williams, "Violent Crime in U.S. Rises for Second Consecutive Year," *New York Times*, September 25, 2017, https://www.nytimes.com/2017/09/25/us/violent-crime-murder-chicago-increase-.html.

105 "Va. State Police Chaplains Resign over Jesus Ban," September 26, 2018.
     https://www.newsmax.com/US/virginia-policechaplains/2008/09/26/id/325568/

106 "Protests against Proposition 8 Supporters," Wikipedia," https://en.wikipedia.org/wiki/
     Protests_against_Proposition_8_supporters.

107 Stoyan Zaimov, "Department of Defense Classified Evangelicals, Catholics as 'Extremists' like Al-
     Qaeda, Documents Confirm," Christian Post, https://www.christianpost.com/news/department-of-
     defense-classified-evangelicals-catholics-as-extremists-like-al-qaeda-documents-confirm.html.

108 Benzion Netanyahu, Don Isaac Abravanel, Statesman & Philosopher (Jewish Publication Society of
     America, 1953) 56.

109 Dore Gold, The Fight for Jerusalem (Regnery Publishing, 2007) 172.

110 Ruthie Blum, To Hell in a Handbasket: Carter, Obama, and the Arab Spring (RVP Publishers), Kindle
     Locations 2162–2164.

111 Elisabeth Elliot, Furnace of the Lord: Reflections on the Redemption of the Holy City (Hodder and
     Stoughton) 50.

112 IRD Press Release, February 27, 2012.

113 Paul Smith, New Evangelicalism (Calvary Chapel Publishing), Kindle Locations 2032–2035.

114 David L. Cooper, quote taken on 3/26/19 from this link: https://www.bibletruths.org/
     the-golden-rule-of-interpretation/.

115 Dr. Ron Rhodes, Northern Storm Rising: Russia, Iran, and the Emerging End-Times Military Coalition
     Against Israel, 139.

116 Dr. Andy Woods, Middle East Meltdown: The Coming Islamic Invasion of Israel, 6.

117 Dr. Mark Hitchcock quote taken on 3/28/19 from this link: https://www.pre-trib.org/pretribfiles/
     pdfs/Hitchcock-TheBattleofGogandMag.pdf, 6–7.

118 Dr. Mark Hitchcock, Iran: The Coming Crisis, 164.

119 Dr. Ron Rhodes, Northern Storm Rising, 151.

120 Dr. Andy Woods, Middle East Meltdown, 9.

121 Joel Rosenberg, Epicenter (Carol Stream: Tyndale House, 2006) 129.

122 Dr. Arnold Fruchtenbaum, Footsteps of the Messiah (San Antonio, TX: Ariel, 2004) 108.

123 Dr. Andy Woods, Middle East Meltdown, 11.

124 Dr. Ron Rhodes, Northern Storm Rising, 154.

125 In my Now Prophecies book, I explain why the USA could be the "young lions" of Tarshish.

126 We thank Ned Bankston for researching the headlines concerning the birds of prey gathering in
     Israel.

127 New American Standard Hebrew and Greek Dictionaries, H7997b: "spoil of those who despoiled."

128 .R. Anderson, Fulfillment of the Prophecy, in The Coming Prince, 10th ed. (Grand Rapids, MI: Kregel
     Classics, 1975).

129 P. Schäfer, History of the Jews in Antiquity, (Routledge, 1995, 2013) 191–192.

130 Josephus, B. J. Translated by Whiston, William. 6.1.1, 7.1.1. (Perseus Project).

131 Ibid., 7.1.1.

132 Mark Twain, Innocents Abroad (London, 1881).

133 T. Herzl, T. (1987). Old New Land, Translated by Lotta Levensohr., M. Wiener, ISBN
     9-781-55876-160-5.

134   First Zionist Congress & Basel Program (1897). (r.d.). Retrieved from https://www.jewishvirtual-library.org/first-zionist-congress-and-basel-program 1897.

135   Kaletsky/Reuters, A. (June 27, 2014). "World War One: First War Was Impossible, Then Inevitable." Retrieved from http://blogs.reuters.com/anatole-kaletsku/2014/06-27/world-war-one-first-war-was-impossible-then-inevitable/.

136   R. Anderson, *The Coming Prince* (p. 56).

137   *Milestones: 1977–1980* – Office of the Historian. (n.d.). Retrieved from https://history.state.gov/milestones/1977-1980/camp-david

138   Statement by President Trump on Jerusalem, December 6, 2017. US Embassy & Consulates in Italy (September 23, 2018). Retrieved from https://it.usembassy.gov/statement-president-trump-jerusalem-december-6-2017?.

139   "What Did Jesus Mean When He Said, 'This generation will not pass'"? (Feburary 21, 2018). Retrieved from https://www.gotquestions.org/this-generation-not-pass.html.

140   M. Neutzling, *The Fig Tree Parable* (Fig Tree Press, 2014).

141   "Winston Churchill: A Founder of the European Union," EU Rope (September 19, 2018). Retrieved from https://eu-rope.ideasoneurope.eu/2013/11/10/winston-churchill-a-founder-of-the-european-union/.

142   "Timeline of European History" (December 20, 2018). Retrieved from https://en.wikipedia.org/wiki/Timeline_of_European_Union_history.

143   John Fleming, *Fallen Angels and Heroes of Mythology*, (1879) 187.

144   Samuel Bradhurst Schieffelin, *Foundations of History: A Series of First Things* (1875) 74.

145   A. W. Pink, *Gleanings in Genesis* (Chicago, IL: Moody Bible Institute, 1922) 93.

146   https://www.pewresearch.org/fact-tank/2017/04/06/why-muslims-are-the-worlds-fastest-growing-religious-group/.

147   https://www.scmp.com/lifestyle/travel-leisure/article/2150526/amazon-drug-tourism-peru-and-colombia-thriving-despite.

148   https://qz.com/quartzy/1411909/the-explosive-growth-of-witches-wiccans-and-pagans-in-the-us/g.

149   https://www.forbes.com/sites/alicegwalton/2018/11/08/yoga-and-meditation-continue-to-gain-popularity-in-the-u-s/#2d858d363782.

150   https://www.fastcompany.com/40410406/is-there-a-crystal-bubble-inside-the-billion-dollar-healing-gemstone-industry.

151   William Jackson, *Sermons Preached in Village Churches*, (1853) 98–99.

152   https://www.nielsen.com/us/en/insights/news/2018/time-flies-us-adults-now-spend-nearly-half-a-day-interacting-with-media.print.html

153   https://techjury.net/blog/time-spent-on-social-media/.

154   https://techjury.net/blog/time-spent-on-social-media/.

155   https://www.wordstream.com/blog/ws/2017/04/20/instagram-statistics.

156   https://www.tubefilter.com/2019/05/07/number-hours-video-uploaded-to-youtube-per-minute/.

157   https://www.omnicoreagency.com/youtube-statistics/.

158   Matthew Poole, *Annotations Upon the Holy Bible,* Vol. 1 (1840) 15.

159   John Murray, *Holy Bible, According to the Authorized Version* [AD 1611], (1877) 61.

160   Reverend John Cummings, *Great Tribulation; or Things Coming on the Earth*, (1860) 171.

161   Simms and M'Intyre, *Antiquities of The Jews*, 11.1, as published in *The Works of Flavius Josephus: The Learned and Authentic Jewish Historian*, (1841) 41.

162   James Glentworth Butler, *The Bible-work: Old Testament,* Vol. 1, (1889) 309.

163   https://www.cnbc.com/2017/03/24/a-record-number-of-americans-are-now-millionaires-new-study-shows.html.

164   https://www.forbes.com/sites/forbespr/2018/03/06/forbes-32nd-annual-worlds-billionaires-issue/#692762610e09.

165   https://www.cnbc.com/2018/07/19/income-inequality-continues-to-grow-in-the-united-states.html.

166   .http://time.com/5508393/global-wealth-inequality-widens oxfam/.

167   https://www.dosomething.org/us/facts/11-facts-about-global-poverty.

168   https://factsandtrends.net/2018/01/16/hope-for-dying-churches/.

169   https://news.gallup.com/poll/210704/record-few-americans-believe-bible-literal-word-god.aspx.

170   https://www1.cbn.com/cbnnews/us/2018/september/most-millennials-believe-the-bible-is-just-a-book-ndash-what-this-group-is-doing-about-it.

171   https://www.christianpost.com/news/only-slim-majority-americans-believe-god-of-bible-worsens-among-those-younger-than-50.html.

172   https://www.independent.co.uk/news/uk/home-news/porn-children-pornography-online-nspcc-half-children-quarter-11-year-olds-a7082791.html.

173   https://www.cheatsheet.com/culture/these-alarming-crimes-are-actually-on-the-rise-in-america.html/.

174   https://www.bbc.com/news/uk-48146305.

175   https://www.opendoorsusa.org/christian-persecution/.

176   https://www.nytimes.com/2018/01/25/opinion/sunday/silicon-valley-immortality.html.

177   https://www.theguardian.com/technology/2019/feb/22/silicon-valley-immortality-blood-infusion-gene therapy.

178   MISSING(27)

179   William Gallogly Moorehead, *Outline Studies in the New Testament, Philippians to Hebrews* (1905) 123.

180   John Cummings, *Great Tribulation, or Things Coming on This Earth* (1860) 175.

Other Titles by Terry James:

RAPTURE READY...OR NOT

Believe it or not, ready or not, the Lord is about to call all Christians into His presence in a stunning instant of time. The Tribulation (Daniel's 70th week) is on the immediate horizon of human history. This book tells why this is the generation that will be *Left Behind*.

Rapture Ready...Or Not: 15 Reasons Why This Is the Generation That Will Be Left Behind

Available on Amazon

DECEIVERS

Just as Jesus foretold, our nation and world is full of *Deceivers*. From fake news in our everyday world, to hellish doctrines now being preached in the pulpits –that first sign to look for, as given by the Lord in the Olivet Discourse, is front and center. Prophecy experts tell you the Truth about the lies that are leading toward the Tribulation.

Deceivers: Exposing Evil Seducers And Last Days Deception

Available on Amazon

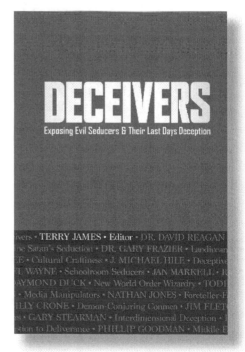

ESSAYS IN APOCALYPSE

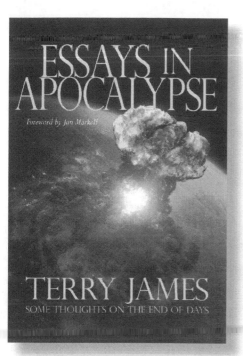

Terry James gives much studied and prayerfully considered analysis of key areas of stage-setting for imminent Bible prophecy fulfillment. Is America Mystery Babylon? Do Donald J. Trump and the "Days of Lot" have anything in common? Is Russia's Vladimir Putin *Gog*? These and other questions are addressed as James dissects critical issues and events of these troubling though exciting days.

Available on Amazon

REVELATIONS

Tyce Greyson goes to Patmos to the cave where the Apostle John dictated the apocalyptic future events of the book of *Revelation*. The television journalist/anchor experiences powerful, supernatural ramifications from things while in the cave high above the Aegean. Thereafter, he, unable to control his subconscious while broadcasting, speaks revelations from heavenly prompting.

Available on Amazon

WWW.RAPTUREREADY.COM

Made in the USA
Lexington, KY
29 September 2019